D1740027

Women's Livelihood Rights

WOMEN'S LIVELIHOOD RIGHTS

Recasting Citizenship for Development

Edited by
Sumi Krishna

SAGE Publications
Los Angeles ■ London ■ New Delhi ■ Singapore

Copyright © Sumi Krishna, 2007

All rights reserved. No part of this book may be reproduced or utilised in any form or by any means, electronic or mechanical, including photocopying, recording or by any information storage or retrieval system, without permission in writing from the publisher.

First published in 2007 by

 Sage Publications India Pvt Ltd
B1/I1, Mohan Cooperative Industrial Area
Mathura Road
New Delhi 110 044
www.sagepub.in

Sage Publications Inc
2455 Teller Road
Thousand Oaks, California 91320

Sage Publications Ltd
1 Oliver's Yard, 55 City Road
London EC1Y 1SP

Sage Publications Asia-Pacific Pte Ltd
33 Pekin Street
#02-01 Far East Square
Singapore 048763

Published by Vivek Mehra for Sage Publications India Pvt Ltd, typeset in 10/13pts Minion by Star Compugraphics Private Limited, Delhi and printed at Chaman Enterprises, New Delhi.

Library of Congress Cataloging-in-Publication Data

Women's livelihood rights: recasting citizenship for development / edited
  by Sumi Krishna.
      p. cm.
  Includes bibliographical references and index.
1. Women's rights—India. 2. Women in development—India. 3. Equality—India.
  I. Krishna, Sumi.
  HQ1236.5.I4W6593   323.3′40954—dc22   2007   2007023771

ISBN: 978-0-7619-3600-8 (HB)   978-81-7829-763-7 (India-HB)

The Sage Team: Sudeep Kohli

Contents

VI. Dignity in Struggle: Lessons from the Past

List of Tables

List of Boxes

Preface

This collection brings together the peer-reviewed work of a deeply engaged group, whose insight and understanding of the different dimensions of women's livelihood, citizenship and development would not normally be found in one volume. *Women's Livelihood Rights: Recasting Citizenship for Development* reflects an ongoing effort towards a dialogue across different disciplines and varied development interventions. A common thread that runs through the contributions is the belief that enhanced understanding through research improves action on the ground and that this understanding cannot come from desk studies, but through empathetic interaction with poor people, including women, and through learning from their struggles.

Women's Livelihood Rights takes forward the issues and concerns of *Livelihood and Gender: Equity in Community Resource Management* (2004). In 2003, the informal group of researchers, women and men who had voluntarily put together *Livelihood and Gender* formed 'jivika,' an e-discussion group.[1] We had different disciplinary and institutional affiliations and had been interacting fairly regularly since late 1999; we hoped jivika, which literally means livelihood, would enable us to continue to share our interests and concerns regarding gender equity in natural resource-based livelihoods and anti-poverty initiatives in South Asia and beyond. By 2005, jivika grew from the initial 20 members to more than 180 fieldworkers, activists, action-researchers, students, teachers, scholars, resource managers and development practitioners. A somewhat fluid inner core of active members has kept up a steady exchange of information, knowledge and experience. Most important is that jivika has facilitated our association as researchers and practitioners, and provided opportunities to share and learn, growing into what some have described as a virtual 'community of practice'.[2]

Women's rights to political and economic spaces have figured regularly on jivika. So, in early 2005, when Kumud Sharma, then president of the Indian Association for Women's Studies (IAWS), invited me to coordinate a sub-theme at the IAWS conference on 'Citizenship, Sovereignty and

Gender' (Goa, 3–6 May 2005), this provided an opportunity to look at the theme of livelihood and gender equity from the perspective of women's rights as citizens. A significant number of the abstracts selected for the sub-theme and published in the *Conference Book of Abstracts* were contributed by jivika members. The brief presentations at the conference and the enriching, wide-ranging discussions brought important issues and new ideas to the fore. It was felt that some of the presentations could be written up as papers and published in a single volume. Others who were not associated with the IAWS Conference were invited to join us in this effort. On the sidelines of jivika, a fairly lengthy process of writing and revising papers followed, as contributors read and responded to one another's work.

Women's Livelihood Rights stands on its own, but may also be viewed as a companion volume to *Livelihood and Gender*. As in the earlier volume, the contributors to this book have brought a critical, gendered perspective to bear on a set of overlapping issues. Most of the chapters deal with detailed empirical case studies; even the few that provide a broader overview have drawn upon the authors' earlier field experiences in locations spread across different states of India. The threads that run through the chapters reflect the interrelatedness of the complex themes that we are addressing. The chapters are grouped into six parts, highlighting a set of overlapping themes: (1) Recognition and resource rights; (2) Work and employment strategies; (3) The challenges of democratic governance; (4) Restructuring institutional systems; (5) Women's collective agency, development and citizenship; and (6) Dignity in struggle: Lessons from the past.

This 'project' (like *Livelihood and Gender*) has been entirely voluntary and unfunded. Working in this way has enormous advantages because we are independent of donor requirements and schedules, and the process is wholly shaped by the participants. The disadvantage is that there are few opportunities for face-to-face discussion, and some gaps are not easy to fill because of our dependence on voluntary contributions from people who lead very busy lives. Nevertheless, I believe that both the process of preparing this volume and the outcome fulfils a significant need in the area of livelihood and gender studies.

I am most grateful to everyone who has participated in this process, generously sharing work and insights, reviewing and revising chapters over many months. Not all the chapters contributed could be accommodated in this volume because of constraints of space and time, but the ideas and the interaction of all are very much part of this book. I would also like to acknowledge the anonymous reviewer who went through the manuscript and the editorial and production team at Sage for their invaluable professionalism.

Sumi Krishna

NOTES

1. The jivika (livelihood) group is open, independent, unsponsored and voluntarily administered; its URL is http://groups.yahoo.com/group/jivika/.

2. Somnath Sen. 'Experiences with Communities of Practice in India'. Inter-cooperation in India. Working Paper 1. [Swiss Agency for Development and Cooperation (SDC), 2005]. www.intercooperation.ch/offers/download/ic-india/wp-1.pdf/view.

1

Recasting Citizenship for Women's Livelihood and Development

An Overview

Sumi Krishna

PRELUDE: HOISTING THE FLAG

In August 1999, I was in coastal Orissa with three young professionals, who were working on a resource management project in the area. It took several hours of travelling by a small motorised boat, down the Mahanadi River almost to its mouth near Paradeep Port and then up a creek to reach our destination. This was a tiny hamlet; let's call it Tanabisu, on a ribbon of land amidst the coastal mangrove forests. It was settled in the 1950s by Bengali-speaking migrants from the Sunderbans area, who had been forced to look for alternative homelands because of successive cyclones in their native West Bengal. Tanabisu consisted of a row of some 20 small mud-and-thatch huts. There was only one *pucca* brick house with a cemented yard for drying grain. A solitary hut belonging to a lower caste family among the migrants stood in the distance near the edge of the creek. Also, apart from the row of huts, but on slightly higher ground, was the dilapidated and snake-infested school hut, rarely used for classes because the teacher only made the long journey to the hamlet once or twice a month. The school hut and the area in front of it served as a common meeting space for men; the women also gathered there to draw water from a shallow hand pump. In the wetland environment of Tanabisu, every household had a pond amply stocked with fish, a thriving vegetable garden of beans, brinjal (aubergine), squashes and leafy greens, besides some livestock (mainly goats) and a hectare of paddy fields or less. Officially, this is forest land under the territorial jurisdiction of the Orissa State Forest Department, but by paying taxes to the State Revenue Department, the residents had wrested for themselves some measure of rights to the land. There were also many individual cases of litigation over the land, which seemed to have gone on interminably in the district and sessions courts. The women's daily work flowed across the threshold of the household and fields. They cooked and cleaned; managed the fish in the ponds as well as the homestead vegetable patches; tended children, goats and poultry; and farmed their small fields with seemingly equal attention. Many of the men had jobs in nearby areas, combining wage employment and farming. Poverty and insecurity made life in this scenically beautiful area very tough; the people literally lived a 'hand-to-mouth' existence, surviving on meagre wages and the produce of the land and water.

We were all up early on the morning of 15 August, Independence Day. Women rushed to finish drawing water from the school hand pump because a flag-hoisting ceremony was to take place. Everyone dressed in their best set of clothes. The men assembled slowly and children, girls and boys, scrambled around the flagpole. There were only a couple of elderly women at the edge of the group. The younger women had gathered at quite a distance; even further away was the lower-caste family, man, woman and children, all watching the proceedings. As an urban educated outsider in a position of apparent authority, my age, gender and caste were not perceived as a barrier to my presence at the flagpole. Indeed, I was invited to hoist and unfurl the flag. I suggested that women should also participate and that one of them might do this instead. After some discussion among the men, I was told that the younger women would watch from a distance as that was the custom. But a few elderly women were called and the oldest among them was chosen to do the honours. The flag was unfurled, the national anthem was sung and everyone cheered.

Later, I talked to some of the women. For the first time in this hamlet, a woman had performed such a formal public function as unfurling the national flag, and this had created quite a stir. I asked the women what independence meant to them. Their instant response was 'freedom from British rule' and the 'right to vote'. To this, they added the right to approach government officials; the right to be 'heard' in court. But what they most wanted from the government, the Forest Department and the law was recognition of their right to reside amidst the coastal forests and cultivate the land that the community had laboured upon for more than a generation. A younger woman said the right to vote did not mean anything without health and education. Others pointed out that the school was virtually non-existent; there were no medical facilities nearby; a sick child or a pregnant woman in labour, who needed immediate medical attention, had to wait for the ferry and be carried a long way. Independence should mean more than just voting, they said.

Listening to them talk, it seemed to me that the women of this isolated hamlet perceived their political rights in independent India and the socio-economic right to livelihood and development as parts of one whole. The 'content' of their citizenship, ritually affirmed in the flag-hoisting, was shaped by universal concepts of nationhood filtered through local history and traditions of inclusion and exclusion, by hierarchies of power and authority both within the community and outside, and by spatial demarcations that were marked by age, gender and caste. For the women of Tanabisu, the issues of marginalised identities, private vis-à-vis public spaces, individual versus group rights and so on, which modern feminist debates have brought into citizenship theory, were lived realities. In their impoverished, water-rimmed hamlet, the unfurling of the national flag on Independence Day seemed to be an affirmation of a citizenship that they hoped would embrace development and ensure the security of their livelihoods.

I. LIVELIHOODS AND CITIZENSHIP

Development and Sustainable Livelihoods

'Development' is a contentious term because it is so variously perceived. Conventionally, development has been seen as national economic growth measurable by the Gross Domestic Product (GDP). Here, however, I use the term 'development' in the broader sense in which I have defined it elsewhere:

> Development is about people, about enhancing their ability and power to direct their own lives, in the context of their environment, their history

and aspirations for the future. Development is not about catching up with other people. But it is about an enlarged range and quality of choices, of lifestyles, of occupations. It encompasses better nutrition, health, education and freedom from oppression and poverty. The process of development involves structural transformations in the organisation of society and the economy. Such a process cannot take place without altering relationships of dominance and subordination, or affecting the interests of different groups within society. Therefore, questions regarding the character, direction and pace of development are fundamentally political questions. (Krishna 1996a: 8)

Prior to independence and more so in the 1960s, there was considerable public debate on alternative developmental paths that would be in the best interests of all Indian people. The social and environmental dimensions of development were also recognised in Indian planning: the need to maintain the health of the soil, to safeguard people's livelihoods and to establish institutional mechanisms for a more participatory, decentralised development. Despite this awareness, the environmental and natural resources (upon which people depended for their livelihoods) were being increasingly undermined. Severe droughts and a food crisis in the 1960s, rising unemployment in the 1970s and the persistence of oppression and poverty led to questioning conventional 'trickle-down' theories of development and to a shift in emphasis to meeting the 'basic needs' of people.

The political questions of development became more sharply etched with the emergence of popular environmental struggles in the 1970s, which focused attention on how different groups of people use and abuse natural resources. In the 1980s, the concept of ecologically and environmentally sustainable development emerged, apparently bridging over conflicts between the environment and development. The publication of *Our Common Future*, the Report of the World Commission on Environment and Development (WCED 1990), gave an impetus to sustainable development, defined as 'meeting the needs of the present without compromising the ability of future generations to meet their own needs'. Even as this became a buzzword in the development debate, it was also widely critiqued (see Krishna 1996a: 252–53).

The more recent concept of sustainable livelihoods is being projected as an advance over sustainable development. For many NGOs and development practitioners, 'livelihood' is a straightforward term, as defined in dictionaries: the means of living and sustenance. For people's movements, such as the Chipko struggle that aimed to protect the hill forests of Uttarakhand, the 'means of living' encompassed the sustainability of the resource base. In the 1970s, the Chipko leader Chandi Prasad Bhatt repeatedly said: 'Saving the trees is only the first step, saving ourselves is the goal' (Krishna 1996b). Such perceptions from 'below', which were rooted in the everyday reality of poor people's lives, influenced the way in which people were thinking and writing about development and contributed to the emergence of the Sustainable Livelihoods Approach or framework in the 1990s. Compared to earlier approaches to 'poverty alleviation' for meeting basic needs and for income-generation in specific sectors, the new emphasis on livelihoods covered a much wider cluster of factors. Chambers (1995) defined livelihood as the 'means of gaining a living, including tangible assets (resources and stores), intangible assets (claims and access), and livelihood capabilities' including coping abilities, opportunities and sundry freedoms.

The broader focus on livelihood rather than on incomes was also projected in the document called *Agenda 21* (United Nations 1992), the non-binding 'Plan of Action' adopted at the 1992 UN Conference on Environment and Development at Rio de Janeiro, Brazil. 'Enabling the poor to achieve sustainable livelihoods' is up-front in the chapter 'Combating Poverty'. It states:

> While managing resources sustainably, an environmental policy that focuses mainly on the conservation and protection of resources must take due account of those who depend on the resources for their livelihoods. Otherwise it could have an adverse impact both on poverty and on chances for long-term success in resource and environmental conservation'. (3.2: 15)

Further, 'The long-term objective of enabling all people to achieve sustainable livelihoods should provide an integrating factor that allows policies to address issues of development, sustainable resource management and poverty eradication simultaneously'. The first programme objective is to 'provide all persons urgently with the opportunity to earn a sustainable livelihood'.

Also in relation to poverty, the 1995 Fourth World Conference on Women at Beijing, China, in its *Platform for Action* (United Nations 1996) urged governments to link macro-economic development policies with the needs of poor women to ensure that development did not adversely affect them; to address the structural causes of persistent poverty; and to provide adequate safety nets, and strengthen state and community-based support systems so that women living in poverty could 'withstand adverse economic environments and preserve their livelihoods, assets and revenues in times of crisis' (Para 58g: 41). It urged multilateral financial and development institutions to create 'an enabling environment that allows women to build and maintain sustainable livelihoods' (ibid.: 43).

In the late 1990s, these concerns provided the impetus for the United Nations Development Programme (UNDP) and other agencies such as the International Fund for Agricultural Development (IFAD), the British government's Department for International Development (DFID), and international non-government organisations (NGOs) such as Oxfam to adopt their own versions of a Sustainable Livelihoods (SL) Approach. The UNDP defines SL as 'the capability of people to make a living and improve their quality of life without jeopardising the livelihood options of others, either now or in the future'. It advocates a poverty reduction strategy in the context of sustainability. This is a narrower definition than that of Chambers', and has resonances with WCED's sustainable development approach.

Development often reinforces local power structures. This has been documented for many different socio-cultural and ecological contexts, exposing the myth of equity in community resource management (see Gujit and Shah 1998; Krishna 1995, Krishna 2004a). The introduction of citizenship into the debate provides an important integrating concept to re-envision development as participatory and people-driven, and to view livelihood as a political right to dignified living rather than simply as a welfare need.

The Construction of Citizenship

Unlike concepts of development and sustainable livelihoods, which are of relatively recent origin, the idea of citizenship has engaged rulers for ages, with political philosophers having attempted to define and categorise citizens. While Buddhist texts of BC sixth to fourth century reflect a dynamic concept of social stratification by which slaves too could become rulers and women were not excluded from the polity, Brahminical patriarchy attempted to forge an inflexible caste framework wherein status was divinely prescribed by birth and lineage. The caste-linked male domination that evolved in the BC first century involved the establishment of high ritual status for upper-caste men and the subordination of women through their seclusion in homes, the concept of *pativrata* (husband worship), forbidding widow remarriage and controlling women's sexuality. According to the *Manusmriti* (attributed to the second century AD), a woman's *dharma* lay in serving her husband as god, and she had no independent existence, or material and religious rights (Chakravarti 1993, 2003). So too in ancient Greece, Aristotle (see *Politics* Book III, Chapter 5, translated by Sinclair 1962) defined citizens as a particular class of men, excluding all those who were constantly engaged in commercial or physical labour. Resident aliens, women and slaves were excluded, as were children, seniors and most ordinary workers. Writing in the BC fourth century, Aristotle argued that all those who may be necessary to the existence of the state could not be considered citizens equally with grown men, and that a citizen in the fullest sense was one who shared the privileges of rule. It is pertinent to note that Aristotle's concept of citizenship reflects his understanding of nature and is seen in his categorisation of that which is 'by nature superior', of mind over body, 'mankind' over animals and male over female. Ownership of property (including slaves) and the right to its produce was the privilege of those considered naturally, biologically, superior due to the possession of rational faculties.

The concept of citizenship is neither universal nor static. However, for over 2,000 years of human history since Aristotle, the denial of women's rationality as the basis for their exclusion from the ownership of property and the privileges of rule has characterised many societies in different parts of the world. For instance, Sundberg (2003: 5) points out that in the nineteenth century, independent Latin American countries established liberal, democratic political systems based on restricted representation:

> Since the colonial era, Latin American societies have been organised by biological and cultural hierarchies that position as inferior women, indigenous people, and people of color with African or Asian ancestry. Limits on women's legal rights have been conceptualised in terms of naturalized accounts of biological differences between men and women, particularly in terms of mental capacity and roles within the family.

She says further that: 'Within the logics of biological and cultural racism, indigenous people, other people of color and illiterate *meztiso* (mixed-race) *campesinoes* (peasants) have been considered unfit to take on rights and responsibilities of citizenship'. Until the mid-twentieth century, full citizenship and formal decision-making was restricted to elite, educated white men who owned property.

In late nineteenth-century Europe and North America, the struggle for suffrage, the right to vote and stand for election was at the centre of the 'first wave' of the modern women's movement. The suffrage movement gained ground as women took on new roles, erasing some of the conventional gendered demarcations of separate spheres of work during and after World War I (1914–18) and following the Russian Revolution (1917). In 1918, the British Parliament granted a conditional right to vote to women over the age of 30 who were householders, wives of householders, occupiers of property with an annual rent of five British pounds and graduates of British universities. A decade later in 1928, women's suffrage was granted on equal terms as men. During the 'second wave' of women's struggles for liberation and equality in the 1970s, feminists argued that the very concept of citizenship was gendered and, furthermore, that the exclusion of women was central to the processes of nation-building, indeed to the very conception of the nation (see Yuval-Davis 1997a, 1997b).

In British India, the struggle for women's rights emerged in the context of self-governance for India within the Empire (Forbes 1998; see also Chatterjee 1989; Sangari and Vaid 1989). In 1918, Sarojini Naidu attempted to persuade the Indian National Congress of the scientific and political rationality of extending the franchise to women, arguing that political participation was a human right, while proffering the assurance that it would 'never' affect women's traditional roles and femininity. She said:

> We ask for the vote, not that that we might interfere with you in your official functions, your civic duties, your public place and power, but rather that we might lay the foundation of national character in the souls of the children that we hold upon our laps, and instil into them the ideals of national life. (Cited in Forbes 1998: 94)

When the women's organisations emerged to articulate the demand for franchise and legal reforms (as in the Hindu law on property rights), the inconsistency of Congress support forced upon them difficult choices between nationalistic and feminist goals. The 'feminist nationalism' that was projected by women and supported by men subordinated gender equality to national politics. Forbes (ibid.: 120) argues that in choosing to subordinate their claims to the national goals, women were not being 'puppets' as some have maintained, but were conscious of the difficulty of the struggle and compromised to get some degree of justice.

The complexity and ambiguity of the women's struggle is evident in the arena of education. Education and law were seen as key factors in the social reform campaigns against child marriage, and those in support of widow remarriage and the abolition of sati. Everyone seemed to agree that education was at the centre of women's emancipation, but this education was envisioned in Brahminical and elitist terms to enhance women's ability to serve the family and the nation more effectively. Many reformist men who played a key role in widening the lives of Indian women through education also fostered ambiguous attitudes among women towards their own emancipation, the freedom of their minds.

Prominent among those who championed women's education in the later nineteenth century was Pandita Ramabai Ranadive (see Chakravarti 1998). As Omvedt (2006: 26) points out, although Pandita Ramabai converted to Christianity, she 'accepted much of the framework of the Brahman intellectuals of the time', the identification of 'India' with 'Hindu', and the Aryan justification for caste hierarchy as 'economic division of labour'. Despite this, says Omvedt, Ramabai was the first to identify 'the Sanskritic core of Hinduism as irrevocably and essentially anti-woman'.

The hegemonic substratum of a Brahminical patriarchy is reflected even more clearly in the lives and work of some of the prominent 'new women' of the late nineteenth century. Tarabai Shinde (ca. 1850–ca. 1910) wrote the defiantly path-breaking treatise *Stri Purush Tulana* on the problems faced by widows and by women in traditional marriages, but accepted that a woman's fulfilment in life lay in her role as wife and mother (see O'Hanlon 1994). Anandibai Joshi (1865–87), the first Indian woman who qualified as an allopathic doctor, was able to do so because she had been married as a child to a fanatic believer in women's education, but she also suffered greatly from his patriarchal convictions, which she upheld to the extent of publicly defending child marriage (see Chitnis 1992: xi). Such defiance of tradition and submission to it also marked the life of

Krupabai Satthianadhan (1862–1894), whose autobiographical narrative *Saguna*, published in 1895, was the first such work in English in India. Her story vividly reflects the influence of a much-loved elder brother and husband in moulding her thoughts to new learning, while reaffirming the conservative values of a married woman in colonial society. Lokuge (1998: 12) writes:

> It is possible to speculate that these women who were so directly caught in the cross-currents of the Indian-British encounter suffered profound conflict and dislocation not clearly explained even to themselves, caused by the collision of recently acquired New-Woman convictions with established ideologies, growing nationalist concerns, and equally significantly, traumatic fear of the unknown.

Aruna Asaf Ali has argued that the 'real liberation' of Indian women can be traced to the 1930s (Masani 1987, cited via Visram in Hardiman 2004: 116). She says that earlier social reformers had not been able to do what Mahatma Gandhi had done when he called upon women to join the freedom struggle, saying that women were better 'symbols of mankind' and better *satyagrahis* than men. Gandhi gave women, including the majority of those in the freedom struggle who were not educated or westernised, tremendous self-confidence: 'At last women were made to feel the equal of a man: that feeling dominated us all, educated and non-educated.' For their part, women applauded Gandhi for his progressive views against child marriage and for equal sexual relationships within marriage, for his advocacy of widow remarriage, his appeal to simple lifestyles that would reduce women's drudgery within the home and his opposition to purdah. Although, some educated women like Dr Lakshmi (Swaminadhan) Sehgal of the INA (Indian National Army) did enter the public arena on their own terms (see Ali 2004), exceptionally exercising freedoms many men of their time could not even think of, middle-class women generally accepted Gandhi's core belief that it was women's duty to uphold the moral values of marriage and society.

In a speech to the Gujarat Educational Conference in 1917, Gandhi said:

> Primary education for the two sexes can have much in common. There are important differences at all other levels. As Nature has made men and women different, it is necessary to maintain a difference between the education of the two. True, they are equals in life, but their functions differ.

It is woman's right to rule the home. Man is the master outside it. Man is the earner, woman saves and spends. Woman looks after the feeding of the child. She shapes its future. She is responsible for building its character. She is her children's educator and hence, Mother to the Nation. (Joshi 1988: 14–15)

Gandhi felt that this 'scheme of Nature' was just and that while women should not be 'kept in ignorance and under suppression', they should not have to earn their living as telegraph clerks, typists or compositors in printing presses. After a certain age, women 'should be taught the management of the home, the things they should or should not do during pregnancy and the nursing and care of children'. Gandhi's views on women's social and political participation evolved over time, but his views on women's education remained much the same.

According to Sarkar (1984: 99), Gandhi astutely blended the 'religious content of nationalism' with feminine virtues of gentility, patience and sacrifice. Gandhian non-violence had a particularly feminine ambience, enabling women to join the freedom struggle without upsetting the essential structure of patriarchy. Gandhi's patriarchal views were not critiqued even by such stalwarts of the women's movement as Sarojini Naidu. As Hardiman (2004: 122) suggests, the 'negative elements' of Gandhi's patriarchy 'were outweighed by the positive social and political benefits he helped achieve for women'. Thus, the Indian woman took 'her place as a worthy yet subordinate citizen of the nation' (ibid.: 105). After independence, government policies and programme approaches to women's education and work extolled women's role in nation-building but denied them rights as full citizens.

Unlike middle-class, upper-caste urban women, in most parts of rural India, the traditional work of poor women, forest-dwellers, peasants and artisans has never been confined to the domestic sphere. In the various pre-independence struggles for resources (as for forest produce in the Kumaon Himalayas in present-day Uttarakhand), women saw the livelihoods of their communities at stake, but rarely raised gender-specific issues within their campaigns, with the only exception of issues like male drunkenness and alcoholism. In the revolutionary Tebhaga movement (1946–47) for rights over the produce of land in pre-Partition Bengal, women peasants participated in large numbers in the struggle, and in some locations emerged as leaders (see Custers 1987). Peasant women joined the movement as 'workers' because they were being sexually and economically exploited by *jotedars* and zamindars, but they also brought questions of gender equality and domestic violence before their male comrades. Panjabi (2000) says:

> The evidence from the women in the Tebhaga movement indicates that they did not enter the movement looking for equality with men. It was not the question of gender politics that brought them into the movement. There was such acute starvation and oppression that the demand for equality was a meaningless concept unless questions of access to food, to shelter, to livelihood were addressed. It was an anti-imperialist and anti-feudal movement. At rock bottom it was a movement against hunger. But what happened next was that as the movement developed more women came into the field of political activism and began dealing with other kinds of problems, further gender demands came in ... and the women's movement developed from within. (p. 81)

Women across social classes came together in the context of sexual exploitation, although in other contexts class also reinforced gender politics.

The revolutionaries, like the Gandhian reformists, sensed that women's power could destabilise patriarchal institutional structures. Like Gandhi, the revolutionary communist groups also grasped the significance of gender equality in nation-building, but were divided on the 'woman question'. Despite the ideological position that women's oppression was caused by class oppression, there was considerable hesitation among the Communists in allowing issues of gender relations and sexuality to be raised within the 'larger' struggles for liberation. In later years, the opposition of Indian women Communists to feminism and feminist groups (for example, Ranadive 1987: 1–34, cited in Sen 2000) would become strident, pushing women's issues to the periphery of the working-class movement. The consequent neglect of the structural aspects of patriarchy, issues of domination and gender-power, property relations and inheritance in the family, have been critiqued from within left-feminism (see for example Jayawardana and Kelkar 1989; Sen 1989).

Redefining Citizenship for Development

Since the early twentieth century, citizenship has been defined in terms of rights in relation to the state. Conventionally, these rights include civil rights (such as freedom of speech, assembly and movement, and equality under the law), political rights (to vote and stand for election), and socio-economic rights (welfare and security). Some rights may cut across the civil, political and socio-economic domains, such as the right to collectively bargain with the state for particular benefits. Under colonialism and discriminatory regimes such as apartheid, as also under post-colonial independent governments, citizenship rights have been denied to many powerless groups. Independence movements have involved struggles for civil and political rights, and the right to control and manage natural resources such as land, water and forests, and the produce from ecosystems. The modern concept of citizenship is based on a liberal framework of individual rights and criteria of individual inclusion and exclusion. Such a concept of citizenship does not easily encompass the rights of citizens in relation to one another or the collective rights of social groups, especially when this relates to the natural resource-based livelihoods of poor peasants, fishers, artisans, and migrant and nomadic people. However, as Yuval-Davis (1997b: 22) points out:

> Once the notion of citizenship is understood as a concept wider than just a relationship between the individual and the state, it could also integrate the struggles of women against oppression and exploitation in the name of culture and tradition within their own ethnic and local communities and transcend the politically dangerous but intellectually sterile debate which took place in the UN conference on human rights in Vienna in 1993 about whether the struggle for human rights should be on an individual or a 'group' level. Power relations and conflict of interests apply within 'groups' as well as between them. At the same time, individuals cannot be considered as abstracted from their specific social positionings.

In the pre-Independence Constituent Assembly debates, Jawaharlal Nehru supported the recognition of woman's rights as an individual and not as a member of a community; yet he saw equity as applying not to the individual but to the community, introducing a complexity that continues to this day. Mazumdar (1998) argues that unlike Gandhi, Nehru did not grasp the political significance of gender equality in nation-building. She says (citing Sarkar 1998) that he also could not understand Kamladevi Chattopadhya's objection that women's fundamental right was for attention and not for protection, and that the concept of protection was patronising.

The Constitution of India takes a complex view of citizenship. It adopts a typical modern liberal approach in recognising all citizens, irrespective of religion, caste or sex, as being fundamentally equal with regard to various individual civil, political and socio-economic rights under the law, and forbids discrimination on the grounds of religion, race, caste, sex and descent, place of birth or residence. Yet, it also recognises that groups within the larger Indian polity have special needs; Article 15(3) empowers the state to make special provisions for women and children, even if this violates the principle of non-discrimination. Apart from this, the Constitution also recognises particular socio-cultural and religious needs and provides for protection by the state. With regard to the special provisions for some of the 'ethnic' north-eastern states, the Constitution clarifies that these would be overriding. For Indian women, what this means is that although the Constitution safeguards their equal rights as individuals and citizens, it also upholds existing patriarchal legal regimes, notably the personal laws of major religious communities, as also the customary laws of socio-cultural groups in north-eastern India, which exclude women from political and jural participation (see Krishna 2004c). Since the majority of these pre-constitutional regimes are not gender egalitarian, this has made women's legal position contentious with regard to marriage and inheritance and ownership of property, especially with regard to land in many parts of India (see Agarwal 1994). (The Hindu Succession Act, enacted nearly half a century ago, regulates inheritance of property in a Hindu 'Undivided Family'; this was amended in 2005 so as to make daughters 'coparceners' in the property. Along with the new Domestic Violence Act, 2006 that ensures a woman's right to residence in the matrimonial home, this may now give some women a fairer share in family property.)

During the 1980s, activist jurisprudence in India extended the fundamental rights recognised by the Constitution, thus giving the concept of rights a deeper and more inclusive interpretation. Most significant for women and men is the right to livelihood, which has been an enforceable right under the Constitution since the 1985 judgement of the Supreme Court upholding the rights of pavement dwellers who were being evicted from the streets of Mumbai (Olga Tellis and others vs Bombay Municipal Corporation). The court held that as the pavement and slum dwellers resided near their places of work, their forceful eviction would result in the loss of livelihood, which would be tantamount to denial of the right to life, as the right to life and the right to work were interdependent. Yet, despite constitutional and legal provisions, in practice citizenship is embedded in webs of power, prestige and authority that create differential rights on axes of class, caste, ethnicity, gender and age. This was unfortunately reflected in another case (Almitra Patel vs. Union of India) in 2000 where the judgement criminalised the poor by holding that if the state facilitated the relocation of slum-dwellers, it would amount to rewarding pickpockets (Ramanathan 2004).

Issues of citizenship entered the development debate only in the mid-1990s and gained ground swiftly by extending the concept of human rights to those who lack entitlements and the means of livelihood. Among the many illuminating reformulations of citizenship are those by Dobson (2003) who envisages a cosmopolitan 'ecological citizenship', Kabeer (2005) who speaks of an inclusive 'global citizenship' that encompasses justice, recognition, self-determination and solidarity, and Roy (2001, 2005) who seeks to foreground a 'gendered citizenship' that does not exclude Dalits, workers, peasants, women and even the environment.

Earlier, feminists had attempted to re-conceptualise citizenship to include 'difference'. Lister (1997) reconciled universalism and difference in a 'differentiated universalism' and Werbner and Yuval-Davis (1999) advanced the concept of a 'multi-tiered citizenship'. Others have included an ethics of care (see Hirschmann 1996; Hirschmann and Stephano 1996; Sevenhuijsen 1998, 2000), and of community organising work and community service (Young 1997). Exploring the linkages between democracy and citizenship in Australia, Curtin (2000: 241) points out that while women 'have belonged as citizens of the Australian nation-state since they gained the right to vote in 1902', they have themselves sought to extend the conception of citizenship beyond the formal right to vote. Initially, they claimed their rights as 'citizen-mothers', arguing for a recognition of their 'difference' from men. When they realised that such a conception excluded some interests, particularly those of Australian Aboriginal women, the strategy shifted to 'seeking equality as workers'. Moving on, women now claim equal representation in political institutions. As Curtin says, 'the way in which demands for the re-conceptualisation of citizenship are framed, very much depends on the historical context'.

It has also been suggested that instead of seeing citizenship conventionally as a means to realise rights, we should see rights as one of the means
to realise equal citizenship (Voet 1998: 73). This has resonances with
Amartya Sen (1999: 36), who sees development in terms of the substantive
freedoms of people, and the process of expanding these freedoms both as
the 'principal means' and as the 'primary end' of development. Perhaps
we could then argue that it is necessary to recast development to deepen
citizenship, even as citizenship is reconstructed to deepen development.
Concepts of inclusive, multi-tiered and gendered citizenship are especially
valuable in countering patriarchal approaches to development and
technocratic attempts to 'de-politicise' development.

II. RESOURCES, WORK, GOVERNANCE, INSTITUTIONS AND AGENCY

Poor people's livelihood rights are increasingly being subverted by the
state and powerful sections of society in concert with global capital and
market forces, resulting in the loss of economic spaces, livelihoods, resources and knowledge, and often the suppression of ways of life and
culture. The livelihood rights of poor and marginalised people are inextricably linked to their right to living spaces, as also to natural landscapes
and ecological-occupational niches. Because of the patriarchal ideologies
that prevail in much of South Asia, all of these spaces are gendered. In
many parts of the country women are primarily responsible for providing
the family food, but do not own and/or control the necessary resource base,
and may or may not have the right to take decisions about resource management. Even among relatively gender-eg...itarian groups, where women
manage resources, they are excluded from political, jural and religious
authority. Processes of modern development and state policies have reinforced existing patriarchal ideologies or introduced new forms of
patriarchy, thus undermining women's rights as citizens. Yet, the struggle
to build upon very narrow and eroding asset bases has also enhanced the
individual and collective strengths of different groups of poor and marginalised women. They have responded to these diverse pressures in novel
ways and have fought to maintain their livelihoods, their work, and their
moral and cultural environments.

Despite the opening up of spaces and the 'limited acknowledgement' of women's rights in the twentieth century, many of the issues have remained unchanged (Mazumdar and Agnihotri 1999; Krishna 2004d). Here, the questions before us are: how can we recast the concept of citizenship for equitable development? And, conversely, how can we transform paternalistic welfare and/or instrumental approaches to women's development so as to advance an empowered citizenship? These questions are critical for poor peasants and other marginalised groups such as shifting cultivators, graziers, fishers and fish-workers, artisans, home-based workers and unorganised labour, all of whom lack the power to claim citizenship. Many complex issues are involved, requiring several different threads of analysis: the economic and political struggles of marginalised groups of women for recognition of their identity as citizens along with their right to access and manage natural, livelihood resources; the importance of access to land and common property resources (such as non-timber forest produce) vis-à-vis familial, institutional and political decision-making spaces; policy approaches to integrating women in governance, development and natural resource policy; women's agency in the context of decentralised, local governance and new local collective spaces (such as savings-and-credit and/or entrepreneurial groups); and women's continuing economic contribution (despite the obstacles to productive work and dignified employment in a globalising world).

While it is difficult to address such a vast canvas in one volume, we have attempted to approach certain key themes (at the field, programme and policy levels) from the point of view of a citizenship that embraces development and of a development that enhances citizenship.

Recognition and Resource Rights

Nation-states in colonial and post-colonial times have variously regulated different occupational groups in an attempt to 'administer' and define the range of their activities, especially with regard to cultivation of crops and access to natural resources. In the late nineteenth and early twentieth centuries, colonial power worked through mapping territories and categorising both people and land within demarcated boundaries.

[The] emerging notion of land as a quantifiable, measurable object of knowledge, as a resource to be controlled and improved in the colonial imagination (Robb 1997: xvi), [was] reflected among other things in the measuring and classification of waste, forest and cultivable areas into distinct geographical spaces. As with other colonised regions during this period, this increasing rigidity was extended into the gradual hardening of boundaries between the tenurial strata. (Misra 2005)

The political attempt to settle various groups into sedentary occupations at particular locations and exclude them from other occupations and areas effectively reduced the range of livelihood choices available to these hitherto mobile groups. The control and appropriation of common property resources, such as land, water and forests by the state in pre-Independence India has now been well-documented. This process has continued, even intensified, affecting all poor communities that depend on land and other natural resources (see Sagari R. Ramdas and Nitya S. Ghotge, Chapter 2, this volume).

Especially vulnerable are the tribal groups of central and southern India, whose subsistence depends on foraging for edible plants and animals from the wild (P. Thamizoli and P. Ignatius Prabhakar, Chapter 4, this volume). Also at risk are people who practice 'nomadic transhumance'—moving seasonally along with their livestock across large distances following the grazing, often living in temporary shelters throughout the year, such as the Deccani herders. So, too, are people like the gender-egalitarian Bhotias of the Kumaon Himalayas (Hoon 1996), who practice 'fixed transhumance'—moving seasonally with their livestock from the lower valleys, where they have permanent winter homes, to higher pastures in summer. Many other adivasi/tribal groups in peninsular and north-eastern India also lead precarious lives as shifting (or swidden) cultivators. In this form of cultivation, the cropped area is 'shifted' after a few seasons by leaving cultivated fields fallow for natural regeneration and moving on to other fields, which are then prepared by slashing and burning the vegetation; in turn, a previously cultivated field would be cleared and replanted in cyclical rotation. Forest dwellers, who depend on gathering non-timber forest produce, are also threatened by arbitrary state regulations on land-use (Neera M. Singh, Chapter 3, this volume). Among those most in jeopardy are migrants/immigrants in precarious ecological niches, such as the women-headed households on the riverine lands of eastern India (Gopa Samanta and Kuntala Lahiri-Dutt, Chapter 5, this volume). Also at risk are the migrants and others in dry semi-arid areas (Sanjay Joshi, Chapter 6 and Chhaya Datar, Chapter 7, this volume).

Yet, all of these fine-tuned livelihood strategies have evolved in response to particularly difficult ecological conditions, and have been modified over time in keeping with external social and environmental factors and the people's own needs and aspirations. The livelihood practices of foragers, shifting cultivators and other forest-dwellers, nomads and migrants are easily targeted in local conflicts over the use and control of resources, or when different arms of the state appropriate or forcibly acquire resources in a supposedly larger national interest. These groups get characterised as 'primitive' and/or are defined as 'illegal'; the 'illegality' of their life-occupations then rubs off on the people themselves, resulting in their being deprived of their tenuous livelihood base and in an erosion of their sense of self.

Despite the relative gender-egalitarianism of many adivasi groups, the women bear the major burden of providing food to the family and therefore access to a sustainable resource base is the most critical for them. As Ramdas and Ghotge point out, it is the women who form 'the backbone of pastoral and shifting cultivation households' and who have also 'led the struggle for legal rights to resources, and to maintaining a way of life and livelihood'. Hence, superficial attempts by the state for 'gender-balance' in programmes are meaningless without addressing the larger political issue of recognition and the right to resources, including women's rights to access and control over livelihood resources, as well as the places where these resources occur and where their evolution has been nurtured over time. Women themselves have also drawn upon their own social networks and struggled to gain political and economic spaces. As Neera Singh comments, by asserting their livelihood rights, women tobacco-leaf gatherers in Orissa have been transformed from 'transgressors' in political territories that had hitherto excluded them to becoming 'citizens of these domains'. The women tobacco-leaf gatherers do not view forests as property over which they have absolute or exclusive rights, but as living resources for which they have certain contractual rights and obligations. In the process of bringing their livelihood issues onto the agenda of a local federation of forest protection groups, they were able to transform the agenda of the federation itself. By doing so they asserted their right to livelihood and gained political space.

For the Irula women foragers in the coastal tract of Cuddalore district, Tamil Nadu, being categorised as Scheduled Tribes (STs) and getting the 'Community Certificate' was perceived as the pathway to fulfilling other socio-economic needs (see Thamizoli and Prabhakar, this volume). The recent public debate and campaign over the provisions of The Scheduled Tribes (Recognition of Forest Rights) Act, 2005, is indicative of the need to reconceptualise citizenship. In a just society the content of citizenship has to be extended to include the political right to recognition of ways of life.

Work and Employment Strategies

Decent work is perhaps the most critical component of citizenship. In the harsh environment of the 'char lands' (shifting mud flats) of the river Damodar in West Bengal, the struggle for livelihood is as relentless for the migrants from Bihar as for the illegal Hindu immigrants from Bangladesh (Samanta and Lahiri-Dutt, this volume). The immigrants were more concerned about being washed away by the river than they were about their legal status. Unlike their Bihari neighbours, the lack of citizenship does mean that the immigrants can never move out of the chars to the mainland, adding to their insecurity. However, the 'levels of poverty of these women do not have a strong relationship with their legal citizenship'. Indeed, the women-headed households are not all alike; on the chars the stresses of poverty are linked more to the number of young children who need care vis-à-vis the number of grown-up and earning members who can contribute to the family income.

Political rights and the legally protected status of citizenship are insufficient without the economic right to resources, work and employment. Rights to food, health, education, indeed the right to life, are dependent on work. Under the Indian Constitution, it is the state's duty to safeguard this right (Articles 39A and 41). A common sense understanding of decent work is that it should be sufficient to lift a family out of poverty. Poverty has many dimensions (see Krishna 2000), although conventionally it has been measured in terms of income alone. The methods of categorising and assessing incomes by the national system of accounting have been controversial. Despite this difficulty, it is now well-established that the recorded decline of poverty in India during the 1970s and 1980s was largely due to government expenditure on relief works and the creation of jobs (see Sen 1996). In the 1990s, with the advent of new economic policies and the reduction of government expenditures, poverty levels stagnated, with the exception of parts of western and southern India, although pockets of poverty continued to persist even in these better-off regions. Poverty has been linked to increasing inequality. Sen and Himanshu (2004) point out that the 'big picture' is that 'the 1990s was the first post-Independence decade when economic inequality increased sharply in all its dimensions'. (In their analysis, inequality had increased in rural areas during the post-Green Revolution period too, but there was 'a tendency for relative food prices to fall' and from the mid-1970s through the 1990s rural inequality decreased. With growth, this led to a fall in poverty levels during that period.) Disparities increased after the early 1990s as food prices increased. Sen and Himanshu (ibid.) further say that 'high initial poverty and population growth seem to have ensured that India's growth revival after 1992 has largely bypassed the poor. The relatively rich did gain and some states did perform better than the others'. They have little doubt that the number of poor increased in the most populated regions, and they see the large shift in the 1990s from food to non-food expenditure, such as on fuel, medicines and conveyance, even among the poor, as indicative of a 'worsening nutrition situation'. This strengthens their argument against excluding numbers of the poor from food subsidies.

According to the 2001 Census, in India as a whole, 52 per cent of males reported themselves as 'workers' compared to only 25 per cent of females. However, only 58 per cent of the male workers were engaged in agriculture and allied occupations, compared to nearly 80 per cent of the female workers. This confirms the casual observations from across the country that the burden of agriculture is shifting to women (a trend that has been termed as the 'feminisation of agriculture'); in certain areas, such as in parts of north-eastern India, this burden is increasingly being borne almost entirely by older women (Krishna 1998a, 1998b, 2005). The National Sample Surveys (NSSs) provide a more comprehensive coverage of work, but neither the NSS nor the census accurately reflects the extent of women's work (see Krishna 2001; Raju 1993; Jhabvala et al. 2003, Krishna 2004a): household chores, home-based work and informal labour in subsistence dairying, livestock rearing, fishing, hunting, cultivating fruit and vegetable gardens, the collection and processing of medicinal plants, seed selection and storage, food preservation, family health care and so on. The pattern of employment in rural as well as in urban India also shows wide differences across social groups. Jeyaranjan and Swaminathan (2005) point out that in the country as a whole, nearly 72 per cent of Scheduled Caste (SC) and nearly 59 per cent of Scheduled Tribe (ST) households depend on wage labour, particularly daily wage labour. The level of self-employment is higher among ST than SC households, but is low as compared to other social groups. As they comment (ibid.: 15):

> Poverty and deprivation in the country is associated not so much with open unemployment but with the quality of employment: informalisation and casualisation of work; high prevalence of child and elderly labour; work with low skills and low capital and hence with low earnings. A person can be employed and still be poor; the issue is not one of exclusion 'but of the nature and terms of 'inclusion'.

Measures of income poverty do not indicate 'how an economy has been able, over time, to build capacities and provide an enabling environment to its citizens for self-actualisation' (ibid.: 23). Apart from the occupational profile, other factors that need to be considered in assessing deprivation include land and its quality, education and health.

Reviewing women's employment over two decades, Banerjee (1995) points out that the government realised quite early on that women responded in very large numbers to state-sponsored work programmes (ISST 1987); the Integrated Rural Development Programme(IRDP), for instance, had a 'very strong component reserved for women'. Although more women did enter the workforce, and this may even have been because the demand for women's labour did increase, women have been mainly employed at lower levels in poorly paid, low-skilled jobs, with low productivity and no prospects for vertical mobility. As Datar (Chapter 7, this volume) points out, the work that women do is drudgery, what no man would like to undertake if possible.

Banerjee (1995) rejects the conventional 'explanation' for women's subordination in the labour market, that is, women's lack of literacy, their domestic responsibilities and the limitations on their mobility, as also the alternative and influential explanation advanced by a section of feminists (see Mies 1998; Mies and Shiva 1994; Sen and Grown 1987;

Shiva 1989). According to Mies and others, in pre-capitalist societies women were able to combine the reproductive work of collecting water, fuel, fodder, et cetera, with production; in capitalist economies, the resources necessary for reproduction are taken away by the state and the market even as productive work and labour are separated from the household, and the ensuing conflict between women's work in the two spheres of reproduction and production increases their subordination. I share Banerjee's reservations with regard to this thesis. First, as she points out, it is ahistorical because there is no anthropological evidence to show that in pre-capitalist societies, including India, women easily combined productive and reproductive work, and that they were not discriminated against. Second, it is not clear that changing the course of development will bring about a harmony in women's reproductive and productive work. And third, the overemphasis on 'nurturing' tasks homogenises women as a group, masking differences of class, community and region. In order to understand the construction of the woman worker, Banerjee (1995) says that we need to analyse the 'primary force' of patriarchy in socialising women, controlling their sexuality and preparing them as a flexible source of labour. Indeed, when the family needs women's wage labour, they do get sent out in large numbers. Patriarchal ideologies subordinate women and restrict their social space through the conventions and practices of marriage and the inheritance of property. State interventions do not counter such patriarchal subordination (this is also reflected in different ways by Kelkar, Chapter 10 and Ramakrishnan et al., Chapter 17, this volume).

Development based on social and economic exclusion only reinforces discrimination, undermining the citizenship of whole groups of people. With India's ongoing economic reforms since the 1990s and the new global forces governing trade, investment and finance, people's decision-making spaces have been eroded, both politically and economically, and different challenges have emerged. As Mazumdar (2005) has pointed out, women's right to livelihood is an economic right, but economic empowerment cannot be bracketed separately from political and social empowerment. 'The right to livelihood is a way by which women can stake a claim as productive persons, but only if women's rights are recognised as human rights can they do so with *dignity*.'

It is against this larger context that we need to view poverty alleviation programmes such as Maharashtra's Employment Guarantee Scheme

(EGS)(Datar, Chapter 7, this volume) and Madhya Pradesh's Employment Assurance Scheme (EAS)(Joshi, this volume). Joshi's study shows clearly that the provisions of even a 'good scheme' like the EAS in Madhya Pradesh are 'too inadequate to make a significant dent on the earnings and the livelihoods of tribal women' in the semi-arid and backward district of Jhabua. As he points out, basic to all development schemes are 'human rights'. The significance of the newly enacted National Rural Employment Guarantee (NREG) Act, 2005, is that it provides for the *right* to employment (see Box. 1.1). However, while it lists a variety of different works, it does not

---

Box 1.1
The National Rural Employment
Guarantee Act, 2005

According to the Constitution of India, the state shall 'direct its policy towards securing that the citizen, men and women equally, have the right to an adequate means of livelihood' (Article 39 A). It also says the state shall 'make effective provision for securing the right to work' (Article 41). Though the NREG Act is an attempt to fulfil these half-a-century old constitutional provisions, it was passed by Parliament only after a sustained campaign and lobbying with political parties. In a period when public policy has been marked by the state withdrawing from providing social security, the new Act significantly recognises the state's responsibility towards its poorest citizens. It guarantees 100 days of wage employment in a year to all rural households in 200 districts across the country. What this means is that any adult in every rural (nuclear) household who is willing to do unskilled 'manual' labour at the minimum wage is entitled to employment on local public works within 15 days of applying for work. If such work is not offered, there is provision for unemployment allowances. The Act gives women special priority, and at least a third of the labourers have to be women. The Right to Food Campaign has described the NREG Act as a 'landmark in the history of social security legislation in India—or indeed, anywhere in the world', and says that it 'promises to be a major tool in the struggle to secure the right to food'. (For details see the website of the 'Right to Food Campaign', http://www.righttofoodindia.org/rtowork/)

envisage the kind of asset ownership that Datar attempted through Maharashtra's EGS. Her attempt to mobilise the women of Osmanabad in drought-prone Marathwada for a collective horticulture scheme was received with scepticism because the poor landless women could not imagine themselves owning an orchard; in their minds, they were labourers, not entrepreneurs.

Democratic Governance and Institutional Systems

In the early 1950s, independent India's nationwide Community Development (CD) Programme had attempted to establish a decentralised administrative system centred around community institutions inspired both by the Gandhian philosophy of Sarvodaya and various initiatives to improve agricultural production (Krishna 2001). The aim was to integrate all aspects of rural life in a holistic process of social and economic transformation. The First Five-Year Plan had emphasised the internalisation of development processes through people's involvement. By the mid-1960s, however, the CD structure and functions were taken over by the bureaucracy and it was more than two decades later that 'community participation' re-entered the development discourse. Although the CD programme aimed to include all men and women, there was resistance on account of caste and gender differentiation. Because the CD model itself was 'constituted by structures of power which had socialised women into silent nurturing, these voices were not heard' (ibid.: 31). Yet, even within the patriarchal structures of patronage, certain collective spaces were created for and by women (such as the *mahila mandals* in different states). The contemporary version of community participation has followed two different trajectories. At one level, it has taken the route of political decentralisation through the Panchayati Raj Institutions (PRIs), in which one-third of all seats are reserved for women under the Constitution (73rd Amendment) Act, 1992, and the Panchayati Raj (Extension to the Scheduled Areas) Act (PESA), 1996. At another level, the explosive growth of NGOs as intermediaries between the communities and the state has effectively de-politicised development. The withdrawal of the state from many areas of development in the 1990s has led to a tussle for space between the elected PRIs and 'civil society' NGOs.

The 73rd Amendment does not apply to parts of north-eastern India that have various customary systems of local governance (as in Nagaland, Meghalaya and Mizoram, and the autonomous district councils that come under the Sixth Schedule). However, they do apply to the state of Arunachal Pradesh (formerly the North-East Frontier Agency, NEFA), strategically located on the India-China border. Till 1987, when Arunachal Pradesh attained statehood, it was directly administered by the Government of India. As in other parts of the region, the state has had a strong military presence and has received large financial outlays. Deepak Mishra and Vandana Upadhyay (Chapter 8, this volume) argue that in the north-eastern region as a whole, the state's relative weakness in protecting property and providing security has led to the emergence of various ethnic groups, which use 'private' means of securing property, contributing to the growth of insurgency. However, uniquely, in Arunachal Pradesh, such conflicts have led to different tribal groups bargaining and negotiating to acquire a larger share of government resources through 'quiet pressure' from within the system. Mishra and Upadhayay say that while community participation is part of the rhetoric of development, this does not reflect the 'elite capture' of governance structures and development processes. They see clear indications of the negative implications this has for marginalised sections among the tribals, including women. They also point to the 'twin dangers' of viewing existing gender relations as egalitarian and of treating all demands for equality as being against tribal traditions.

Education and the law are critical dimensions of democratic governance. The traditional subordination of women and their exclusion from decision-making persists even in Mizoram, where conventional demographic and economic indicators reflect more gender equality than elsewhere in India (see Krishna 2005b). Analysing processes of socialisation and the value system of tribal groups, B. Lakshmi (Chapter 9, this volume) shows how traditional gender stereotypes in Mizoram are now being reinforced by development, the modern education system, school languages and textbooks.

Whether it is governance, education, inheritance of property, or resource policy, the perception that the community is homogeneous and that legal/institutional changes will bring about gender equality is increasingly being questioned. Meghana Kelkar (Chapter 10, this volume) argues that the agricultural research, education and extension network form a vast institutional system geared towards enhancing productivity through a 'unidisciplinary mode of research and technology transfer' that excludes women's agricultural knowledge and skills. The question is not just of including women farmers in policy and programmes, but of understanding that the agricultural network is a 'gendered institution' that is especially resistant to change. Advocacy for 'gender mainstreaming' remains at the level of rhetoric, serving to mask the instrumentalist approach of the state and interests of the elite. Similarly, Seema Kulkarni (Chapter 11, this volume) points out that the new water policy environment seeks solutions to the water crisis through institutional reforms such as the decentralisation of resource management, but is resistant to women's 'potential to challenge the existing property relations and the division of labour'. So, although women are accepted as members of village drinking water and sanitation committees, they are unrepresented in the water user associations (WUAs) whose membership depends on holding land in the command areas of a particular irrigation project, thereby effectively keeping out women and the landless. She says the real issue for women is not just more access to water, but 'to demand a space that can challenge the structures of patriarchy'. Indeed, grassroots women's movements in southern Maharashtra are doing this (see Kulkarni 2005).

In many parts of India the 'elite capture' of state resources has led to the emergence of a speculative land market, especially in rural areas in the vicinity of urban centres. This has led to the encroachment and usurpation of common lands, affecting poor women's access to land and common productive resources. The question of women's individual and collective right to land has rarely been taken up within local struggles on the ground, and this is so across the political spectrum. However, research that has grown out of the women's movement has underlined the importance of land ownership to enhance women's power to take decisions within the family. The extensive work done by Agarwal (1994) has shown that ownership of and control over land is the single most important economic factor in women's well-being and empowerment. More recent work (Panda and Agarwal 2005) shows that women's ownership of land has a positive impact on reducing domestic violence. Land ownership is also critical in facilitating access to farm credit and other inputs. Women's subordinate position in relation to men forms the basis of various Hindu laws related to marriage, adoption and the succession or guardianship of children.

Following sustained campaigns by the women's movement, the law on the inheritance of property has now been reformed. The Hindu Succession (Amendment) Act, 2005, removes gender inequalities in the inheritance of agricultural land (see Box 12.1).

A few of the more progressive states had introduced legal and administrative measures by the 1980s to give women a share in property (such as 'joint *pattas*', title deeds in the names of both the husband and the wife). The central budget for 2005–6 gave women concessions with regard to property registration. Extrapolating data from a larger study on watershed development in Karnataka, M. Indira (Chapter 12, this volume) found that women's title to land had not as yet given them a greater say in decision-making relating to production, marketing, purchase and sale of assets, or control over money. Indeed, earning an income seems to have been more significant for women than owning land. Similarly, Geethakutty's (2006) survey of a randomly selected group of farming women in Thrissur district in Kerala found a relatively high proportion of women who owned land in their own names or held it jointly with their husbands. Yet land ownership, whether by inheritance or purchase, did not seem to have much impact on women's ability to access farmer-support services. The farming women perceived the potential for activities only in those spaces that were intended for women alone, notably the Self Help Groups (SHGs). 'General institutions' like cooperative societies were not viewed as women's spaces. Moreover, both land-owning and landless women did not perceive landownership as important either for livelihood or their own status. This has resonances with the attitude of the poor women of Osmanabad, despite the geographical and socio-economic distance that separates the drought-prone, backward hinterland of Maharashtra from the green fields and waterways of Thrissur. These micro studies should not be read as indicating that land ownership is not important, but they do show that having title deeds to land in their names may not always be sufficient to enhance women's livelihoods and position.

Gender-just laws do facilitate change, but the transformation of social practice is a much more difficult process. Consider the case of Goa (a Portuguese colony till its liberation and union with India in 1961). Civil law in Goa follows the Portuguese Civil Code, established over a century ago in 1867, which makes the registration of marriages compulsory for all communities and assures married women a share in their husband's property (Shaila Desouza, Chapter 13, this volume). As all property is considered to be held jointly, a husband cannot sell his property without the consent of his wife. Sons and daughters get an equal share of family property. Despite such gender egalitarianism, there are many ways of circumventing the law. Unless a wife insists that her name be included in the land records, which is a rare occurrence, it will be solely in the husband's name. He then only has to conceal the fact of his marriage to dispose of the property. Desouza points out that the law has not enabled women to access economic resources because it has not been 'assimilated into the lifestyle of the people'. Legal and social reforms have to go hand-in-hand.

Women's Collective Agency and Struggles

In classical economic thought, women's agency has been simply defined as the capacity of a female economic agent for rational decision-making. Across many cultures, it was long believed that women lacked rationality because of their biological attributes and that, therefore, they were not fit to participate in public affairs. One of the early tasks of the suffragette movement was to establish that women were rational, discriminating beings who were indeed fit to vote and stand for election. Since then, feminists have expanded the concept of agency to encompass other aspects of empowerment, including the power to make life choices and define the meaning of things. Women's agency (as exercised by individuals and by groups of women) is a significant aspect of their gender identity, sexuality, economic independence and socio-political participation in institutions of governance. As individuals and as members of groups, women are deprived of their agency in multifarious ways by the state, by their own communities and even within people's political struggles of which they may be a part. Poor tribal women are disempowered as both tribals and women (see Bhaskaran 2004); so too poor Dalit women are disempowered as Dalits and as women (see Bama 2005). 'Interlocking patriarchies' (Anandhi 2002) ensure that Dalit women are rarely able to claim their legitimate political rights as citizens. Even as new spaces in local governance and resource management open up for women, patriarchy systematically destroys women's agency, their livelihoods and their capacity for self-determination, thus advancing the process of subordination (see Krishna 2004a, d, 2007).

Over the last decade and a half, certain clear trends, which have had an enormous and varied impact on the development sector in India, have been discernible. First, there has been political decentralisation (through the 73rd and 74th Amendments and PESA): this is, of course, not the same as democratisation, but it has paved the way for a realignment of power at the 'grassroots'. Second, the opening up of spaces in civil society for non-government intermediaries to serve as an interface with people (for instance, in the provision of basic services) has brought about a renewed emphasis on 'participatory' approaches to development. Third, the promotion and extraordinary growth of women's micro-economic activities through formal associations (SHGs) for micro savings-and-credit and micro-enterprise schemes have posed new challenges for women's development and women's citizenship. Micro-credit may not have reached the poorest women or contributed significantly to sustainable development, but women's collectives (including SHGs in some areas) have begun to serve as an effective interface for women to articulate and claim rights, and perhaps even to deal with male-dominated village panchayats.

Indeed, this has also been the experience with the *sangha*s of the Mahila Samakhya (MS) programme in many states. The MS programme is unusual in its feminist, transformatory emphasis. In keeping with Paulo Freire's ideas of education as empowerment, it attempted to change gender stereotypes through reflection and action in a common space. Although the programme has been criticised for its lack of focus on livelihood and economic problems, there is abundant evidence from states like Karnataka showing that sanghas have enhanced women's sense of self-worth and their ability to define their own roles in local affairs. They have given women a legitimate collective *bedike* (platform), which fulfils a deeply felt need for women's space, and provided crucial support for the elected women representatives in the panchayats (Krishna 2004b, d). Many a sangha has also sought to translate this into a concrete physical space, a *mané* (house). Vinalini Mathrani and Vani Periodi (Chapter 14, this volume) have shown how women negotiate the tortuous process—extending over months and years—of establishing their own mané, acquiring the land, constructing the structure, managing the funding and, not the least, overcoming entrenched male resistance. The women's mané is a symbol of their independence and a medium through which they exercise collective citizenship.

Gender-specific spaces like the women's mané, which are outside the private gendered spaces of the household, alter notions of the private and the public, even if they are unable to challenge existing gender relations in the family or gender roles in the community. In certain circumstances, especially where NGOs facilitate the process, women's groups have also been able to enter political spaces. Mandakini Pant (Chapter 15, this volume) reviews the role of women's SHGs in bringing women's voices into the planning process at the level of the panchayats in the economically backward areas of Madhya Pradesh, Uttar Pradesh and Uttarakhand. She suggests that the SHGs covered by the study have provided poor and marginalised women information, a social network and the motivation to make panchayats more responsive to their needs and concerns. These are not small gains in a context in which even statutory representation in local bodies does not necessarily translate into meaningful and participatory democratic governance (see Mohanty and Tandon 2006). Like the MS programme, the Women's Development Programme (WDP) in Rajasthan was conceived as a transformatory development intervention that focused less on tangible assets. It sought to question patriarchal perceptions of women as inferior and limited in their abilities. As Shobhita Rajagopal (Chapter 16, this volume) points out, this was unusual in a state with a feudal, patriarchal past that continues to govern its present. The burden of the programme was carried on the shoulders of the *sathin* (literally, woman friend or companion) who served as a village change agent, mobilising women around a range of human rights and livelihood issues such as the right to grazing land and fair wages. On the other hand, Rajasthan's District Poverty Initiative Project aims to improve the incomes of women and men through livelihood activities such as tailoring, basketry and rope-making. While women's visibility and mobility increased, their voices continued to be excluded from institutional spaces.

There is increasing concern that seemingly progressive development interventions speak the language of empowerment, but take instrumental approaches to women's participation (see Batliwala and Dhanraj 2004; Krishna 2007; Raju 2005). Even the WDP's intention to improve women's participation was deeply circumscribed, as Ramakrishnan, Lobo and Kapur (Chapter 17, this volume) point out. Within a few years of the programme's inception, there was an 'unannounced shift in orientation' as 'centralised policy planning and a top-down approach reappeared'. Sathins were reduced to functionaries in government development programmes and their workload increased, but the official perception of them as volunteers persisted. The sathins' unionisation and their collective struggle for minimum wages created a backlash in the form of intimidation and attempts at suppression. The sathins had fought patriarchal feudal practices through mobilising groups of women, but their own citizenship was threatened; the programme that was intended to empower women turned oppressive when the women began to raise political issues of entitlements. As Ramakrishnan, Lobo and Kapur say, 'ideological mists in the development sector' cannot simply 'be analysed away', but 'have to be challenged through collective action'. Women's struggle against exploitation is 'two-fold but integrated ... as women and as workers'. Economic and socio-political empowerment are mutually reinforcing processes.

III. ENHANCING CITIZENSHIP TO ENSURE LIVELIHOOD RIGHTS

The right to vote has not changed the marginalised position of the women in Tanabisu. As internal migrants their right to land and livelihood has been constantly under threat, and as women they have been excluded from public spaces, denied even the right to participate in hoisting the national flag on Independence Day. For many poor women like them who are 'free' to work outside the domestic space, this in itself does not bring the right to decision-making or liberation from the traditional constraints of patriarchy, but rather may even exacerbate oppression in both public and domestic spaces, contributing to what Kannabiran (2005) has called 'the violence of normal times'. Gendered critiques of the liberal concept of a 'universal' citizen have helped counter essentialist approaches (whether conventional or celebratory) that see all women as one, united by their biological identity. Women are not a homogeneous group; it is critical to recognise and encompass differences among women. Individuals are embedded in social groups and marginalised in multifarious ways, both as individuals and as members of a group. Oppression, too, takes on many forms undermining the entitlements of people both as individuals and as groups. So, even as we reject essentialist conceptualisations of women's identity, we need to recognise gender justice as a fundamental human right and strive to ensure that the state takes responsibility for equitable development through public policy and the law. Development cannot be truly participatory and people-driven if the structural aspects of patriarchy, issues of domination and gender-power, and property relations and inheritance in the family are not addressed. Legal reforms facilitate access to economic resources, but need to be assimilated into people's lives. The question is not just of including women in policy and programmes, but of unravelling the gendered structure of patriarchal institutions that are notoriously resistant to change. If the content of citizenship were to be extended to include the right to recognition of ways of living and livelihood, women could take their legitimate space as productive human beings who are entitled to dignity as a political right, and not simply to protection and welfare. Theoretical attempts to define a contextual, multilayered and gender-just citizenship that deepens the content of development are fraught with difficulty. However, there is much to be learnt from the collective struggles of poor women, from action and dialogue on the ground. Feminist politics has to network strategically with other struggles to counter the enormous resistance to altering the patriarchal social fabric and work towards recasting citizenship for a gender-just development that ensures women's livelihood rights.

REFERENCES

Agarwal, Bina. 1994. *A Field of One's Own: Gender and Land Rights in South Asia.* Cambridge: Cambridge University Press.

Anandhi, S. 2002. 'Interlocking Patriarchies and Women in Governance: A Case Study of Panchayati Raj Institutions in Tamil Nadu', in Karin Kapadia (ed.), *The Violence of Development*, pp. 425–56. London: Zed Books.

Ali, Subhashini. 2004. 'A Life in Service', *Seminar*, August.

Bama (translated from Tamil by Lakshmi Holmstrom). 2005. *Sangati: Events.* New Delhi: Oxford University Press.

Banerjee, Nirmala. 1995. 'Women's Employment and All That', *The Administrator*, XL(3): 53–70.

Batliwala, Srilatha and Deepa Dhanraj. 2004. 'Gender Myths that Instrumentalise Women: A View from the Indian Frontline', *IDS Bulletin*, 35(4): 11–18.

Bhaskaran (translated from Malayalam by N. Ravi Shankar). 2004. *Mother Forest: The Unfinished Story of C.K. Janu.* New Delhi: Women Unlimited.

Chakravarti, Uma. 1993. 'Conceptualising Brahamanical Patriarchy in Early India: Gender, Caste and State,' *Economic and Political Weekly.* 3 April.

————. 1998. *Rewriting History: The Life and Times of Pandita Ramabai.* New Delhi: Kali for Women.

————. 2003. *Gendering Caste: Through a Feminist Lens.* Kolkata: Stree.

Chambers, Robert. 1995. 'Poverty and Livelihood: Whose Reality Counts', *Environment and Urbanization,* 7(1): 173–204.

Chatterjee, Partha. 1989. 'The Nationalist Resolution of the Women's Question', in K. Sangari and S. Vaid (eds), *Recasting Women: Essays in Indian Colonial History,* pp. 254–68. New Delhi: Kali for Women.

Chitnis, Suma. 1992. 'Introduction', in S.J. Joshi, *Anandi Gopal* (translated from Marathi and abridged by Asha Damle, originally published 1962), pp. v–ix. Kolkata: Stree.

Curtin, Jennifer. 2000. 'The Gendering of "Citizenship" in Australia', in Andrew Vandenberg (ed.), *Citizenship and Democracy in a Global Era,* pp. 231–44. Hampshire and London: Macmillan Press.

Custers, Peter. 1987. *Women in the Tebhaga Uprising: Rural Poor Women and Revolutionary Leadership (1946–47).* Calcutta: Naya Prokash.

Dobson, Andrew. 2003. *Citizenship and the Environment.* Oxford, UK: Oxford University Press.

Forbes, Geraldine. 1998. *Women in Modern India.* The New Cambridge History of India, IV(2) Cambridge, UK: Cambridge University Press.

Geethakutty, P.S. 2006. 'Land Ownership Alone Does Not Engender Farm Livelihoods: A Note on Three Village Panchayats in Thrissur, Kerala', (Unpublished paper).

Gujit, Irene and Meera Kaul Shah (eds). 1998. *The Myth of Community: Gender Issues in Participatory Development.* New Delhi: Vistaar Pubications.

Hardiman, David. 2004. *Gandhi in His Time and Ours: The Global Legacy of His Ideas.* London: C. Hurst and Co. Publishers.

Hirschmann, Nancy J. 1996. 'Toward a Feminist Theory of Freedom', *Political Theory,* 24(I): 46–67.

Hirschmann, Nancy J. and Christine Di Stephano (eds). 1996. *Revisioning the Political.* Princeton, NJ: Princeton University Press.

Hoon, Vineeta. 1996. *Living on the Move: Bhotiyas of the Kumaon Himalaya.* New Delhi: Sage Publications.

ISST. 1987. *Status of Women's Employment.* Vol.1. New Delhi: Institute for Social Studies Trust (mimeo, cited in Banerejee 1995).

Jayawardana, Kumari and Govind Kelkar. 1989. 'The Left and Feminism', *Economic and Political Weekly,* 23 September: 2123–26.

Jeyaranjan, J. and Padmini Swaminathan. 2005. 'Understanding Persistent Poverty in India', Report for the Humanist Institute for Co-operation with Developing Countries, the Netherlands. Bangalore: Hivos.

Jhabvala, Renana, Jeemol Unni and Ratna M. Sudarshan. 2003. *Informal Economy Centre Stage: New Structures of Employment.* New Delhi: Sage Publications.

Joshi, Prabha (ed.). 1988. *Gandhi on Women.* Ahmedabad: Navjivan Trust and New Delhi: Centre for Women's Development Studies.

Kabeer, Naila. 2005. 'The search for Inclusive Citizenship: Meanings and Expressions in an Interconnected World', in Naila Kabeer (ed.), *Inclusive Citizenship: Meanings and Expressions.* New Delhi: Zubaan.

Kannabiran, Kalpana (ed.). 2005. *The Violence of Normal Times.* New Delhi: Women Unlimited.

Krishna, Sumi. 1995. 'It's Time to Clear the Cobwebs: The Gender Impact of Environmentalism', *The Administrator*, August: 93–104.

———. 1996a. *Environmental Politics: People's Lives and Development Choices.* New Delhi: Sage Publications.

———. 1996b. 'The Appropriation of Dissent: The State vis-à-vis People's Movements', in T.V. Satyamurthi (ed.), *Class Formation and Political Transformation in Post-Colonial India* (Social Change and Political Discourse in India, Vol. 4). New Delhi: Oxford University Press.

———. 1998a. 'Arunachal Pradesh', Case Study in M.S. Swaminathan (ed.), *Gender Dimensions in Biodiversity Management*, pp. 148–81. New Delhi: Konark Publ. Pvt. Ltd.

———. 1998b. 'Mizoram', Case Study in M.S. Swaminathan (ed.), *Gender Dimensions in Biodiveristy Management*, pp. 182–210. New Delhi: Konark Publ. Pvt. Ltd.

———. 2000. 'The Impact of the Structural Adjustment Programme on Gender and Environment in India', in CWDS (eds), *Shifting Sands: Women's Lives and Globalization*, pp. 173–234. Kolkata: Stree.

———. 2001. 'Introduction: Towards a 'Genderscape' of Community Rights in Natural Resource Management', *Indian Journal of Gender Studies* (Special Issue: Gender and Community Rights in Natural Resource Management.),. 8(2): 151–74.

——— (ed.). 2004a. *Livelihood and Gender: Equity in Community Resource Management.* New Delhi: Sage Publications.

———. 2004b. 'A "Genderscape" of Community Rights in Natural Resource Management', in Sumi Krishna (ed.), *Livelihood and Gender: Equity in Community Resource Management.* New Delhi: Sage Publications.

———. 2004c. 'Gender, Tribe and Political Participation: Control of Natural Resources in North-Eastern India', in Sumi Krishna (ed.), *Livelihood and Gender: Equity in Community Resource Management*, pp. 351–76. New Delhi: Sage Publications.

Krishna, Sumi. 2004d. 'Knowledge Systems, Equity and Rights: A Dialogue with Vina Mazumdar', in Sumi Krishna (ed.), *Livelihood and Gender: Equity in Community Resource Management*, pp. 425–31. New Delhi: Sage Publications.

———. 2005. 'Gendered Price of Rice in North-Eastern India', *Economic and Political Weekly*, XL(25): 2555–62.

———. 2007. *Genderscapes: Revisioning Natural Resource Management*. New Delhi: Zubaan.

Kulkarni, Seema. 2005. 'Looking Back, Thinking Forward: Women and Landless People's Access to Irrigation—the Khudawadi Experience', in S. Ahmed (ed.), *Flowing Upstream: Empowering Women through Water Management in India*. Ahmedabad: Centre for Environment and Education.

Lister, Ruth. 1997. 'Citizenship: Towards a Feminist Synthesis', *Feminist Review*, 57 (Autumn): 28–48.

Lokuge, Chandani. 1998. 'Introduction', in K. Satthianadhan, *Saguna: The First Autobiographical Novel in English by an Indian Woman*, pp. 1–17. New Delhi: Oxford University Press.

Mazumdar, Malabika. 2005. 'Women's Right to Livelihood and its Positive Linkages with Human Development', (Unpublished paper).

Mazumdar, Vina. 1998. 'An Unfulfilled or Blurred Vision? Jawaharlal Nehru and Indian Women', Occasional Paper No. 30. New Delhi: Centre for Women's Development Studies.

Mazumdar, Vina and Indu Agnihotri. 1999. 'The Women's Movement in India: Emergence of a New Perspective', in Bharati Ray and Aparna Basu (eds), *From Independence Towards Freedom: Indian Women Since 1947*. Gender Studies Series, pp. 221–38. New Delhi: Oxford University Press.

Mies, Maria. 1998. *Patriarchy and Accumulation on a World Scale: Women in the International Division of Labour*. London: Zed Books Ltd.

Mies, Maria and Vandana Shiva. 1994. *Ecofeminism*. New Delhi: Kali for Women.

Misra, Sanghamitra. 2005. 'Changing Frontiers and Spaces: The Colonial State in Nineteenth-Century Goalpara', *Studies in History*, 21(2): 216–46.

Mohanty, Ranjita and Rajesh Tandon (eds). 2006. *Participatory Citizenship: Identity, Exclusion, Inclusion*. New Delhi: Sage Publications.

O'Hanlon, Rosalind. 1994. *Tarabai Shinde and the Critique of Gender Relations in Colonial India*. Madras: Oxford University Press.

Omvedt, Gail. 2006 (rev. ed., first publ. 1995). *Dalit Visions: The Anti-Caste Movement and the Construction of an Indian Identity*. New Delhi: Orient Longman.

Panjabi, Kavita. 2000. 'Intervention: Transcribed Proceedings of the Workshop on "Regional Histories of Women: The Eastern Region", 25 and 26 February, 1999, Calcutta'. Organised by Indian Association for Women's Studies, School of Women's Studies, Jadavpur University and WSRC, Calcutta University.

Panda, Pradeep and Bina Agarwal. 2005. 'Marital Violence, Human Development and Women's Property Status in India', *World Development*, 33(5): 823–50.

Raju, Saraswati. 1993. 'Introduction', in Saraswati Raju and Deipica Bagchi (eds), *Women and Work in South Asia: Regional Patterns and Perspectives*, pp. 1–36. London: Routledge.

———. 2005. 'Limited Options: Rethinking Women's Empowerment "Projects" in Development Discourses: A Case from Rural India', *Gender, Technology and Development*, 9: 253–71.

Ramanathan, Usha. 'Illegality and Exclusion: Law in the Lives of Slum Dwellers', IELRC Working Paper 2004–2, International Environmental Law Research Centre. http://www.ielrc.org/w0402.pdf.

Robb, Peter. 1997. *Ancient Rights and Future Comfort: Bihar, the Bengal Tenancy Act of 1885 and British Rule in India*. Richmond, Surrey: Curzon.

Roy, Anupama. 2001. 'Community, Women Citizens and a Women's Politics', *Economic and Political Weekly* (Special Issue on Review of Women's Studies), 36(17): 1441–47.

———. 2005. *Gendered Citizenship: Historical and Conceptual Explorations*. New Delhi: Orient Longman.

Sangari, Kumkum and Sudesh Vaid. 1989. *Recasting Women: Essays in Indian Colonial History*. New Delhi: Kali for Women.

Sarkar, Tanika. 1984. 'Politics of Women in Bengal: The Conditions and Meaning of Participation', *The Indian Economic and Social History Review*, 21(1).

Sen, Abhijit. 1996. 'Economic Reforms, Employment and Poverty: Trends and Options', *Economic and Political Weekly*, 31(35): 2459–78.

Sen, Abhijit and Himanshu. 2004. 'Poverty and Inequality in India-II: Widening Disparities during the 1990s', *Economic and Political Weekly*, 39(39): 4247–63.

Sen, Amartya. 1999. *Development as Freedom*. New Delhi: Oxford University Press.

Sen, Gita and Caren Grown. 1987. *Development, Crises and Alternative Visions: Third World Women's Perspectives*. New York: Monthly Review Press.

Sen, Ilina. 1989. 'Feminists, Women's Movements and the Working Class', *Economic and Political Weekly*, 29 July: 1639–41.

———. 2000. 'The Women's Movement in India', Booklet. Secunderabad: Azad Reading Room.

Sevenhuijsen, Selma. 1998. *Citizenship and the Ethics of Care: Feminist Considerations on Justice, Morality and Politics*. London and New York: Routledge.

———. 2000. 'Caring in the Third Way: The Relation between Obligation, Responsibility and Care in *Third Way* Discourse', *Critical Social Policy*, 20(1): 5–37.

Shiva, Vandana. 1989. *Staying Alive: Women, Ecology and Survival in India*. New Delhi: Kali for Women.

Sinclair, T.A. 1962. *Aristotle: The Politics*. (Translated with an Introduction). Hammondsworth, UK: Penguin Books.

Sundberg, Juanita. 2003. 'Conservation and democratization: Constituting Citizenship in the Maya Biosphere Reserve, Guatemala', *Political Geography*, 22: 715–40.

38SUMIKRISHNA

United Nations 1992. *Agenda 21*, adopted by the United Nations Conference on Environment and Development. Rio de Janeiro, Brazil, 3–14 June. UN Division for Sustainable Development. http://www.un.org/esa/sustdev/documents/agenda21/english/agenda21chapter3.htm

———. 1996. *Platform for Action and the Beijing Declaration*. Fourth World Conference on Women, Beijing, China, 4–15 September 1995. New York: United Nations Department of Public Information.

Voet, Rian. 1998. *Feminism and Citizenship*. London: Sage Publications.

WCED 1990. *Our Common Future*. Report of the World Commission on Environment and Development. New Delhi: Oxford University Press.

Werbner, Pnina and Nira Yuval-Davis. 1999. 'Women and the New Discourse of Citizenship', in Pnina Werbner and Nira Yuval-Davis (eds), *Women, Citizenship and Difference (Postcolonial Encounters)*, pp. 1–38. London and New York: Zed Books.

Young, Iris Marion. 1997. *Intersecting Voices: Dilemmas of Gender, Political Philosophy, and Policy*. Princeton, New Jersey: Princeton University Press.

Yuval-Davis, Nira. 1997a. *Gender and Nation*. Reprint, 2004. London: Sage Publications.

———. 1997b. 'Women, Citizenship and Difference', *Feminist Review*, 57: 4–27.

I

Recognition and Resource Rights

2

Whose Rights? Women in Pastoralist and Shifting Cultivation Communities

A Continuing Struggle for Recognition and Rights to Livelihood Resources

Sagari R. Ramdas and Nitya S. Ghotge

Swidden or shifting cultivation (*podu, jhum, bewar, kumri*) and pastoralism, seemingly unrelated livelihood choices and lifestyles, emerged similarly thousands of years ago in extremely harsh ecological niches, where settled plough agriculture was difficult to practise: pastoralism in arid and semi-arid areas and shifting cultivation in hilly, forested terrains. Both systems have a relationship to land that is not centred on private ownership. Both forms of land use depend upon mobility, flexibility and vary across space and time. They also share a common vulnerability, as they are threatened primarily by contradictions between and conflicts with the policies of the state.

Despite 200 years of the state's attempts to squash these livelihoods and its refusal to recognise them as legitimate systems of land use, the reality on an all-India basis is that the land area and numbers of families engaged in both pastoralism and shifting cultivation have increased (Satapathy et al. 2003). As we argue in this chapter, the pre- and post-colonial state has consistently attacked and interpreted pastoralism and shifting cultivation as being ecologically destructive, economically inefficient and ill-suited to 'modernity'. In the context of this ongoing struggle between the state and the communities, it is women, the backbone of pastoral and shifting cultivation households, who are most vulnerable in a situation where these communities continue to have no assured legal rights to the natural resources on which they critically depend for their livelihood. Simultaneously, women are in the forefront of the struggle for legal rights to resources, a way of life and livelihood. In this chapter, we draw on our work with pastoralists in the Deccan and shifting cultivation communities in the Eastern Ghats of Andhra Pradesh to demonstrate the common thread of insecurity and struggle linking women from communities whose very livelihood and existence continue to be questioned by the state.

THE COLONIAL BACKGROUND

The drastic restrictions on traditional community use of natural resources has been conclusively traced by historians to the imposition of state control over forests and other natural resources during the second half of the nineteenth century, when the colonial state began to extend its laws and models of private property and state monopoly over natural resources throughout India. The complex, mutually sustaining relationship between agriculture, forests and pastoral areas was radically transformed. The colonial state systematically appropriated all categories of land, declaring these as 'reserved', while drawing boundaries and creating systems of taxation for community use (Murali 1995; Pouchepadass 1995). Pastoralists and shifting cultivators were seen to be the last remnants of an uncivilised past; aggressive steps were taken to ensure that they conformed, and were settled and confined to one location to lead an 'honest livelihood'. To illustrate:

> The hill people were described as wild, roaming and ignorant, most having only hatchets and no draught cattle, incapable of engaging in productive agriculture on account of their material poverty. (Rangarajan 1996: 98)
>
> In South Canara the Malai Kudigals (inhabitants of hills) were described by the Collector in 1820 as 'a miserable class of human beings' ... and whose 'wretched and only means of support was kumri cultivation'. (Pouchepadass 1995: 129)
>
> Those who have not understood the economic problems of the hill tribes are often heard to state that the tribesmen resort to Podu because they are lazy and expect quick return (Report on the Socio-Economic Conditions of the Aboriginal Tribes of the Province of Madras). (Aiyappan 1948: 15)

'These erratic and wasteful clearings', exclaimed the first Inspector-General of forests, Dietrich Brandis, 'give unsettled habits to the people, and make all improvements of their moral and material well-being difficult if not possible.' (Guha 1994: 25)

And, in a similar vein, on pastoralists:

In Colonial description pastoralists were represented as lazy, improvident, 'wretched' as cultivators, lawless, wild, mean and cowardly. They were associated with all that was considered evil, ugly and miserable. (Bhattacharya 1995: 70–71)

They are utterly devoid of energy and are the most apathetic, unsatisfactory race of people I have ever had anything to do with. They will exert themselves occasionally to go on cattle stealing expeditions or to plunder some of the quite well-conducted Arians ... but their exertions are seldom directed toward a better end. (Ferozepur Settlement Report, 1853: 4, quoted in Bhattacharya 1995: 71)

During the last famine, most of the States with reserved forests threw them open to free grazing, but the invasion that followed produced lamentable results, and the GoI have observed that in future famines all grazing should be strictly controlled and that the sheep and goat should be excluded, the injury caused by goats being all out off proportion to the relief offered to the people. (Revenue and Agriculture [Famine] File No. 94, Dec. 1905, pp. 10/8, quoted in Kavoori 1999: 148)

The Banjaras (traditional grazers/pastoralists across the Deccan Plateau) were perceived as a threat to the state and subjected to police surveillance and legal persecution. (Satya 2004: 75).

Researchers have vividly described the dominant colonial worldview and discussed the perspective that both pastoralism and shifting cultivation were inherently ecologically destructive, and that pastoralists and shifting cultivators needed to be settled. (See, for example, on pastoralism: Bhattacharya 1995; Kavoori 1999; Saberwal 1999; Satya 2004; and on shifting cultivation: Guha 1994; Jyotishi 2003; Pouchepadass 1995; Pratap 2000; Rangarajan 1996)

The colonial state introduced the Criminal Tribes Act, 1871, to take legal action against 'wanderers'. It implemented Forest Acts, imposed systems of taxation on grazing lands and expanded settled agriculture, severely curtailing the mobility and restricting the traditional resource use of grazing grounds by pastoralists and forests by shifting cultivators. The colonial state used these means to settle the shifting cultivators and pastoralists once and for all. As Bhattacharya (1995: 84) describes it: 'Nomads, vagabonds and wanderers were thus to be disciplined and settled. .... They had to belong to a marked territory —a village, a district, a province'. Pastoralists could graze cattle on a village common only 'by becoming a proprietor and an agriculturist'. It was repeatedly emphasised in official discussions that 'It is to be distinctly understood that the Government of India do not desire that grazing should be looked upon primarily as a source of income' (Cited in ibid.: 169). Further, Murali says:

> Colonial scientific conservation policy denied the needs of local communities at two levels. At one level, it denied the tribals their traditional subsistence living by banning shifting cultivation and the collection of minor forest produce ... . At a second level, the peasantry in the settled agriculture regions—both wet and dry ecological zones were deprived of their traditional grazing facilities. By encroaching on small forests, the government stripped many peasants of their grazing facilities. (1995: 101)

Among both communities there was silent resistance against these restrictions, as well as open forms of rebellion against the state. None of the restrictions succeeded in wiping out these forms of livelihoods and land use, which persisted.

A salient feature of all these discourses is their almost universal silence on the women within these communities and the impact such dramatic restrictions had on them. Based on our own knowledge of the pivotal role of women in these production systems, we hypothesise that women must have both borne the brunt of violence and been in the forefront of the resistance to the state.

POST-INDEPENDENCE: SHIFTING CULTIVATORS AND PASTORALISTS

Post-Independence the attitude of the Indian state to these forms of livelihood has been no different from that of the colonial state. Indeed, struggles between the pastoralists/shifting cultivators and the state have only heightened and sharpened, with the state continuing to view these practices as 'pernicious' and the prime cause of environmental degradation, and seeking to make those involved lead sedentary lives with no further delay. As quoted by Rao and Casimir (2003: 2) as recently as 1999, an anthropologist (Bharara 1999) opined, 'The nomads in the present times ... are a menace to the whole society and their sedentarisation is imperative. [With sedentarisation] administration and exercise of control become easy.'

Shifting cultivation, however, continues to be widely prevalent in the hills of north-eastern India, as also in pockets in Andhra Pradesh, Chhattisgarh, Madhya Pradesh, Maharashtra and Orissa. It is estimated that there are nearly 607,540 families engaged in shifting cultivation, spread across 2278,000 hectares. Between 1956 and 1985, the area under shifting cultivation increased by 81.2 per cent, and the total population involved also increased by 12.6 per cent. Of the total area under shifting cultivation, some 87 per cent is located in north-eastern India, followed by Orissa and Andhra Pradesh (Darlong 2004).

In India, roughly 7 per cent of the population is nomadic, consisting of about 500 communities (Rao and Casimir 2003: 1), of which barring 1–2 per cent, a predominant proportion are pastoralists (ibid.: 33–34). While there are no clear estimates of the extent of land area under this form of livelihood in India, it is clear that a vast number of people stretching from the sheep and goat-herding Bakarwals of Kashmir to the migratory duck-herders of Tamil Nadu are engaged in some form of pastoralism.

Impact of Post-Independence Forest Policies

Post-Independence, the various Forest Acts and policies have been no different from what we saw in the colonial period. The National Forest Policy (NFP), 1988, hailed for its apparent pro-people stance, took the same old colonial position that both grazing and shifting cultivation were the primary causes of forest destruction.

On Shifting Cultivation: 'Shifting cultivation is affecting the environment and productivity of the land adversely. Alternative avenues of income, suitably harmonised with the right land-use practices, should be devised to discourage shifting cultivation. Efforts should be made to contain this cultivation within the area already affected, by propagating improved agricultural practices. Area already damaged by such cultivation should be rehabilitated through social forestry and energy plantations'.

On Grazing: 'In the absence of adequate productive pasturelands and a grazing policy, forests have become the major source of grazing and fodder. It is estimated that around 60 per cent of the livestock (about 270 million) graze in forests. These include traditional sedentary village livestock and migratory animals herded by ethnic graziers. Additionally, graziers collect about 175 million tonnes of green fodder, annually, by lopping and harvesting grasses. This also adversely affects regeneration of forests'.

'Grazing in forest areas should be regulated with the involvement of the community. Special conservation areas, young plantations and regeneration areas should be fully protected. Grazing and browsing in forest areas need to be controlled. Adequate grazing fees should be levied to discourage people in forest areas from maintaining large herds of non-essential livestock'.

'The rights and concessions, including grazing, should always remain related to the carrying capacity of forests. The capacity itself should be optimised by increased investment, silvicultural research and development of the area. Stall-feeding of cattle should be encouraged. The requirements of the community, which cannot be met by the right and concessions so determined, should be met by development of social forestry outside the reserved forests'.

The above extracts from the 1988 Forest Policy read no differently from any of the writings of the colonial administrators. Grazing needs to be controlled by levying a grazing fee; shifting cultivation is to be discouraged through alternative avenues of income and 'improved settled agriculture'.

All legal and policy measures prior to the NFP, 1988, such as the Wild Life (Protection) Act, 1972, the Indian Forest Act, 1927, and the Forest (Conservation) Act, 1980, also placed severe restrictions on these communities, resulting in loss of livelihood, shelter and food. Indeed, community involvement in managing forests through the Joint Forest Management (JFM) programme, launched with much fanfare in the 1990s, has only made it easier for the forester to police the pastoralist and appropriate land used by shifting cultivators. In the name of forest protection today, it is the village elite (who often head the forest protection committees) who fine the grazier, ban lopping and raise plantations on shifting cultivation fallow lands.

Yet another crisis in this ongoing struggle for survival and rights arose in May 2002, when the Union Ministry of Environment and Forests announced its intention to evict encroachers in forests. Nearly a million adivasis and other forest-dwellers, or partially forest-dependent dwellers such as pastoralists, were once again exposed to the vulnerability of existence. The eviction order resulted in driving more than 100,000 families from their homes (Campaign for Survival and Dignity 2005). A nationwide mobilisation against these evictions and a demand for the legal recognition of the rights of forest-dwelling and forest-dependent communities was yet again an expression of the ongoing resistance and fight on the part of these communities against the retrograde policies, and for a recognition of the livelihood strategies that are a rational response to a variety of ecological, economic, political and social circumstances.

Here, we describe the state's attempts at 'sedentarising' and 'settling' shifting cultivators and pastoralists in the 1980s and 1990s. The state aimed at settling communities through development projects that claimed to further women's empowerment. In reality, 'achieving gender balanced development' was only a ruse to sidetrack women from the critical issue of claiming their rights to their land. We also discuss women's experiences and responses to this through the eyes of women podu farmers in Andhra Pradesh and women pastoralists of the Deccan.

Women's Resistance and Fight for Space

The Case of Adivasi Podu Cultivators in Andhra Pradesh: In Andhra Pradesh, podu, a form of shifting cultivation, is the sole source of livelihood for about 70,000 households spread across an area of 103,000 hectares located primarily in the four north coastal districts of Srikakulam, Vizianagaram, Visakhapatnam and East Godavari. Between 50 per cent and 75 per cent of the land in these districts is classified as forests. About 84 per cent of all forests in Andhra Pradesh are located in what is known as the Tribal-Sub Plan area. Forest policies of the colonial state resulted in highly restricted areas for communities to practise podu. Post-Independence, they continue to have no legal rights to these lands, most of which are legally classified as reserved or protected forests. Shifting cultivators have continued to practise this form of farming as if they were 'thieves' and 'law-breakers' in the eyes of the law, are in a constant state of

fear of being 'caught', continuously having to bribe forest officials to survive, and are at the receiving end of state violence. In the late 1970s and
1980s, there were strong adivasi movements all over the state, demanding
settlement of long outstanding rights in forest areas. In 1987, the state
government declared its intention to settle these rights, but never did so.[1]
Till the early 1980s, shifting cultivators had to contend only with the forest
officials. In the 1980s, the Forest Department and the Integrated Tribal
Development Agencies initiated social forestry programmes to actively
encourage farmers to raise horticulture trees on their own lands.

In the early 1990s, the process of settling farmers through development
programmes continued through a project funded by the International
Fund for Agricultural Development (IFAD) to the tune of US$ 20 million.
Apart from raising horticulture species on lands, there was a clear focus
on targeting women, through the formation of Self-Help Groups (SHGs),
to take the lead in implementing development plans that would ostensibly
provide an 'alternative livelihood' to podu.[2] Simultaneously, in 1994, the
ground was set and necessary government orders modified[3] to launch
the Joint Forest Management (JFM) programme, funded heavily with
World Bank money (Rs 3,650 million between 1994 and 2000). On the
face of it, this was to involve people in managing the forests, but the actual
agenda of the state was to recover what the state defined as 'encroached
land',[4] a large chunk of which was forest land under cultivation. The state
actively sought the help of 'communities' of tribals organised under forest
protection committees, the Vana Samrakshana Samitis (VSS), to oust
other tribal communities, that is, podu cultivators, by putting those lands
under 'VSS protection' and raising plantations on them. Again, what stands
out is the huge emphasis that was placed on 'including women in Vana
Samrakshana Samitis' and on 'having equal representation of man and
woman in the Samiti'. They were promised huge returns from these forestry efforts and, of course, were attracted to the immediate availability of
some wage labour generated through forestry activities that had to be
carried out according to forest working plans. Andhra Pradesh forestry
officials and advocates of JFM are extremely proud that this is the only
state in India with 'gender balanced' forestry programmes. *It is almost as
if gender balance in such development programmes was, and is, used as a
ploy or as a cover to marginalise the more fundamental issues of settling the
communities' rights to resources and recognising a different way of using
resources.*

The Forest Department stated openly that this land was 'voluntarily' handed over by the people and that through the JFM they were able to successfully reclaim 37,000 hectares of encroached land in the Vishakapatnam circle. This was ostensibly because people had happily gone in for *bhoodhan* (gifting of land) and returned it to the Forest Department. The protests by some NGOs against such eviction and their arguing for a rehabilitation and resettlement package for the adivasis did not address the real issue: settling all outstanding adivasi claims on forests and giving them legal recognition to podu. The demand for rehabilitation was happily accepted by the World Bank, who upped their next instalment of funding to the tune of US$ 108 million for the forestry project, this time under the name of Community Forest Management (CFM). It must be noted that the rehabilitation and resettlement policy under CFM, officially announced through a government order, reinforces the state's fundamental opposition to both shifting cultivation and settling the outstanding claims on the forests:

> It was generally felt that shifting cultivation and the encroachment into the forest for cultivation are not good practices and they need to be discouraged. The shifting cultivators and encroachers into the forest should be motivated to leave the practice and surrender lands encroached upon for cultivation. (Government Order MS 10)

The complete hollowness of the so-called voluntarily participation, the horrific ramifications it had on women, as also the central role of women in leading the resistance to the state's taking over their land came to light when podu farmers organised under the leadership of adivasi movements in Andhra. This was as part of the wider response of adivasi and other forest-dwellers' movements against the most recent attempt to evict the so-called 'encroachers'[5] (Andhra Pradesh Adivasi Aikya Vedika and Yakshi 2004; Campaign for Survival and Dignity 2003). The testimonies of adivasis and other forest-dwellers brought to light the subtle and not-so subtle state violence, as also the manner in which the state, through the agency of the VSS, is using the local village elite to perpetrate violence and do the policing. It also brought to light the forms of resistance used by women.

Women Podu Cultivators Fight for their Right to Practise Podu: Pallamguda village (Gannela Panchayat, Araku Valley, Visakhapatnam

district, Andhra Pradesh) consists of 37 households of Paringi Poraja
(a 'primitive' tribal group), Goud and Valmiki. The following is the tes-
timony of Ms Gobbu Mitti, a podu farmer of Pallamguda:

> We were 25 families doing podu in the forests. In 1994, the Forest Depart-
> ment officials visited the village and urged us to establish a VSS committee.
> We opposed the idea and decided not to establish a VSS. We told the forest
> guards that our lands were located in the forests surrounding the villages;
> our animals graze in the forests, and thus if we start a VSS, our source of
> livelihood and survival will go, as the guard told us that we had to protect
> these lands, and stop grazing our animals and cultivating the land.
>
> When we opposed the Forest guards, they went to the neighbouring
> villages Ramkrishnanagar and Kussigoda, and persuaded them to establish
> a VSS on these forestlands, where we do podu. Soon the VSS began to plant
> trees and saplings on our lands, and established a nursery to produce
> saplings. In 1995, as soon as this happened, we women led the others in
> our village to uproot the saplings from our lands and prepared the land
> for cultivation. VSS committee members from the other two villages along
> with Forest Department officials visited Pallamguda village. At that time
> we women of Pallamguda were preparing the land for sowing our crops,
> and the FD representatives forcibly confiscated our implements: our
> hoes, digging sticks, axes, etc. They forced us to walk to the forest office,
> where they made us stand in the rain all day. In 1996, two policemen
> visited our village and threatened us saying, 'You are illegally cultivating
> forest land and must come to the police station'. No one went. In 1997, 15
> policemen visited the village and threatened us, saying they would arrest
> us if we persisted in doing podu. However, we women resisted, and con-
> tinued to carry out podu. In 2002, once again the VSS committee members
> came to Pallamguda village and burnt our agriculture implements. In
> 2003, the same VSS committee went to our fields and burnt our field
> houses/huts and the wood, which people store on their lands. Whenever
> we pass these neighbouring villages en route to the market, the villagers
> threaten us, and say they will attack and kill us unless we stop podu and
> hand over our lands to the VSS. We, however, will never leave our land
> and will continue to do podu here.

Farmers from this village also testified at the *jan sunwai* (public hearing)
on Forest Rights held at Delhi in 2003 (Campaign for Survival and Dignity
2003).

The 'settling' of shifting cultivators continues in the new 'globalised regime' through newer modes of extracting commercial profits from forests to serve the needs and interests of the powerful, namely, 'environmental services'—carbon-sink projects and raising bio-diesel plantations. Countries and companies have a license to pollute in exchange for buying 'virtual' emission-reduction through financing forestry projects outside of their country. This ensures that the former can continue with their own polluting behaviour, while forest-dwellers and other forest-dependent communities are forced to sacrifice their traditional livelihoods in exchange (Caruso and Reddy 2005). A recent feasibility study, *The Clean Development Mechanism and Village-based Forest Restoration*, carried out in Adilabad district, Andhra Pradesh, concludes that women's SHGs are the most appropriate institution to carry out carbon offset projects, since they are 'dynamic, accountable and transparent' (cited in ibid.: 8). The Adilabad study specifically enumerates the pressures on forest resources in Andhra Pradesh as (in order of importance): first, the large and growing human and cattle population; second, uncontrolled grazing of cattle in forests; and third, 'encroachment' of forest lands (an estimated 90,000 hectares of forestland has been encroached upon illegally in the last 20 years) and conversion of forest lands for podu (swidden) cultivation.

By 2004, the first climate change related carbon trading project had already been implemented in the tribal village of Powerguda, Adilabad district, where the women's SHG was given a certificate and US$ 645 in order to offset emissions produced by a World Bank workshop (on climate change) held in Washington D.C. The women's group (set up through the IFAD programme discussed earlier) had been persuaded to grow *Pongamia* (Indian oilseed) tree plantations on forest lands, and were running a unit to press and extract bio-fuel produced from the Pongamia seeds. The women were completely unaware of the reason they had received the money, and had no idea about the ramifications of carbon trade and the relationship of their SHG activities with climate change (Caruso and Reddy 2005).

In January 2005, the Forest Department of Adilabad announced a scheme of Rs 20 million, which they termed 'voluntary re-clothing of podu lands', to regularise the 'encroachers', through models of alternative cultivation of either bio-diesel plantations of Pongamia species, bamboo, or other Non-Timber Forest Produce (NTFP) crops on podu lands.

Adivasis would be provided wage employment by the government for ploughing, trenching, pitting and planting saplings on their podu lands.

Women Shepherds of the Deccan: Spread across the three states of Karnataka, Maharashtra and Andhra Pradesh, the traditional shepherds (Kurma, Kurba and Dhangar), as well as newer entrants into this livelihood of sheep and goat-rearing, are dependent on migration and mobility in search of fodder and water for varying periods of time through the year. While there are families (including women and children) in northern Karnataka who are perennially mobile, there are others who migrate for six to nine months in the year, with the women and children usually staying back home and caring for the land. There are yet others who practise local migration, in which they are away from home for, maybe, one or two months.

Common grazing resources have all but disappeared; most have been converted to private property, while others have been declared as protected areas (wildlife sanctuaries and national parks) or covered with non-fodder mono-crop plantations such as eucalyptus. In all the three states, the common experience of these shepherds is that the Forest Department (FD) and other members of the VSS continuously harass them. The FD or VSS arbitrarily impose a tax or fine on the shepherds who graze their animals in the forest. Most often the fine is in the form of animals, with each shepherd having to give the FD or VSS chairman a live animal in exchange for permission to graze their flock in the forest. The VSS committees have unilaterally declared that 'lopping is a bad practice' and that they must go into the forest without an axe. Members of several VSS committees have confiscated the axes that women use to lop fodder. FDs of these states continue to go out of their way to dig trenches around forests (supposedly to harvest water) and plant thorny bushes (supposedly to stall soil erosion), which actually end up blocking grazing routes and access routes to watering holes in the forest. The shepherds have to carry on their day-to-day lives and graze their animals secretly, as if they were thieves, slipping in and out of forests, hoping they will not be caught.

In some areas like Andhra Pradesh, the state has particularly targeted goats, to the extent of making material conditions especially difficult for the people to herd goats, thus forcing communities to sell them (see Ramdas 2000). It goes without saying that this 'anti-goat' stand has hit women the most, as rearing goats has always been an extremely vital component of their livelihood. Smaller livestock like sheep, goat and poultry are probably the only 'asset' they own (unlike land), and over which they make independent decisions.

The absence or scarcity of common property resources has meant that for large parts of the year, the shepherds are dependent on negotiating terms of grazing and penning their sheep on the land of landlords. In doing so the shepherds, particularly the women, are also subjected to all kinds of violence from settled landowners, who are increasingly unhappy to have them on their land. Land development projects, such as watershed development, have similarly placed severe restrictions on the mobility of the shepherds. All this has severely constrained women and men, forcing many to sell their stock. Being on the move all the time also means that they have little voice when it comes to representing their concerns in formal institutions of local governance such as the panchayat, which through the 73rd Constitutional Amendment has been authorised to look into issues of resource use at the level of the Gram Sabha.

Very few pastoralist women have become members of government-initiated women's SHGs, or hold membership in any of the 'committees' for forest management or watersheds. Indeed, many have consciously chosen to boycott these committees/groups, as they have realised that not only do these spaces have nothing to offer them, they will further restrict their access to resources—something which again mirrors the response of podu farmers vis-à-vis VSS committees. Again, the state has used the tactic of divide and rule; by including other elite and powerful 'non-pastoralists' and through a nominal representation of women in the village resource management committees, they are able to pit the committees against the pastoralists, ensuring that the conflict between settled farmers and the migratory groups is accentuated. Thus, while it is the Forest Department who would advise the committee on a decision taken at the village level, it is finally the village committee that interacts directly with the pastoralists. The committees have become an extended arm of the Forest Department, and more often than not agree with the stance of the department rather than that of the people.

The people's forms of protest and resistance have included herding their animals purposefully on plantation areas that are protected either through a forest protection or a watershed committee and continuing to carry their axe to lop fodder, sometimes deliberately using wrong lopping methods intended to damage a tree as a sign of their non-cooperation with the state. Needless to say, it is women who are directly attacked by the forest guards, and/or the VSS committees or landlords. It is once again the women who stand up and resist this, as we see in the words of Woteri Naguramma, a woman shepherd of Bangarammanaidu Kandriga village, Chittoor district, Andhra Pradesh, narrating an incident which occurred in the summer of 2005:

> Like everyday, I went to the forest to graze my goats. I have 30 goats. I was using my lopping stick to lop branches of fodder for my animals. Suddenly, the forest guard appeared in front of me, and threatened me. He said I was forbidden to graze my animals in the forest, and was not allowed to rear goats, as there was now a VSS in the village and through that the forest was out of bounds. He forcibly snatched away my lopping stick. I told him that I have been grazing my goats in this forest since many years, as had my mother and her mother too. He did not listen. I ran all the way back to my village and told the others. The next day the entire 'sangham' (group) of women and men came with me to the forest. We found the forest guard and we caught him and tied him to the tree and we left him there for a couple of hours to teach him a lesson. We told him we would not untie him till he handed back the lopping stick, and till he promised never to threaten us again. Since that day, we have grazed our animals without any interference but we are not sure how long this will last; is it till the next guard comes?

Saving Indigenous Seeds and Breeds:
A Form of Resistance

A favourite strategy of the state to 'settle' these communities has been to force new technologies onto them in the name of 'improved productivity, efficiency and modernisation'. Thus, livestock development policies and programmes have consistently argued for replacing the 'large number of useless non-descript low producing indigenous stock' with 'improved high producing breeds of superior genetic potential imported from the West'. So we have Jersey cows in place of indigenously-bred Khillar cattle, and Marino Rams introduced into flocks of Deccani breed. They also argue that these improved varieties need not be grazed, but can be 'stall-fed'.

The preferred strategy for controlling grazing within existing forestry policies is vividly illustrated in the revised Forest Policy for Andhra Pradesh, which was announced by the Andhra Pradesh Forest Department in April 2002 through G.O. MS 34. An entire section (3.1.2) is devoted to the issue of grazing and states:

> The present policy of free grazing in the forests is detrimental to regeneration and establishment of vegetation. There is need for reasonable restrictions on grazing. *Further the burden of scrub cattle on the already scarce fodder resources needs to be reduced by upgrading the cattle stock, and encouraging stall feeding ... there will be coordinated efforts with the Animal Husbandry Department of the Government of Andhra Pradesh to improve the quality of livestock in the forest fringe areas so that the number of cattle heads will be reduced.* (Emphasis added)

Similarly, in the context of shifting cultivators, as we saw clearly, the attempts through, for instance, the IFAD interventions have been to introduce Green Revolution technologies—high yielding seeds, monocropping and rehabilitating podu land through plantations of cashew nut and coffee on the shifting cultivation fallows. Once again, this practice is reflected in policy, with the 2002 Forest Policy of Andhra Pradesh devoting a separate section (3.1.3) to 'Encroachments and Podu', wherein it is stated:

> [T]he traditional shifting cultivation practiced by Tribals, is transforming into settled agriculture. Such type of cultivation is resulting in land degradation and unsustainable agriculture leading to poverty and increasing demand for land again for further cultivation ... *there is urgent need to educate the tribal on sustainable farming ... access to improved agriculture practices for these tribals needs to be made available.* (Emphasis added)

Replacing seeds and breeds, and forcing people to lose control over their genetic resources are perhaps the ultimate forms/modes by which the state takes control of natural resources, thus permanently alienating communities from their means of production.

Ironically, in the context of both seeds and livestock breeds, it must be noted that women play a crucial role in saving the primary germplasm essential for subsequent production—seeds for sowing in the case of shifting cultivators, and young stock of sheep and goat breeds in the case of the pastoralists. Incredibly, despite the efforts of the state to settle and alienate these communities from their means of production, seeds of local crops grown through shifting cultivation and local breeds such as the Deccanni sheep have been sustained and still persist, nurtured and cared for by the women of these communities over decades. Given the kind of violence and restrictions on livelihoods that we have witnessed over the years, this hold on genetic resources must also be viewed as a form of resistance to state diktat, where, despite all odds, women are holding on boldly to perhaps the only means of production they can fearlessly say is theirs. So women podu cultivators conserved seeds from year to year, persisted with podu and have not meekly submitted to the Forest Department's efforts to replace podu with plantations; nor have they become wage labourers and worked for the VSS/FD. Similarly, their pastoral sisters have adamantly refused to shift to what the state views as eco-friendly livestock, namely, 'crossbred stall-fed cows', but have stuck to rearing their own sheep and goat breeds under grazing systems, despite strong opposition from the state. In both these production contexts, women have been instrumental in protecting and innovating with knowledge, practice and genetic resources, which they have handed down to future generations.

CONCLUSION

Resistance and violation of these laws and community resource management regimes are treated as a 'law and order' problem, with the guilty being punished accordingly. What stands out is how the state violence mirrors colonial methods and is primarily oriented towards depriving people of their means of production and thus their livelihood, confiscating the adivasi women's podu digging sticks and the pastoralist's axe. Other forms of violence include burning standing crops and denying their animals access to drinking water, which has become a private resource. The appropriation by the state (and now by private corporate capital) of the little land, forest, water and genetic resources to which these communities have access continues at an ever-increasing rate, particularly in the current ideology of economic growth in the context of privatisation and globalisation. A serious concern is that as long as these communities are not granted clear legal rights to these resources, rights that recognise the complex land-use patterns, all talk of involving communities (and women) to sustainably manage, conserve and regenerate these lands, and to make these systems more 'efficient' is a wasteful exercise.

Women are demanding clear legal rights for their communities so as to continue to practise their livelihoods and use natural resources in these specific ways. Another point of concern is the way in which women are being used by the state in the name of equal participation and gender-balanced development to sidetrack the issue of rights and divert their attention from the struggle for the right to means of production and livelihood to artificial, virtual livelihoods, such as earning through carbon trade from growing forests or the trade in biodiversity and other germplasm. The experience of the Joint Forest Management is a clear example of this.

In mid-2005, a Bill to recognise the rights of adivasis and other forest-dwellers (including pastoralists and local graziers) to the forests was drafted and placed before Parliament.* While serious flaws, which need critical attention still exist within the draft, it is a historic step towards resolving the century-long conflict between forest communities and an authoritarian, corrupt and repressive forest bureaucracy. This means that perhaps for the first time in the last 200 years, these women will lead slightly less insecure lives. However, almost immediately after the Bill was first drafted, the Union Ministry of Environment and Forests (MoEF), including the Forest Department and other wildlife lobbies, reacted (as was expected) negatively. Their response is summed up succinctly by the following statement of an activist wildlife conservationist and a member of the Tiger Task Force (which was recently constituted by the MoEF under the instructions of the prime minister):

> The situation is bad enough with all the restrictions, and now the draft Bill makes a mockery of all conservation efforts. Give them land rights today and expect total chaos as their population grows. Traditional pastoral or nomadic lifestyle is not viable in many parts of India due to the decreasing land-people/livestock ratio. Tribals were wrongly stripped off their rights under the colonial rule. But we can't unlive history and it will be a much greater mistake today if we dream of restoring the pre-colonial situation. Instead, we must share the economic fruits of our mega-diversity with the locals and address their livelihood concerns. (Reported in *The Indian Express*, 29 April 2005)

---

* The Scheduled Tribes (Recognition of Forest Rights) Act, 2006.

Yet again, the statement only reaffirms and echoes the concepts, perspectives and attitudes of the colonial state and the subsequent post-colonial perceptions of the Indian state.

It is clear that for the women shifting cultivators and pastoralists, their struggle is far from over. It is not only a struggle for legal rights to resources, but also for recognition and acceptance of a livelihood strategy that has for so long been viewed as ecologically destructive and 'inefficient'. These women, who have been the target of the violence carried out by the forest bureaucracy, are clearly demanding a recognition of their rights, a way of livelihood, and for a just and fair access to resources. We must acknowledge that the survival of the forest landscape and that of the forest/forest-dependent communities is mutually interdependent.

It is time that we critically analyse, unravel and address current development efforts within the context of people's livelihoods and natural resource use. These efforts are being unconditionally supported and extolled as unique and path-breaking examples of involving women and addressing gender issues but are effectively marginalising the larger questions of women's rights to resources and control over resources. Women will continue to organise and voice their demands for livelihood rights as part of a long continuum that stretches back over 200 years.

ACKNOWLEDGEMENTS

We thank Madhusudhan, who is working with the Adivasi Peoples Movements in Andhra Pradesh, for his invaluable insights and inputs on the struggle of podu farmers and the larger struggle of adivasis for their rights to livelihood resources.

We have drawn upon our work with ANTHRA and its database on medicinal and fodder plants. The database programme was designed by ANTHRA using Oracle software, to manage information documented by ANTHRA between 1996 and 1999 in an action-research project 'Documentation of Ethno-veterinary Practices'. (The database is maintained at ANTHRA-Hyderabad, A-21 Sainikpuri, Secunderabad–500094, Andhra Pradesh, India.)

NOTES

1. In 1987, the Ministry of Energy, Forest, Environment, Science and Technology, Government of Andhra Pradesh, issued a memo (Memo No. 26531/For I/87-1,

dated 28.12.1987) in connection with the assignment of forest lands to local tribals who were cultivating or residing in reserved forest lands prior to 1980. The memo said that the date on which forest legislation had come into force in 1980 would be accepted as the cut off date, and the local tribal occupation of reserved forestlands prior to 1980 should be regularised. While this process is on, the forest department should not evict local tribals. The principal chief conservator of forests was also requested to take up the question of demarcation of forest boundaries immediately on a permanent basis, in consultation with the revenue department.

2. The IFAD supported project known as APTDP was evaluated in the 2001 'Completion of Evaluation Report of April 2001', in which they admitted that project interventions resulted in enhanced food production, but increased vulnerability to drought because of the dependence on irrigated agriculture at the expense of traditional techniques, which included built-in measures to counteract periodic drought conditions. The environmental impact of the application of non-organic inputs for HYV paddy cultivation in low-lying lands such as chemical fertilizers, pesticides and herbicides is a serious concern'. Ironically, the report concludes that the potential for 'organic agriculture methods' should be explored, particularly in context of the expanded market for organic produce. Another sincere admission is that the intervention resulted in the marginalisation of women from agriculture. Independent studies also found that while farmers planted horticulture crops, they cleared new forest areas to continue with the practice of podu.

3. Memo No. 26531/For/I/87 dated 3.11.95: instructions to suppress earlier note of 1987 to regularise lands. The memo now says that these lands will be managed under JFM and intensive plantations.

4. Andhra Pradesh has 325,000 ha. of land that is stated to be encroached.

5. In May 2002, the MoEF issued a circular to all state forest departments requesting them to prepare time-bound action plans to evict encroachers from the forest. Due to the wide-scale mobilisation across the country, this could not materialise as planned. The campaign for dignity and survival has successfully contested this, while also demanding comprehensive legal recognition of rights.

REFERENCES

Aiyappan, A. 1948. *Report on the Socio-Economic Conditions of the Aboriginal Tribes of the Province of Madras*. Madras: Superintendent, Government Press.

Andhra Pradesh Adivasi Aikya Vedika and Yakshi. 2004. 'Adivasis Demand Owner-ship, Management and Resource Use Rights to Land in Forests in 5th Schedule Areas. A Status Report and Charter of Demands Submitted to the Parlia-mentary Standing Committee on Social Justice', November 2004.

Bharara, L.P. 1999. *Man in the Desert: Drought, Desertification and Indigenous Knowledge for Sustainable Development.* Jodhpur: Scientific Publications.

Bhattacharya, Neeladri. 1995. 'Pastoralists in a Colonial World', in David Arnold and Ramchandra Guha (eds), *Nature, Culture and Imperialism: Essays on the Environmental History of South Asia.* New Delhi: Oxford University Press.

Campaign for Survival and Dignity. 2003. 'Endangered Symbiosis: Evictions and Forest Communities', Report of the Jan Sunwai (Public Hearing), 19–20 July 2003.

———. 2005. 'The Scheduled Tribes (Recognition of Forest Rights) Bill, 2005. Our Stand'.

Caruso, Emily and Vijaya Bhaskara Reddy. 2005. *The Clean Development Mechanism: Issues for Adivasi Peoples in India.* UK: Forest Peoples Programme.

Darlong, Vincent. 2004. *To Jhum or Not to Jhum: Policy Perspectives on Shifting Cultivation,* p. 143. Guwahati: The Missing Link (TML), Society for Envir-onment and Communication.

Guha, Ramchandra. 1994. 'Fighting for the Forests: State Forestry and Social Change in Tribal India', in Oliver Mendelsohn and Upendra Baxi (eds), *The Rights of Subordinated Peoples,* pp. 20–37. Delhi: Oxford University Press.

Hanumantha, V., N.K. Acharya and M.C. Swaminathan. 1998. *Andhra Pradesh at 50.* Hyderabad: Data News Features Publication.

Jyotishi, Amalendu. 2003. 'Institutional Pluralism: Case of Swiddners in Orissa', in Rajendra Pradhan (ed.), *Legal Pluralism and Unofficial Law in Social, Economic and Political Development.* Kathmandu: ICNEC.

Kavoori, Purnendu S. 1999. *Pastoralism in Expansion: The Transhuming Herders of Western Rajasthan.* Delhi: Oxford University Press.

Murali, Atluri. 1995. 'Whose Trees? Forest Practices and Local Communities in Andhra, 1600–1922', in David Arnold and Ramachandra Guha (eds), *Nature, Culture and Imperialism: Essays on the Environmental History of South Asia.* Delhi: Oxford University Press.

Pouchepadass, Jacques. 1995. 'British attitudes Towards Shifting Cultivation in. Colonial South India: A Case Study of South Canara District 1800–1920', in David Arnold and Ramachandra Guha (eds), *Nature, Culture and Im-perialism: Essays on the Environmental History of South Asia.* Delhi: Oxford University Press.

Pratap, Ajay. 2000. *The Hoe and The Axe: An Ethnohistory of Shifting Cultivation in Eastern India.* New Delhi: Oxford University Press.

RTF. 1987. *Report of the Task Force to Evaluate the Impact of Sheep and Goat Rearing in Ecologically Fragile Zones, 1987*. New Delhi: Government of India, Ministry of Agriculture, Department of Agriculture and Cooperation.

Ramdas, Sagari. 2000. 'A Scapegoat? Goats are not the Greatest Enemies of the Environment', *Down to Earth*, 9(1), 31 May.

Rangarajan, Mahesh. 1996. *Fencing the Forest: Conservation and Ecological Change in India's Central Provinces, 1860–1914*. Delhi: Oxford University Press.

Rao, Aparna and Michael J. Casimir (eds). 2003. *Nomadism in South Asia*. Delhi: Oxford University Press

Saberwal, Vasant. 1999. *Pastoral Politics: Shepherds, Bureaucrats, and Conservation in the Western Himalaya*. Delhi: Oxford University Press.

Satapathy, K.K., B.K. Sharma, S.N. Goswami and N.D. Verma. 2003. *Developing Lands Affected by Shifting Cultivation*. New Delhi: Department of Land Resources, Ministry of Rural Development, Government of India.

Satya, Laxman D. 2004. *Ecology, Colonialism and Cattle: Central India in the Nineteenth Century*. Delhi: Oxford University Press.

3

Transgressing Political Spaces and Claiming Citizenship

The Case of Women Kendu *Leaf-Pluckers and the Community Forestry Federation, Ranpur, Orissa*

Neera M. Singh

'*Ama peta jaluchhi, ame jaha kahibu, sambhalibaku padibo*' (Our bellies are on fire; what we say will have to be honoured).

— K. Nahak

A day after the world celebrated International Women's Day on 8 March 2005, women from Ranpur block sat in dharna in front of the Orissa State Legislative Assembly. They were in the state capital, Bhubaneswar, to press for their demand for opening state collection centres for kendu leaves (KL) in their area.

The leaves of kendu (*Diospyrus melaxylon*), also known as *tendu* or *timbru* in other parts of India, are used for wrapping beedis; the sale of KL is a major source of livelihood for local people in central India. In Orissa, the trade in KL is the monopoly of the state; the 'Kendu leaf wing' of the Orissa Forest Department procures KL through government collection centres, called KL phadis. Ranpur block in Nayagarh district is among those areas where, despite the availability of KL, there is no government collection centre. In the absence of KL phadis, women are at the mercy of private traders who operate 'illegally', offering only a fraction of the prices fixed for KL by the state government.

Women from Ranpur have been demanding collection centres for kendu leaves since 2000. After repeated attempts to place their demands before the administration, they finally decided to stage a protest in front of the State Assembly. For seven days from 9–15 March 2005, women stayed put on the streets, braving the heat and rain. For most of these women, this was probably their first visit to Bhubaneswar; and possibly the first time that they were away from their families for so long. In their own way, they were celebrating their arrival into the political arena and were demanding to be heard as citizens.

This dharna was part of a continuing struggle waged by the women from Ranpur block for their livelihood. As part of this struggle, these women have traversed political territories, and created spaces in which to be political actors and assert their citizenship. This chapter traces their struggle to establish KL phadis in Ranpur, and analyses how women navigate existing and newly created political spaces to assert their livelihood rights. It also explores how women and other actors leverage different images and representations in this struggle, and bridge conservation and livelihood concerns.

Orissa has large-scale community initiatives to conserve and manage forests. Further, community forest protection groups have come together in the form of federations. These federations, however, tend to be male-dominated, and do not always represent the needs and priorities of women (Singh 2002). However, Ranpur block is an exception, where a federation of forest protection groups, the Maa Maninag Jungle Surakhya Parishad (MMJSP), has made special efforts to involve women. This has brought women's forest-based livelihood issues to the fore in the agenda of the Parishad. This chapter discusses how space for women within the Parishad has brought women's livelihood issues onto its agenda and has contributed to improving the effectiveness of the Parishad's advocacy efforts.

Two stories unfold here. One relates to the transformation of the Parishad and its agenda. The other is the struggle of women themselves to assert their livelihood rights and their transformation from transgressors into different political territories to citizens of these domains. I use ethnographic material from different federation meetings, advocacy events including the dharna in front of the State Assembly, and interviews and extended conversations with the agitating women to explore the complex interweaving of their notions of political rights, citizenship and the accountability of their representatives; and what this struggle has meant to them at both individual and collective levels.

BACKGROUND

Ranpur block in Nayagarh district of Orissa is a drought-prone area; and forest-based livelihoods play a critical role in the lives of the poor, especially adivasis and Dalits. Almost 35 per cent of its geographical area is recorded as forest. More than 50 per cent of forest land is under the control of the revenue department. Landlessness is high in the block, with almost 39 per cent of the households being landless (in the case of Scheduled Castes and Tribes, landlessness is more than 70 per cent). As in other forested areas in Orissa, local dependence on forests is high. This dependence has shaped community responses to forest degradation in the form of community-based conservation initiatives. The block has 231 revenue villages; about 187 communities (including hamlets) are involved in conserving forests through community-based arrangements for protection and management (Vasundhara 2003). As elsewhere in Orissa, these community forest management systems (CFM) are self-initiated, having evolved as a local response to the degradation of forests and to threatened forest-based livelihoods. While some of the villages have been protecting forests from the 1960s, most other CFM groups emerged during the early 1980s. A significant number of community forest management efforts have come up during the last five years or so, due to the efforts of the MMJSP to stabilise and further spread community-based forest conservation.

These CFM groups display enormous ingenuity, creativity, environmental ethos and responsibility. At the same time, they are not free from the politics of exclusion and elite dominance. It has been a cause of concern that these community-based arrangements reflect local power structures, within which women and other forest-dependent poor have limited say in decision-making. As a result, it is often felt that the livelihood concerns of the forest-dependent poor sometimes get undermined in the process. In this area, the situation is beginning to change with women playing an important role in the community forestry federation. Here, I trace the process of this change.

MAA MANINAG JUNGLE SURAKHYA PARISHAD: ORIGIN AND EMERGENCE

The MMJSP is a federation of forest-protecting villages in Ranpur block. This federation emerged in 1997 after a series of meetings and consultations at the level of villages and clusters of villages, in which issues confronting forest protection groups were discussed. Vasundhara, a Bhubaneswar-based NGO working on community forestry issues, played an important role in facilitating the process. At the time of its formation, about 85 villages came together to form the MMJSP. Over the years, the membership of the Parishad increased to 137 communities in 2003, and to 187 communities in 2005. These forest protection communities include revenue villages, settlements (hamlets), or groups of villages.

In this area, there were also pre-existing examples of clusters of villages coming together to extend mutual support for protecting forests. To co-ordinate inter-village cooperation, cluster-level committees such as the 'Sata Mouza Jungle Surakhya Committee' (seven villages' forest protection committee), 'Sulia Sata Bhaya Jungle Surakhya Samukhya' (Sulia seven brothers' forest protection group), 'Dhani Pancha Mouza Jungle Surakhya Committee' and 'Dasa Mouza Jungle Surakhya Samiti' came up. These were groups of villages that had come together to protect a common or contiguous forest patch, and had evolved rules and regulations to this end. Although the history of how these villages came together is different, the common drivers were the dependence of several villages on a commonly shared and used forest patch, the need for collaborative arrangements to minimise conflicts over use and boundaries, and to be able to effectively protect the patch from outsiders.

Such cluster-level forums helped strengthen community-based forest protection efforts and were more effective in protecting forests from un-regulated use, both within these villages as well as from outsiders. While such cluster-level committees arose from a more immediate need of collective arrangements to protect a forest patch that was not necessarily easily divisible amongst individual villages, these provided useful examples for collective action at higher spatial scales. These examples also demonstrated the advantages of networking and working together to strengthen community forestry initiatives and to resolve conflicts.

These early networking examples provided directions and lessons for the formation of the Parishad. For almost a year, during 1996–97, Vasundhara staff facilitated meetings at the village and cluster levels, where community members expressed the need for networking and for a collective forum. According to community leaders, they felt that such a forum would help in resolving inter- and intra-village conflicts, and in increasing their collective strength to deal with external threats. Following this, in 1997, around 85 villages came together to form a loose network, which was named the Maa Maninag Jungle Surakhya Parishad, in honour of the local deity, Maa Maninag, and the Maninag hill and forest.

In the initial phase, the Parishad was dominated by men and there were hardly any women present at the meetings, as has been the usual case with other CFM groups and federations. The discussion on women's involvement at one of the Parishad's initial meetings is illustrative. At a meeting in 1997, when Parishad members were discussing the structure and tentative byelaws, they were not very forthcoming with any special provisions for the representation of women and other marginalised sections such as Dalits and tribals. Staff from the facilitating organisation, Vasundhara, gently nudged, 'What about women, do you want to keep any special stipulations on women's representation? What about Dalits and tribals?' The response from the federation leaders was: 'But these are people who destroy forests! If we allow them in, or give special consideration to their interests and needs, the forest will be gone in no time.' A very heated discussion ensued. 'Is this really the case, and can forests be protected by ignoring the needs and interests of these forest dependent sections?' The federation leaders discussed this till late in the night. The next morning, the secretary of the Parishad shared their decision, 'We discussed this issue at length. We will include women (that is, make special provisions for their representation). Otherwise, *it will not look nice*. Nowadays, most agencies/organisations insist on women's involvement. There are also reservations for women at different places, including the panchayats. Against this backdrop, it will not look nice if we do not include women. So, we have decided that we will keep women (make provisions for their involvement)'.

The Parishad has come a long way from the time they included women as part of a cosmetic 'look good' strategy. Here, I discuss this process of transformation. This section is based on an analysis of the records of the

Parishad, as well as interviews with its leaders and staff of the facilitating organisation, Vasundhara.

WOMEN'S PRESENCE, REPRESENTATION AND INFLUENCE IN THE PARISHAD

As already mentioned, in the initial years the Parishad leaders were not particularly interested in having women on board. This is not surprising, considering that women are generally absent from management arrangements pertaining to forest protection at the community level. This has been the case with other community-based endeavours as well and reflects the existing social power relations, especially gender relations within communities, which makes the effective participation of women and also that of Dalits and adivasis difficult.

Records of eight meetings were available for 1997, the initial year of the Parishad's existence. No woman was present at any of these meetings. Women were also conspicuously absent from the initial meetings when the decision to form the Parishad was taken. Gradually, from 1998 one or two women started attending the working body meetings of the Parishad. Among the earlier participants were women who were either brought in by male relatives or were from higher castes. Once the space for women was opened up, however, this soon changed with tribal and Dalit women participating in greater numbers. The space for women's participation was created by instituting a sub-group within the Parishad, an informal body that consists of women and meets every month. This group was called the Central Women's Committee, but women refer to these meetings as '*mahila* (women's) meetings' or as '*Athraha tarikh* meetings', that is, meetings held on the 18th of every month.

The Vasundhara staff felt that the lack of women's presence in the Parishad was a cause for concern. Vasundhara was committed to bringing in women, and to promoting their active involvement in forest management and decision-making. At the same time, they did not want women's participation to be an external imposition, and were committed to gradual but steady progress in this direction. As a first step, the organisation committed to having more women on the staff and as part of the facilitating team at Ranpur. One senior woman staff member, as well as a woman community organiser, specifically focused on strategies for improving women's involvement.

After the marginal participation of women at the Parishad meetings in 1998, at one working body meeting in May 1999 it was decided to form a women's sub-group within the Parishad to work on women's involvement in the organisation. It had also been noticed in the earlier meetings that women hardly spoke when they were present in a small minority in meetings dominated by men. Hence, it was considered important to create a space within the Parishad's structure where women could meet and discuss their concerns. There were no women present at the meeting where the decision to form such a sub-group was taken, but it was this continuing absence of women from these meetings that prompted this step.

This meeting was followed by another on 9 July 1999 to discuss the strengthening of different cluster-level forms and to plan for women's meetings at different villages. This was attended by only one woman and nine men. In July and August 1999, meetings were held with women in different villages. Following this, on 26 September 1999, the first 'women's committee' (sub-group) meeting was held. At this meeting, the role of women in environmental protection, the need to have a women's sub-group within the Parishad, as well as the aims and objectives of the Parishad were discussed. Of the 25 participants, seven were women. This was followed by another meeting of the women's committee. In many of these initial 'women's meetings', men spoke and tried to patronise women, encouraging them to participate and speak up.

With women coming forth in greater numbers at different Parishad meetings, more of them were included when the working body and executive committee of the federation were reconstituted in 2000. The new working body now included 12 women and the executive committee had four women. Table 3.1 shows the changes that took place over time in the Parishad's governing structure. In 1997, when the MMJSP was formed, the ad hoc committee comprising 24 members did not include any women. However, prior to the registration of MMJSP and following the discussion on the involvement of marginalised sections including women, three women, two tribal and one Dalit were included. This inclusion was more notional. During 1999–02, the working body was reconstituted to include 57 persons; of these 19 were women. In 2003–04, the next working body consisted of 71 persons, of whom 30 were women. The current

Table 3.1
Changes in Maa Maninag Jungle Surakhya Parishad's
Governing Structures over Time

	1997–2000						2000–02						2002–05					
	GC		SC		ST		GC		SC		ST		GC		SC		ST	
Body	M	W	M	W	M	W	M	W	M	W	M	W	M	W	M	W	M	W
Working Body	24	0	2	1	1	2	33	11	1	3	4	5	49	12	1	8	2	11
Executive Committee	6	0	1	1	0	1	9	1	1	1	0	1	13	1	0	2	0	2
Advisory Body	5	0	0	0	0	0	5	2	0	0	0	0						

Note: GC: General Category; SC: Scheduled Caste; ST: Scheduled Tribe; M: Men; W: Women.

working body, constituted in 2004–05, has 84 members, including 31 women. Thus, there has been a dramatic increase in the membership of women in the working body. Similarly, the representation of tribals and Dalits in the working body has been increasing. The initial nine-member executive committee had only two women. In early 2006, there were four women in the current executive committee of 17, but no women office bearers.

THE ATHRAHA TARIKH MEETINGS

As mentioned earlier, women's meetings are held on the 18th of every month. This is a fixed date for an 'open house' for women who want to come in. The meetings provide an open space for discussion on various issues. The degree of 'openness', in terms of women being able to bring different issues forward, depends on the presence or absence of strong facilitators. From 2000, these meetings have been presided over by women; usually it is the same person who is invited to chair every time. While a woman presides over the meetings, when the male leaders of the Parishad are present, they end up doing far more facilitation. From my own participation in and observations of these meetings, it appears that the absence of the male leaders of the Parishad and that of a strong facilitator usually helps women to take on the task of 'facilitating' or managing without too much of facilitation. Participation of women is freer when the space is left open to them, with the facilitators either absent or taking a back seat. Such situations tend to create an environment that is less threatening for women who want to speak and articulate their concerns. A heavily structured meeting or a rigid agenda can hinder the free flow of ideas and feelings. A strong facilitator can conduct the meetings more 'efficiently', in terms of reaching decisions faster, but broad-based participation and consequently ownership of these decisions cound be lacking even though the decisions are made efficiently.

For women who attend regularly, the 'athraha tarikh' meetings provide an important outlet and platform from which to venture into the public domain. Issues of collective concern are discussed here, and they feel that they have a means to pursue these concerns and find solutions to common problems. Observations of these meetings also reveal that they play an important role in terms of providing a space to socialise, exchange news and generally connect with other women. What gets discussed outside of the meeting agenda is as important for women's advancement as political actors as the formal discussions in the meetings. In the meetings, when women discussed the non-availability of KL phadis in their area and the course of action to deal with the problem, the process was critical as it helped them get a sense of agency, and acquire skills to negotiate through political spaces and assert their democratic rights.

The growth of individual women leaders over the years has also resulted in their taking on the leadership at the village level, intervening on behalf of women who are marginalised, protesting against unfair decisions at the community level and negotiating for better deals at the time of selling forest produce. In small focus-group discussions with women on the experience of attending these regular meetings, it emerged that not only has the process been important for the women leaders, but it has also been so for other women in the village, who now feel secure in the knowledge that they have a fellow woman as a leader who can fight on their behalf. These women's meetings have thus played an important role in fostering leadership skills amongst women, giving them confidence, which then comes handy in mixed group meetings and helping them venture into other public spaces.

KENDU LEAVES AND LOCAL LIVELIHOODS IN THE RANPUR CONTEXT

Kendu leaves are an important source of livelihood for the poor in central India, especially during the lean summer months when few other sources of employment exist. In Orissa, the trade in KL was 'nationalised' in 1973 to protect the interests of KL pluckers by eliminating middle-men and to maximise revenues from the trade. A number of studies indicate the high degree of local dependence on KL for livelihood in the state.

In Orissa, it is estimated that about 30 million person-days' work is created by KL collection within a short span of three to four months. Given the state monopoly in KL trade and the absence of state-operated phadis, KL collectors are left with almost no option but to sell their labour to private illicit KL traders, who offer them only a fraction of the price fixed by the government. In Ranpur block, about 5,000 persons, mainly women from about 113 villages, suffer because KL phadis are not available. The problems faced by these KL pluckers were first raised in a meeting of the women's sub-group of the Parishad.

Prior to nationalisation in 1973, there were 10 phadis operated by private traders in the Ranpur area. After nationalisation, there were two to three phadis in the area; these were closed down after a few years, apparently at the behest of private traders. There continue to be many private *beedi* companies operating in the area. A recent survey conducted by the MMJSP (December 2004–January 2005) shows that there is plenty of KL available in the area. In this survey, 974 pluckers were interviewed in 41 sample villages. Of the 240 villages in Ranpur block, 125 villages are involved in KL collection. About 3,100 households and 15,800 people depend on KL for subsistence, and the income from KL provides critical subsistence for about two months. It is estimated that approximately 8,000 quintals of KL are collected in the area (most traded 'illicitly'). The average income from KL at the rates offered by private traders in the 2005 season was Rs 1,560 per household and it is expected that opening of KL phadis can enhance this income by an additional amount of Rs 1,350 per household.

The problems that KL pluckers face in the absence of KL phadis in the area were brought forth at a women's meeting in 2000. Raising the issue of forest-based livelihoods, the women repeatedly emphasised that it was not enough to simply protect forests; they also need to work towards improving the incomes of women (especially from forest products). As part of these discussions, the specific issues and problems of KL pluckers came up. At a meeting of the Central Women's Committee (CWC) on 18 January 2001, it was decided to undertake advocacy to address the problems of KL pluckers in Ranpur block. Accordingly, at this meeting a sub-committee was formed to work on the KL issue. This sub-committee met later in the month, and in the process of discussions at various levels it was decided to conduct a rally to advance the demand of the KL pluckers in the area to open up KL phadis.

Consequently, on 3 April 2001, about 2,000 women from 95 villages held a demonstration at Ranpur, the block headquarters, and rallied to the office of the *tahsildar* and Forest Range Officer to give a memorandum demanding the opening of KL phadis in the area. Later, on 12 April 2001, at a state level workshop on KL, MMJSP also placed the issue before the Chief Minister of Orissa, who promised to look into the matter. Following the advocacy efforts by the MMJSP, a survey was undertaken in 2001 by the KL wing of the Forest Department to ascertain the availability of KL in the area and the feasibility of setting up KL phadis. Following this feasibility study, the KL department submitted a report identifying 20 viable phadis in Ranpur block. In 2002, the government established two KL phadis and promised to open more in the coming year. The government's promise to establish phadis was met with an overwhelming response and the poor pluckers voluntarily took up bush-cutting operations. Even though two phadis were sanctioned, the government constructed one phadi house and a school building was used to store the kendu leaf in Pimpala (the location of the second phadi). In 2003, the phadi in Pimpala was shifted to Dengajhari, where community members voluntarily contributed their labour and materials to construct the phadi house. These two phadis benefited about 600 poor households.

Through the MMJSP, women KL pluckers continued advocating for more phadis. They met higher officials in the KL department, as well as the local Member of Legislative Assembly (MLA) and the Member of Parliament (MP). With these efforts going in vain, the women decided to undertake another rally at Ranpur. On 10 November 2004, about 2,000 Dalit and adivasi women gathered to demand the setting up of 18 phadis as per the government's earlier commitment. Efforts to contact the local MLA and MP continued. Simultaneously, a rigorous media campaign was conducted to bring the problems of KL pluckers to mainstream attention.

The administration has been stating that the leaves in the Ranpur area are of inferior quality and that there have been some problems with marketing of KL in general throughout the state in the past few years. The MMJSP, however, feels that the major determinant of the quality of leaves is the lack of investment in bush-cutting. In the absence of bush-cutting operations in the area, the quality of KL has been deteriorating. Moreover, with KL trade being nationalised, it is the government's responsibility to arrange for procurement centres because the State is the sole procurer of KL in Orissa. Women KL pluckers in the area have also pointed out that the neglect of the KL phadis and lack of proper storage have also led to deterioration in the quality of the leaves.

In March 2005, after receiving no response from the administration with regard to the opening of phadis, the women decided to hold a sit-in demonstration in front of the State Assembly. Thus, from 9–15 January 2005, women representatives from 200 villages in Ranpur sat in front of the State Assembly to demand the opening of KL phadis; 19 women representatives and a few male office bearers of the MMJSP came to Bhubaneswar for this dharna. Interestingly, many of the women who came for the dharna were active leaders from the areas where phadis had already been opened. They, however, felt that it was their responsibility to continue to extend solidarity to other women and ensure that the demand for additional phadis is fulfilled.

REPRESENTATIVES, POLITICAL SPACES AND CITIZENSHIP

The local representative to the State Legislative Assembly happens to be a woman; she also holds a ministerial charge. The women from Ranpur were particularly hurt by her apathy during the process of demanding for KL phadis, and especially during their experience of staging a dharna at Bhubaneswar. At the time of elections, during which the demand for phadis was very much on the electoral agenda, she had moved around in the area asking for votes from women, invoking 'sisterhood'. However, this 'Apa' (elder sister) changed after she won, she paid no attention to this demand. According to one woman leader, after becoming an MLA she does not recognise them, 'We are still the jungle-people, while she has become an urban dweller'.

When the women went to Bhubaneswar to stage a dharna before the State Assembly, while other MLAs stopped by to talk to them about their demands, this MLA sent raw chuda (puffed rice) to them. The women were quite hurt at what was seen as an insensitive gesture. Instead of visiting them personally and taking into account their long-standing demand for phadis, she simply sent chuda. Women responded with, 'We have brought enough food with us, to last us for 15 days, what will we do with this chuda?' Someone else added, 'She sent us raw chuda, maybe because she is now a minister, she has forgotten how to roast chuda. When we leave this place, we will go and give her some roasted chuda, and some sugar and bananas to go with it'. In the cacophony of responses, someone else said, 'She is not a woman. If she were a woman she would have understood our pain. She is a man.'

Ideas of femininity, sisterhood and citizenship made a complex weave in the responses and in how the women viewed the woman MLA. When she had approached them for votes, they had been truly taken in by her role-play of Apa; and had harboured expectations that she would understand their needs and concerns and would connect with these needs as a woman. When that did not happen, the grudge against her was not only for being a failed 'representative', but for being a failed woman. At another level, there was also resentment against her for being able to escape the drudgeries of being a woman—she no longer has to roast chuda and she moves about in the male world just like a man. My guess is that these responses would have been different in the case of a male MLA. In the case of the woman MLA, the expectations and the connections were somehow deeper and hence the stronger disappointment and anger upon her failure as their representative.

After six days of sitting in dharna in front of the State Assembly, the women went to meet the local MLA at her residence. The following account is based on interviews with the women leaders.

Yesterday when we went there (her residence) to meet her, her peon asked us to sit. She came out of her home and straightaway headed towards her car. Quickly we went after her and said Namaskar (paid regards) and stood before the car.

MLA: *Maa mane, kana hela?* [Elderly women, what happened?]

KN: You are asking what happened, as if you do not know. From 9th we are here, today it is 14th. Adivasi and Harijan from Ranpur are sitting here; we are on the road. So many newspapers have taken out our story, and still you ask what happened. So many MLAs have visited us and you have done nothing on this till now.

MLA: How do you know what I have or have not done?

KN: If you would have raised the issue in the Assembly, we would have read about it in the newspapers. Other MLAs and ministers' news cover the pages of the newspaper, whereas nothing has come out in the newspaper on this.

MLA: Don't you know that ministers don't raise questions in the Assembly?

KN: I don't know when you became a minister. I only know that you are our MLA.

MLA (very rudely): Who the hell are you, what is your village's name?

KN (replied confidently): I am Kuntala, from Mardakote Village

MLA: Since when have you started showing leadership?

KN: Why are you saying so, why are you not concerned about the hardships of the poor?

MLA: I will not listen to you, get lost.

KN (thought): Of course, I will leave. I have not come to stay at your place.

By this time another woman leader intervened and told about the matter politely, and the MLA said, 'Fine, I will listen to you, and not to (KN)'.

After the entire episode, all the other women stood by KN and went on to say that the MLA showed that she was not a woman, rather she was a very unfair man.

However, following this encounter, the MLA called representatives of the MMJSP for another meeting in the evening, and after some discussion and pressure from women due to the dharna, the media coverage, et cetera, the administration agreed to open one more phadi in the area. The opening of one more phadi was seen as hardly a cause to celebrate (given the demand for 18 phadis), but women felt that they would at least not have to return home empty-handed.

For many women, this was the first time they had stepped out and were away from their families for so long. Some of them said that this was the first time that people from their area, Ranpur, had come to Bhubaneswar for their demands. This placed a substantial burden on them, as they were the first to venture out into the streets of the state capital. There was a sense of responsibility, which was conveyed when they spoke about their protest as being the first of its kind. Hence, they felt that they had to have something to tell back home.

WOMEN'S PARTICIPATION AT THE COMMUNITY LEVEL

In MMJSP, women's participation at the block and cluster levels has increased over the years, while it still remains difficult at the community level. For example, consider the case of Mardakot, a small village with tribal and Dalit hamlets. In Mardakot, women play a leadership role in the forest protection initiative; and in the vicinity, there are other examples of women leading forest protection efforts. The area also has an all women cluster committee comprising of five villages. Bisika Jani from Mardakot is a prominent woman leader, who presides over the CWC meetings. She talks animatedly of how she called a village meeting to discuss some important issues related to the participation of Mardakot in forest protection currently being done by Dengajhari village. However, in the same village, 'village' meetings are an all-men affair. On seeking clarification, we found that the village meeting that Bisika Jani convened comprised only of women. She referred to this as the 'village sitting together', and while we sat talking thus, the other half of the village, the male village was having a 'village meeting'. The village remains clearly segregated along gender lines, even while women's action in community affairs appears far more active when viewed from the outside.

At the community level, the barriers are more difficult to surmount in many respects, with caste and gender identities being more deeply ingrained than at other spatial scales. While Bisika Jani is a leader at the MMJSP meetings in her own right—she is probably viewed as a tribal leader—in her own village, she is also so and so's wife, sister-in-law, et cetera. Another active member of the cluster-level committee said shyly that her son was the secretary of the Village Committee, and 'if I walk into the village meeting, he will say that my mother has become very modern/ aggressive'. There were also fears of being labelled as someone who picks fights by raising issues or asking questions in public spaces.

On repeated probing into what hinders women from attending the village meeting while they go all over the state and meet all kinds of people (some of them had also been to Bhubaneswar for the dharna), they said that it would be all right if they went (to the village meeting) with us (outsiders). Often it is easier to bridge the barriers with the help of outsiders.

In another case of the Das Mauja (group of 10 villages), there are no women in the group-level committee. The Das Mauja has been protecting forests for over 25 years. A committee of about 20 persons, two representatives from each village, sits together every Sunday evening to run the collective forest management endeavour. This traditional committee had no representation of women, while in recent years the committee has included three women, who remain as members for the benefit of outsiders. When this committee was approached by the Forest Department for formalisation under the Joint Forest Management programme, the stipulations for a JFM committee led them to include three women. Or, as one of the members of the Das Mauja Committee told us, 'We have included women since this (having women on board) is the "requirement" of outsiders (external agencies with whom they interface)'. The cluster committee continues to meet every week on Sunday, starting at six or seven in the evening and continuing till late at night. It is obviously very inconvenient for women to attend these late evening meetings, especially as this involves travel from neighbouring villages. It is only when outsiders, the Forest Department or some NGOs, convene the meeting that the women are called in; otherwise the male members take the signatures of women members instead of 'bothering' them ('after all the women are busy with so much work at home').

According to a survey undertaken by Vasundhara and MMJSP, only about 20 per cent of the villages involved in forest protection have any women representatives in the village committee. From the information available for 111 villages in Ranpur, it is seen that women's representation in the village community forestry committees is as low as 6.8 per cent. Representation of Scheduled Tribes and Scheduled Castes is equally low, and stands at 15.5 per cent and 6.7 per cent respectively. These figures might not reflect the true situation of women's participation, as in the case of women's membership on the Das Mauja Committee.

Thus, women's participation at the community level continues to be problematic, constrained by existing socio-cultural taboos on women's presence and participation in community affairs. In many villages in

Ranpur, the forest protection committee organises an annual feast to celebrate their collective effort to conserve forests. According to the elders involved in forest protection, this is done so that the children and the youth can become involved in the community forestry efforts. As with other similar community feasts, women remain absent. After everyone has finished eating, the surplus food is sent to women's homes. Women's absence from formal occasions where community-based forest conservation is celebrated and furthered seems at odds from the otherwise very active association of Dalit and tribal women with forests.

While women's active involvement remains elusive at the community level, the opening up of space within the block-level Parishad has led to animated participation at the higher levels. It is almost with a vengeance that women seek their space in higher-order organisations, something that is denied to them within the confines of their own villages. Their participation at these other forums also leads them to demand the opening up of space within their own villages. A woman leader, Kuntala Nahak from Mardakot, described an occasion when she had refused to sign on a village resolution that according to her was not a fair representation of events. She seemed to have been the only one who had bothered to read it so carefully and had had issues with the wording of the resolution. In the case of the Das Mauja, the women from one of the Dalit villages who are active within the Parishad have started questioning the practice of putting their signatures without participating in the meetings. This is, however, a gradual process of change and a process that needs to be aided by opening up of spaces at different levels. Even gestures such as representational quotas create spaces that democratise decision-making in the long run.

DISCUSSION

Democracy is much more than voting rights, periodic elections and delegation of power to elected representatives. Beyond an ensemble of formal democratic institutions, democracy is also a normative process that helps define interactions within societies. For more effective democracy, democratic practices need to spread throughout the society, governing not only the relationship between the state and citizens, but also that between citizens and among their associations.

Habermas suggests that the moral legitimacy of binding laws can only be due to their origination as the outcome of a discursive process through which citizens engage in self-determination through open and rational discourse (Deflem 1996). He proposes the concept of deliberative democracy, which is built on the foundations of communicative reason and communicative rationality (Habermas 1996). Put simply, this suggests that all those whose basic interests are affected by a decision ought to be included in the deliberatively democratic process. Feminist scholars have further built on this concept of deliberative democracy to bring in a more explicit focus on inclusion, social justice and an attention to difference as a resource (see Benhabib 1996; Young 2000).

The feminists' call for inclusion comes from their experiences of exclusion in different forms—exclusion from basic political rights and opportunities to participate, and exclusion from an unhindered vantage point from which to re-imagine the future. In today's context, inclusion has to go beyond equal voting rights to the additional conditions of deepening political inclusion, such as attention to modes of communication, social differences and pluralism, representation, civil organising, and the borders of political jurisdictions (Young 2000). Not only should all those affected be nominally included in decision-making, but should also be included on equal terms. Young (ibid.) further suggests that the path to more socially just outcomes for deliberative democracy needs to pay explicit attention to the values of self-development (along the lines of Amartya Sen's emphasis on capabilities) and self-determination. Both self-development and self-determination are often restricted by institutional constraints, which further entrench power differentials and the ability to constrain the choices and actions of others. Furthering institutional conditions for promoting self-development and self-determination of members of society is, thus, one of the means of furthering social justice and substantive democracy.

Deep democracy also calls for a more robust concept of citizenship, in which citizens are active political actors at different scales, defined not only through their relationship with the state, but also through their relationship with each other. Yuval-Davis (1999) posits citizenship as a multilayered construct, with the citizenship in collectivities in the different layers—local, ethnic, national, state, cross- or trans-state and supra-state—getting affected, and often at least partly constructed, by the relationships and positionings of each layer in a specific historical context. Marshall (1950, 1981) defines citizens as 'full members' of a collective or community. Women have to generally struggle to be accepted as full members of a community or collective, starting from the domain of the family to various other collectives and the state.

The case of Ranpur illustrates women's attempts to claim citizenship at various levels. By leveraging their increasing acceptance as full members within the Parishad, these women try to break into political spaces at the community level to which they otherwise have limited access. Separate women's meetings have provided them institutional space to nurture their self-development and the self-determination that helps them to do so. The fallouts of the process of self-development and self-determination are also visible in terms of how women become politically more active in different political arenas. In the process, the nature and quality of deliberations taking place within the Parishad have been transformed and so has the quality of the outcomes of these deliberations. For example, the kendu leaf problem would not have appeared on the radar of the Parishad in the absence of women's deliberation. Women's presence and deliberations have helped transform the agenda of the Parishad and there is a deepening of democracy in the process.

Political inclusion needs to move beyond the simple presence of all those affected by certain decisions at the time of decision-making, to providing equal opportunities to be heard and to influence outcomes. This is a tough call and requires close attention to the forms of internal exclusion that result from, among other things, subtle institutional norms such as expressions that are privileged or are more likely to be heard, the agenda-setting processes, the burdens of past exclusion and power relations. Facilitation for expanding democratic spaces has to pay close attention to such forms of internal exclusion and inclusion. Simply creating institutional spaces for women's presence is not enough; the constraints that hinder the process of their expression, self-development and self-determination have to be eased out as well. Deepening of democracy and maturing of women as political actors and full citizens at multiple layers are challenges that require all our imagination and untiring work.

ACKNOWLEDGEMENTS

This paper draws on my dissertation research, 'Democratising Forest Governance: Emergent Community Forestry Federations in Orissa', as a Ph.D. candidate at the Department of Community, Agriculture, Recreation and Resource Studies, Michigan State University, USA. The fieldwork for this research was supported by the International Dissertation Research Fellowship of the Social Science Research Council, USA; and the American Institute of Indian Studies, USA. My earlier work and ongoing discussions with colleagues from Vasundhara have been particularly useful. I am especially grateful for the generous offer of time and the insights that women and men from villages in Ranpur have shared with me. Thanks to Arundhati Jena for her research assistance and help with transcribing interview notes and translation of meeting records.

REFERENCES

Benhabib, S. 1996. *Democracy and difference: Contesting boundaries of the Political.* Princeton, NJ: Princeton University Press.

Deflem, M. 1996. *Habermas, Modernity, and Law.* London, Thousand Oaks: Sage Publications.

Habermas, J. 1996. 'Three Normative Models of Democracy', in Seyla Benhabib (ed.), *Democracy and Difference.* Princeton, NJ: Princeton University Press.

Marshall, T.H. 1950. *Citizenship and Social Class.* Cambridge: Cambridge University Press.

———. 1981. *The Right to Welfare and Other Essays.* London: Heinemann Educational Books.

Singh, N.M. 2002. 'Federations of community forest management groups in Orissa: Crafting new institutions to assert local rights', *Forests, Trees and People Newsletter*, 46 (September).

Vasundhara. 2003. *Maa Maninag Jungle Surakhya Parishad: An Overview.* Mimeo.

Young, 2000. *Inclusion and Democracy.* Oxford, New York: Oxford University Press.

Yuval-Davis, N. 1999. 'The "Multi-Layered Citizen": Citizenship in the Age of "Glocalization"', *International Feminist Journal of Politics*, 1(1): 119–36.

4

Legal Identity and Natural Resource Management

The Foraging Irula Women of Killai, Cuddalore District, Tamil Nadu

P. Thamizoli and P. Ignatius Prabhakar

'Who are we? We are deprived of our identity and we are lost' (Chorus of voices at a meeting on 27 August 1998, in the Irula settlement, MGR Nagar).

A historical analysis of tribal citizenship in the Indian subcontinent reveals the constraints and difficulties that tribal groups have faced and the struggles that they have undergone. The efforts by different tribal groups to obtain legal identity continue in various parts of the country even in the present time. The traditional foraging nature of many tribal groups, their relative isolation and their existing notions of territoriality are not consonant with practical efforts to establish and formalise their legal identity. The tribal communities have their own cognitive concepts of identity and citizenship, as also of rights and livelihoods. Ignoring their identity and refusing their legitimacy provide very little or no scope for the representation of these groups and their participation in the 'mainstream'. The relationship between the individual and the state has been differently conceptualised across historical moments and geographical regions. Class, caste, ethnicity, gender and age intersect with notions of the role of individuals and/or communities, their status and legitimacy and, subsequently, with citizenship. Rights have to be universal, but social and economic exclusion and oppression act as barriers to achieving this; in addition, the prevailing value system reinforces the inherent economic, social and gender bias. The gradual gaining and enforcement of rights would lead to improved welfare and enhancement of the livelihood status of the community, and of the women within the community.

This chapter traces a multilayered process. We start by discussing aspects like awareness, services and the institutions related to the lives and livelihoods of the Irulas living in the Killai area, a coastal belt around the Pichavaram mangroves in Cuddalore district, Tamil Nadu. We then outline the process by which the Irulas of MGR Nagar, a hamlet near Pichavaram, gained the approval of the state government, and also focus on their entitlements and rights over the resources that they use. Finally, we attempt to understand the effect of the new identity gained by the Irula women of Killai.

Field (1998: 432) says, 'Analysis of identity requires anthropologists to uncover and describe the specific historical conditions producing elements of identity, attending their dynamically continuous transformation. It also encourages ethnographers to transform their relationships with local intellectual informants in the direction of collaboration and exchange'. Indigenous movements speak the language of historical continuity and stake their claim for collective identity upon this. Field (ibid.: 198) further emphasises such an approach and the possible collaboration of academics and indigenous leaders in the case of the `Unacknowledged tribe'.

The Irula tribal group lives in the recently developed settlements in the Killai area, located at the tail end of the perennial river Cauvery. The government of Tamil Nadu had not recognised their tribal identity and refused to accept their legitimacy. So, this group of Irulas had not been given the 'Community Certificate' issued to individuals belong to Scheduled Castes, Scheduled Tribes and Other Backward Communities. The community certificate issued by the revenue departments of respective state governments provides legal recognition of identity and community status. Without the certificate the Irulas could not benefit from the special constitutional provisions for Scheduled Tribes, available in Tamil Nadu and the rest of the country (See http://india.gov.in/govt/constitutions_india.php and http://tribal.nic.in/schedule1.html).

This denial of their tribal identity was keenly felt, with the constant question, 'Who are we'? Despite a long and hard struggle on the part of the people to legitimise their tribal status, they did not succeed. Later, the Chennai-based NGO M.S. Swaminathan Research Foundation (MSSRF) facilitated the process and recorded the stages through which the group eventually achieved their legitimate status.

SUBSISTENCE ECONOMY AND MARGINALITY
IN A MULTICULTURAL CONTEXT

The Irulas are the second largest tribal group in Tamil Nadu, concentrated in most of the northern districts of the state. The group is known by several local names such as Irular, Iruligar, Iruligas, Villiar, Arava Yenadi and Pambukaran. Traditionally, the tribal group has been managing its subsistence economy by small gaming and gathering in the dry and deciduous forest areas, or through working as labour on agricultural farms. The traditional Irula settlements near the Pichavaram mangroves in Killai are semi-permanent and small in size, and are composed of only a few households. Apart from these tiny settlements, a few scattered huts are located in private coconut groves.

At present, the livelihood of the Irulas depends primarily on groping by hand in the mangrove creeks and canals to gather fish and prawns juveniles. They also very occasionally hunt wild animals in the slushy mangrove forests. The other traditional fertile grounds for Irula foraging are the harvested paddy fields; they hunt rats by opening up the burrows and gathering the paddy grains stored in them. On the one hand, due to changes in the local environment, the group has developed new skills, adaptability, and new subsistence and economic practices in the contemporary situation. On the other hand, the slow process of settling down has created social stability, which has enabled them to mobilise as a group, discuss matters more regularly, feel their collective identity and arrive at a consensus to take decisions pertaining to the common issues of the community.

The traditional farmers and fishers in the region are the two dominant neighbours with whom the tribal Irulas have developed working relationships. The Irulas work in the paddy fields and casuarina plantations of the farming groups, and share the mangrove resources with the traditional fisher groups. The complete absence of a political relationship with the external systems and government institutions, and their economic dependency on other communities, created an environment where they maintained an absolute silence. The inception of a sedentary life for at least one section of the population and the emergence of independent economic activities, like groping for prawn and catching fish in the mangrove waters, gradually helped to develop their collective identity.

Not having been a part of any mainstream social institutions, the Irulas themselves, however, were neither aware of the purpose nor knew the values of these institutions. They were also ignorant of the details of the special provisions available to socially and economically marginalised groups, and the social responsibility of the state institutions.

Historically, the group has been kept outside the boundaries of the Hindu caste system and an identity has been imposed on them from the Hindu perspective engrossed with purity and pollution. The other groups perceive the Irulas as rat-eaters, snake-catchers and nomads, who are 'submissive', 'ignorant', 'dirty' and worshippers of local deities. The caste groups in the region identify and address the Irulas as *Vedar* or *Vettakaran*, which means a nomadic group involved in small gaming. Even though the Irulas were not happy about the pejorative identity imposed on them, their marginal position never gave them the courage to react and openly express their resentment. The communication between the other castes and the Irulas is always instruction-based, with the Irulas being expected to listen and respond. Their submissiveness ensured a frictionless co-existence of the Irulas with other local communities. Similarly, the government administration, which is responsible for ascertaining and legitimising the cultural identity of the group, also refused to recognise them as Irula. However, the Irulas refused to accept the government's listing of them in the Schedule Caste category, which is a kind of de-cultured absorption at the lowest end of the Hindu social hierarchy. When government officials asked for any recorded proof against which to consider the Irulas' request for a community certificate, they were unable to produce any records. Our own interactions and observations in the Killai region showed that modern processes like democratisation, education and the implementation of developmental programmes by the governments had not touched the Irula population.

SOCIAL MOBILISATION AND COMMUNITY IDENTITY

The Irulas' longing for recognition of their identity led to their developing a common voice. During the recent past, after the move towards a semi-sedentary life and the establishment of MGR Nagar, the first settlement in 1978, some of the Irulas of this area were able to mobilise themselves. They made attempts to initiate a dialogue with the institutions of the state. During that process, NGOs were identified as the only potential supporters. But in the initial phase, NGOs were unable to produce any authentic evidence and could not succeed in helping the Irulas to establish their identity. Without a community certificate, the Irulas encountered critical practical problems in their daily lives. They were unable to get ration cards (to buy grains at subsidised rates from the government shops of the Public Distribution System), or send their children to school. They were also deprived of any special benefits from government programmes meant for tribal groups.

Several interactions with government officials at different levels, from the Village Administrative Officer to the Regional Revenue Officer, who are responsible for issuing the community certificate, did not yield any positive result. As the villagers were not able to provide strong evidence due to their nomadic past, their request was repeatedly declined. When it was mentioned that some of the Irulas continued to practise rat-hunting, the official was not convinced. The official's attitude of searching in the present for a conventional document for past practices and his lack of understanding of the dynamics of a socio-cultural system determined the negative response.

It was during the colonial period that tribal groups all over India were listed for the first time. In subsequent years, the list was modified a little, with some additions and omissions. Article 366 (25) of the Constitution of India refers to Scheduled Tribes as those communities who are scheduled in accordance with Article 342 of the Constitution; the Scheduled Tribes are the tribes or tribal communities who have been declared as such by the President through a public notification. The criterion for defining the word 'tribe' is not spelt out in the Constitution, but some of the essential characteristics of these communities are: primitive traits, geographical location, distinct culture, shyness when it comes to contact with the community at large; and economic backwardness. Anthropologists are multi-vocal in defining the word 'tribe' in the Indian context; however, elaborating this historical discourse is beyond the scope of this chapter.

The official tribal list in Tamil Nadu, which was compiled a long time ago, is a slightly modified version of that prepared by the British. According to this, there are no tribal groups in Cuddalore district. The present list for Tamil Nadu consists of 36 tribal groups. Even though Irulas are included as one of these groups, *their presence in Cuddalore district is not recorded.* Consequently, in the official view, the community is not entitled to a community certificate legitimising their status as a tribal group and entitling them to the special provisions of the central and Tamil Nadu governments. The Irulas had no official 'place' in the district due to the lack of any serious efforts to alter the list and also due to their own nomadic life. The officials were, therefore, hesitant or blatantly refused to deal with the issue. Even the 1991 Census has no record of Irulas in the district, although for the last two decades the Irulas have been requesting members of local bodies, visiting government officials and politicians to recognise their status as a tribal group.

COASTAL WETLANDS MANAGEMENT AND LEGITIMACY OF TRIBAL IDENTITY

The Pichavaram mangrove wetland on the southeast coast of India occupies an area of 1,357 hectares, bordering the Vellar estuary in the north and the Coleroon estuary to the south of Cuddalore district. The Vellar-Coleroon estuarine complex comprises the Killai backwater and Pichavaram mangroves. The renewable natural resources in the Pichavaram mangrove wetland can be divided into two major categories: (*a*) aquatic resources; and (*b*) forest resources. The local communities use forest resources mainly for grazing and fuel wood collection, which has now been declared illegal. About 30 species of prawns, crabs and molluscs, and 200 species of commercially important fish have been harvested from the Pichavaram mangrove ecosystem.

MGR Nagar is the first permanent Irula settlement and falls within the Killai panchayat. It was established during the mid-1970s. When the then Prime Minister Indira Gandhi had declared an Emergency in the country in 1975, a development programme known as the '20 point programme' had been launched. One of the 20 points was for the release of bonded labour. This enabled the Irulas in the region to be released from the local landlords under whose control they had been working for generations as virtual bonded labourers. As a part of the programme, the government allotted about four acres of *porombokku* land for the Irulas to establish their first permanent hamlet. MGR Nagar has 136 households and a population of 494. The settlement lies close to the mangrove forests. The residents own no assets and manage their livelihood through fishing in the mangrove waters. In the beginning there were only around 20 families settled here, but later the number of families gradually increased and reached the present strength.

The MSSRF, an NGO involved in participatory action research and development, has facilitated a project in the area for evolving Joint Mangrove Management with the active involvement of the major stakeholders, including the local mangrove-dependent communities and the Tamil Nadu Forest Department. The objectives of the project are to check the further degradation of the mangrove ecosystems and restore the degraded mangrove areas with the participation of all the stakeholders. It also aims to modify the relationship between the user groups and the wetland ecosystems and to reduce the anthropogenic pressure exerted by the communities living close to the mangrove wetland by involving the community to explore and ensure sustainable utilisation of the mangrove resources.

Chambers (1997: 183) has warned against the bias of professionals while implementing a project involving community as the major stakeholder. He has pointed to the attitude of professionals who assert their own 'reality', ignoring and failing to appreciate the perceptions and views of the local people; and has argued for the need for major reversals to share people's realities. Cultures have different goals and needs to meet. These needs are sometimes complementary to that of other cultures or groups and sometimes not. No cooperation can be expected from local communities unless the problems and threats related to the basic requirements in their lives are addressed. It is necessary to assist communities to develop alternatives to compensate for the restrictions imposed upon them by the authorities, particularly in the use and management of natural resources. Hence, it is essential to strike a balance between the objectives of the project and those of the people. Past experiences have clearly showed that there will never be a 'blueprint recipe' for natural resource management problems, as in every specific situation, the priorities and strategies would be different. The significance of such an approach has been noted and appreciated by researchers and activists.

In order to understand the local people's perception on different issues, identify their major concerns and also decide the interventions for follow-up action, several exercises of Participatory Rural Appraisal (PRA) were organised at the start of the project with the active involvement of Irula men and women. This created an enabled environment for the community to actively participate in the process. The Irulas' sense of lacking an identity and not having the Community Certificate was first among their major concerns, which were listed on the basis of PRA results. Mangrove management only ranked fourth.

Prior to developing the microplan to address the concerns identified through PRA, the Irulas had formed an informal community-based organisation called the Village Development and Management Committee (VDMC), in which all adult men and women of the village became members. The VDMC functions according to a set of rules and regulations evolved by the members of the group. It provides a forum for discussion and for arriving at a consensus, and sets the agenda for action and assuming collective responsibilities. The forum facilitates the linkages of the community with other government developmental agencies and financial institutions. After a detailed discussion, a microplan was prepared by the VDMC to approach the district revenue officials to solve the community certificate problem. The plan consisted of the steps to be taken, the time and expenditure necessary, the officials to be met, and the individuals from the community and the MSSRF who would be responsible to undertake these different tasks. The visits and meetings undertaken by the villagers and the project staff were done as per the microplan and many of the issues raised by the officials were clarified. After several meetings with the Revenue Divisional Officer (RDO) at Chidambaram, the taluk headquarters, it was decided to opt for a departmental enquiry and simultaneously to prepare an ethnographic document with the support of subject experts. These meetings helped the officials to understand some of the concepts of cultural groupings and identity, ethnography and the 'essential elements' of tribal ethnography. It was suggested to the RDO that because there was no record available to prove the Irulas' tribal status, an ethnographic profile could fill the gap and provide an authentic 'proof' to decide the community's Scheduled Tribe status. The Department of Anthropology, University of Madras, was involved in preparing the supportive ethnographic profile and the profile was submitted to the RDO

(Thamizoli and Sudarsen 1998). The RDO then paid a personal visit to the settlement to conduct an enquiry with the Irula women and men separately regarding their cultural characteristics and ancestral linkages. He listened to descriptions of the history of their foraging past and the traditional hunting practices, and also witnessed a mock demonstration. Following the visit, the RDO fixed a date and paid another visit with his subordinates. An *oormariyal* (village-level ban on fishing and any other economic activity) was declared by the village leaders to enable the entire village, women and men heads of households, to gather at a common place. Each and every case was cross-checked with the entire community gathered and the community certificate was distributed by the RDO to all household heads.

After some time, an attempt was made to elicit the different perceptions of the men and women of MGR Nagar about the impact of some of the elements of the mangrove management project. The different activities were assessed at the individual, family and community levels. About 20 women and 20 men were approached to elicit the significance of the community certificate (see Table 4.1).

The women of MGR Nagar perceived the community certificate as the best result of the interventions, as it could bring benefits at the individual, family and community levels. On the day the certificates were distributed, when an elderly woman, who was also the head of her household, was asked what she would do with the certificate, she answered: 'What a meaningless question you are asking? It is a treasure; I will lock in the trunk (box) that we have at home'. Agreeing that it was indeed a

Table 4.1
Perceptions of Women and Men Regarding the Significance
of the Community Certificate

	Individual		Family		Community	
	Women	Men	Women	Men	Women	Men
School	–	–	15	10	15	16
Community Certificate	19	4	19	15	20	18
Mangrove Restoration	9	–	9	5	15	10
Savings	15	9	16	13	–	5
Leader-skill	10	4	–	–	6	–
Information Access	15	9	–	–	–	–

Source: Thamizoli (1999). 'Report of the Workshop on Social and Gender Audit'.

treasure to be carefully preserved, we tried to probe what she could do with it. She replied curtly, 'In the future, occasions will come, and it will enable us to achieve something in our life, which otherwise would not at all be possible'. Another woman said that she was protecting the certificate as she would her son. All of the women said that what had happened that day would stand for all time, eternally (*ithu kaalathukkum nikkum*).

TRIBAL FISHER'S COOPERATIVE AND FISHING RIGHTS

The fishermen in the surrounding hamlets claim traditional fishing rights in the mangrove waters. They have traditional, strategic spots where they get a good catch of prawns. These spots are used cyclically, the same site being visited every 10 days. Only the traditional fishermen, who are members of the fishermen's cooperative society, enjoy the fishing rights, through an annual lease. With their newly acquired legal identity, the women and men of MGR Nagar have been able to form and register the 'Irular Meen Pidippu Sangam', with the support of the District Fisheries Department. Irula women form almost 50 per cent of this tribal fisher cooperative. The major advantage they have gained from the cooperative society is the legitimate right to fish in the mangrove water, which was previously denied to them by the traditional fishing communities living in the surrounding hamlets. It is pertinent that the results of a PRA exercise, 'Livelihoods: Matrix Ranking,' conducted with groups of Irula men and women, showed that fishing in the mangrove backwaters was the most preferred job among the major livelihood options available to them.

Another major gain is that they have become members of a Tamil Nadu state-level Irula network, called the 'Irula Thozhilalar Sangam' (Irula Labour Organisation). Through this network, the Irulas of MGR Nagar receive traditional fishing boats and nets for fishing. These assets are given to the households on a joint ownership basis. Both husband and wife are involved in fishing, and work as a pair in the mangrove waters. The support of different organisations contributed to completely eliminating groping by hand in the mangrove creeks, a method that meant immense drudgery for Irula women. Until 1999, all Irula women gathered prawns and fish, mainly prawn juveniles, by sitting immersed for long hours in the mangrove creeks, just keeping their heads above the water, groping by hand in the slush for the catch. According to the women's daily routine (as reflected in the PRA exercise done earlier), they went to the mangroves by 8:00 a.m. and were in the water till 3:00 p.m. Other domestic activities consumed the rest of their day, with virtually no time for leisure. However, as the men and women now use boats and nets for fishing, the women's groping method has been gradually eliminated, as mentioned earlier. The women perceive this as the most significant positive change that having the certificate has brought. The other advantage is that men and women are compensated for any damage caused to the boats by a natural event. The society promotes savings among its fishermen and fisherwomen members by providing a complementary fund with a ratio of 1:2. It has also helped them acquire land to construct houses, which are jointly owned by husband and wife, and to buy boats and nets as asset-building for livelihood promotion. Apart from this, the Tamil Nadu Adi-Dravidar Housing and Development Corporation (THADCO), Cuddalore, has recognised the Irulas as a Scheduled Tribe and is consulting with them about schemes to which they are entitled.

ROLE OF WOMEN IN MANGROVE FOREST CONSERVATION

The Irula men acknowledge that the women show more concern for mangrove forest management. Whenever an Irula woman comes across a mangrove propagule in the forest, she collects it and plants it in an appropriate place. She would never want to miss a chance to develop a mangrove tree. The Irulas' commitment to preserve and manage the mangroves is reflected in a statement made during a focus group discussion: 'When we are young, mother's milk saves us and when we grow, mother mangrove feeds us'. The active involvement of Irula women and men in the process of project implementation and, subsequently, in the management of the identified mangrove restoration area (85 hectares), along with the Forest Department officials, helped them gain good expertise in mangrove restoration methods. The Forest Department now employs Irula women and men as resource persons in the restoration programme being carried out in other parts of Tamil Nadu. This new skill has created a new opportunity for employment and income for the Irulas. The Forest Department's support in the form of the revolving fund given to the VDMC has helped to promote other income-generation activities for the Irula women like crab fattening, selling prawns and running petty shops. It has also been encouraging the Irula women to take up the fish vending business, which has hitherto been a monopoly of traditional fisherwomen.

EDUCATION AND OTHER OPPORTUNITIES

The community certificate has paved the way for Irula children to have access to education. In the past, Irula children were not allowed to go beyond primary education due to the lack of a certificate. The community certificate is the proof that indicates the community name in school records, but because no family had the certificate, they could never continue with their education beyond the primary level. Now the certificate helps the children to go onto middle and high school, and continue with their education without this hurdle. It has also helped children to get the special fee concessions and other facilities meant for tribal students. The certificate also enables all households in the hamlet to get family ration cards, which can be used in locally designated ration shops to buy subsidised food grains, provided by the Public Distribution System.

The experience of MGR Nagar also helped the district Revenue Department to see it as a precedent and provide the community certificate to Irulas in other hamlets located in the same region.

Ethnic identity is dynamic, not static; hence, the real issue is not about preserving a static culture, but rather one of promoting a cultural autonomy, which will allow people to redefine their identity without compromising their dignity. For the tribal societies in India, this implies integration in the larger society, but not necessarily by losing their cultural distinctiveness.

CONCLUSION

The changing physical landscape and social and political environments of the Irulas created the pressure to define their identity. For small minority groups such as the Irulas, it is a major problem to maintain respect for and control over their traditional knowledge and practices, while at the same time engaging with non-traditional knowledge and asserting the validity of new bases of identity. The lack of any documentary evidence as authentic proof to negotiate with the institutions of the state and to establish their cultural identity is a drawback. It is in this context that the Tamil Nadu administration's recognition and acceptance of ethnography, as a tool to record particular cultural markers of tribal identity, assumes significance. The 'new identity' has started helping the Irulas to develop new relationships, institutions and to make changes in their livelihoods. It has created major changes in the lives of Irula women due to the new rights and assets that reduce their drudgery, enhance their active participation in fishing activities, allow them to diversify to other economic activities and finally gain access to and control over resources. The impact would expand to other areas in the future, such as the government schemes related to women's access to livelihoods, education, health and human rights. .

ACKNOWLEDGEMENTS

The authors acknowledge the support of the MSSRF mangrove conservation project team; the late Professor V. Sudarsen, Department of Anthropology, Madras University, for his active involvement in the preparation of the Irula ethnography; Sumi Krishna and R. Rengalakshmi for their patience in going through the draft of this chapter and for valuable comments; the Indo-Canadian Environment Facility (ICEF), which provided financial support to the project; and finally, to the villagers of MGR Nagar who shared with us the whole process.

REFERENCES

Chambers, R. 1997. *Whose Reality Counts? Putting the First Last*. London: Intermediate Technology Publications.

Field, L.W. 1999. 'Complications and Collaborations Anthropologists and the "Unacknowledged Tribes" of California', *Current Anthropology*, 40(2): 193–209.

Government of India. National Portal of India: Government: Constitution of India. http://india.gov.in/govt/constitutions_india.php.

Government of India. Tribal schedule. http://tribal.nic.in/schedule1.html.

Thamizoli, P. 1999. 'Report of the Workshop on Social and Gender Audit'. Chennai: M.S. Swaminathan Research Foundation (unpublished).

Thamizoli, P. and V. Sudarsen. 1998. 'Ethnographic profile of the Irular of Pichavaram, Cuddalore District, Tamil Nadu: A tool to find out tribal identity', Unpublished report. Chennai: M.S. Swaminathan Research Foundation.

II

Work and Employment Strategies

5

Marginal Lives in Marginal Lands

Livelihood Strategies of Women-Headed, Immigrant Households in the Charlands of the River Damodar, West Bengal

Gopa Samanta and Kuntala Lahiri-Dutt

INTRODUCTION

The women of the charlands (see Box 5.1) comprise a more disadvantaged group when compared to men. However, those households headed by divorced, deserted or widowed women are even more deprived and marginalised than the rest. Such households are known to be the poorest of the poor because of their low human capital, low bargaining power and restricted social and economic mobility (Datta and Hossain 2003). A report of the Asian Development Bank (2001) noted the widespread occurrence of poverty among women-headed households in the Indian subcontinent; over 95 per cent of women-headed households in Bangladesh are below the poverty line. The charland inhabitants of West Bengal, living in extremely vulnerable environments, are generally poor because they do not have assets such as landed property. Therefore, their livelihood is greatly dependent on the number of members in the household who are able to earn. Women-headed households are even poorer because the absence of adult male earning members places the responsibility of running the household solely on the women. Not only are they poorer, but in general, compared to other low-income households, women-headed households are also more vulnerable, living in uncertainty and powerless to control their destinies. They are marginalised in char

Box 5.1
Charlands

The chars are riverine landmasses rising above the water level. Rivers carrying large quantities of silt and flowing sluggishly over the plains create these fluvial deposits. Riverine chars may be on the river beds (when a river has a braided channel), or may appear as attached spits near the banks. The largest char in the world, Majuli, is an island formed by the Brahmaputra in central Assam. The silt-laden Himalayan rivers descending onto the Gangetic plains leave behind tracts of such land, commonly known as *diara* in north Bihar and eastern Uttar Pradesh.

The charlands are highly vulnerable to frequent floods and bank erosion due to shifting river channels. The physical characteristics inherent in the ecology of char formation make the charlands one of the most fragile environments in the world. This vulnerability of the physical environment makes chars risky and disaster-prone places. Newly formed charlands are more fragile than the older ones; their edges may be eroded at any time by the river currents. Even old charlands may be lost to the unpredictability of a river, with fields and dwellings disappearing in a matter of days. Some chars may gradually turn into permanent human settlements along the river courses, depending on the silt properties and the velocity of river currents. These chars are literally and figuratively on the margins of human habitation. The newly emerging chars, on the borderlines of land and water, are legally non-existent till they are officially recorded. The use of these lands throws up unique questions of environmental dynamics and management (EGIS 2000). The ecological fragility leads to human insecurity and vulnerability, which are key factors behind the persistent poverty in these charlands, confirming Wisner's (2003) observation that poverty and vulnerability are correlated.

The nature and causes of poverty in the charlands are complex and interlinked (Ashley et al. 2000). Yet, people do live on chars, especially in developing countries such as India and Bangladesh. To live in this hostile environment, people take risks and have to develop lifestyles to cope with the river's fluctuations. The competency of the chouras—people living on chars—to adapt to what is commonly seen as an insecure environment offers a problematic. The chouras are very poor migrants, both from elsewhere in India and across

(*Box 5.1 continued*)

(Box 5.1 continued)

international borders, who have struggled hard to transform the chars into habitable and cultivable lands.

There are innumerable chars in deltaic Bengal and the Damodar is no exception, although human intervention in the river system is more responsible for char formation in this river. The Damodar river has been notorious for its shifting courses and has created an inland delta while joining the Hooghly through its innumerable distributaries (Bagchi 1944). Its floods had become legendary and people began to call it 'the sorrow of Bengal'. To improve the situation, the Damodar Valley Corporation (DVC) was established in 1948 for multipurpose water resource development. The DVC, though partly successful in reducing the frequency of floods and in providing irrigation water through a canal network to agricultural fields, has brought many changes in the physical environment in both the upper and lower reaches of the valley. Extensive natural forests were cleared in the upper catchments for the construction of reservoirs. As a result, the siltation rates have been much higher in the reservoirs, but at the same time the release of coarser silt through the sluice gates has led to the formation of chars on the riverbed downstream.

society with respect to income-generating activities, social status, health and children's education. Their poverty also affects their ability to provide for adequate self-protection, and as a result they are less able to create safe conditions during floods and riverbank erosion. However, the support of networks and the social capital of kinship relations are the chief mechanisms that women-headed households use to mobilise resources and cope with contingencies (Valdivia and Gilles 2001).

The women heads of households are aware of their low status within the charland social milieu and, hence, are engaged in a daily struggle to secure their means of survival. Their livelihood strategies emanate from their experience of living in poverty, from working out solutions to the daily problems of life in the specific and difficult location of the char and from their attitudes to life, which are rooted in cultural traditions.

Set against this background, our research agenda seeks to examine the livelihood strategies of women who head their households in the charlands of the Damodar River in West Bengal. The more specific objectives are to analyse the impacts of their vulnerable locations on these livelihood strategies, bringing the essence of the place into focus. This in turn raises the issue of 'belonging', of the attachments of a particular set of women to a particular place that forms a very specific context. In the case of the Damodar chars, the extreme poverty, as well as in some cases the non-citizen identity, act as critical elements in increasing their vulnerability to reduced livelihood choices. Finally, in this study we have also tried to understand the perceptions of these women regarding the changing and hostile environment of the charland as a place of residence. Our research also explores the role of social capital, generated out of kinship and community relations, in the livelihoods of poor women-headed households. Participatory research methods, which offer a creative approach to information sharing, have been used to understand the livelihood strategies of poor women-headed households living on the Gaitanpur char. In recent years, participatory methods that emphasise a 'bottom-up approach' have become significant in social research. The participatory approach is based on field visualisation, interviewing and group discussions promoting interactive learning, shared knowledge and flexible yet structured analysis (IDS 1997).

We selected char Gaitanpur, located on the Damodar riverbed in Burdwan district, West Bengal, for a micro study of the livelihood strategies of women-headed households. Extending over an area of 2.5 sq. km, it is essentially a strip of land running in a north–south direction. Burdwan town, the district headquarters, populated by nearly 285,000 people in 2001, is located 3 km north of this char and provides an important market for both the labour and the products of the char inhabitants. The relative position of this particular char on the riverbed has changed several times due to the frequent shifting of the thalweg (that is, the main flow channel) within the river. Bhattacharyya's 1998 study of the Damodar refers to Dickens' map of 1854 showing Gaitanpur as a marginal bar (that is, a char attached to the south bank of the river). Until the 1950s, it was located on the south bank of the river, separated by a small drainage channel from Gaitanpur village, of which it was a part. The Survey of India map of 1970 showed it as a mid-channel bar (an island char). During the devastating flood of 1978, the course of the river completely changed; Gaitanpur again became an attached char, but it was now attached to the north bank of the river. Since then it has remained more or less in the same position, although minor inundations and bank erosion are common hazards.

Our study is entirely based on fieldwork methods, mainly qualitative observations and primary data collection, but also uses quantitative methods. The survey results reported here are part of an ongoing, larger study. For the purpose of this chapter, we covered each of the 11 women-headed households presently living on the Gaitanpur char (see Table 5.1). We interviewed each woman and recorded these conversations. They were transcribed later to understand the livelihood strategies in view of the personal histories of the individuals. We also met the women-headed households in a group discussion, in which nearly half of them partici-pated. The focus of the group discussion was again on their livelihood strategies, especially in the lean season, on coping with the vulnerability created by the floods and continuous river erosion, and their own percep-tions of their identity as 'illegal-citizens'. All the names given are real and have been used with the consent of our participants.

THE POVERTY OF WOMEN-HEADED HOUSEHOLDS

Women-headed households have been the subject of considerable debate among academics and policy makers, with regard to their definition, the increasing trend of women-headship, the relationship between this and poverty, and for targeting them in policies for poverty reduction. The literature presents them as the 'poorest of the poor' (Jahan 1995; Lahiri-Dutt 2000), and as less able to invest in health and education of their chil-dren (Folbre 1991; UNDP 1995, United Nations 1996; World Bank 2001). However, across countries and regions, women-headed households do not constitute a single homogeneous group that is poorer than male-headed households. Typically, the group includes widows, divorced women, single women, abandoned women and women whose husbands have out-migrated in search of employment. The percentage of women in each category differs across countries, cultures and regions of the world, and also across time (Joshi 2004). Barros et al. (1997) are of the opinion that women-headed households are a heterogeneous group and that there are strong regional variations. In their study in urban Brazil, they have found that on an average, female-headed households are not necessarily always the vulnerable groups. Indeed, some are quite well-off, whereas others are very poor and vulnerable. This diversity in social status and economic standing must be recognised while examining women-headed households.

Table 5.1
List of Women Heads of Households

Name	Origin	Status	Age	Length of Stay in Char	No of Children	Agricultural Land	Source of Income
Sunita Sarkar	Bangladesh	Widow	42	9 years	3	Nil	Wage labour
Dipa Sarkar	Bangladesh	Deserted	41	11 months	4	Nil	Wage labour
Kakali Sarkar	Bangladesh	Deserted	40	8 years	3	Nil	Wage labour
Kajalrani Mondal	Bangladesh	Husband missing	43	6 years	4	Nil	Wage labour
Padmabati Sardar	Bangladesh	Widow	51	8 years	3	Nil	Wage labour
Tulsi Barui	Bangladesh	Widow	55	14 years	4	Nil	Wage labour
Tukurani Ray	Bangladesh	Circumstantial head	39	12 years	4	2 *bigha*	Leasing out land and wage labour
Aloka Mohali	Bangladesh	Deserted	32	10 years	1	2 *bigha*	Farming own land
Sundaria Mahato	Bihar	Widow	43	7 years	3	1.25 *bigha*	Leasing out land and wage labour
Dhaneshri Mahato	Bihar	Widow	50	35 years	3	1 *bigha*	Leasing out land and wage labour
Dasania Mahato	Bihar	Widow	35	20 years	3	Nil	Petty trading

Source: Field survey.

Developmental agencies as well as academics are concerned about the rapidly increasing proportion of households headed by women in the total number of households, both in developed and developing countries (for example, see Buvinic et al. 1991; Wojtkiewicz, et al. 1990). In South Asia, too, various social factors have led to a high rate of desertion, leading to the situation in which the woman is forced to take up the responsibility of running the household as well as earning cash incomes to sustain the family. Out-migration of males often leaves women in rural areas; they become the virtual heads of their households. It is widely argued that women-headed households are more vulnerable to risk, economically less viable, socially less connected and poorly integrated and, above all, are enmeshed in a social and economic context that is less than optimum for the growth and the development of mothers and children alike (Arias and Palloni 1999). Several studies have shown that women-headed households are the most disadvantaged group in their respective societies. Ashley et al. (2000), in their livelihood assistance scoping study of the Bangladesh charlands, have identified married women who lose their husbands as one of the most vulnerable groups in Bangladesh society. Vecchio and Roy (1998) state that female-headed households face institutional and social discrimination outside the home, limiting their access to income-generating resources. Akinsola and Popovich (2002), in their study on the quality of life of the families of women-headed households in Botswana, have shown that these families experience significant poverty, with subsequent health threats and poor quality of life with respect to food, shelter, clean water and a safe environment.

The nature and causes of women-headed households are different across countries. In developed countries, women-headed households generally include women who are divorced, separated, single unmarried mothers and widows. In contrast, women-headed households in Asia (Islam 1993; Mencher 1993), Africa and South America are households headed by widows, 'left-behind' women and women who have migrated to urban areas (Joshi 2004).

The validity of the earlier claims of a relationship between a higher incidence of poverty and women-headed households has, however, been questioned by several studies (see, for example, Chant 1997; Louat et al. 1992; Rogers 1995; Varley 1996). Quisumbing et al. (1995) also raised doubts regarding the often-claimed association between female headship and higher poverty. From their study in 10 developing countries, they concluded that the difference between male- and female-headed households among the very poor households is not large enough to state that one group is unambiguously worse-off or better-off. In a similar study, Quisumbing et al. (2001) again found that the relationship between female headship and poverty is strong only in two out of 10 developing countries—Ghana and Bangladesh.

The debate clearly points to the need for greater policy attention towards women-headed households, as their economic disadvantage and triple burden (of running households on single earning, gender discrimination in the labour market and time pressure) are indeed a reality. Our study of women-headed households does not fit into any of the debates outlined above, but explores the unique struggle of non-citizen women-headed households in the specific context of the vulnerable environment of the charlands. We defined women-headed households as those units of residence and domestic consumption comprising adults and children living together without a male, able-bodied earning adult to look after them and where the main earning member of the households are women. Such women are marginal in the true sense of the term as well as the poorest in all respects. Their marginality is the central focus of our study, which examines the relationship between the vulnerability induced by the environment of the char and the unauthorised migrant identity of the inhabitants.

VULNERABILITIES OF THE CHAR ENVIRONMENT

The physical character of the Gaitanpur char is somewhat different from the other chars located in the active delta region of the Ganga–Padma and other rivers in deltaic Bengal. Regular flooding, an important characteristic of the chars of lower Bengal, is absent here. Gaitanpur was flooded only by knee-deep water during the last major flood in 1978. The problems related to recurrent and annual inundations, shifting lands, and the consequent regular conflicts accompanying the re-demarcation of land that has been covered by sand and alluvium, are less intense in this char. Therefore, Gaitanpur provides a comparatively more secure environment than the Bangladeshi chars (see Baqee 1998), one in which migrants can settle, while at the same time presenting a marginal environment in which established local communities may not wish to live. Property boundaries have become more or less permanent, which offers residents a slightly safer, if not an adequate livelihood.

The poor households living on the char are vulnerable to natural calamities such as floods and riverbank erosion, or to socio-economic factors such as a fall either in production or in the market price of crops, or to illness. These multiple vulnerabilities experienced by the char dwellers are the underlying causes of the chronic, persistent and extreme poverty in the charlands (Brocklesby and Hobley 2003). However, the opposite is also true: most of the char inhabitants live in the chars because of their severely restricted choice. Poverty is also the cause of the vulnerabilities faced by char dwellers.

Erosion of the banks, rather than floods, has a greater impact on people's lives in the Damodar charlands. Erosion is a frequent but irregular danger, and creates catastrophic livelihood shocks as households lose their land, shelter and other assets. The film of loamy soil on chars is only about three to six inches thick above the substantial layer of sand. This loosely packed silt and fine sand is highly susceptible to erosion, and the consequent loss of agricultural land poses a serious threat to the residents. Bank erosion reached its peak during the 1978 flood when half the char was lost to erosion. Some households have been displaced by erosion as many as three times during their stay on this char.

Diseases and illnesses of various types, especially among the earning members, bring vulnerability to the extremely poor households in the charlands. Women-headed households with only one earning member become more vulnerable in the event of ill health. Children's illness due to malnutrition is a recurrent problem in the poorer households, affecting both the expenditure and the income of the household negatively. Working women cannot work if their children fall ill. As a result of their staying at home, the family income decreases and at the same time the daily expense increases because they have to purchase medicines. Illness of the sole earning women members of households engaged in daily labour leads to extreme vulnerability. Women-headed households rarely have significant savings with which to run the household for a length of time without an income. In such periods of crisis, women usually seek help from their friends, relatives and neighbours. Sometimes they borrow money or seek advance payments from the farmers in whose farms they work. This sort of advance payment often takes a heavy toll and sometimes leads to exploitation as the women have to work at a lower wage to compensate the lender for the interest on the loan amount.

WOMEN-HEADED HOUSEHOLDS

The 11 women-headed households in char Gaitanpur, out of a total of 199 households (Table 5.1), is not a very high proportion when compared to the rate in both developed and developing countries (20 and 33 per cent respectively). Among the 11 households, eight are headed by illegal migrant women from Bangladesh and the rest by Bihari women who were relatively earlier settlers. They are *de jure* heads (widows and deserted women), that is, women who are legal and customary heads of their own households with full control over their household incomes and expenditures. However, a *de facto* head (married woman heading her household in the absence of her husband), whose husband lives permanently in Bangladesh with his first wife, noted that she too runs her own household, although the man visits her once or twice a year.

The women's ages range from 32 to 55, averaging 40–45, which matches the findings of other scholars (Vecchio and Roy 1998). In some cases they had come to the char with their husbands, who later either died or left them destitute. In other cases, they came as widows with their children and have close family ties nearby on the char. The average family size of these households is four to five persons. A large family, comprising mostly underage children, means more dependents on women, thereby increasing their livelihood burden.

Due to poverty and a lack of significant amounts of landed assets, all except one of the 11 women are agricultural wage labourers. Generally, they are landless with limited cattle resources. Four households have small pieces of cultivated land that they lease out, which adds a significant income of Rs 800–1,000 per crop per bigha (a variable measure of land area, about a third of an acre) to the household's overall earnings. The landowning households are relatively better-off than those that are entirely landless. One woman does petty trading of vegetables in the nearby Burdwan town.

Some women have lived on the char for 10 to 15 years, whereas others are relatively new to the char. Although they are illiterate, their children's education is a high priority for them. However, in most cases they cannot continue their children's education beyond the primary level because of acute poverty. Women with grown-up children usually encourage them to earn money to supplement the household income. The situation is slightly easier when a woman has an older son who is able to fulfil the income-generating role of an adult male member in the household. This son gradually takes over as the head of the household as the earning capacity of the woman diminishes.

LIVELIHOODS IN POVERTY

Women household heads are engaged in low-paid, casual jobs that unfortunately yield uncertain incomes. With little or no formal support from the state, the women are forced to devise innovative ways and means to stay alive under the hostile circumstances. They work from dawn to dusk without rest as they are the only income-earners of their households. All the domestic chores of the household are considered the responsibility of the women in addition to other physical work, making them doubly burdened. In addition to this enormous physical strain, they have to put up with a high level of mental stress because of their perennial anxiety to meet the bare minimum needs of their families. They are marginal to the charland society at large and, sometimes, also inside the households. It is very easy to exploit their labour at a low wage as they are forced to take loans or advance payments from farmers to cope with the lean season crises. They are rarely invited to village meetings, which are mostly organised with the male members of each household. Inside the households, they usually take decisions. However, the situation changes for the women heads with grown-up sons who take over the responsibility of decision-making for the household as soon as they begin to earn.

Agricultural wage labour is the main livelihood activity of the women-headed households in the charlands. They have developed the skills necessary for all sorts of farm work at par with men and the wage rates are the same (Rs 50 per day in 2004). Even 10- to 15-year-old girls from these households work as labourers and get the same wages during the period of potato harvesting in February–March, when there is a huge demand for labour. However, the nature of the jobs offered is gender-coded, thus restricting the scope of work as well as shrinking the household income. For example, women do not till the land with animal-driven ploughs, or carry bundles of crops from the fields to courtyards.

Job opportunities for agricultural labour are seasonal, as tracts of land remain fallow in summer (April to June). Double cropping is practised all over the charland, whereas multiple cropping is limited to only 26 per cent of the farms. The sandy soils of the char have a high water requirement. Therefore, only a section of farmers who have shallow and submersible pumps can tap the groundwater and produce multiple crops. During the kharif or monsoon season (July to October, elsewhere the main cropping season), poorer farmers leave their lands fallow as they lack the capital to organise their own minor irrigation. In fact, the main cropping season in the char is the dry season in winter and early summer (October to March), when temperatures are lower. During this time a number of vegetable crops, such as brinjal (eggplant), cauliflower, cabbage, carrot, pea, spinach and mustard, are produced.

The seasonality of agricultural activity also arises out of the fear of crop damage due to flooding. Floods are a recurrent natural hazard that always accompanies life in the charlands. It is to cope with the risk of losing crops due to inundation that lowland farmers usually keep their lands fallow in the rainy season. In winter, in case of rains in the upper catchments areas, the river may fill up with water from the upstream reservoirs. This sudden increase in water level ruins the winter vegetables cultivated on the lands recovered from the abandoned river channels. Coping with seasonal employment is not as easy for women as it is for male agricultural labourers. Men have a diversified basket of wage labour to choose from, whereas all the alternatives are not always open to women. Men can also easily switch over to other off-farm seasonal labouring activities available locally outside the charland. The women are at a disadvantage as they cannot take up such opportunities because, apart from being solely responsible for earning from outside the home, they also have to undertake domestic chores within their homes. Lean seasons, therefore, are harder for women than men.

The chief strategies adopted by women to cope with the crises of the lean season comprise fishing in the river, growing vegetables for household subsistence in the courtyard, and shared livestock rearing and selling livestock resources, especially poultry and goats. They are also dependent on the collection of subsistence resources from common property. Requesting errand jobs on farms in exchange for only rice, without a wage, is also commonly practised. The informal loans taken from male farmers are repaid with labour during the cropping season. In case of the repayment of a prior loan, the women are usually exploited, either in the wage rate paid or in the number of free job hours for repayment.

The collection of fuel and fodder, mostly from the fallow areas of the charland, is another time-consuming livelihood activity. Households possessing cattle usually prepare a special dung cake for fuel, which comprises a coat of cowdung around jute straw. The poorer households without any cattle have to depend entirely on wood, catkin grasses, crop residues, dried weeds and bush, rice bran, et cetera, for fuel throughout the year. The dried leaves and branches of trees are also used as fuel. However, women use the branches of trees from their courtyards only in times of severe fuel crisis, such as in the rainy season, when they have no other sources or stock of fuel. Fuel wood or jute straw sometimes serve as supplementary fuels.

Women who own small pieces of cultivable land usually lease these out for cash. Petty trading of vegetables is also free from lean season crises of livelihood, but entails more skill and initiative. Dashania Mahato is the only woman who has taken up such trading, but her economic status is better than that of others. In her words:

> My husband passed away, leaving behind three children. I started petty trading then. I work for 365 days in a year. I do not have to depend on others. I have married off two daughters on my own. My son goes to school. I do not allow him to work to help me. I am looking forward to the future; when my son will grow up and start earning, I will give up this hard work.

Women's livelihood burdens and hardships increase during the monsoonal flow of the river. The level of the river rises steadily during the rainy season, although major floods have not taken place (except in 1978 and 1998) due to the construction of the DVC dams upstream. However, the sudden release of water from reservoirs do cause short-term flooding and inundates the chars. The loss of household essentials, the increased chore of bringing drinking water from distant areas, rebuilding houses, et cetera, add to the hardship of women's lives. It has been noted that floods undermine some of the women's well-being because of their dependence on economic activities linked to their homes (Khondker 1996), and the losses of harvest and livestock make livelihood difficult for women-headed households that depend on cattle and chicken for their cash income (Baden et al. 1994).

STRESSES AND BURDENS

Both physical and mental stresses are usually very high for the women who are heads of their households. Our conversations with the women were often interrupted by their deep sighs: long working days, short lunch breaks, lack of rest, excessive work and poor nutrition characterise their lives. Vickery (1977) noted that the 'double day' economic burden makes all women-headed households time poor, lacking in leisure time (Rosenhouse 1989), and causing an intergenerational transmission of disadvantages through nutrition deficiency, illiteracy and the children having to labour (Buvinic and Gupta 1997). All these characteristics of women-headed households are notable in the charland areas. Kakali Sarkar narrated the time stress:

> I work from dawn to dusk without rest and leisure. Nobody is there in the home to share my domestic duties. Night is the only time for rest. For that reason I dislike summer nights. Winter nights are most welcome to me because of their longer duration. Longer winter nights offer me longer period of rest from my heavy physical burden.

Similar sentiments were expressed in conversation with us by other women heads, who are tired of heavy manual labour to earn their household's livelihoods.

Poverty takes its toll on the health of women, who often do not get the nutrition sufficient to compensate for the heavy physical labour done by them. The nutritional deficiency makes their children physically weak and unwilling to take up physical labour. Sundaria Mahato said: 'My 18-year-old son cannot do the jobs on the farm that I can do easily. He is weak and as a result becomes tired even with a little work. He does not want to work as an agricultural labourer as it requires strength'. Children of women-headed households not only suffer from malnutrition, but are also often illiterate or have low levels of education. It is not easy to support the education of a child; in Dipa Sarkar's words:

> My daughter is going to the village primary school. But, I cannot purchase text books, cannot afford to arrange the private tuition for her. How will she become educated? She has to look after the house when I am at work. Getting education is not possible for the children of poor people like us.

The relatively younger women with young children are usually burdened with more domestic responsibilities. If there is no other female member in the family, infants are often taken to the place of work and laid on the bund of the field. Tukurani Ray, the only *de facto* household head on the Gaitanpur char, started working in the fields just five days after the birth of her fourth daughter:

> My husband lives in Bangladesh with his first wife. He occasionally visits us. When I gave birth to my youngest daughter, I had nobody to look after me except my little daughters. We did not have sufficient food for about a month. So, I had to begin working without taking time to recover my health. This lack of rest left me weaker. Nowadays I feel exhausted soon after working in the field under the high sun.

Her expression proves that in spite of her husband's existence (although his visits are very rare), her livelihood stresses are no less than those of the widowed or deserted women heads.

The domestic burdens of the charland women are increasing as the availability of fuel material is becoming scarcer with the expansion of agricultural land. Several women-headed households use local material such as dried-up bushes and cowdung for fuel. In the early years of settling on the Gaitanpur char in the late 1980s and early 1990s, there was no dearth of subsistence resources as the charlands were sparsely populated. However, the common property resources have been shrinking continuously as more people have settled on the chars. The demands for fuel and fodder are increasing at rates faster than the increase in the population, leading to increased work burdens for women, particularly the household heads.

SOCIAL CAPITAL FOR LIVELIHOODS

Monetary and physical support from either kin or neighbours play an immense role in the livelihoods of women-headed households on char-lands. The survival of poor women in such extremely vulnerable areas is possible because of this support and help. Help from kin often serves to meet daily livelihood needs; the fresh catch of fish from the river and cooked food are also supplied from the parents' house. In the lean season, the period of crisis, the help of others is frequently needed. Such help may take the form of borrowing rice or foodstuff, or cash. Being women, access to private loans from local moneylenders is restricted and hence during emergencies, they approach male neighbours to act as guarantors.

A significant level of crisis occurs when they have to marry off their daughters; this requires a large amount of money for the dowry and to feed the neighbours. Dipa Sarkar points out that having relatives near-by helps: 'My father and my brother arranged my daughter's marriage. I had not to think of it at all'. Community networks play important roles at such times. The village headman, who is also a local panchayat member and political party leader, usually makes it a community responsibility to raise funds for such occasions. The community also helps in kind with foodstuffs and goods as well as by the informal loans given on request by the relatively better-off farmers. Tulsi Barui recollected her daughter's wedding:

> When I arranged my elder daughter's marriage, I asked the community leader for help. He organised a meeting in which he asked for help from individual household heads. They promised to extend their help in the form of either cash or kind, which was listed in that meeting and they kept their word. The rest of the money I arranged through a loan from my employer, a farmer. I paid off this loan by working for him over the years. However, without the help of my community I could never have arranged my daughter's marriage.

Contingent situations that occur during floods are also overcome with community help. Men help by carrying the movable assets away to safer areas on the embankment. Sometimes mud huts are washed away by flood waters. Women are then forced to take shelter in the open verandas of other people's houses. Again, the huts are constructed quickly with the help of community members after the floodwater recedes. Most of the women we spoke to confessed that their survival is ensured by the human capital generated out of social relations. This is not uncommon for poor people in difficult situations, but in chars the value of these networks cannot be overstated. The lack of citizenship and the illegality of existence make such intra-community social capital essential for survival.

CITIZENSHIP AND ACCESS TO RESOURCES

Being illegal migrants, the char women have neither legal rights over local resources, nor do they have access to the state support system for poor women, such as the schemes for poverty alleviation and widow's pension. Many of these women came to the chars with their husbands or settled with the help of their kin already living on this char. The women have diverse perceptions regarding their lack of citizenship. Some of them, like Dipa Sarkar, are not particularly concerned about their non-citizen identity. According to her:

> We are living on this charland far away from the mainland society because of the lack of citizenship. We are poor, illiterate people who can earn only by doing manual labour. Doing manual work as a labourer does not require any citizenship document. Therefore, I do not want to spend money and time in collecting that piece of paper.

However, many men pursue the local channels and are successful in obtaining valid papers for themselves and their families. Unlike men, women heads of households have difficulty accessing the informal networks through which citizenship documents are obtained. Sumita Sarkar told us bitterly: 'We have neither money nor any adult male in the household to do the rounds for obtaining Indian citizenship documents. Like me, my children will also remain non-citizens'.

Another group of women is eager to obtain Indian citizenship documents, but as women they cannot access the informal networks necessary for this. They are aware of the problems related to their non-citizen status. Tulsi Barui made it clear:

> We do not get any economic support from the local panchayat as we are non-entities to the Indian Government. If we cannot arrange our legal

citizenship, then we cannot move out of this char. We are stuck here; my children will also suffer due to this. They will not get any job in India even if they get some education.

CONCLUSION

Living in the chars means a relentless struggle for the women household heads. However, because of their poverty and, in some cases, their legal identity as non-citizens, they have no option of getting away from this highly vulnerable land. They bear the double burden of work to sustain their families, but that work often remains unacknowledged. However, not all of them can be put in a single and universal category according to their social and economic status. A section of them were uprooted from Bihar and have migrated to the Damodar charlands due to extreme poverty. The other section comprises lower-caste Hindus who have illegally migrated from Bangladesh. The levels of poverty of these women do not have a strong correlation with their legal citizenship. Women of both origins work hard from dawn to dusk to meet the minimum livelihood needs of their households. However, marked differences are observed in their perceptions of the insecurity of life in the charlands. Whereas they consider themselves distinctly better-off here than they were in their original homes because of the religious persecution they had faced, the Bangladeshi women suffer from insecurity as they have neither a voter's identity card nor a ration card to establish their claims on the charlands. They are more concerned about the homelessness caused by floods and river bank erosion. Their inability to go to the mainland outside this char to obtain a better and more secure livelihood limits their livelihood options drastically.

Women heads of households have different levels of poverty, individual problems and situation-specific livelihood strategies, which are in no way identical to each other. Within women-headed households, the level of poverty varies with the number of earning members in the household. For example, women with grown-up children have lower livelihood stresses than younger women with young children. Moreover, in the charland environment, poverty is not solely associated with women-headed households. In our field survey of the charlands of the Damodar

River, we had come across a number of male-headed households that are also poor and vulnerable. The lack of citizenship documents adds a critical dimension to these stresses by reducing the options open to them for earning a secure livelihood. The women heads of households have a knowledge of struggle and means of survival that stems from their experience of living in poverty, from working out solutions to the daily problems of life in a specific and difficult location, and from their cultural traditions. In the charlands of the Damodar, they cope with a hostile environment of floods and river erosion by drawing upon their experience of having lived in more or less similar environmental conditions elsewhere in India or in Bangladesh.

In conclusion, we note the relationship between the cross-border movements of people in eastern India, the question of securing livelihoods and gender, as outlined in this small case study. The location of the community forms a unique setting—a vulnerable environment with just about enough resources to somehow scrape a living—providing an important geographical element in understanding the livelihood strategies of women-headed households. Here, we see the importance of locality, the key characteristic of place, playing a major role in influencing the activities of two sets of translocal women. The focus of our attention is on how, in the shifting sands of the chars, they build a sense of community in securing livelihoods for themselves and their families. The chars are not deterritorialised in the process; although neither locality nor community are rooted or 'natural' identities, through their livelihood strategies, women-headed households are creating new forms of economic citizenship enmeshed in a complex interplay of culture and power.

REFERENCES

Akinsola, Henry A. and Judith M. Popovich. 2002. 'The Quality of Life of Families of Female-Headed Households in Botswana: A Secondary Analysis of Case Studies', *Health Care for Women International*, 23: 761–72.

Arias, Elizabeth and Alberto Palloni. 1999. 'Prevalence and Patterns of Female Headed Households in Latin America: 1970–1990', *Journal of Comparative Family Studies*, 30(2): 257–79.

Ashley, Steve, Kamal Kar, Abul Hossain and Shitabrata Nandi. 2000. 'Bangladesh: The Chars Livelihood Assistance Scoping Study for Poor People—The Role of Agriculture', Draft Paper. London: DFID.

Asian Development Bank. 2001. *Country Assistance Plans: Bangladesh*. Manila: ADB.

Baden, S., C. Green, A.M. Goetz and M. Guhathakurata. 1994. 'Background Report on Gender Issues in Bangladesh', *BRIDGE Report 26*. Sussex: Institute of Development Studies.

Bagchi, Kanangopal. 1944. *The Ganges Delta*. Calcutta: Calcutta University.

Baqee, Abdul. 1998. *Peopling in the Land of Allah Jaane: Power, Peopling and Environment, The Case of Charlands of Bangladesh*. Dhaka: The University Press Limited.

Barros, Ricardo, Louise M. Fox and Rosane Mendonca. 1997. 'Female-Headed Households, Poverty, and the Welfare of Children in Urban Brazil', *Economic Development and Cultural Change*, 45(2): 231–57.

Bhattacharyya, Kumkum. 1998. 'Applied Geomorphological Study in a Controlled River: The Case of the Damodar Between Panchet Reservoir and Falta', Ph.D. Thesis. Burdwan: The University of Burdwan.

Brocklesby, Mary Ann and Mary Hobley. 2003. 'The Practice of Design: Developing the Chars Livelihoods Programme in Bangladesh', *Journal of International Development*, 15 (7): 893–09.

Buvinic, Mayra and Geeta Rao Gupta. 1997. 'Female-Headed Households and Female-Maintained Families: Are They Worth Targeting to Reduce Poverty in Developing Countries?' *Economic Development and Cultural Change*, 45(2): 259–80.

Buvinic, Mayra, Nadia H. Youssef and Barbara von Elm. 1991. 'The Vulnerability of Households Headed by Women: Policy Questions and Options for Latin America and the Caribbean.' United Nations: Economic Commission for Latin America and the Caribbean.

Chant, Sylvia. 1997. 'Women-Headed Households: Poorest of the Poor? Perspectives from Mexico, Costa Rica and the Philippines', *IDS Bulletin*, 28(3): 26–48.

Datta, Dipankar and Iqbal Hossain. 2003. *Reaching the Extreme Poor: Learning from Concern's Community Development Programme in Bangladesh*. Dhaka: Concern.

Dreze, Jean. and P.V. Srinivasan. 1997. 'Widowhood and Poverty in Rural India: Some Inferences from Household Survey Data', *Journal of Development Economics*, 54: 217–34.

EGIS. 2000. *Riverine Chars in Bangladesh: Environment Dynamics and Management Issues*. Dhaka: The University Press Limited.

Folbre, Nancy. 1991. 'Women on Their Own: Global Patterns of Female Headship', in Rita S. Gallin and Anne Fergusen (eds), *The Woman and International Development Annual*, Vol. 2. Boulder CO: Westview Press.

IDS. 1997. 'PRA and Gender.' Sussex: Institute of Development Studies.

Islam, Mahmuda. 1993. 'Female-Headed Households in Rural Bangladesh: A Survey', in J.P. Mencher and A. Okongwu (eds), *Where Did All the Men Go?* Boulder, CO: Westview Press.

Jahan, Rounaq. 1995. *The Elusive Agenda: Mainstreaming Women in Development.* London: Zed Books.

Joshi, Shareen. 2004. 'Female Household-Headship in Rural Bangladesh: Incidence, Determinants and Impact on Children's Schooling.' Centre Discussion Paper No. 894, Economic Growth Centre. New Haven: Yale University.

Khondker, H.H. 1996. 'Women and Floods in Bangladesh', *International Journal of Mass Emergencies and Disasters*, 14(3): 281–92.

Lahiri-Dutt, Kuntala. 2000. 'Struggle and Survival: Female-Headed Households in a Low-Income Area of Burdwan Town, India', *Asian Profile*, 28(2): 137–47.

Louat, F., M.E. Grosh and J. van der Gaag. 1992. 'Welfare Implications of Female-Headship in Jamaican Households', Paper presented at the International Food Policy Research Institute-World Bank Conference on 'Intra-Household Resource Allocation: Policy Issues and Research Methods', Washington, D.C.

Mencher, J.P. 1993. 'Female-Headed Households, Female-Supported Households in India: Who Are They and What Are Their Survival Strategies', in J.P. Mencher and A. Okongwu (eds), *Where Did All the Men Go?* Boulder, CO: Westview Press.

Quisumbing, Agnes R., Lawrence Haddad and Christine Pena. 1995. 'Gender and Poverty: New Evidence from 10 Developing Countries.' Discussion Paper No. 9, International Food Policy Research, Food Consumption and Nutrition Division.

———. 2001. 'Are Women Overrepresented Among the Poor? An Analysis of Poverty in Ten Developing Countries', *Journal of Development Economics*, 66(1): 225-69.

Rosenhouse, S. 1989. 'Identifying the Poor: Is "Headship" a Useful Concept?' World Bank Living Standard Measurement Study, Working Paper No. 58.

Rogers, B. 1995. 'Alternative Headships of Female Headship in the Dominican Republic', *World Development*, 23.

UNDP (United Nations Development Programme). 1995. *Human Development Report.* New York: Oxford University Press.

United Nations. 1996. *Food Security for All, Food Security for Rural Women.* Geneva: International Steering Committee on Economic Advancement of Rural Women.

Valdivia, Corinne and Jere Gilles. 2001. 'Gender and Resource Management: Households and Groups, Strategies and Transitions', *Agriculture and Human Values*, 18(1): 5–9.

Varley, A. 1996. 'Women Heading Households: Some More Equal Than Others?' *World Development*, 24: 502–20.

Vecchio, Nerina and Kartick C. Roy. 1998. *Poverty, Female-Headed Households, and Sustainable Economic Development.* Westport: Greenwood.

Vickery, Claire. 1977. 'The Time-Poor: A New Look at Poverty', *Journal of Human Resources*, 12: 27–48.

Wisner, B. 2003. 'Sustainable Suffering? Reflections on Development and Disaster Vulnerability in the Post-Johannesburg World', *Regional Development Dialogue*, 24(1): 135-48.

Wojtkiewicz, Roger A., Sara S. McLanahan and Irwin Garfinkel. 1990. 'The Growth of Families Headed by Women: 1950–1980', *Demography*, 27(1).

World Bank. 2001. *Engendering Development: Through Gender Equality in Rights, Resources, and Voice.* New York: Oxford University Press.

6

Migrant Tribal Women's Struggle for Livelihood

A Study of the Employment Assurance Scheme in Jhabua, Madhya Pradesh

Sandeep Joshi

INTRODUCTION

The creation of employment opportunities has always been an important objective of development planning in India. The relatively higher growth of both the population and the labour force has led to an increase in the volume of unemployment and underemployment from one Plan period to another. The development of rural areas has been an abiding concern of successive governments ever since the adoption of planning in India. Policies and programmes have been designed and redesigned with this aim (Aziz 1994). The problem of rural poverty was brought into sharp focus during the Sixth Plan (1980–85). The Seventh Plan (1986–90), too, emphasised growth with social justice. It was realised that a sustainable strategy of poverty alleviation has to be based on increasing productive employment opportunities in the process of growth itself. (Chadha and Sharma 1997)

Rural development implies both economic betterment of people and greater social transformation (Visaria et al. 1996). Over the years, rural development has emerged as a strategy designed to improve the economic and social life of a specific group of people—the rural poor. It involves extending the benefits of development to the poorest among those who seek a livelihood in the rural areas. In India, eradication of poverty and reduction of income inequality have been among the most important objectives of the Plans. As is well known, economic growth alone will not necessarily reduce poverty unless the spread of additional income favours the deprived classes and is accompanied by improvements in social indicators. It may, therefore, be desirable to enquire into the distribution of the generated income at the micro level. The impact of adjustment and stabilisation policies may get reflected in a number of indicators, like the consumption of goods, levels of health, morbidity, and school enrolment and dropout rates.

Specifically designed anti-poverty programmes for the generation of both self-employment and wage-employment have been in existence in order to enhance the capabilities of the poor and downtrodden groups of the society. Development efforts encompass improved productivity, expansion of employment opportunities and reduction in disparities in income and wealth, with the objective of establishing a society which has acceptable levels of food, shelter, education and a healthy environment. State interventions related to the quality of life of the socially and economically disadvantaged include: an array of constitutional and legal measures; positive discrimination in government employment as well as in elected representative bodies through reservation; budgetary support through the special component plan (SCP) approach; special programmes of health and education; priority in all rural development; slum improvement and anti-poverty programmes for the Scheduled Castes (SCs)/Scheduled Tribes (STs); and technological changes such as the conversion of dry latrines to flush latrines so as to release the people engaged in traditional occupations such as scavenging.

Approaches towards rural development and poverty alleviation have undergone several changes since the inauguration of the Community Development Programme, the first ever nationwide attempt at rural development, initiated in 1952. The rural poverty alleviation programmes can broadly be grouped in four categories: (a) Wage Employment and Infrastructure Development Programmes; (b) Self-Employment and Entrepreneurship Development Programmes; (c) Special Area Development Programmes; and (d) National Social Assistance Programmes (Joshi 2000).

WAGE EMPLOYMENT PROGRAMMES

A major problem in the rural areas of India is chronic seasonal unemployment and underemployment. A large number of people depend on wage employment for their livelihood as they have no assets or have grossly inadequate assets. Such people have virtually no source of income during the lean agricultural season, when employment opportunities shrink. Wage employment programmes as an approach to poverty alleviation have been conceived to mainly provide additional gainful employment to the unemployed and underemployed. Such employment also helps in the creation of durable assets. The economic logic of wage employment programmes is that in an economy characterised by inadequate capital stock and surplus human power, the programmes help to reduce unemployment and underemployment, and at the same time facilitate capital formation (Hirway 1986).

In 1961, the Rural Manpower Programme was initiated as a wage employment programme to provide seasonal employment for 100 days to the needy target groups. Another scheme of a similar nature, but with a wider coverage, the Crash Scheme for Rural Employment, was launched in 1971. The Food for Work Programme, which was later renamed the National Rural Employment Programme (NREP), was started in 1977 by utilising the available surplus stocks of food grains to create rural infrastructure. It became an integral part of the Sixth Plan and remained operational until March 1989 as a centrally sponsored programme. Later, in 1983, a new scheme called the Rural Landless Employment Guarantee Programme (RLEGP) was launched. Financed by the central government and implemented by the states, it remained in operation until March 1989. In 1989–90, NREP and RLEGP were merged to create the new national wage employment programme, Jawahar Rozgar Yojana (JRY). A salient feature of JRY was that its financing as well as planning and implementation functions were devolved to the elected village panchayats. That scheme was expected to ensure better utilisation of funds. In addition, the cost of administering the programme was expected to decline.

The main features of the wage employment programmes in India have been: (*a*) creating gainful employment in the rural areas; (*b*) creating community assets for direct and continuing benefits to poverty-prone groups; (*c*) supporting and giving a boost to the economic activity in rural areas, leading to rapid growth of the rural economy; and (*d*) improving the overall quality of life in the rural areas. Thus, the emphasis was on dealing with the problem at the local or the village level with the object of providing work during the slack agricultural season and as close as possible to the homes of the persons concerned. (Dandekar: 1996)

EMPLOYMENT ASSURANCE SCHEME

The Employment Assurance Scheme (EAS) was introduced in 1993 (on 2 October, Mahatma Gandhi's birthday) in those rural blocks of the country where the revamped Public Distribution System (PDS) was in operation. The scheme now covers all rural blocks in the country. The primary objective of the EAS is to provide gainful employment for 100 days during the lean agricultural season through 'manual work' to all able-bodied adults in rural areas who are in need and desirous of work, but are unable to find it. The secondary objective is the creation of economic infrastructure and community assets for sustained employment and development. The EAS is open to all rural people below the poverty line. Preference is given to members of Scheduled Castes, Scheduled Tribes and freed bonded labourers; and at least 30 per cent of employment opportunities are to be reserved for women. While works under other programmes (besides the EAS) could be taken up during any part of the year, these were preferably to be started during the lean agricultural season. The works under the EAS are required to be taken up only during the lean agricultural season. The Government of India felt the need to merge the different programmes for wage employment in rural areas to take care of food security, additional wage employment, and for village infrastructure at the same time. This has led to the announcement of a new wage employment programme, namely the Sampoorna Grameen Rozgar Yojana (SGRY), with effect from 25 September 2001. Though the EAS and JGSY have been merged with this new programme, the funds are released separately to avoid any kind of confusion in their implementation at the grassroots level (Government of India 2002).

Schemes like the EAS can be more effective in tribal areas as the tribals migrate in the lean season in search of labour opportunities to sustain their livelihoods. This migration ranges from working as agriculture labour in adjoining rural areas to working on construction sites in distant urban locations. Most tribals move within the state to growth centres like Indore, Hoshangabad and Harda, or in adjoining states, to Bilaspur in Chhattisgarh, Dhulia and Nagpur in Maharashtra, or Vadodara, Surat and Ahmedabad in Gujarat.

By and large, the employment opportunities available to the migrants are the worst paying, involving high exploitation and requiring the least skills. Migration affects the households, leading to a break in their family lives, the non-availability of social security systems like education, health facilities, group solidarity and subsidised food grains from the PDS. The living conditions of migrants in their urban destinations are very poor, affecting their health and, hence, productivity. Many times they are also forced into a debt trap by contractors who give them advances for the next season to ensure the availability of their cheap labour in the future. As soon as the season begins, the contractors pack them off to distant locations to work as agricultural labour, construction workers, or in other labour-intensive industries, where relatively low skills are required. Tribals are preferred over others as they are less demanding and are in a more vulnerable position (Joshi: 1999).

In such a situation, tribals need such programmes that assure them employment in their homeland. It will help in redressing the balance of social, economic and political power a little in favour of the downtrodden classes. However, a study of the impact of state intervention through programmes for the poverty-stricken tribal women is of special import-ance, not only for public policy, but also to know the grassroots realities.

This chapter seeks to examine the effectiveness of the EAS in the tribal Jhabua district of Madhya Pradesh and explores measures that can make state intervention in support of the women more effective.

METHODOLOGY

The chapter is based on a study undertaken by the author in Jhabua district on the 'Overall Working of Employment Assurance Scheme'. The main objectives are to examine the organisational and administrative set-up under the Panchayati Raj system in relation to the EAS; to examine the impact of the programme on the women beneficiaries in terms of changes in occupational status, income and employment; and to review the progress of work and assess the overall impact of the scheme on the tribal women of the district.

Two blocks were selected on the basis of their having a higher proportion of 'beneficiaries' of the scheme. From each block, 10 gram panchayats and from each gram panchayat 10 women 'beneficiaries' of the EAS, that is, 200 women in all, were to be selected for the study. However, due to the non-availability of women beneficiaries of EAS, a sample of only 170 could be selected and interviewed. A few selected issues, which have a direct bearing on the status of employment in the study area, have been taken up for analysis and interpretation. These issues deal with the number of working months in a year, the actual number of working days, duration of employment at the migrated location, months in which the EAS should be carried out, reasons for migration, family card, facilities, working hours in a day, wages paid under the EAS, duration of employment under the EAS, earning from the EAS and the problem of migration.

Employment as Casual Wage Labour

An attempt is made to ascertain the actual number of days the women work as casual wage labourers in a year. In order to get a correct and nearly accurate picture, they were asked to mention separately the number of working days both in a week and in different seasons. After the necessary calculations, the data has been split into four categories. The data reveals that only 14.7 per cent women labourers get work for 10–12 months; 37.05 per cent respondents get work for only up to three months. If we include those in the second category (four to six months), we find that 70 per cent respondents of the sample do not get opportunities to work as wage labourers for over six months. This shows the non-availability of adequate employment opportunities in the district (see Table 6.1).

Table 6.1
Employment as Casual Wage Labour

Employment as Casual Wage Labour	Respondents	
	No.	Per cent
Up to 3 months	63	37.05
4–6 months	56	32.95
7–9 months	26	15.30
10–12 months	25	14.70
Total	170	100.00

Employment through the EAS

What is important is that the employment must be gainful as well as sustainable. As far as the implementation of the EAS during the lean agricultural season is concerned, a large number (47.05 per cent) of beneficiaries found employment for only up to 15 days and 30 per cent respondents for between 16–30 days. In other words, only 77.05 per cent of the total sample could find employment only for about 30 days. The percentage of those who found employment for between 76–90 days is very small (5.32 per cent). This analysis indicates that employment has not been provided to the tribal women to the required extent (see Table 6.2).

Table 6.2
Employment through EAS

	Respondents	
Employment through EAS	*No.*	*Per cent*
1–15	80	47.05
16–30	51	30.00
31–45	12	07.05
46–60	14	08.23
61–75	04	02.35
76–90	09	05.32
Total	170	100.00

Employment at Migrated Locations

As employment opportunities in the district are very few, the tribals need to migrate to nearby cities/states in search of employment. It is important to note that tribals always migrate as a family group. An attempt was made to estimate the duration of employment of tribal women when they migrate to other places. Only 5 per cent respondents migrate for a period exceeding three months. The majority of tribal families migrate only up to a period of 60 days in a year, as 77.2 per cent of the respondents from our sample stated. They also stated that at the migrated locations, they were subject to some of the worst exploitation. On the basis of the data, it can be said that the tribals migrate only for a specific and short duration when employment opportunities in the district cease to exist. They do prefer to return to their homes as soon as they find the possibility of employment. It is, therefore, important to ensure that employment opportunities during the lean agricultural season, spread over almost eight months, are available within the district (see Table 6.3).

Table 6.3
Employment at Migrated Location

Employment at Migrated Location	Respondents	
	No.	Per cent
1–30	37	36.60
31–60	41	40.60
61–90	18	17.80
More than 90	05	05.00
Total	101	100.00

When the EAS should Provide Employment

As there is a provision stating that work should be carried out in the lean agricultural season, the selection of months during which the work under the EAS should be carried out is very important. The respondents were asked about their preference. According to the responses received, 55.9 per cent beneficiaries were of the opinion that the EAS activities should be carried out from March to June because it is during this period that they do not have any work. Another 43.5 per cent held the view that during the months from November to February, works under the EAS should be undertaken (see Table 6.4). The divided responses to this question indicate that tribals need employment for almost eight months in a year, particularly in the months from November to June.

Table 6.4
When EAS should Provide Employment

When EAS should Provide Employment	Respondents	
	No.	Per cent
March–June	95	55.90
July–October	01	00.60
November–February	74	43.50
Total	170	100.00

Indeed, during the lean agricultural season, it becomes difficult for the majority of tribals to get two square meals a day. Non-availability of any kind of work compels them to migrate to other places in search of a job.

Reason for Migration

Jhabua district is plagued by water scarcity. Consequently, the tribals cannot remain engaged in agricultural work for the entire year. They have to find other avenues to meet their requirements. Keeping this situation in mind, an attempt was made to find out why the tribals migrate. The major reason for their migration is non-availability of wage (paid) employment in the village during the lean agricultural season, according to 84.15 per cent of the respondents. However, 15.85 per cent said that they migrate because they get higher wages in the big cities (see Table 6.5).

Table 6.5
Reason for Migration

	Respondents	
Reason for Migration	*No.*	*Per cent*
Wage rates are higher	16	15.85
Non-availability of wage (paid) employment in the village during lean season	85	84.15
Total	101	100.00

These responses regarding the migration of tribal women clearly point to the need to implement schemes/programmes which generate wage employment for a larger number of people and for a longer duration. These are sufficient grounds for the implementation of the EAS or any wage employment programme in a district like Jhabua, which is drought-prone and over-exploited. Greater attention should be paid to area-specific schemes in such districts. It is crystal clear from the data that inadequacy of employment during the lean agricultural season is a major causal factor compelling mass migration from the district. Taking this practice into consideration, it is imperative to provide them with employment all year round, which will also ensure stability in the economic conditions of the tribals and of the district as a whole.

Family Card

The issue of family cards is an important requirement under the EAS. Every family consisting of husband, wife, children and other dependants, whose adults are registered for work under the scheme, have to be issued with a family card immediately in the prescribed form. This card contains details of family members and the employment provided to each registered person under works sanctioned by the EAS or under other Plan or non-Plan schemes (that is, newly-initiated schemes). Data relating to this requirement are very discouraging, with 97.64 per cent of the total respondents replying in the negative (Table 6.6). The reasons for the cards not being issued are: (*a*) that officials, particularly field staff, take the fulfillment of the formalities for granted; (*b*) villagers, particularly women, are not aware of the formalities to be fulfilled; and (*c*) the lackadaisical approach of the elected representatives and officials.

Table 6.6
Family Card

| Family Card | Respondents | |
	No.	Per cent
Yes	04	02.36
No	166	97.64
Total	170	100.00

Facilities

As per the guidelines of the EAS, at each work site certain facilities have to be provided. The responses of the workers with regard to each such facility were collected during the field work. An examination of the data presents a picture of the dismal performance of the implementing agencies concerned, as out of five facilities, only one, drinking water, was provided according to 75.29 per cent of the respondents. The rest of them stated that even drinking water was not available at the work site. As far as indicating the minimum wages prescribed for unskilled work and the schedule of rates at the work site are concerned, responses are very disheartening, as 100 per cent of the respondents replied in the negative. The facilities of first-aid and creches for the small children of workers were also not provided, according to almost all respondents (Table 6.7). This clearly indicates that the implementing agencies are not serious about providing these facilities to female workers. The women have no knowledge about the different provisions of the various schemes that are meant for them; this results in their being exploited in one way or the other.

Table 6.7
Facilities

Facilities	Respondents			
	Yes	*Per cent*	*No*	*Per cent*
Drinking water facility	128	75.29	42	24.71
First-aid	05	02.95	165	97.05
Creches for small children of workers	01	00.60	169	99.40
Trial pit indicating the norms of output for the minimum wages prescribed for unskilled work	–	00.00	170	100.00
Schedule of rates applicable in the area	–	00.00	170	100.00

Working Hours in a Day

To understand the level of exploitation that a wage labourer has to face, we enquired into the number of hours a woman is required to work in a day. As per the responses of the labourers, 93.50 per cent said that they worked eight hours a day under the scheme. There are only 1.80 per cent and 4.70 per cent who are of the view that they work for more or fewer hours (10 or six hours, respectively). It seems that their views differ because of their inability to estimate the actual period that they remain at work (see Table 6.8). It can be said that so far as the working hours are concerned, the women are working as per the rules.

Table 6.8
Working Hours in a Day

Working Hours in a Day	Respondents	
	No.	*Per cent*
6 hrs	08	04.70
8 hrs	159	93.50
10 hrs	03	01.80
Total	170	100.00

Wage Paid under the EAS

Payment of wages to the labourers is an important aspect of any scheme. It becomes all the more important in the case of the EAS, which is primarily meant for the generation of employment for needy rural groups during the lean agricultural season. Keeping this in mind, the respondents were asked to state the actual wages they received per day under the scheme.

According to their responses, 38.80 per cent received Rs 41–43, whereas 34.10 per cent say that they got Rs 40 and 27.10 per cent got Rs 44 or more (see Table 6.9). It is important to mention here that the Panchayat and Rural Development Department of the Government of Madhya Pradesh, Bhopal, vide its letter no. 7070/22/V-7JRY of 17.5.99, has communicated to all agencies/departments concerned to pay Rs 50.50 per day to all the un-skilled labourers as per the Minimum Wages Act, 1948. However, the actual amount of wages received by women is very low compared to their legal entitlement.

Table 6.9
Wage Paid under EAS

S.No.	Wage Paid under EAS	Respondents	
		No.	Per cent
1.	Up to Rs 40	58	34.10
2.	Rs 41–43	66	38.80
3.	Above Rs 44	46	27.10
	Total	170	100.00

It is also necessary to note the delay in the payment of wages. Under the EAS, the wages should be paid every week. However, particulars collected from the implementing agencies of the district revealed that there were delays ranging from 15 to 300 days in the payment of wages. On the basis of this information, it can be said that the labourers in Jhabua district do not get their wages as per the government orders and Minimum Wages Act, 1948. The tribal women labourers are not aware of the prescribed minimum wage rate, which has resulted in this sad state of affairs.

Duration of Employment under the EAS

The crux of the EAS is that those who are in need of and seek employment will get assured wage employment for 100 days during the lean agricultural season. It is in this context that an attempt has been made to ascertain the actual number of days of employment generated under the scheme. It is disheartening to note that the majority of beneficiaries (45.30 per cent) found employment for only between one and 15 days, and 30 per cent got 16–30 days of work. Thus, under the scheme, 75.30 per cent of the total respondents found employment for less than a month. There are only 8.20 per cent who could get work for 61–90 days. However, there was no one in the sample who got work for the full 100 days as envisaged in the scheme. This leads to the observation that the scheme is resource-driven rather than demand-oriented. The objective set out for the scheme appeared to be high-pitched compared to the resources made available by government (Table 6.10).

Table 6.10
Duration of Employment under EAS

S.No.	Duration of Employment under EAS	Respondents	
		No.	Per cent
1.	1–15	77	45.30
2.	16–30	51	30.00
3.	31–60	28	16.50
4.	61–90	14	08.20
	Total	170	100.00

Earnings from the EAS

The total earnings of the respondents from the EAS is an important aspect by which one can know their actual earnings, particularly during the lean agricultural season when all other sources of income dry up. Analysis of data pertaining to the earnings under the EAS makes it clear that a large number (46.50 per cent) earn only up to Rs 700, which cannot be considered enough for them to sustain themselves by any means. Of the rest, 32.30 per cent earn Rs 701 to Rs 1500, and there are only 15.30 per cent who earn more than Rs 2,501 from EAS activity (see Table 6.11). On the basis of the analysis of the data, it can be said that the majority do not

Table 6.11
Earnings from EAS

S.No.	Earnings from EAS	Respondents	
		No.	Per cent
1.	Up to Rs 700	79	46.50
2.	Rs 701–1500	55	32.30
3.	Rs 1501–2500	10	05.90
4.	Above Rs 2501	26	15.30
	Total	170	100.00

get adequate wages. Apart from this, the amount is not given to them in a timely manner and they have to visit the officials/authorities concerned several times to get their legitimate wages.

Impact on Migration

The non-availability of employment for unskilled women is an important reason for the large-scale seasonal out-migration from Jhabua district. Has the EAS helped to curb this forced migration of tribals? It is encouraging to note that 79.40 per cent of our respondents see the EAS as greatly helpful in curbing the rate of migration. Only 20.6 per cent respondents said that the scheme did not help to check the migration of tribals (see Table 6.12). It can be said that though the EAS has helped in curbing migration, it is only on a small scale, and the migration of tribals still takes place on a large scale. The most important reason for such a situation is that under the scheme, only one person from a family is employed at a time, whereas in tribal areas both the husband and wife work together. This is a cause for concern, requiring a serious attempt at curbing at least a part of this forced migration. Considering the responses, it can be inferred that there is a strong and urgent need to look into the overall procedure of providing employment to the tribals, and ensuring them work during the lean agricultural season for at least 100 days and to at least two persons from a family (a male and a female).

Table 6.12
Impact on Migration

S.No.	Impact on Migration	Respondents	
		No.	Per cent
1.	Yes	135	79.40
2.	No	35	20.60
	Total	170	100.00

CONCLUSION

This study reveals that the provisions under the EAS in Madhya Pradesh are inadequate to make a significant dent on the earnings and the livelihoods of tribal women. The scheme is being executed through contractors at some places in violation of the central government guidelines, the norm of 60:40 for the ratio of wages: materials are not maintained, genuine muster rolls are also not being maintained by the gram panchayats. Further, at some places no inventory of assets was kept and it was difficult to ascertain whether the asset created was for the community (public) or for the individual (private). However, the quality of assets created under the EAS was found to be reasonably good in many cases. Also, due to the inability of the state government to contribute its matching share in full, the state was not able to avail of the full central allocation for this programme. Thus, the performance of the EAS has not been up to the expected levels of employment generation and asset creation.

Measures that Need to be Taken

Though the state has intervened in many ways to help tribal women earn their livelihood and ensure their right to work as citizens, at the grassroots level the efforts have not yielded the desired results as is evident from the findings of the present study. The EAS is a good scheme, but its implementation is not satisfactory, which is apparent from the responses of the tribal women. A few suggestions are made here to make it more effective insofar as the amelioration of the present conditions of tribal women is concerned.

First, the findings of the study underline the importance of strengthening the local Panchayati Raj Institutions (PRIs), which alone can act as effective delivery mechanisms because they will ensure people's participation at various stages of implementation of the programmes and bring transparency in the operation of the schemes. PRIs can play an important role in improving the efficiency and effectiveness of the schemes, and in plugging leakages. Institutions of local self-governance (PRIs) that respond to the needs of poor rural women, encourage their mobilisation and are open to social audit can be expected to provide a better delivery system for poverty alleviation programmes.

Second, migration is one of the most crucial problems that the district has to face every year, particularly during the lean agricultural months. It is, therefore, imperative that special provisions should be made for districts like Jhabua. The district authorities should be asked to prepare some long-term plans so that the funds are utilised in such a manner as to provide employment to the tribals to meet their needs in their homelands, and also create assets that would prove to be income generating as well.

Third, there is a strong need to inform tribal women about the provisions of the various schemes that are meant for them. It is found that the majority of the women in the district are not aware of the various provisions and schemes. Due to this, they either come to know only whatever the officials want to communicate to them or remain unaware of the developments. There must, therefore, be a network of channels and agencies providing information about the various schemes having specific provisions for women.

Fourth, it is necessary to appoint staff, particularly technical staff, for satisfactory implementation of the EAS. The staff should be both for planning and advertising the EAS activities systematically, and for the proper execution of the EAS works at the work sites. The present staff strength does not seem adequate in the district. It is also found that officials pay little attention to issues relating to the women.

Fifth, it is suggested that the National Rural Employment Guarantee Act, 2005, should also include skilled work, so that the employment generated is not just temporary for 100 days, but could also be sustained by including agro-processing, on-farm processing, embroidery, weaving, printing, toy making and so on.

Basic to all developmental efforts for the uplift of the downtrodden is a respect for their human rights; respect for their right to equality and equal opportunity, the right to life with dignity, the right to enjoy the rights guaranteed by our Constitution. Statutes and schemes are important, but they become meaningless in the absence of commitment to enforce or implement them. Projects and programmes for the uplift of women would remain on paper, or would get derailed, unless the agencies charged with the responsibility of implementing them are not only sensitised but also made effective. The role of women's organisations and activists in the sensitisation of government functionaries is of great importance in this regard.

The newly enacted National Rural Employment Guarantee Act, 2005, provides for the enhancement of livelihood security of the households in rural areas of the country through at least 100 days of guaranteed wage employment in every financial year for every household whose adult members volunteer for unskilled manual work. This Act not only covers almost all the provisions present in the erstwhile Employment Assurance Scheme, but some more provisions have also been incorporated in it. However, keeping in view the findings of the present study, it can be concluded that only a more stringent implementation of the Employment Guarantee Act, and that too in a scientific manner, will help the downtrodden to get employment when it is needed most and thus come out from the clutches of poverty. This would ultimately be helpful in improving the living standards of the tribals, along with the prospects for economic development of the district as a whole.

REFERENCES

Aziz, Abdul (ed.). 1994. *Poverty Alleviation in India: Policies and Programmes.* New Delhi: Ashish Publication House.

Chadha, G.K. and Alakh N. Sharma (eds). 1997. *Growth, Employment and Poverty: Change and Continuity in Rural India.* New Delhi: Vikas Publishing House Pvt. Ltd.

Dandekar, V.M. 1996. *Population, Poverty and Employment.* New Delhi: Sage Publications.

Dantwala, M.L. 1996. *Dilemmas of Growth: The Indian Experience.* New Delhi: Sage Publications.

Government of India. 2002. *Annual Report: 2001-2002.* New Delhi: Ministry of Rural Areas and Employment.

Hirway, Indira. 1986. *Wage Employment Programmes in Rural Development.* New Delhi: Oxford University Press and IBH Publishing Co. Pvt Ltd..

Joshi, Sandeep. 1999. *IRDP and Poverty Alleviation.* Jaipur: Rawat Publications.

―――. 2000. *Panchayat Raj Institutions and Poverty Alleviation.* Jaipur: Rawat Publications.

Visaria, P., N.A. Majumdar and T.R. Sundaram. 1996. *Dilemmas of Growth: The Indian Experience.* New Delhi: Sage Publications.

7

Restructuring the Employment Guarantee Scheme
Efforts to Provide Livelihood Opportunities through Women's SHGs and Horticulture in Maharashtra

Chhaya Datar

INTRODUCTION

A tangible impact of the women's movement has been in separating 'woman' as a productive actor in her own right within the 'household', which had formed a basic building block for economists when it came to understanding the functioning of the national economy. Gender disaggregated data on the workforce has become an accepted practice. The inclusion of 'Code 93', which enumerates women's work of fuel wood and fodder collection, in the format for census data collection, has been another achievement of feminist economists. However, acceptance of woman's status as an economically productive unit of society is still lagging behind her political status as a citizen who can influence the political processes. Even as the enumeration of her work has begun slowly, there are very few efforts to provide her with work security and an independent income. The work she does is still drudgery, leftover work that no man would like to undertake. An important feature of woman's work situation is 'lack of mobility', which has escaped the attention of planners. The Employment Guarantee Scheme (EGS) in Maharasthra indirectly addressed this issue; it was noticed that many more women than men flocked to the rural construction sites. After 27 years of the EGS, for the first time the National Rural Employment Guarantee Act, 2005, has specifically targeted women.

Inheritance and ownership of land are the most critical issues within the existing personal laws of major religious communities. These regimes impinge upon the core of women's status, that is, their access to livelihood security. Even when changes were made in the Hindu inheritance laws, these did not automatically become applicable to women from the land-owning class because, under the Indian Constitution, the inheritance of agricultural land was governed by various state-level tenurial laws that were gender unequal. The 2005 Amendment to the Hindu Succession Act made women's land rights equal to men's across the states. While Indian women have the right to work, it has required continuous struggle to gain the right to ownership and inheritance. The growing phenomenon of the feminisation of poverty can be attributed to this reality; the fact that when she is divorced or deserted, she owns nothing except the responsibility of children. All her labour vested in establishing the home and providing stability to the family go unrewarded. She is left only with her constitutional 'right to work'.

My concern is with how women can gain the 'right to develop assets through access to natural resources'. Land rights are a feminist dream, which may take time to realise. The Shetkari Sanghatana in Maharashtra had asked its members to donate half an acre of land to be legally recorded in the wife's name, which she should be free to cultivate as she wants. Such gestures are always welcome, but they cannot change the revenue map of India. However, there are many other ways through which to create women's access to land and fulfil their right as citizens to dignified livelihoods.

BACKGROUND

There is a critical debate raging over whether micro-credit, as proposed by the World Bank and other international funding agencies, sufficiently empowers women in the long run or whether it is a diversion from the demand for land rights and a structural change in the asset-holding pattern in the country. We need to explore cases where women have indeed acquired land, through struggle or other mechanisms, including purchase, and have managed these lands independently. Such cases could show that access to land is a priority for secured livelihood and also point the direction to bringing about incremental structural change.

The deficiency of micro-credit programmes is that these very rarely help to create assets for the majority of women who are either landless or possess small plots. The interest rates are too high, the loan amount is very small and the duration of repayment is very short for the woman to be able to create a surplus from that particular enterprise and repay the loan. Her repayment comes from other sources of income such as the labour she and her family perform on the other sites. Nevertheless, rarely does the asset become viable enough to be self-sustaining, that is, to be able to pay for the labour cost of maintaining the asset. The micro-credit programme has been successful only when it is properly organised by NGOs with backward and forward linkages and the mobilisation cost is borne through some other source of funding.

Through my own experience of interacting on a small scale with Self-Help Groups (SHGs), I realised that if micro-credit activity were combined with payment for the labour cost of developing an asset (say, a plot of land for fodder, horticulture or biofuel cultivation), then the asset would be sustained. The loan obtained from the SHG could then be utilised as investment for small equipment, water delivery systems and so on. This could also have potential for structural changes in the access to land and land rights. I then looked at Maharashtra's EGS, which had already addressed some of these ideas. EGS was meant for landholders and small farmers, but its provisions could also apply to women's groups, SHGs or an individual woman member of an SHG. In my understanding, an SHG is only a vehicle for bringing women together as their livelihood resources are shrinking. It cannot be a tool to launch women in the marketplace to compete with other powerful actors, or to make their living in the competitive world without any assistance.

This chapter is the outcome of a small study that I undertook in Osmanabad district of Maharashtra to explore whether the scheme of horticulture funded through the EGS since 1991 could be utilised in the manner I had visualised, and whether women SHG members were willing to undertake the operations under the scheme, becoming entrepreneurs, that is, horticulturists.

Maharashtra is proud of its Employment Guarantee Act, 1977 (EGA), which enabled the government to levy special service taxes on salaried persons and a cess on certain other taxes[1] in order to mop up revenue intended exclusively for creating unskilled employment for marginalised people. In the drought-ridden areas of Maharashtra, the labour force has a large component of Scheduled Castes (SC) and Scheduled Tribes (ST). Women comprise 50 per cent of the labour on the EGS sites. Unfortunately, despite the very laudable objectives of helping to regenerate natural resources and facilitating better access to fuel, fodder and water, especially for women, the structures built through the EGS did not have a notable ripple effect on the subsistence economy of Maharashtra. Due to the careless implementation of the construction works at many sites, the EGS did not help develop assets that could sustain the supply of water as well as fuel and fodder. For a few years during the last decade, the EGS had lapsed into an almost non-existent programme, declaring that all the possible sites for construction work under the scheme were exhausted and that there was no more demand for the EGS work.

During the last three years the government has suddenly woken up to the need to provide employment under the EGS because of successive drought years in many parts of Maharashtra. The EGS had earlier been acclaimed for its 'food for work' programme that provided partial wages through food coupons, which workers could use to obtain food through a well spread network of ration shops. However, the official Public Distribution System (PDS) has been weakened by the government's new economic policies. When the Supreme Court (in response to a Public Interest Litigation) ordered all state governments to implement eight food security programmes,[2] Maharashtra did not emerge as the state providing the most efficient machinery in India.

RESTRUCTURING OF THE EGS AND WOMEN'S ACCESS TO DEVELOPED ASSETS

Against this background, Maharashtra is now restructuring the EGS. This is the time to recognise women's contribution and provide them the opportunity to develop assets that they could maintain and use. In this new phase, the state government should also restore the EGS' vital environmental objective (as mentioned in the EGA) of regenerating natural resources and safeguarding common property resources, which are fast being encroached upon. The government can ensure the sustainability of the resources by allowing marginalised people and women to develop and use these for their livelihood. Restructuring access to natural resources has been started with the Joint Forest Management (JFM) programme. Similarly, there is tremendous scope for allocating access to the assets developed under the EGS, especially to women. 'Social forestry' plots could be given to the women who have worked on those plots earlier. After paying a certain lease amount to the gram panchayat, the women should be able to earn their livelihood, using the fodder and timber from these plots and caring for their regeneration. This could become an entrepreneurship venture for them.

Water rights and the water delivery system also need to be organised through the SHG loans or the Swarna Jayanti Grameen Rojgar Yojana (SGRY). As per the record published by the Maharashtra Remote Sensing Centre (Nagpur), a total of 4,955,473 ha of wasteland is available in Maharashtra. This land could be handed over to the women's groups (or to individuals) who wish to undertake horticulture or fuel and fodder production by linking up with the micro-credit groups. The horticulture programme implemented through the EGS did succeed to some extent in some areas such as the Konkan, but the benefits did not accrue to the women because the programme was for those who had land in their own names. Women can benefit if they are given the wastelands and some funds to organise the water delivery system.

At present, the EGS funds are being used for sericulture by small plot holders under the justification that it provides employment to women. However, it is the men who benefit as the land is in their name. There is a need to encourage women entrepreneurs and landless women, who could come together and organise the land-based activity. For example, they could lease a plot of community land and plant guava trees, which are least prone to plant diseases and pests. Guava trees bear fruits after three years. The Mahila Arthik Vikas Mahamandal (MAVIM), an official organisation for the economic development of women, should provide marketing support so that the guavas could be supplied to food-processing companies. There could be a pulp-processing factory in every district and chilled pulp could be transported for packing in tetra-packs. Such an activity could come under the EGS horticulture programme. For three years, a group of five women could get daily wages under the EGS for asset development. Once fruit-bearing starts, the group could become financially independent. An EGS-SHG link is very important for promoting entrepreneurship among rural women. The Bharatiya Agro Industries Foundation (BAIF)[3] already has a *wadi* (homestead) programme for women who have their own land to plant mango trees. Similarly, MAVIM, with the help of NGOs, could develop a systematic guava tree programme.

ELABORATION OF A HORTICULTURE SCHEME UNDER THE EGS

The Maharashtra Agriculture Department (Commissioner for Horticulture, 2002) has listed achievements under the EGS-funded horticulture scheme as follows: by March 2002, the scheme included 24 kinds of fruit trees and covered 1,014,100 ha. During the previous 11 years, it has provided Rs 8,025.10 million as subsidy towards labour cost, amounting to 222.60 million labour days. The scheme reached 36,000 out of 40,412 villages in Maharashtra. Of the total land under horticulture (including earlier private efforts), 656,000 ha produced 8,788,000 tonnes of fruit, yielding Rs 57,450 million to farmers. This activity needs to be compared with what happened during the same period within the mainstream EGS scheme, which is supposed to provide employment to hundreds of thousands of landless and small farmers in Maharashtra during the lean season and droughts. The diversion of funds to private beneficiaries is a serious deviation, although it is justified under the plea that the activity is labour-intensive and, thus, the benefits accrued are only that of labour cost, which is an aim of the EGS. The usual EGS activity also generates community assets such as percolation tanks and linking roads. However, the benefits of these assets can be judged only indirectly. The horticulture scheme is the only one where assets are generated for the individual farmer.

It is also necessary to assess how efficiently this money was used, the delivery system, corruption in terms of false claims and whether the scheme benefited the targeted small farmers. I had access to the evaluation report of the scheme, prepared in 1996. This shows that the survival rate of the trees is reasonable and, thus, false claims for reimbursement of labour cost are fewer. The majority of farmers were satisfied with their income from the orchards. Each said that intercropping helped during the gestation period of the development. Later, marketing could be a problem with a few farmers because fruits are a perishable commodity and cold storages are not affordable (which is a practice with grape producers who export their produce). Once the orchard is developed, it does not require too much water.

I visited eight beneficiaries of the scheme and got detailed information of their experiences with different fruits. None had kept any systematic record of the cost incurred: the amount of water required each season, or the annual income from the orchard. But through detailed discussions we could understand how beneficial this asset could become, despite water shortage, which was a major problem mentioned by everyone, particularly against the backdrop of three years' continuous drought in the Marathwada region. The average income per acre, per year after deduction of labour costs and watering were: Rs 20,000 for *chiku* (sapodilla or sapota), Rs 12,000 for guava, and between Rs 10,000 and Rs 20,000 for mango.

NORMS FOR THE BENEFICIARY TO ACCESS THE SCHEME

Any individual in whose name there is a land record can avail of the scheme. If the land is under tenancy contract, the tenant's signature is required. The tenant can also avail of the scheme, provided her/his name is on the land record as a tenant. The scheme is applicable for land between 0.20 ha and 4 ha in extent. In the hilly and rocky Konkan area, however, the land coverage could be up to 10 ha. The farmer has to undertake the responsibility of digging trenches, applying manures and pesticides, watering and so on. The grant is meant for labour cost and also the partial cost of materials such as saplings, fertilisers and some pesticides. The grant would cover 100 per cent of the labour cost and 75 per cent of the material cost. The entire material cost would be covered for Dalit, tribal, marginal and small farmers (as defined by NABARD). The grant period covers three years. In the first year, it provides the material cost and reimburses labour costs as recorded in a register. During the next two years, labour cost would be reimbursed after assessing the survival rate of saplings (90 per cent for orchards with water; 75 per cent for dryland orchards). Thus, the progress and the growth of the orchard are monitored for the first three years as the asset is developed. The labour cost during this period is borne through the EGS funds.

EVALUATION OF ORCHARDS BEFORE 1996

The horticulture department has set out norms for the labour days per hectare required for a specific fruit orchard, with EGS wage rates. Similarly, norms have been set out for the material cost of a particular orchard. The water requirement varies from region to region. However, the report has also produced tables for a few fruit varieties regarding the waterings in the summer period for three successive years. The water quantum is very essential to decide whether or not a farmer is eligible for the grant. Tables 7.1–7.4, computed on the basis of information in the 1996 evaluation, provide information about the viability of these orchards. Overall, the expenditure is less than the grant (Table 7.1).

The expenditure on *ber* (*Zizyphus mauritiana*) orchards alone is more than expected. Very few plantations have exceeded the average expenditure pattern. It appears that the agriculture department has calculated cost on the basis of more labour days than are actually required as an incentive to farmers (Table 7.2). It is also interesting to note that not much family labour is involved; rather, outside labourers have been employed. Thus, the scheme complies with its main aim of providing employment to the landless or marginal farmers. Unfortunately, there is no record about

Table 7.1
Grant and Average Expenditure on Plantation

Fruit Variety Total Plantations (75% alive)	Grant per Hectare (Rs)	Average Expenditure, per Hectare	Plantations Involving More than Grant Amount (%)
Mango saplings	12,712.00	4,719.77	2
Mango (grafted)	14,602.00	10,489.50	3
Guava	11,030.00	4,724.60	0
Pomegranate	13,008.00	7,535.48	8
Custard apple	8,970.00	2,695.43	1
Ber	7,324.00	7,592.84	20

Source: Evaluation Report of the Employment Guarantee Scheme, Maharashtra Agriculture Department (Commissioner for Horticulture), 2002.

Table 7.2
Details of Working Days and Family Labour Days

Fruit Variety Total Plantations (75% alive)	Per Plantation Labour Days per ha		
	Grant for Labour Days	Actual Average Labour Days	Actual Family Labour Days
Mango saplings	581	147.94	38.00
Mango grafted	596	314.99	189.70
Guava	409	131.00	33.00
Pomegranate	488	316.89	57.08
Custard apple	415	125.00	28.00
Ber	294	309.00	29.58

Source: Evaluation Report of the Employment Guarantee Scheme, Maharashtra Agriculture Department (Commissioner for Horticulture), 2002.

whether the outside labourers were men or women. They are likely to be men because digging trenches is treated as 'men's job' and the maximum labour days must have been spent on trenches.

Young saplings require more waterings as their roots are not developed. Table 7.3 gives the percentage of plantations receiving waterings. Around 60 per cent of all plantations have required a maximum of 16–20 waterings during the three summer months. Very few plantations have required to be watered more than 21 times. Our interviews also confirm that while assured water is necessary, it is a myth that heavy watering is required. During the third summer, the water requirement comes down drastically (see Table 7.4). Except for grafted mangoes and ber, which required more than 21 waterings (35.51 per cent for mangoes and 23.23 per cent for ber), other plantations need much less water.

Based on the above information, I was convinced that this is a good scheme and that women in the SHGs would be able to implement it by taking some amount of loan to tide them over the initial expenses. Instead of working as agricultural or construction labour, a group of five women could come together in this venture, invest their time and money, and be paid for their daily labour. There were a few glitches, which were noticed when we visited the orchards and farmers related stories about the grant being paid late or in a lump sum at the end of each year, and not in the short intervals that would enable the farmer to pay labourers and pay the costs of electricity, pumping water and so on. This made us aware of the need for capital for recurring expenses. However, these were considered administrative problems, which could be sorted out once the commitment was made to build assets for the poor women.

Table 7.3
Details of Irrigation during First and Second Summers
(1990–91 and 1991–92)

Fruits	Plantations Showing Number of Waterings	Plantations Showing Number of Watering Rounds (%)					
		0	1–5	6–10	11–15	16–20	More than 21
Mango saplings	175	17.71	26.86	30.29	13.71	8.57	2.86
Mango grafted	111	9.91	00.90	15.32	13.51	24.32	36.04
Chiku	4	–	–	50.00	50.00	–	–
Guava	7	–	28.57	28.57	28.57	14.29	–
Pomegranate	82	2.44	14.63	17.07	14.63	4.88	46.34
Custard apple	12	58.33	8.33	25.00	8.33	–	–
Ber	91	16.48	23.08	24.18	8.79	4.40	23.08

Source: Evaluation Report of the Employment Guarantee Scheme, Maharashtra Agriculture Department (Commissioner for Horticulture), 2002.

Table 7.4
Details of Third Summer Irrigation after Plantation (1992–93)

Fruits	Plantation showing number of given watering rounds	Plantations showing number of watering rounds (%)					
		0	1–5	6–10	11–15	16–20	More than 21
Mango saplings	143	26.57	23.08	25.87	14.69	7.69	2.10
Mango grafted	107	16.82	1.87	14.02	10.28	21.50	35.51
Chiku	4	50.00	–	25.00	25.00	–	–
Guava	7	–	14.29	42.86	14.29	28.57	–
Pomegranate	80	48.75	7.50	17.50	11.25	11.25	7.50
Custard apple	11	63.64	9.90	27.27	–	–	–
Ber	90	25.56	21.11	15.56	10.00	4.44	23.23

Source: Evaluation Report of the Employment Guarantee Scheme, Maharashtra Agriculture Department (Commissioner for Horticulture), 2002.

RESEARCH METHODOLOGY

The major problem was how to approach women and stimulate their
imagination to make them believe that with the loans available from the
SHG, they could think of something else other than goats, cows and buffaloes as their assets. The area selected was Osmanabad district, which is
a dryland area and figures prominently on the map of the EGS. Moreover,
I was visiting the district and the rural campus of the Tata Institute of
Social Sciences as part of my job. The funds allotted were very modest.

Earlier, I had planned an elaborate and scientific design such as the
collection of data on wasteland in nine talukas of Osmanabad district

and also on the different types of SHGs scattered all over the district, functioning under NGOs or government programmes. Our idea was that once the data was obtained, the horticulture under EGS could be promoted more vigorously in areas where the ideal conditions such as the availability of wasteland as well as strong SHGs exist. But that proved elusive because the government officers were reluctant to share data with us, either because they did not have it or because of red tape. Hence, the data on all the talukas could not be obtained. This was despite the computer centres in every district, established by the National Informatics Centre (NIC). Gathering data and feeding it appears to be a slow process, and according to the head of the district computer centre, there is very little response from the taluka-level offices. So, I had to be satisfied with whatever we could get.

It was decided to make a presentation to NGO representatives. Some of them would like the idea, and they might invite me and my colleague to speak to their women SHG members. This workshop proved very important because we also organised another presentation by the women members of the Deccan Development Society (DDS) from Zahirabad (Andhra Pradesh). The DDS has motivated Dalit women for the last 20 years to cultivate a piece of land (either leased, or bought with the help of government funds) and has helped them for three successive years with the cost of manuring and ploughing. The money is to be returned in kind, out of the produce, to the local grain bank and distributed at a fixed price to whoever wants it. The DDS made a short film on this Alternative Public Distribution System (APDS), which was screened as part of the workshop. Four women and one agriculturist from the Krishi Vigyan Kendra, run by the DDS, were invited to share their experience. Representatives from 25 organisations in Osmanabad district were present. The district agricultural officer was also invited to elaborate on this scheme.

This helped us to inspire some of the NGO representatives to use SHGs as a vehicle to promote the idea of access to land and develop long-term assets such as orchards. We had presentations in 18 villages, screening the DDS film at many places. This stirred a lot of discussion on whether it was possible for women to make a success of this scheme. We could collect data from some of the SHG members, although it was not possible to go into details in the time available. But we got a glimpse into our constituency. A total of 185 women in nine villages filled our forms. Only

70 women had some land, which does not give us landholding size. The majority were landless. Only 39 women claimed to have farming as a basic category for income, while 110 earned their income from wages. Nine earned their main income from salaries, having salaried persons in their families. In 142 families, there was only one woman as a working member, whereas in 122 families there was only one working man. In 23 families, more than one woman was earning money, compared to 35 families with more than one earning man. Women had a strong presence as workers and earning members in the family.

In all, 61 women came from families earning less than Rs 2,000 a month, while 92 earned less than Rs 1,000; 32 of the women did not report on this. Of the 185 women, 106 had BPL cards and 75 did not; 27 women said that their families have taken bank loans: seven had repaid the loan, 16 were either in the process of doing so, or may have been defaulters. Of the 103 women who had taken the saving group loan, 70 had borrowed more than Rs 1,000 and the rest below Rs 1,000, and of these, 26 women had returned the loan and 67 were in the process of returning it. The loans were mainly for illness, house repairs and, in a few cases, for family farming. SHG activity was apparently not very strong, in terms of the availability of loan funds. Among all these 185 women, there was no major income-generating activity.

We could not get much background information on the villages as it was very difficult to meet the *gram sevaks* or *talathi* in the village. We tried to meet them at the taluka offices during their monthly meetings. But even with an appointment, on the particular day they would not be there to share the information. So our village proformas could not be filled.

WOMEN'S VOICES

Our interaction with the women on the matter of accessing land for orchard cultivation is presented below in their own voices.

On the Availability of Land

The majority of the women did not have land of their own and were worried that nobody would give land on lease to poor women. The *gairan* (wasteland under the Revenue Department) is available, but is far away in hilly terrain:

Who would walk that distance everyday!

Some of us go for work on the construction site at a long distance by public transport, but then the wages are higher there. For agricultural work, wages are not that high and hence it is not affordable to go by public transport. Also, if the gram panchayat makes the revenue fallow land available on lease, then when the Sarpanch changes, he would undo what has been done by the earlier Sarpanch and she/he would cancel our lease. Whatever efforts we would have put in would go waste. We do not believe that the lease would last for 10–15 years.

What about the fencing? If the land is far away then who would secure it? We may not be able to stay there at the spot. The private horticulturist stays there himself or appoints the saldar (labourer on annual contract) who stays there. Stealing of fruits is an important concern for us.

We are aware that once the trees are fully grown one guava tree or chiku tree bears 10–20 kilo of fruits per day in the season. It is a good business but we do not have land. And we do not believe that we can acquire the piece of land.

Even though the Sarpanch is in favour of allotting a piece of waste land to the SHG, we know that the people in the village would not like it. They would destroy our plantation as they have done in the past when some Dalit families encroached upon the land and started cultivating it.

In our Ansurde village, the Sarpanch is very keen to make the experiment a success. He is willing to give two plots of land to two SHGs. He offered 5 acres of land to each group. (There was a good discussion about which piece is better and how the plots should be formed so that both the SHGs would get some land, which is black and fertile.)

On the Security of Leased Land

Gairan plots are a contested issue in the Marathwada region. The major concern pertained to the quality of the gairan or wasteland that they were likely to be offered. Women from five (out of 18) villages had a very negative perception of the land. They felt that such rocky land would be of no use for any plantation. Making trenches by digging was not possible without blasting. They asserted that the wasteland around the village was so hilly that they would not be able to climb it and would be unable to do any work there.

> Already some of us have encroached upon the gairan, but the titles have not been given to us by the government. We are fighting for that. We cultivated the land for two years and both the years the high caste farmers allowed their cattle to graze in our plots and all our investment and labour went waste.

> The high caste farmers in the village are opposed to the idea of allotting the gairan plots to the Dalit landless labourers. They are afraid that once we have our own land we would bargain for better wages when we work on their farms.

> We need to first secure the gairan plots in our own names and then we can think of horticulture as an option.

> If you are supporting our demand for the distribution of gairan to the landless, then we are happy to work with you. We would think that you would compliment our movement of Jameen Adhikar Andolan.

> It is possible that tomorrow our fruits too would be stolen under the pretext that it is a common land.

> Gairan is usually wasteland, a little rocky plot, and it would be quite difficult for us to dig trenches for the tree plantation. We may not afford to pay for digging work.

> That is not true. Some of us go on Employment Guarantee Scheme and have done work on rocky land. It is not more difficult than that. Our men folk too would help us to dig.

On the Availability of Water

The next point of discussion concerned the availability of water. We had made posters based on the evaluation report and our interviews with the nine orchard owners. We made the point that while water was a crucial resource for any land-based activity, the amount of water required was reasonable and would not be that difficult to obtain. The need for water is a myth; judicious use could bring down the quantity of water required for such plantations. However, there were stronger negative responses with respect to the availability of water than there were for the availability of land. The main demand was that water first be assured for any land-related activity, and only then could any new programme be conceived. Some of them showed willingness to fetch water, if available, by using pitchers. But water does not exist. A borewell or ordinary well has to be the first priority. This cannot be done with the loan available through the SHG, as it is a big amount.

Without an assured source of water it would be difficult to search for water and then we would be forced to get a pitcherful of water for each plant and do the watering. Without a close source of water, we may have to hire a bullock cart and get a barrel for watering the plants. It would be too costly an affair to keep the plants alive during the summer period.

We don't have water for drinking and so how can we ask for water for plantation. In many villages women depend upon tankers to fetch water and then how can one think of getting water for plantation.

To get a tanker of water is itself like a battle everyday and we have to wage so many conflicts. To nurture an orchard is a dream for us.

Even if there were a plantation of jatropha, it would require some water at least for the first two years.

Some women narrated their experiences of planting mango trees in their fields. They were willing to water them by carrying water physically from a distance everyday. Even then, the plants did not survive. They realised that it was not easy to nurture a plantation.

As you suggest we can take loan from the SHG for arranging a pipe-line, but it takes three to four years to start getting profit from the orchard, then how can we repay the loan in time. There is a rule of repayment in time otherwise we need to pay fine.

We do understand that we can make a facility of some storage and thus get water to be used during summer. But tanker water is too costly and where can we get that kind of money?

Nobody is willing to sell water in the summer. Last year when there was a shortage of drinking water, then the people pressurised a farmer to cut his water to the sugarcane fields and provide for drinking water to the villagers.

As you said, we understand that we can take intercrops such as peanuts or sunflower, so that we can get some income in the gestation period of plantation. But that also requires some water.

I have 40 mango trees. Last year I purchased water in summer and paid Rs 100 every week for eight weeks and took care that my three-year-old plants survived. I personally watered each tree with a pitcher. We kept earthen pots at the roots of every plant and filled these pots so that it acted as a drip. It takes hard work but in the long run it is beneficial.

In my village there is a borewell owned by the panchayat and as long as light (electricity) is there, water continues to flow and gets wasted. I always feel that if we use that water and channel it to the plantation we can do wonders.

In my village, no hand pump works anymore. They have dried up. Where can we get water? There is no community well. Only some farmers have private wells. There is land but no water.

There is a storage tank built on the land of our village but it is far away and we cannot access it easily but the villages downstream are able to access it and they have built lifts on that tank. Our gram panchayat is very lazy. You must help us to get that water.

Women in our village are very hardworking. We can make the orchard a success if we get water. Along with saplings, if the agriculture department also provides us with water facilities, then we can grow an orchard.

The women of Balajinagar Lamantanda (a hamlet of a nomadic tribe) said that there was a small tank in the village, but they suspected that the gram panchayat would not allow them to draw water from it. The sarpanch of Ansurda was willing to give land as well as water to women members of the SHG. He insisted that two acres of land could be brought under plantation first and, once it was found successful, more land could be made available. Water shortage is a real thing. Massa village women were optimistic, and said, *If we use drip like saline bottles very little water would*

be utilised and also we would save labour cost. We can get loan from the
SHG and invest.

On Marketing and Sale

Where could we sell these fruits? Do we need to go to the market yard for that? Can we understand the dealings in the market yard? Is there any assurance of prices for our fruits, such as guava? In case we get a very low price it would be really sad because it means that so much time and energy is wasted, apart from having a loss.

Cannot government ensure that it would arrange a purchase of all the produce? If we fail to sell the produce our men folk are likely to get angry.

Is there any storage facility provided by the government for keeping the fruits fresh, if it is not sold on the same day?

The local market cannot take so much produce. It has to be on a big scale.

If we start going to the market yard, the men folk in the family would be annoyed and are likely to beat us. What is the solution for that?

As we do not have knowledge of the market yard, we can take some male family member along and pay him daily wages.

In Belwadi village, women said that they were worried about not having a good road, which could become a barrier to getting any vehicle to the village to transport the produce.

On Intercrops

Your suggestion of taking intercrops for first three years, to earn some money during the gestation period, is a good idea. But it won't make much difference.

No. I feel we can divide the plot and cultivate vegetables during at least rainy season. If we sell it together it will make profit.

We need training and consultation for these crops. Most of us are agri-cultural labourers, but have never taken any decisions.

On Payment Rules for the Grant

We have always depended upon the cash wages. If we are supposed to cultivate vegetables, we need to work every day, but the profit would come after two months. We need to wait to earn cash, which is not possible for us. We need consumption loans.

The SHG cannot give us consumption loans.

If we need to wait one year to get the first instalment, we cannot afford that. We would have to work in the horticulture plantation and hence we cannot go for other wage work. How can we feed ourselves? Our husbands won't like this idea. They would not permit us to take the scheme.

Our husbands are drunkards and do not earn much. Our wages are the core of our livelihood resources.

Women in Keshegaon and Ansurda Villages who Wanted the Scheme:

What kind of agreement would be required between the village panchayat and the women's group or individual farmer? What should be the minimum period of the agreement for the government to consider allotment of the horticulture scheme?

If there are two groups who are willing to work, how can you ensure that both groups would get the land on lease? Women from two groups would not like to come together due to lack of trust in each other.

Does the scheme include compensation for pests or any other diseases affecting the plantation during first three years?

If the saplings are burnt due to drought, would the government ensure that at least a second lot is given free of charge? Is there any insurance scheme for this?

Would the panchayat consider cancellation of rent if the plantation did not materialise?

If the land is given to the collective, then the losses have to be borne collectively. However, we doubt whether there exists that maturity among women and whether they would not blame each other for sharing loss.

Women's Suggestions for Amending the Scheme

We would like to suggest that if the government is allotting the scheme to women, then it must also provide weekly wages to us. If the saplings do not survive at the end of the first year, then the wages can be stopped.

We do not trust the government. Its payment never comes in time. Our loan from the SHG would not last long.

No farmer pays us on time. We have to beg for a month or two. Hence, I am agreeable if the government promises to pay us after every two months.

We as farmers are willing to accept the drought situation and if crops fail we do not blame anybody. We take the loss. In this scheme, we have to make payment for rent, for water and also work without wages. If this horticulture fails we cannot take the loss. Here we are required to invest money first. We are not willing to take the risk. We feel that it is government work and hence the risk should be borne by the government, not us.

The agreement should be in the name of the women's group. If anybody wants to take the scheme individually, then her name should be there on the land title. We would insist that the husband should divide his land and give a plot to his wife.

It is a difficult and expensive proposition. Lot of bribe is required and then only the title is changed.

There are many privately owned fallow lands, which can be used for this purpose. But our husbands are opposed to this idea. They do not mind keeping it fallow but would not like it to be used for this kind of experimentation.

Sometimes we feel that it is better to give individual loans through SHG and earn interest, which can be distributed among the members. We do not want to invest money and also work hard so that we get more profit. This is risky.

On Collective Work versus Individual Work

In all villages, women expressed doubts about whether they could work together and develop a feeling of collective ownership towards this enterprise.

In Upsinghe village, we had done an experiment of cultivating small plots of land collectively. But it failed. Women do not stay together.

We are a highly individualistic lot. If one woman comes late one day, another would cite that as an example and would come late tomorrow.

That is the reason why farmers do not lease us the fallow land. They know that nothing would be produced out of the land.

So, it would be appropriate that the wasteland could be given on lease individually and not collectively. Then the responsibility could be pinned down. It won't become a 'sarakari kam' (government work).

If we stick on and show that there is a profit in the enterprise, then women would definitely stay together. It appears to be a good scheme, where the government appears to provide the basic resources.

I suggest that we divide the responsibility of trees among all the members and then the sense of ownership would come. There would be competition, which would prompt everybody to do better. We should sell the fruits together, so that the cost of transport, et cetera, would be shared.

We are sure that if land plots are available our men would not allow us to have the title of the land in our name. We are willing to do horticulture but the land is to be given in the name of men.

Some of us have sufficient land of our own. Can we take the scheme on our own land and grow fruits?

I feel that we can do horticulture and also have a goat each because we can get enough leaves and fodder for the goat, once we have the orchard.

In our SHG group of 10 women, six have farms of their own. So, we do not go for agriculture labour. If we take the plot for horticulture collectively how could it be managed? Those who would work would get wages from the group, but those who do not work, would they be able to get a share of the profit or not?

We must have courage. Courage to take risk, otherwise we would never succeed. Once we come forward we would find a way to solve issues. (Ansurda village)

I find that this is the best scheme. It provides us wages for work and also assets such as horticulture, which would provide profit, year after year.

We have devsthan (community temple) land and also some water in the well. I will try to convince the trustees of my community to donate the land to our SHG and we would plant the orchard. I am sure if I take the initiative other women would follow. This is a good idea. You must help me to talk to the trustees of the temple. (Naldurg, Jai Durgamata Group)

I like the scheme because the government is willing to provide wages, saplings, pesticide, and will not charge any interest on all this money. There is some hard work, but it is worth it. We need to find out a piece of land and water, which can be done within village. (Keshewadi)

Demand for Other Assets

To tell you the truth, we are keen to get buffaloes and goats. Ultimately, it does not cost us to maintain them. They can graze as we work. Sometimes we end up sending our children to graze them.

What about children's education? Our daughters do not go to school.

But I can make money out of the cattle. If I get a semi-crossbreed buffalo, I can get five litres of milk and make khoya by evaporation. I can make two kilos of khoya. Milk sells for Rs 8 per litre. Khoya sells Rs 60 per kg.

The advantage of cattle is that we can sell it in a crisis. It is an asset, which is personal. I do not have to ask even my husband.

Income out of sale of goats is always woman's income. She can buy gifts for her brother's wife and her parents.

Those who earn Rs 100 on brick kilns would not like the idea of working in horticulture. But those who are agricultural labourers like us would definitely see benefit in this scheme.

ANALYSIS

The women were surprisingly articulate and had opinions on each issue related to the enterprise of horticulture under the EGS. They touched upon almost every aspect of implementation and analysed the factors involved for the successful adoption of the scheme. The responses were varied, with most pointing out the negative side of each provision of the scheme. Who were the negative respondents? It was not possible for us to distinguish the background of the respondent every time and see the correlation between the landholding and the negative or positive tone of the response. Our detailed data (not included in this chapter) on the background of the respondents and SHGs in eight villages shows clearly that the majority of members are landless, or possess marginal land. That, perhaps, explains their cautious approach every time they expressed their opinions.

We were also overwhelmed by the cynicism of the responses, particularly against the background of the film on Dalit women that we had used to stimulate the discussion. The DDS film was made very crisply, presenting the story of 1,000 women who have been part of the campaign for 'autonomy over production, over seeds, over market'. The campaign had culminated in the building of the APDS. The DDS helped the women to take over fallow lands, their own or lands leased from the panchayats, or plots bought with the money acquired through an Andhra Pradesh government scheme. The boldness of the Andhra women was inspiring. The same women were themselves present when the workshop was organised for NGO leaders (to enable us to hold meetings with the SHG members in the villages where they are working). The women's stories were powerful and everybody praised this experiment. However, when we visited the SHGs, the idea of owning an asset, or setting up an enterprise, was not greeted with excitement. The identity as a labourer was so deep-rooted among the women that the possibility that they could have the inner potential and ability to manage an orchard had never crossed their minds. We realised that unless this became a campaign, the women would never aspire towards mustering the energy to accept the challenge of becoming entrepreneurs.

The women knew of the physical availability of gairan land, but were also aware of the social barriers to their access to the common land. Since 2000, the Dalit women had been part of the ongoing 'Jameen Adhikar Andolan' (Land Rights Movement) in the Marathwada region. In 1991, the government had attempted to regularise encroachments on gairans through a government resolution, but the implementation was haphazard and disillusioned the Dalits. When the movement gathered momentum, several Dalit families tried to cultivate village common lands, but were foiled by high-caste farmers.

The women were clear about the issue of security of the leased land. They said that the government should offer cheap loans so that they can possess land, which would allow them to feel secure. Apart from the social barriers to accessing land, the more important issue was the availability of water. This overshadowed all other issues. Surprisingly, in this region of Maharashtra there has been no 'Pani Adhikar Andolan' (Water Rights Movement), or even a struggle for access to community wells for productive uses. Assured water is the key in any attempt to enhance productivity of the land by using water judiciously, and bringing public and private fallow lands under cultivation. The women's thinking is crippled by water scarcity, for which they find no solution.

In two villages, Keshegaon and Ansurda, where the sarpanches were very supportive, the women appeared very keen to know all the details of the scheme and asked about the kind of agreement required. The Sarpanch came with us to meet the collector to ask for land for the women. However, the collector said that gairan was being demanded by everyone and he could not favour women over others.

The women's interest in the marketing aspects was very welcome. They wanted to know the viability of the scheme and were concerned about the possibility of getting compensation or insurance cover in the likelihood of the plantation being devastated by pests. The women were aware of their own limitations and their incapability of negotiating in public life, in the markets. They wanted some assurance of purchase, or, in economic terms, forward linkages, before they take up the activity of producing the fruits. They also expressed concern about the problem of transportation, as some villages did not have proper roads.

The possibility of intercropping was suggested as a part of the scheme, till the trees grow and start yielding money. Women were aware that this activity would also require some amount of investment and asked where the money would come from. Their major concern was regarding wages for their work. They realised that if the grant was given only after the inspection for the survival rate, the scheme was not meant for them, but only for rich farmers. Indeed, they did not bother to check out the scheme because their experience showed that only rich farmers or absentee farmers could afford to wait for the grant to be delivered at the end of the year, which was supposed to be payment towards wages. The real marginal farmer, who would put her own labour in the orchard but would not get wages till the end of the year, would face a problem of survival.

The women also realised that the key to making the scheme work for them was to ask for weekly, or at least monthly, wages, which would enable them to develop a sense of ownership and not be tempted away by some good wage-earning opportunity. However, they could not answer the agriculture officer about why the women should be trusted more than the men farmers. In the past, the men farmers had taken money by showing false records of hiring labour, but had not nurtured the trees and had simply explained that the plants had dried out. Women were shocked to hear the dirty ways of corruption. But they were convinced that if the officers came to make payments every month, the women could not cheat them. At one point, they indicated that there might be connivance between the officer and the farmer. Their argument was that if this is the scheme under EGS, then it should follow the rules of EGS payments.

On the one hand, women expressed keen concern about the agreement to be made in their names but, on the other, some were afraid that their men would not appreciate this idea. Some women were looking forward to getting the piece of private land in their own name so that they would be eligible for the scheme. Women's desire for land could be noticed through these discussions, although they are still far behind when it comes to upholding the demand of the women's movement elsewhere for the inheritance of land rights.

Most disturbing was the lack of collective spirit among the women. Only in Keshewadi and Ansurda was the idea of land to be given to the SHG appreciated, and they talked of taking turns in working in the orchard and getting wages. Some agreed that those who needed work would be allowed to work for wages; while others would participate in decision-making and would share the profit when it was earned. Many of these women had been engaged on EGS work on percolation tanks, roads and, sometimes, the nurseries of the Forest Department. None of them had been a member of any union or organisation, but at least they had been associated with the NGO for some time and had been part of SHG activity. However, the SHG activity does not appear to inculcate the spirit of collectivity among them. Indeed, it sometimes encourages competition among members with regard to accessing loans. The strongest voice was for individual activity.

Moreover, very few women had a long-term view of the business and its advantages. Except the women of Keshewadi and Ansurda, very few were aware that risk-taking is important to increase income, not just through wages, but also through assets, that is, through investment. The Dalit women, who were all landless labourers, were only concerned about wages in the short-term. The lesson learnt from this interaction was that it might not be possible to build a cooperative spirit of entrepreneurship among landless labourers. The DDS experiment also shows that the majority of women purchased land individually and cultivated it individually. Very few did it collectively. But the DDS has been supportive all along, for the last 20 years, in 75 villages. They provided the funding as well as capacity building support with concerted efforts at organising women. What we noticed here was a 'base line' mindset before an attempt to shape it took place. We concluded that we could not take this as a negative response.

The women distrusted the government machinery. The delivery system is so weak and partisan towards the wealthy that the women have lost hope of change occurring in their lives through the government schemes. Promoting SHG activity is one of the several strategies the government wants to pursue to alleviate poverty. Poor women have to cross many hurdles to access funds that could generate sustainable assets. This has resulted in scepticism about any new idea that is to be implemented through the government machinery.

Policy and Administrative Issues

In our discussions, the Commissioner for Agriculture, Maharashtra, was appreciative of the idea, but was sceptical about the political will of the government to allot the gairan plots to women. He was also doubtful about their ability to manage the orchards. He felt strongly that the fruit-processing activity was the best for women, either as a home-based activity or through small powered units at the taluka or district centre. He advised us to take it up with NABARD and MAVIM to prepare proposals for such enterprises and sanction loans to the SHGs to take up the processing activity. He felt that they should develop marketing linkages with the bigger consumer industries that produce juices, jams, et cetera. On the whole, it appeared that women were perceived basically as workers in small factories, but not as farmers who can act independently as entrepreneurs.

The grant is given as payment towards labour, as it is money provided under the EGS to supplement and sustain the income of marginal farmers. However, if the payment is only disbursed at the end of the year, how can a marginal farmer sustain herself through the year, look after the orchard and take up an intercrop? To avoid cheating, the scheme requires monitoring the condition of survival of 75 per cent of the saplings, but this contradicts the basic aim. Of the nine orchards that we visited, only two were managed by family labour; all the others belonged either to rich farmers or absentee farmers residing in the city. This is the biggest lacuna, and unless this is removed, the scheme cannot be considered as an EGS compatible with the involvement of SHGs. Women need monthly support towards payment of their labour. Indeed, we were told that the grant has not even been given at the end of the year for the last two years because of the cash crunch faced by the government. In 2004, the Zilla Parishad staff had been paid in a lump sum for two previous years.

The Maharashtra government should issue a government resolution about the gairans, allotting the plots to SHGs and not to individual members. NGOs, along with gram panchayats, should be given the responsibility of organising, motivating and also monitoring. NGOs could be given some funds as incentives to cover their travel costs. The gram panchayat should allow water from the community wells to be used for this purpose. SHGs should take the responsibility for setting up pumps and laying pipelines. The Agriculture Department needs to make separate rules for SHG collectives and, after monitoring growth, disburse the labour cost every month. NABARD and MAVIM should prepare proposals for setting up processing units in each district and also develop linkages with the big industries that cater to consumers. When a sizable number of orchards are created in one taluka or district as part of a campaign, these processing units would become a viable alternative to direct selling in the local market. The women's movement should look at this activity as providing a synergic opportunity for SHGs to bring about structural changes in land access. Access to land as a right to livelihood and to increase the income of poor women has to be an immediate short-term goal.

NOTES

1. The following taxes/cess on taxes are imposed to collect funds for the EGS: professional tax on salaried people in Maharashtra; levy on irrigated land; levy on commercial buildings in the cities; additional tax on motor vehicles; additional tax on education tax; and surcharge on sales tax.

2. The eight food security schemes are: National Midday Meal Scheme; Targeted Public Distribution System; Antyoday Anna Yojana; Integrated Child Development Services Programme (ICDS); Annapurna Yojana; National Old Age Pension Scheme; National Maternity Benefit Scheme; and National Family Benefit Scheme.

3. BAIF is a major NGO working across five states and is mainly helping tribal people to increase the productivity of their land and cattle and build their management capacities.

III

The Challenge of Democratic Governance

8

In the Name of the Community
Gender, Development and Governance in Arunachal Pradesh

Deepak K. Mishra and Vandana Upadhyay

With increasing appreciation of the role of institutional factors in the process of economic development, there has been a greater realisation of the significance of democratic and humane governance for equitable and sustainable development. India's northeastern region is not only one of the least developed but also one of the most ill-governed parts of the country. The continuing presence of insurgency and violent ethnic conflicts in the region has clouded discussions on the political economy of development of the region. While ethnic conflicts, militant secessionist movements and insurgency are often described as the result of the lack of development initiatives on the part of the central and state governments, the underdevelopment or deceleration of the economies of the Northeast is often explained in terms of the presence of insurgency and conflicts. Based on the experience of a relatively peaceful state, Arunachal Pradesh, this chapter attempts to explain the manifold linkages between the political economy of development and the crisis of governance in the region. The central argument is that as a consequence of the ethnicisation of the development discourse, the rights of various marginalised groups, including women, suffer in fundamental ways, which often gets concealed in highly generalised notions of the relatively egalitarian social order in tribal societies. A number of gender-sensitive indicators of development throw up disturbing evidences of the marginalisation of women in various spheres in the state, particularly in recent decades.

The chapter is organised as follows. After a brief introduction to the salient features of the development experience in Arunachal Pradesh, we have discussed the emerging gender relations in this predominantly tribal state on the basis of a few indicators. The next section presents manifestations of the crises in governance, after which the implications of these processes for women have been discussed. Concluding observations are in the final section.

THE DIFFICULT TRANSITION: ASPECTS OF THE POLITICAL ECONOMY OF DEVELOPMENT

Given the historical legacy of relative isolation and underdevelopment, the progress made by Arunachal Pradesh on the economic front in a comparatively short span of a few decades is quite impressive. During the entire period of 1971–2001, for which data is available, the Net State Domestic Product (NSDP) has registered an average annual growth rate of 7.34 per cent per annum. Although the growth rate was much higher in the 1970s (7.07 per cent) and 1980s (7.81 per cent) than it was in the 1990s (4.54 per cent), given the low levels of initial development, difficult ecological preconditions and geo-political constraints of being a border state, the development of the economy may seem satisfactory in overall terms (Upadhyay and Mishra 2005).

The structural transformation of the Arunachal economy is manifested through an increasing diversification of the workforce, emergence of a modern non-farm economy, rapid urbanisation and gradual integration with the regional and national economy. However, it is important to note that in the last three decades, the contribution of manufacturing has never exceeded 7 per cent of the state's income. The share of the secondary sector has gone up from around 20 per cent in 1970–71 to only 23.65 per cent in 2001–02, while that of the tertiary sector has increased substantially during the same period from 20.48 per cent in 1970–71 to 41.68 per cent in 2001–02. The share of the primary sector has decreased from around 60 to 35 per cent during the same period. The key aspect of the changing sectoral composition of the state lies in the fact that the expansion of the service sector has been almost entirely driven by government-sector activities. Public administration alone contributed around 14 per cent of the NSDP of the state in 2001–02 (GoAP 2006).

The 1990s seems to have reinforced the structural imbalances of the state's economy. Apart from the relatively slow growth of the NSDP during this decade, Arunachal's dependence on the service sector in general and on public administration in particular increased substantially.[1] As such, industrialisation never really had a firm footing in the economy; however, the restrictions imposed on the timber trade by the Supreme Court of India led to the closure of many timber-based industries.

Like many other states of northeast India, Arunachal Pradesh continues to remain heavily dependent upon central government assistance. Between 1990–91 and 1998–99, the ratio of annual net transfers to NSDP remained as high as 78.05 per cent. In 1998–99, only 1.5 per cent of the revenue expenditure could be generated from its own tax revenue (Sachdeva 2000). The predominant role of the state as the prime economic actor and the dependence of the state government on central government aid and loans have crucially conditioned the pattern of development in Arunachal Pradesh over the past decades.

Although a comprehensive analysis of the development process in Arunachal Pradesh is beyond the scope of this chapter, some aspects of it can be selectively looked at for a better understanding of the challenges before the state. First, along with the monetisation of the exchange process and gradual commercialisation of the economy, interpersonal inequalities in the distribution of income, assets and opportunities have grown manifold. While the elaborate networks of redistribution and reciprocity prevented the emergence of inequality in the traditional economy of the communities, under the mutually reinforcing influences of the market and the state, the gradual economic differentiation of the indigenous population has led to the emergence of a neo-rich, upwardly mobile class in Arunachal. Occupationally, this group belongs to the trading and business community, contractors or government services, but the most important aspect of their emergence is their access to the resources of the state. Second, the spatially uneven process of development within the state has created new challenges and constraints. Typically, the districts or areas bordering Assam and areas near the urban, administrative centres have better infrastructural facilities than those in the interior. Arunachal has been the home of a number of tribes and sub-tribes, and many of them had limited mobility beyond their well-defined local boundaries. Inter-regional disparities in the state, therefore, have an additional implication—in many cases and up to a certain extent, this may reflect inter-tribal disparities. Third, although until recently it has been relatively free from secessionist violence and insurgency, its development performance has not been satisfactory, particularly in terms of human development indicators. Among the eight northeastern states, Arunachal Pradesh occupied the second position in terms of per capita NSDP in 1990–91 and is fifth in terms of consumption expenditure, but according to the *National Human Development Report: 2001* (Planning Commission 2002), it was at the bottom of the Human Development Index (Table 8.1). In terms of the Human Poverty Index, except Mizoram, its position is the worst in the region. In 2001, it had the lowest literacy rate among all the northeastern states as well as the highest urban-rural gap and the highest gender gap in literacy. In terms of enrolment, drop-out rates and school availability, its performance, in a comparative perspective, has hardly been satisfactory (Table 8.2). Further, in terms of the health status of the population, Arunachal Pradesh's performance has been less impressive than many other states of the region (Table 8.3). As the brief analysis in the following section shows, the increasing inequality among men and women, when viewed in a comparative perspective, is clearly one of the serious problems associated with the modern growth process.

While it is always possible to explain away this relative under-performance by citing many historical, geographical and economic constraints, any forward-looking strategy of development for the state has to address these issues in their entirety as well as in terms of their local specificities.

Table 8.1
Human Development Indicators

States	Per capita NSDP 1998–99	Per capita Consumption Expenditure	HDI (1991)	HPI (1991)	Gender Disparity Index (1991)
Arunachal Pradesh	12335 (4)	672.31 (3)	0.328 (8)	47.40 (2)	0.776
Assam	8826 (8)	473.42 (8)	0.348 (7)	46.29 (3)	0.576
Manipur	10504 (6)	596.36 (5)	0.536 (2)	39.82 (6)	0.815
Meghalaya	11090 (5)	639.13 (4)	0.365 (6)	49.41 (1)	0.807
Mizoram	13479 (1)	935.53 (2)	0.548 (1)	26.47 (8)	0.770
Nagaland	12408 (3)	1005.99 (1)	0.486 (3)	41.30 (5)	0.729
Sikkim	12645 (2)	559.97 (7)	0.425 (4)	38.59 (7)	0.647
Tripura	9613 (7)	589.50 (6)	0.389 (5)	42.71 (4)	0.531
All-India	14395	590.98	0.381	37.42	0.676

Source: Planning Commission, Government of India 2002.

Table 8.2
Educational Attainments

States	Literacy Rate 2001	Urban-Rural gap in literacy 2001	Gender gap in literacy 2001	Enrolment ratio for age group 6 to below 11 years 1991	Drop-out rates in classes I–IV 1998–99 (p)	No of primary schools per thousand population (1997–98)
Arunachal Pradesh	54.74 (8)	30.48 (1)	19.83 (1)	61.5 (7)	46.89 (5)	8.21 (5)
Assam	64.28 (6)	24.84 (3)	15.9 0(4)	63.4 (6)	41.56 (6)	8.62 (4)
Manipur	68.87 (4)	14.71 (8)	18.17 (2)	71.9 (4)	52.59 (2)	8.69 (3)
Meghalaya	63.31 (7)	30.12 (2)	5.73 (7)	55.4 (8)	62.44 (1)	13.38 (1)
Mizoram	88.49 (1)	15.89 (7)	4.56 (8)	77.6 (1)	51.82 (4)	11.17 (2)
Nagaland	67.11 (5)	22.96 (4)	9.85 (6)	70.0 (5)	35.94 (8)	6.80 (6)
Sikkim	69.68 (3)	17.15 (6)	15.27 (5)	74.9 (2)	41.30 (7)	6.72 (7)
Tripura	73.66 (2)	19.28 (5)	16.06 (3)	73.2 (3)	51.95 (3)	4.14 (8)
All-India	65.20	20.85	21.61	62.1	39.58	5.04

Source: Planning Commission, Government of India 2002.

Table 8.3
Health Status of the Population

States	IMR	Under 5 Mortality Rates	Percentage of Women with Anaemia
Arunachal Praesh	63.1	98.1	62.5
Assam	69.5	89.5	69.7
Manipur	37.0	56.1	28.9
Meghalaya	89.0	122.0	63.3
Mizoram	37.0	54.7	48.0
Nagaland	42.1	63.8	38.4
Sikkim	43.9	71.0	61.1
Tripura	–	–	59.4
All India	67.6	94.9	51.8

Source: National Family Health Survey-II.

ECONOMIC DEVELOPMENT AND GENDER RELATIONS

It is extremely difficult to make generalisations regarding the position of women in Arunachal Pradesh and the changes in this, primarily because of two reasons: first, given the extraordinary diversity in the socio-economic conditions, institutional arrangements and cultural ethos of the women belonging to different tribes and sub-tribes of the state, and the paucity of in-depth studies on various aspects of gender relations, it is very difficult to arrive at valid conclusions on the basis of the few variables for which reliable estimates are available. Second, in the absence of earlier benchmarks, it is difficult to understand the magnitude and the processes of change.[2] However, we have attempted to discuss a few indicators of women's well-being and empowerment to point out that irrespective of the initial conditions of women in the traditional society, the development process has created conditions under which women have not only been able to participate and utilise the emerging opportunities, but also face new hurdles in various spheres of the rapidly changing socio-economic milieu. The intention is not to deny the significant progress made by women in various fields, but to recognise the significant gaps that remain to be bridged. The following analysis, based largely on the available secondary data, is far from exhaustive, but is intended to provide a preliminary insight into the complexities of the transition process in terms of its relationship with gender relations in the state.

We start with a discussion on the sex ratio. A lower sex ratio typically represents a lower social status of women, which creates conditions for discrimination at various levels. Dreze and Sen (1995) feel that it also captures the extent of intra-household gender inequalities. Although the sharp decline in the sex ratio in India has been a cause for concern, at a disaggregated level there are significant regional variations. Regions with a higher percentage of Scheduled Tribe (ST) populations are typically found to have a higher sex ratio, reflecting a lesser degree of gender discrimination (Rustagi 2000). The sex ratio, which declined from 862 to 859 between 1981 and 1991, increased to 893 in 2001. The sex ratio, however, cannot be taken as a reliable measure of women's well-being because of the discrepancies arising out of in-migration. In order to isolate the effects of migration, if we separately consider the sex ratio among the ST population, which largely consists of the indigenous population, a steady decline is noticed from 1,013 in 1961 to 998 in 1991, although it has increased to 1,003 in 2001 (Table 8.4). While sex-selective migration may have contributed to the overall low sex ratio in the state, the child sex ratio (CSR), which is less likely to be affected by migration has also registered a sharp decline from 982 to 964 between 1991 and 2001. This decline has been sharper in rural areas than in the urban areas. Notably, the CSR in

Table 8.4
Sex Ratio in Arunachal Pradesh: 1961–2001

| Year | All Population | | | S.T. Population | | |
	Total	Rural	Urban	Total	Rural	Urban
1961	894	894	–	1013	1013	–
1971	861	881	457	1007	1009	765
1981	862	881	629	1005	1010	803
1991	859	880	728	998	1004	921
2001	893	914	819	1003	1000	1020

Source: Census of India: Various Years.
Note: In 1961 there was no urban centre in the state.

Arunachal declined by 18 points during 1991–2001, which is the same as the fall at the all-India level.[3] It is also significant that in 1991, the CSR among the ST population was 976, which was lower than that for all social groups. At a disaggregated level, only Papum Pare, Lower Subansiri and Upper Siang (that is, three of the 13 districts in Arunachal) have experienced an increase in CSR during the last decade (Table 8.5). Descriptively speaking, the decline in the overall sex ratio among the ST population during 1961–91 can be explained in terms of gender gaps in education and income: women are less literate and have less command over resources than men, and probably because of gender inequalities in terms of access to emerging opportunities, the sex ratio among the ST population declined during a period of rapid economic growth and transformation.[4] However, the low child sex ratio in the tribal population cannot be explained in terms of differential literacy or income. The only plausible explanation, then, can be in terms of discrimination against female children. Many studies, however, point out that discrimination against female children is relatively less severe in predominantly tribal societies. The low and falling CSR in Arunachal Pradesh thus needs further investigation. It also explains the difficulties in arriving at conclusions regarding the condition of women on the basis of a few summary measures, in a state characterised by an extraordinary level of socio-cultural diversity as well as unevenness in the process of development.

In 2001, the Female Work Participation Rate (FWPR) in Arunachal Pradesh was 36.54 compared to the national average of 25.63. Urban FWPR has registered a steady increase in the state even as the overall FWPR has consistently declined in the past decades, although the decline of 0.95

Table 8.5

District-wise Child Sex Ratio in Arunachal Pradesh: 1991–2001

Districts	1991			2001		
	T	R	U	T	R	U
Tawang	965	965	NA	948	948	948
West Kameng	970	973	932	955	956	952
East Kameng	1036	1036	NA	1035	1027	1058
Papum Pare	934	942	924	978	967	990
Lower Subansiri	970	978	947	1005	1013	945
Upper Subansiri	1005	1005	NA	985	985	985
West Siang	997	1008	921	950	949	953
East Siang	1008	1007	1009	958	945	1003
Upper Siang	967	967	NA	1010	1010	NA
Dibang Valley	994	1008	906	946	947	939
Lohit	968	980	912	933	927	966
Changlang	987	987	NA	954	958	912
Tirap	946	940	1054	941	933	1000
Arunachal Pradesh	982	986	946	964	960	980

Source: 1991—District Census Handbooks, Census of India, 1991, Series-3, Arunachal Pradesh, Part XII-A&B; 2001—Provisional Population Totals, Paper-2 of 2001, Census of India 2001, Series-13, Arunachal Pradesh.

Note: NA implies that there was no urban population in the district.

was not very significant during 1991–2001 (Table 8.6). In 2001, FWPR in the districts was found to be negatively correlated with the female literacy rate and the percentage of the urban population to the total population, but positively correlated with the proportion of the ST population in the total population. During 1991–2001, the age-specific WPR of the 15–19 age group declined by close to 11 percentage points, compared to 2.9 for the 15–59 age group. There could be various factors behind the decline in work participation among relatively younger females, particularly in the rural areas, ranging from expansion of educational opportunities to decline in *jhum* (shifting/slash-and-burn) cultivation and the changing gender distribution of work in families.

Another significant dimension of women's work in Arunachal Pradesh is the relatively high proportion of marginal workers among the female workers.[5] In 2001, 8.13 per cent of the total female workers were marginal workers, while among the males the percentage was only 4.60. Of the total marginal workers in the state, 61.23 per cent were females in 2001. The relatively higher proportion of females among marginal workers signifies the additional constraints women face while entering 'productive'

Table 8.6

Work Participation Rates in Arunachal Pradesh: 1971–2001 (percentages)

		1971	*1981*	*1991*	*2001*
All Populations	Male	63.14	58.63	53.76	50.69
	Female	51.28	45.67	37.49	36.45
	Total	57.65	52.63	46.24	43.97
Rural	Male	62.78	58.50	53.69	51.13
	Female	52.27	47.64	40.86	41.33
	Total	57.88	53.42	47.69	46.47
Urban	Male	70.32	60.24	54.18	48.99
	Female	10.58	11.62	11.95	16.69
	Total	51.57	41.47	36.39	34.19

Source: Census of India, 2001, Series-13, Arunachal Pradesh, Provisional Population Totals, Paper-3 of 2001.

Note: Figures for 2001 are based on provisional population totals.

work, as well as the patterns of household risk management where women's labour serves as the 'buffer' during bad times to meet unexpected shortfalls in consumption or earnings.

In terms of occupational structure, although women have been gradually moving out of agriculture and allied activities, they lag behind men in the extent of shifts to the secondary and tertiary sectors. In 1971, among the total male main workers, 68.78 per cent were engaged in the primary sector; only 0.66 per cent were working in the secondary sector; and the rest, 30.56 per cent, were in the service sector. By 1991, the share of male workers in the primary sector had come down to 54.60 per cent, but had risen to 12.34 per cent in the secondary sector and to 33.06 per cent in the tertiary sector. In contrast, the distribution of female workers in different sectors in 1971 was 97.11 per cent, 0.14 per cent and 2.75 per cent in the primary, secondary and tertiary sectors respectively. In 1991, 89.93 per cent of female main workers were still engaged in the primary, 2.21 per cent in the secondary and 7.87 per cent in the tertiary sectors. Preliminary estimates from the 2001 Census data suggests that the percentage of total female main workers engaged in the primary sector continues to remain as high as 81.70 per cent in the state, although their share in the service sector has gone up to nearly 13 per cent (Table 8.7). Thus by all counts, the occupational diversification of women workers in the state has lagged behind that of men. Even when they are employed in non-agricultural occupations, particularly in the government services, a higher proportion of women workers are to be found in the lowest ranks of the job hierarchy.

Table 8.7

Sectoral Distribution of Industries in Arunachal Pradesh: 1971–2001

Areas		Primary				Secondary				Tertiary			
		1971	1981	1991	2001	1971	1981	1991	2001	1971	1981	1991	2001
Total	M	68.8	63.21	54.6	51.54	0.65	13.13	12.3	14.54	30.56	23.7	33.06	33.93
	F	97.1	95.11	89.9	81.70	0.14	2	2.21	5.74	2.74	2.89	7.87	12.55
	T	80.4	75.28	67.4	62.27	0.44	8.92	8.66	11.41	19.12	15.8	23.9	26.32
Rural	M	72.3	68	62.3	64.59	0.55	11.85	11.1	12.18	27.15	20.2	26.57	23.23
	F	97.4	96.1	92.6	89.04	0.11	1.74	1.87	4.47	2.5	2.16	5.52	6.49
	T	82.9	79.08	74.1	74.14	0.36	7.87	7.5	9.17	16.72	13.1	18.37	16.69
Urban	M	5.39	6.75	6.72	6.70	2.58	28.25	20.1	22.63	92.03	65	73.18	70.67
	F	46	30.6	22.5	15.40	5.75	18.93	10.7	17.22	48.26	50.5	66.85	67.39
	T	8.01	9.25	8.86	8.40	2.78	27.27	18.8	21.57	89.21	63.5	72.32	70.03

Source: Census of India, various years.

Note: The figures for 2001 are based on provisional estimates.

While the share of female workers in the service sector has expanded more than that of male workers during 1971–2001, this growth has also been accompanied by a ghettoisation of women workers in the lowest-paid jobs.[6] In recent years, women belonging to indigenous tribal communities have started entering the urban informal markets in limited numbers, mainly in petty trading and in hotels and restaurants (Upadhyay 2005).

Access to formal education has been among the most important determinants of social mobility in the state. The gender gap in educational attainment clearly reveals the emerging disparity between males and females in the changing socio-economic milieu. The female literacy rate for Arunachal Pradesh was only 43.53 per cent according to the 2001 Census, much lower than the national average of 53.70 per cent. Arunachal has made rapid progress in raising female literacy from only 14.02 per cent in 1981 to 43.5 per cent in 2001; however, the female literacy rate in rural areas is as low as 36.90 per cent and the rural-urban gap in female literacy continues to be very high.[7] Between 1981 and 1991, literacy among the female ST population went up from 7.31 to 24.94 per cent, whereas the total adult female literacy rate in the state rose from 11.01 to 23.59 per cent. In rural Arunachal Pradesh, however, female literacy in 1981 was only 19.13 per cent, much below that of other northeastern states. Although Arunachal has made significant progress in the past, its performance in comparative terms has not been very impressive. Considerable inter-district variations exist in female literacy rates, from 60.4 per cent in Papum Pare to 28.8 per cent in Tirap, and 28.6 per cent in East Kameng. The gender gap in literacy in Arunachal Pradesh as per the 2001 Census is 20.3 percentage points, lower than the national average of 21.61 (Table 8.8).[8] The gap between male and female literacy rates in the state declined very slowly during 1981–2001. In rural areas, the gender gap in literacy is sharper than that in urban areas, remaining at 20 per cent during the past two decades. This needs to be addressed in all future initiatives.

According to the 1991 Census, the percentage of working children in the age group of five to 14 years was marginally higher in Arunachal Pradesh (5.7 per cent) compared to the national average (5.4 per cent), but had declined from 1981, when it was at 11.3 per cent. The percentage of working girl children continued to remain higher than that of boys in both rural and urban areas. In 1991, 6.7 per cent of girls and 4.6 per cent of the boys were working, as against 13.2 per cent of girls and 9.5 per

Table 8.8

District-wise Gender Gap in Literacy in Arunachal Pradesh: 1991–2001

	Gender Gap in Literacy Rate	
Districts	1991	2001
Tawang	35.82	30.28
West Kameng	19.81	22.83
East Kameng	23.67	23.77
Papum Pare	22.47	16.92
Lower Subansiri	17.55	17.36
Upper Subansiri	20.34	18.85
West Siang	18.01	15.07
East Siang	16.74	16.00
Upper Siang	21.97	19.92
Dibang Valley	22.64	18.55
Lohit	22.81	21.20
Changlang	24.80	22.90
Tirap	24.92	24.52
Arunachal Pradesh	21.76	20.30

Source: Census of India, 2001, Final Population Totals, 2001.
Notes: (i) Literacy rate is the percentage of literates to total population aged 7 years and
above.
(ii) Adult Literacy Rate has been estimated as percentage of literates among the
15+ population.

cent of boys in 1981. The incidence of girl child workers was considerably
higher in rural areas than in urban areas of the state. In comparative
terms, the percentage of working girl children was higher than in any
other northeastern state, with the exception of Meghalaya and Mizoram.
The percentage of working girls in the 5–14 age group is clearly not an
adequate measure of the extent of the prevalence of child labour, but it
does indicate that girls face significant disadvantages at a very early stage
in their lives. Special attention has to be given to the additional constraints
faced by girl child workers in programmes aimed at the elimination of
child labour.

According to the *National Family Health Survey* (*NFHS*)-II (IIPS and
ORC Macro 2002), 18.3 per cent of children in the age group 6–14 years
were not enrolled in school—14.1 per cent of the boys and 22.7 per cent
of the girls. In the age group 6–10 years, the gender gap in school attendance was even wider. Among the boys who never attended schools, the
distance of the school from their homes was the most important reason,
followed by 'not having interest in studies'. Among the girls the most

important reasons were: being required to do household work (30.8 per cent), schools too far away (16.1 per cent) and the cost of education (10.5 per cent). Only 0.7 per cent boys considered education unnecessary, compared to 5.6 per cent girls. A higher percentage of girls cited sibling care as the main reason for not joining schools. Marriage was cited to be the main reason for discontinuing education in the case of 13 per cent of out-of-school girls.

In Arunachal Pradesh, the educational infrastructure continues to be inadequate, but its expansion over the past three decades or so has been impressive. As a result, girls today have better access to schooling than they had in the past. Between 1981 and 1991, the enrolment ratio among girls aged 6–11 went up from 24.1 to 33.4 per cent, while among those aged 11–14 it improved from 28.5 to 53.7 per cent (Planning Commission 2002). However, girls continue to have comparatively less access to higher education.[9] Improvements in enrolment do not guarantee access to adequate levels of education. The drop-out rates in relatively underdeveloped regions are very high, more so in the case of girls. The drop-out rate in Classes I–V for girls in Arunachal Pradesh has come down substantially from 72.2 per cent in 1981–82 to 45.10 per cent in 1998–99. This is still higher than the national average, but unlike in many other states, the drop-out rate for girls has been less than that for boys. Similarly, for girls the drop-out rate in Classes I–VIII has reduced from 83.60 per cent in 1981–82 to 65.86 per cent in 1998–99. However, in Classes I–X, girls in the state have a higher drop-out rate than boys.[10] This seems to indicate that the pressure on girls to drop out of school is especially high after they reach middle school.

There is some evidence to show that unlike in many other parts of India, the intra-family distribution of food and nutrition in Arunachal Pradesh does not show any systematic gender bias. According to the India Nutrition Profile (1998), the average consumption of foodstuffs in Arunachal was nearly the same among boys and girls, except in the age group 4–6 years, where the average consumption was lower among girls for all foods except pulses. Among adults, the average consumption was similar among males and females. While the average intake of cereals, green leafy vegetables, roots and tubers, and other vegetables were above the suggested levels of a balanced diet for all age groups, the intake of pulses, milk and its products, fat and oils, as well as sugar were below the mandatory level. The percentage of severely undernourished children was found to be marginally higher among girls than boys, but the percentage of moderately malnourished children was higher in the case of boys.[11] Thus, so far as the overall nutritional status is concerned, no serious gender discrimination was found. A crucial aspect of the food consumption pattern in the state is the high average consumption of leafy vegetables, roots and tubers as well as fish and meat, not only in comparison with the national averages but also compared with the neighbouring states. A substantial proportion of these items are collected from forests and jhum fields. Women's nutritional status is related to their participation in forest-related activities and access to forest resources. Women's access to forests and other Common Property Resources (CPR) is intrinsically linked to their micro-level strategies for risk minimisation, mutual support and solidarity in a high-risk ecological-economic context. Along with the gradual privatisation of these resources, the food and nutrition security prospects of households in general and the access of women and girls to food and nutrition in particular need to be carefully monitored in the future. An analysis of the *NFHS-II* data suggests that, contrary to the findings in other parts of India, in the northeastern region, female children have a nutritional edge over male children (Rama Rao et al. 2004).

Notwithstanding the significant efforts that have gone into establishing the modern health care system in the state, it must be emphasised that the access of women in general and that of rural and poor women in particular remains very low in comparison with the national average. According to the *NFHS-II*, only 40.5 per cent of mothers received three ante-natal check-ups and 34 per cent of births were assisted by trained personnel. There is a great deal of rural-urban disparity as well as a high concentration of these services in the few urban, administrative centres.

Women's Participation in Household Decision-making

The overwhelming dominance of the patriarchal value-system denies effective rights of participation to women in various spheres. Structural inequalities in terms of relative deprivations in earnings, education, employability and overall well-being create strong barriers to the informed and effective participation of women in decision-making, so far as the majority of the women are concerned. Moreover, the internalisation of patriarchal values by women themselves, through the processes of social-isation and other means, makes the articulation of women's independent voices more problematic and difficult. In societies facing the challenges of modernisation and possible integration into other dominant cultures, there is generally a strong emphasis on preserving a real or imagined 'pure', 'indigenous' culture. In such sharply polarised discourses on identity and culture, women's rights and concerns are often relegated to the background.

It is difficult to explain the status and position of women in Arunachal Pradesh in general terms. Given the substantial influence of traditional mores, community institutions and regionally differentiated socio-cultural practices, there are significant variations in the status of women within the indigenous communities. Traditional social differentiations as well as newly emerging economic differentiations within these communities also impact on the position of women from different strata. In addition, migrations from different parts of the country, education, mass entertain-ment, media exposure and external cultural influences have been shaping gender relations in the changing social milieu.

In the traditional value system of the communities, the relative suprem-acy of adults in general and male adults in particular vis-à-vis children was near universal. Among some of the indigenous communities of Arunachal Pradesh, experienced old adults commanded greater respect and played a decisive role in decision-making. The changing values, disintegration of old family systems and differences in the worldview of the young and the old have, in varying forms and degrees, been changing the balance of power and authority within households and clans.

So far as gender differences in intra-family decision-making are con-cerned, any generalisation about the entire state, given the degree of inter-community heterogeneity, is bound to be partial. Gender relations in many migrant families, though not completely immune from the influences of the general social milieu of the state, are largely governed by the social conditions of the state or country of their origin as well as by their relative social position in terms of a caste-class hierarchy within the original society. Among the indigenous communities, too, there is a great deal of difference in the relative position of women in decision-making, though by and large it is argued that women enjoy greater autonomy in tribal commu-nities. It is, however, equally important to note that in some communities in Arunachal Pradesh, male dominance is quite high. Within those communities where women have some control over household decision-making, this participation is almost always within well-defined and differentiated spheres of action and socially sanctioned parameters. The data generated by *NFHS-II* has to some extent captured these complexities.

In comparison to other parts of India, women in Arunachal Pradesh seem to enjoy greater freedom in terms of mobility and decision-making in some spheres. According to the *NFHS-II*, among the female respondents, 84.1 per cent decide what items to cook, but when it comes to obtaining health care for themselves, only 32.1 per cent of women take the decision alone and 35.9 per cent do so along with their husbands. So far as decisions regarding purchasing jewellery or other major household items are concerned, only 15.7 per cent decide on their own, while 56.8 per cent do so along with their husbands. While 22.5 per cent of women take their own decisions about visiting and staying with their parents or siblings, 49.1 per cent decide along with their husbands, and for 22.2 per cent the decision lies exclusively with their husbands. Among women who earn cash incomes, 46.2 per cent take decisions on their own about how to spend it, while 38.9 per cent decide with their husbands and 13.6 per cent have no freedom to decide how they would spend their own earnings. The survey also reveals that 46.8 per cent women do not need any permission to visit markets, 53.7 per cent do not need any permission to visit friends or relatives and 78.6 per cent have some access to money. There is no consistent rural-urban divide: while more rural women participate in decisions about cooking and personal health care, a comparatively higher proportion of urban women participate in decisions about purchasing jewellery or staying with parents or siblings. Urban women also have greater access to money. It is interesting to note that educated women and those having a high standard of living have less freedom of mobility, although they have comparatively greater access to money than illiterate and poor women.

Political Participation of Women in Arunachal Pradesh

Throughout the world, in varying forms and degrees, there exists a considerable gap between men and women in terms of their access to political power. However, as the Human Development Report (UNDP 1995) points out, significant progress has been made towards greater political participation of women at various levels. The need for political reforms to provide greater access to women in the decision-making process can hardly be overstressed. Gender equality cannot be achieved through a set of policies and programmes alone; more fundamentally, it calls for a re-structuring of the political, economic and socio-cultural goals and priorities. Given the unequal distribution of resources and opportunities between the sexes, women's empowerment has to be assigned a central place in the agenda of social transformation.

Over a span of less than 50 years, the road to parliamentary democracy in Arunachal Pradesh has been more or less smooth.[12] Democratic political processes, institutions and practices have been gradually accepted by the tribal communities, but the establishment of formal institutions of liberal democracy has not been smooth or uniform within various parts of the state. The capture of political processes by the elite has been one of the fundamental aspects of governance in Arunachal Pradesh (Mishra and Upadhyay 2004). In the post-Independence period, the most crucial aspect of political development that needs pressing attention is the near complete marginalisation of women in politics.

At present, there are no women representatives either in the Parliament or in the Arunachal Pradesh legislature. In the past, the share of women members in the Legislative Assembly has never exceeded 5 per cent. The highest number of women members in the 60-member Assembly has only been three. No woman member has ever been elected to the Lok Sabha. In the last 25 years, there was only one woman Member of Parliament from the state who was elected to the Rajya Sabha. Thus, in terms of repre-sentation in the formal structures of political power, women in Arunachal Pradesh remain completely marginalised.

Even today at the grassroots level, it is the traditional village chief and the village councils that play a crucial role in conflict resolution and ad-ministration of justice. These institutions are considered democratic and participatory in spite of the considerable diversity in their power, areas of operation and modes of decision-making. Women are hardly al-lowed to play any role in these traditional institutions, although in recent years there have been some attempts to provide them some space. The percentage of women village-chiefs was only 1.13 per cent in the state. In eight districts (out of 13), there was not a single woman village-chief. The share of women village-chiefs was highest in Dibang Valley and that was only 2.20 per cent. However, the introduction of the three-tier Panchayati Raj system, along with 33 per cent reservations for women, has altered women's participation in grassroots-level political institutions. For the state as a whole, women's shares at the village, intermediate and district panchayat levels were 39.60, 34.99, and 33.82 per cent, respectively, in the panchayat elections of 2003.[13] Reservation of seats for women in decentralised institutions of governance may play a catalytic role in gradually eliminating gender bias in the sharing of political power in the state.

Women's share in top managerial and professional positions is considered one of the indicators of their empowerment. Unfortunately, we do not have any data on the relative shares of males and females at such top positions. Anecdotal evidence suggests that there is hardly any presence of women at these apex decision-making levels. Given the low levels of industrialisation and the thin presence of the private corporate sector in Arunachal, the share of women in top-level decision-making can be assessed indirectly by looking at their share at the top levels of the bureaucracy. In the top levels of civil administration, women's share was found to be only 6.66 per cent in 2000–01 (Upadhyay and Mishra 2005).

Violence against Women

Economic prosperity and human well-being require efficient, just and non-discriminatory rule enforcement and monitoring mechanisms. One of the key determinants of a healthy and just social order is its treatment of vulnerable social groups and individuals. Increasingly, the significance of human security[14] is being stressed as a key element of human development, particularly in the context of conflict-ridden societies.

Crimes against women are among the most traumatising and politically explosive subjects in India. In the political mobilisations of (and against) social groups, cruelty against women has been used as a forceful political weapon; so, women are not just victims of individual acts of violence. Violence against women significantly affects various aspects of their overall well-being, such as self-esteem, mobility, psychological and emotional capabilities, as well as the freedom to lead a normal and healthy life. Conventional development indicators, even the human development ones, have been criticised for their neglect of this aspect of women's well-being (Hirway and Mahadevia 1996). Although the degrees and nature of violence directed against women vary across regions, classes and cultures, it is important to note that often women feel more insecure in cities that are the most developed and have good communications.

There are various problems in quantifying the extent of violence directed against women. First, for a variety of reasons, such as the attached social stigma, distrust in legal mechanisms, fear of retaliation, et cetera, most crimes against women go unreported. Second, it is often seen that some forms of violence are justified within the structure of socially-sanctioned value systems, beliefs and practices. Many of these forms of violence go unnoticed and are scarcely recognised as crimes or violence. Domestic violence, for example, is rarely treated as a crime, even by the victims themselves. According to *NFHS-II* data, it has been found that domestic violence is widespread even in the northeastern states. The study reveals that in Arunachal Pradesh, of the total respondents, 61.5 per cent had been beaten or physically mistreated at least once in the past 12 months, while 13.1 per cent had been beaten many times during that period. Tolerance and experience of domestic violence act as significant barriers to women's empowerment.

In Arunachal Pradesh, traditional community laws and institutions continue to play a vital role in conflict resolution and administration of justice at the village level.[15] The simultaneous existence, overlapping spheres of action and fuzzy boundaries between the formal and informal legal frameworks make the situation all the more complex. The incidence of both reported crimes and crimes against women are by and large on the rise. The share of crimes against women has gone up from less than 5 per cent of total crimes in the early 1990s to more than 6 per cent during 1998–2002. The distribution of crimes against women across districts is highly skewed: West Siang reported 20 per cent, East Siang 15.25 per cent and Papum Pare 14.83 per cent. In 2000–02, crimes against women, as a proportion of the total crimes, was highest in East Siang, closely followed by West Siang and lowest in West Kameng. When we estimate the rate of crimes against women, that is, the number of reported crimes directed against women per 10,000 population, West Siang followed by East Siang and Dibang Valley have the highest crime rate, and West Kameng the lowest (Table 8.9).

Table 8.9
Crimes Against Women: 2000–2002

Districts	As % of Total Crime	Per 10,000 Population
Tawang	8.97	1.103
West Kameng	2.80	0.402
East Kameng	8.54	1.985
Papum Pare	4.92	1.916
Lower Subansiri	6.43	1.091
Upper Subansiri	6.11	1.504
West Siang	9.59	2.987
East Siang	9.97	2.748
Upper Siang	8.02	1.298
Dibang Valley	8.53	2.142
Lohit	5.11	0.906
Changlang	4.24	0.558
Tirap	3.53	0.465
Arunachal Pradesh	6.89	1.595

Source: The Director General of Police, Government of Arunachal Pradesh, Itanagar.
Note: Calculations are based on average of three years—2000, 2001 and 2002.

It is difficult to draw conclusions regarding the security of women on the basis of these official statistics, partly because they may reflect a trend towards higher *reporting* of crimes rather than higher *incidence*, as the legal and policing infrastructure in the state is at an early stage of development. When we look at the composition of crimes against women during 2000–02, we find that 41.74 per cent of the total cases were of molestation, 28.18 per cent concerned kidnapping and 22.67 per cent rape; cruelty by husbands and relatives accounted for 6.35 per cent. It may be noted that the nature of rape, according to NGO activists, has undergone a change in Arunachal Pradesh. In the past, there were many cases of rape in the form of forced marriages, but in recent years, as elsewhere, rape is a brutal assault on women.

Women typically become easy targets of violence in areas of prolonged and chronic conflicts. In those parts of the state where there has been a recent upsurge in insurgency, women face constraints not only in terms of violence but also in terms of a denial of opportunities and options, which would otherwise have been available to them under normal circumstances.[16] That there has been no documentation of the condition and sufferings of women in these districts points to the fact that these violent conflicts have seldom been seen through the eyes of the victims, particularly women, even in the mass media and academic discourses.

Two major steps need to be taken urgently by the government and civil society in Arunachal Pradesh to reduce crimes against women. First, concrete steps have to be taken to prevent the occurrence of such crimes by making policing and law enforcement more responsive and accountable in both rural and urban areas. Second, awareness-building and gender-sensitisation campaigns are necessary both for law enforcing agencies and the general public in order to reduce the number of unreported crimes against women. There is also a need to prepare a more comprehensive and gender-sensitive database of the complaints lodged and actions taken on harassment of women by the formal and informal institutions.

THE CRISIS OF GOVERNANCE: MANIFESTATIONS AND CHALLENGES

For a long time, the underdevelopment of the northeastern region as whole has been seen in terms of a real or perceived lack of adequate central assistance to the region. Some scholars have described the Northeast as an internal colony of the Indian state. Partly in response to such popular discontent, successive central governments have been announcing large financial packages for individual states, as well as for the whole region. However, it is being widely recognised that such financial packages, in the absence of an appropriate institutional strategy for their implementation and monitoring, has not only resulted in powerful individuals and groups siphoning off the funds but has also discredited the Indian state in the eyes of the public. Against this backdrop, there is an urgent need to make governance transparent, accountable and non-discriminatory (Mahbul ul Haq Human Development Centre 1999).

As already discussed, Arunachal Pradesh has undergone a transition to electoral democracy in a comparatively short period. As elsewhere in the developing areas, and particularly in tribal areas, the establishment of formal institutions of liberal democracy has not been smooth and uniform in all parts of the state. Given the absence of insurgency and militancy, a high level of participation in elections and a smooth change of governments, it would probably be correct to conclude that democratic processes and institutions have taken firm root in Arunachal Pradesh. Nevertheless, many key aspects of good governance are clearly absent. Some of these problems are common to all developing societies; a few others are generally found in almost all states in the Northeast, while some others are unique to Arunachal. We shall argue that the specificities of mal-governance, as outlined below, have profound implications for the survival and dignity of marginalised groups, including women.

Property Rights

First and foremost, it is important to point out that some fundamental aspects of the market-enabling role of the state, that is, demarcation and safeguarding of property rights, and an efficient contract-enforcement mechanism, are not being given due importance. Given the heterogeneity of property right formations in Arunachal, the transition to private pro-perty rights has not been complete; but more importantly, the privatisa-tion of communally held property has, by and large, proceeded without any legal backing of the state. In this *informal* transition to private property rights over land and forests, for example, one section of the population has been able to use the institutional vacuum to their advantage. They have acquired wealth in the form of urban land, land for plantation and cultivation purposes, or have been able to use common village resources like forests for private benefits (Mishra 2001). This inadequate demarca-tion, recognition and safeguarding of communal property has ultimately resulted in an increasing concentration of income and wealth, as well as a weakening of the traditional institutional mechanisms.

Contract Enforcement

The contract enforcement mechanism in Arunachal is weak not only be-cause of a weak administrative and policing apparatus but also because the effective separation of the executive and the judiciary has not yet been completed. Even in the state capital Itanagar, the government has been unable to stop mass encroachment on government land. This generally perceived weakness of the government in everyday activities has some obvious implications for marginalised and exploited groups, particularly in terms of their fallback positions and strategies to counter discrimin-ation. Since it is known that the state apparatus would not be interested in or capable of enforcing the contracts, the weaker parties, which, depending on the circumstances, may include a wide category of people from hapless migrant labourers or women to outside businessmen, tend to either surrender before the demands of the stronger parties or look to various non-state agencies, including militant outfits, civil society institutions, powerful individuals, surrendered militants and even traditional institutions, for dispute settlement.

Corruption

Given the negligible presence of the industrial sector and the low levels of development of private enterprises, access to government jobs and contracts are the only means to a better living standard. The overwhelming dominance of the government sector, along with other factors, has created a thoroughly unproductive rent-seeking economy in the state. The political economy of development administration can perhaps be best described as a *distributional coalition* of varied and competing interests. Political entrepreneurs routinely distribute favours, like contracts, as a means to secure support bases or create channels of patronage. The small size of the electorate, particularly in assembly constituencies, puts extra pressure on politicians to cater to the demands of the people. In democracies, such a situation should encourage accountability to the citizens. However, since accountability structures and rule-enforcement mechanisms are weak, politicians find it convenient to garner support by distributing favours. At times the relatively easy access of ordinary people to ministers and political leaders gives the impression of an egalitarian political culture in the state. While that may sometimes be so, primarily because the traditional bonds of community and fellow-feeling have not been erased altogether, in many cases such a show of loyalty is cosmetic rather than substantial. Cementing and sustaining such bonds requires some investment in cash and kind on the part of the politicians, but instead of making governance transparent, such transactions make corruption acceptable and hence weaken the collective rights of the people. Over a period of time, along with the well-known problems of 'government failure', corruption in general and the appropriation of public resources for private benefits in particular have become the hallmark of government-sponsored schemes. The substantial control exercised by a well-coordinated and powerful group of elites who routinely speak on behalf of their community makes any general movement against corruption, or corrupt members of the group, extremely difficult because such attacks could be seen as an attack on the community and because of which the community is expected to defend such individuals and their actions.

Fiscal Accountability and Discipline

The perpetual financial dependence on the central government has several implications for governance in Arunachal Pradesh. First, the inability to mobilise resources has meant that many of the developmental programmes have not been conceived at the state level. Inadequate attention to local specificities and peculiarities in the designing and implementation of centrally-sponsored schemes has not only resulted in the failure of these programmes but has also reduced the faith of the people in the government machinery. Second, the central and the state governments have paid inadequate attention to monitoring the spending of public money. Although development expenditure constituted 72.98 per cent of the total public expenditure in 1998–99 in Arunachal (Planning Commission 2002: 290), a lack of transparency and ineffective monitoring, coupled with the politics of populism, has resulted in mounting dead-weight losses and an ever expanding administrative apparatus. Another aspect of the problem is the popular misconception of government activities as 'job creation' activities rather than developmental initiatives.

Lack of Credible Opposition

Until recently, electoral politics has been characterised by the dominance of a single political party. The tendency of the members of opposition parties to join the ruling party and the en masse switching of loyalties has ensured that there has been virtually no opposition to question and scrutinise the decisions of the ruling party. If state-funded development initiatives have resulted in the unholy nexus between politicians, bureaucrats and businessmen, the absence of a strong opposition and public scrutiny has strengthened the black economy of corruption. For all practical purposes, the government-sponsored schemes have been treated as a mechanism for generating private benefits at the cost of the public.

Freedom of Press

A key requirement for ensuring accountability and transparency in governance is the presence of a free and fair press or mass media. In Arunachal Pradesh, the number, circulation and impact of the mass media in general and the print media in particular are severely limited. However, the existing newspapers have not been able to act objectively and without fear. There have been frequent cases of intimidation, physical attacks and violence directed against the media by powerful organisations. This has seriously undermined the freedom of the press and has also weakened the scope for democratic accountability and transparency.

Community Participation

In relation to the much talked about question of 'community participation in governance', Arunachal Pradesh provides a rather unusual case where the emphasis (or at least the rhetoric) on integrating the community with administration predates the current emphasis on the term in the overall framework of neo-liberal reforms. Indeed, it was one of the key elements in the Nehru-Elwin framework for tribal development, particularly in the erstwhile North-East Frontier Agency (NEFA). The framework was unambiguous in its emphasis on the democratic content of traditional institutions and the need to strengthen these institutions rather than replacing them with new, alien structures (Elwin 1957). To what extent was the invocation of community participation in development matched by the effective participation in governance? This is, of course, a pertinent question. It is important also to note that without democratising community-based institutions, in an increasingly differentiated and fragmented socio-economic milieu, community participation may just result in the participation of the elite in the name of peoples' participation. In the absence of adequate mechanisms for democratic accountability, the 'pluralisation' of the state (in the sense of increasing the role of non-state entities in the process of decision-making and implementation of developmental programmes) is not always an unmixed blessing.

Democratic Governance and the Politics of Identity

A key aspect of the development process in the entire Northeast is the complex interrelationship between the crisis of identity, security and underdevelopment (Madhab 1999). The politics of identity and difference has an overwhelming significance in this multi-ethnic region (Fernandes 1999; Gohain 1996). Without venturing into an analysis of the underlying causes and manifold consequences of the prolonged and, more often than not, violent conflicts surrounding the politics of identity in northeast India, we limit the following discussion to some aspects of it which have vital implications for the governance and development of the region, with a particular focus on Arunachal Pradesh.

At the outset, it is important to note that 'ethnicity is not a primordially given essence, but the outcome of complex socio-cultural and political processes of labeling and identifying people' (Peters 1998: 400). The politics of identity and difference in Arunachal Pradesh, like it is elsewhere, is not just a relic of the past, but a product of the state-led drive for modernisation and growth. As Dasgupta observes in the wider context of India, 'It is the developmental activity of the centre conducted in a democratic setting of political competition that initially reinforced the politics of identity' (1991: 150). The creation, popularisation and consolidation of an Arunachalee identity from amongst the numerous tribal communities who inhabited the region and whose official nomenclature itself has undergone a few changes, have been facilitated as well as moulded by the progressive modernisation of the economy, the polity and the society itself.

An important paradox noticed in the governance of the Northeast in general is the apparently strong presence of the Indian state, reflected through the heavy military and financial presence on the one hand, and its relative weakness in safeguarding the basic rights and security of the people in their everyday life, on the other (Baruah 2004b). This weakness in safeguarding property rights and enforcing contracts typically paves the way for the emergence of ethnic groups who provide private means of securing property rights (Bates 1998). Unlike many northeastern states where this has resulted in the proliferation of numerous insurgent groups defending the interests of specific ethnic communities, in the case of Arunachal Pradesh it has led to competition and bargaining among different tribal groups in order to acquire a larger share of the government's resources—a form of 'quiet pressure' exercised from within the system. Nevertheless, the state's weakness when it comes to strictly enforcing the rules of the game has provided non-state sources of power and authority with ample scope to exercise considerable control over the everyday politics of survival and accumulation.

The politics of identity in Arunachal in terms of its impact on governance can be analysed at two distinct levels: first, the politics of difference that clearly distinguishes the indigenous tribal people of the state from all 'outsiders', including migrants from neighbouring countries and different states of India; and second, the inter-tribal distinctions among indigenous communities of the state. The implications of these two forms of identity politics for the development process, though interrelated and overlapping in some aspects, are different from each other.

The anxieties of the indigenous tribal population regarding the changing demographic composition of the state (the share of the tribals in the total population was 64.2 per cent in 2001) and also the contentious issue of the settlement of the Chakma-Hajong and other refugees in the state have led to a strong articulation of 'son-of-the-soil' demands on many issues. Key to the development process in the state is the constant inflow of migrants, not only as government servants but also as construction labourers, tenants, traders and workers in different sectors. While migrant workers, both skilled and unskilled, have played an important role in the economic development of the state, with increasing unemployment among the youth in the state, the demand for local control over jobs, contracts and other resources has intensified. Historically, these aspirations have to some extent been accommodated within the broad parameters of democratic governance and have also helped in protecting the interests of the local population. However, the politics of affirmative action by the state in the presence of such politicisation of ethnicity and ethnic difference has led to a replacement of civic rules by rules of difference—a process that, according to Sanjib Baruah, has created a 'crisis of citizenship' in the Northeast[17] (2003, 2004a).

At another level, the competitive politics of ethnic difference among the different tribes of Arunachal Pradesh has led to a complex and multi-layered process of articulation of collective identity. The establishment of hundreds of associations, groups and institutions on the basis of community and territorial aspirations has further consolidated this process. This has led to competitive pressure being placed on the state for the recognition and fulfilment of these aspirations. On the positive side, it has led to an awareness of and active participation by non-state agencies in governance; but at times, it has also led to mutual antagonisms between various groups as well as increasing the burden on the administrative apparatus, affecting its efficiency and productivity. The spirals of identity-based politics of recognition, beyond a point, are bound to be in conflict with the universalistic principles of citizenship and democratic governance.

Again, as has happened elsewhere, the benefits of identity-based mobilisation of public opinion have not necessarily been shared equitably within the groups in whose name the demands for more resources from the governments have been placed. Ethnic claims and ethnic action, although claimed to be designed to serve the ethnic collectivity, may in practice serve the mobilisers more than the collectivity for which they speak (Dasgupta 1991: 145–46). It is generally the traders-politicians-bureaucrats within the groups who have cornered a substantial proportion of the gains of such collective articulation of demands. Often, the principles of democratic rights, equality and justice, which are invoked when demanding benefits for such ethnic or identity-based groups, are not necessarily considered legitimate while discussing the rights of underprivileged groups or individuals within the ethnic group itself. The systematic privileging of ethnic or community-based demands over individual rights is not necessarily conducive for deepening democracy or ensuring civic governance (Collier 1998).

Another significant implication of such circles of difference and identity for good governance is that 'ethnic fractionalization' undermines economic performance by inhibiting the development of social capital and trust, and thereby raising transaction costs, although to some extent it may help build trust within the ethnic groups (Horowitz 1998). As the resources of the state become scarce, competition intensifies and, for multi-ethnic states like Arunachal Pradesh, such competitive politics of recognition and difference will have grave implications for the future. The consensual mode of decision-making, which has been followed in the past by ruling political combinations to keep inter-ethnic conflicts under check, will lose its relevance in the context of the rising costs of consensus-building among groups with a heterogeneity of interests, some of which might be mutually exclusive, or at least conflicting (Jayal 1997).

The role of civil society in checking autocratic and undemocratic tendencies within the state apparatus and also in democratising governance is well recognised (Edwards 2000). The civil society in Arunachal Pradesh is still in an early evolutionary phase, and in this fluid and transitional stage, only tentative comments can be made about some of the manifested tendencies. First, it is important to note that in terms of the sheer number of publicly announced civil society institutions (CSIs), Arunachal Pradesh has perhaps one of the highest per capita incidences of such institutions. Superficially, it gives an impression of a vibrant civil society tradition. However, most of these institutions are particularistic in their objective, exclusionist in their membership and narrow in terms of their concerns and aspirations. The politics of identity—community-based or geographical—forms the basis of many of these institutions. Quite a few of them are formed in the context of specific issues and concerns, but some of the CSIs like the Arunachal Pradesh Women Welfare Society (APWWS) have not only been active for a long time but have also been engaged in sustained campaigns for gender justice and democratisation of governance.[18]

Second, many CSIs in the state deliberately or otherwise follow the state's agenda as well as its modus operandi—a fact that is perhaps common in the case of many 'dependent societies'. Commenting upon the Northeast in general, an observer notes that 'militarisation itself implies systematic dissolution of the civil society and its reconstruction in the image of the military, and correspondingly, fostering [*sic*] upon the population, the ideology and culture of the military' (Barbora 2002: 1291). Given the dominance of the state apparatus in different spheres, the CSIs to some extent follow the language and logic of the bureaucracy.

Between Mal-governance and Identity Politics: A Note on Implications for Gender Relations

As the relatively isolated communities of Arunachal Pradesh are being exposed to new forms of economic, political and social organisations, cultures and ideas, enormous changes are also taking place with regard to the construction of acceptable social norms and practices, many of which have tremendous implications for gender relations in general and the position of women in particular (Upadhyay and Mishra 2005). The sheer enormity of these far-reaching changes and the speed with which they have been introduced have unsettled many of the age-old institutions, beliefs and practices. The life-worlds and worldviews of the communities have been transformed in diverse and complex ways. The transitions in gender relations, both at the individual and the collective levels, are yet to be documented and analysed by researchers. Further, the wide variations across space, altitudes and communities make any generalisation patently difficult. What follows therefore is just a description of a few issues that need to be further studied, discussed and contextualised. There are even some doubts as to the appropriateness of the 'concepts' and terms that have been used to describe the social phenomena concerned. Nevertheless, our interactions with women and activists have made us realise that these questions need to be posed to understand the complexities of the situation in which women of Arunachal Pradesh find themselves. It is interesting to note how the systematic privileging of community over citizenship, the willingness of the state and to some extent that of civil society institutions, to differentiate citizens on the basis of their identity has influenced the articulation of gender-related issues and concerns. A few examples listed below should unfold the multi-level implications of the crisis of governance and the politicisation of ethnicity for the gender questions in the state.

In many indigenous communities of Arunachal Pradesh, the bridegroom's family has to make some payments, generally in terms of *mithuns* a local breed of partially domesticated cattle resembling gaur, pigs, ornaments and other valuables. Like in many other tribal communities, this practice was rooted in the traditional context, where the loss of a working hand was seen to be compensated through such an exchange at the time of marriage. The practice is often seen as indicative of a better social status of women, particularly when contrasted with the system of dowry prevalent elsewhere. Recent and more careful research, however, has questioned such causal interpretations. With modernisation, the attitude towards this practice has been changing. Is bride price in the changing context a recognition of women's productive contribution to the household economy, or is it a devaluation of women's position? A comparatively recent phenomenon is the payment of dowry by some among the better-off sections of the society. Objections are also being raised against the use of the term 'bride-price' for marriage gifts on the grounds that even the girl's family have to reciprocate with gifts for the bridegroom's family. A related problem is that of child marriage. In some cases, parents of girl children take the bride price in advance and the girl is 'booked' for marriage. Such a practice obviously denies the basic rights of the girl. There are indications, though, that this practice is on the decline.

In many communities in Arunachal Pradesh, polygamy has been in practice for a long time. Although we do not have dependable data on the proportion of polygamous marriages in the state, informed observers feel that the system is dying out. However, a 'new polygamy' can be seen in recent years, where polygamy is fast becoming a status symbol among the neo-rich and the elite. Women's groups in the state have voiced concerns about the rise of such cases among the educated elite. However, such protests are always brushed aside by the elites who state that polygamy is part of the tradition of tribal communities and is also sanctioned according to community laws.

There is a great deal of variation in the traditional community laws governing the lives of people in rural areas of the state. Many of these laws affect women's well-being and rights. In recent years, there have been attempts to codify these laws. However, some women activists feel that there is an urgent need for careful codification of these laws in the light of the changing social context and gender justice. In spite of their best efforts to influence the outcomes, the process of codification will definitely open up a new arena of struggle for the traditionalists and those advocating basic human rights for women and others.[19]

Evidence from different parts of the world suggest that the transition from collective to private ownership over land usually results in the concentration of private ownership over resources in the hands of the men. Arunachal Pradesh has been undergoing this transition during the last few decades. As there has been no cadastral survey in the state, it is difficult to estimate the pattern of ownership over land.[20] Moreover, access to land is governed and monitored by the village communities with little interference from the state machinery, notwithstanding the recent efforts to codify land ownership and management laws. Given women's marginalised position in the traditional community-based institutions, women get disinherited as community resources, particularly land, are privatised. Generally, the inheritance laws of the communities of Arunachal Pradesh do not allow women to inherit landed property (Pandey et al. 1997).

Livelihoods in Arunachal Pradesh, like in many other states of the Northeast are critically dependent upon 'environmental entitlements'.[21] A study based on a household-level primary survey in four villages of West Kameng district[22] found that almost all the households rely on multiple sources of livelihoods. In the study villages, the significance of the forest resources lies in their centrality as an additional and dependable source of livelihood, particularly for smoothening consumption, so as to remove fluctuations.[23] Needless to say, women and children play an important role in gathering forest resources for both domestic consumption and commercial use. The declining forest cover, particularly the degradation of forest near the settlements, has meant extra work. Participation in non-farm agricultural labour markets, especially for the rural poor, is not in terms of a permanent occupational shift, but can be explained as being among the 'livelihood gathering' efforts on the part of the deficit households. The large and semi-medium farmers, on the other hand, concentrate more on agriculture, trade and commerce activities. There is a gender dimension to this process as well—when male workers in small and marginal holder families move out to non-farm activities like government service or petty business, female workers tend to spend a comparatively higher percentage of their working days on farming and forest activities. Another micro-study found that while male workers tend to spend a higher percentage of their working days as agricultural wage labourers, the trend is reversed in the case of the percentage of working days spent in all types of wage labour, both agricultural and non-agricultural, because of the relatively higher participation of female workers in the non-farm wage labour market (Mishra 2002a). Given the substantial dependence of women on forest resources and related activities, the weakening of the institutional management of these communally-owned and managed resources obviously has significant gender implications as well (Krishna 2001).[24] For all their so-called 'democratic ethos', these traditional institutions for the management of CPRs were completely male-dominated.

Over the past decades, a large number of migrant women workers have been working in various sectors in Arunachal Pradesh. Many of them are engaged in the unorganised sector (Upadhyay 2002b). Like elsewhere in the country, unorganised-sector workers are deprived of social security provisions. Further, in the road construction sector, female workers, who often live in 'labour camps', are deprived of basic health care and other facilities. There have been cases where their employers and co-workers have exploited them. As they are considered members of the 'outsider' community, their grievances as women generally take a backseat.

IN LIEU OF A CONCLUSION

The fundamental challenges facing the government and civil society in Arunachal Pradesh today include the tasks of secularising governance and democratising development. The goals of building capabilities, expanding choices and safeguarding freedoms cannot be achieved unless the development process is made more inclusive and participatory. The often talked about, but least implemented, bottom-up approach to development is likely to suit the aspirations of the people in this state, which has so much cultural and ecological diversity. However, there is an urgent need to develop a transparent and non-discriminatory framework for governance, which in turn requires effective monitoring mechanisms and accountability at all levels. While there is always scope for enhancing public investment in the development of physical and social infrastructure, a mere announcement of financial packages without an institutional strategy ensuring proper utilisation of the funds will only reinforce the existing cycles of corruption, inefficiency and perpetual dependence. The role of civil society in this transformation can hardly be overstressed.

The question of identity and cultural distinctiveness of the indigenous people in the state is an issue that needs urgent attention and its relationship with the political economy of development has to be examined in greater detail. As Dipankar Gupta has argued, 'Since the demand for cultural protection carries legitimacy only in the constitutional democratic regimes, the resolution of these issues can also be done only within a modern liberal democratic structure. Tradition is not a reliable ally in such circumstances' (1999: 2313). The task is obviously complex, and requires a group of 'cultural entrepreneurs' with a vision for the future and a belief in democratic principles.

The gender question in Arunachal Pradesh has to be viewed in the context of the twin dangers of portraying the existing gender relations as *egalitarian* and that of clubbing all demands for equality as being against tribal traditions. As long as civil society continues to follow the basic framework of identity politics and categorises people on the basis of their identity, the gains from popular mobilisations are going to be fairly modest. A selective invocation of democratic principles and a hierarchical categorisation of the victims would, in the final analysis, perpetuate discrimination and exclusion. It is high time that the democratic credentials of those seeking 'justice for the community' are brought under critical scrutiny. The more such voices come from within the community, the better. This, in a sense, is the fundamental challenge before those who wish to struggle for a just and democratic order. 'Finding a way to liberalise a cultural community without destroying it' is the task that the liberals face in a number of multi-ethnic contexts (Kymlicka 1989: 170, quoted in Gupta 1999). In Arunachal Pradesh, the key challenge to developing a non-discriminatory framework for governance without compromising the basic collective rights of the indigenous population is to be able to address particularistic demands within the framework of universal norms. This, by all counts, is a tough challenge before the decision makers of today and tomorrow.

NOTES

1. During 1990–91 to 1995–96, the share of manufacturing in NSDP at current prices declined from 5.11 to 3.27 per cent, while that of public administration increased from 13.52 to 14.15 per cent (Bezbaruah and Dutta 2001).

2. These problems are not unique to the study of the position of women in society. One of the major problems associated with understanding the process of social change in Arunachal Pradesh, as in many other similar contexts, is that the paucity of written accounts and the extreme biases that are reflected in whatever written accounts are available make any objective assessment a complex matter. Apart from the divergence between the oral memories of the indigenous tribes and the 'outsiders' during the colonial period, in recent times, too, much of the writings by indigenous and non-indigenous scholars, notwithstanding the innate difficulties in using such categories, are coloured by various shades of romanticism, populism, distrust or plain

misunderstanding. This section draws on our earlier work in GoAP 2006, and Upadhyay and Mishra 2005.

3. Among the northeastern states, Sikkim, Tripura and Mizoram have registered an increase in CSR during the same period, while the decline in other states of the region has been less severe than that in Arunachal Pradesh.

4. The census operation started in the state in 1961, but the figures of the 1961 Census are not considered reliable. Improvements in data collection and low reliability of the data from earlier censuses make the analysis of inter-temporal variations especially difficult.

5. In 1991, of the total marginal workers in the state, 87.31 per cent were female and only 12.69 per cent were male. Of the female marginal workers, 96.44 per cent reported household duties to be their main activity. Most of the marginal workers were engaged in agriculture—the percentages of cultivators and agricultural labourers among female marginal workers were 82.44 and 15.33, respectively.

6. Even without going into the details of the underlying causes, it is safe to presume that in a context where the service sector in general and government service in particular have been the primary sources of alternative employment, the differential access to education itself creates conditions for such gender disparities in the quality of employment within the sector. In 1991, while 55.9 per cent of the male main workers were illiterate, 87.9 per cent of the female main workers were illiterate. In rural areas, the percentage of illiterates among female main workers was as high as 90 per cent. Only 1 per cent of female main workers had studied up to the graduation level and above. Even among the women workers who were engaged in non-agricultural sectors, the percentage of illiterates was as high as 54.06 in 1991. Among the female main workers working in 'other services' in Arunachal Pradesh, mainly those engaged in the government sector, 41.67 per cent were illiterate and 11.82 per cent had studied till the primary level or below. Among the female workers in other services, only 11.16 per cent had studied up to more than the higher secondary level in 1991. This means that even when there is a limited degree of diversification of occupation among the female workers, they typically get jobs in the low-skilled, low-earning end of the spectrum.

7. Between 1981 and 1991 there was a decline in the urban-rural gap, both for male and female literacy rates, but the decline in the urban-rural gap was sharper for male literacy than it was for female literacy. However, during the 1990s the urban-rural gap in female literacy came down very sharply.

8. *The National Family Health Survey (NFHS)* data for 1998–99 shows that the median year of schooling among males in Arunachal Pradesh was 4.4, while

that for females was only 2.1. It is important to mention that the survey found the median years of schooling for females in the state to be the lowest among all northeastern states (IIPS and ORC Macro 2002: 25–29).

9. The sex-ratio among students first increased from 787 girls per 1,000 boys at the pre-primary level to 830 girls at the primary and 903 girls at the middle-school levels. The sex ratio then declined fast at the secondary and tertiary levels, dropping further to only 222 girls per 1,000 boys at the university level.

10. The drop-out rate of girls in these classes is also high in Arunachal Pradesh in comparison with Assam, Manipur, Meghalaya, Mizoram and Nagaland (Planning Commission 2002).

11. *NFHS-II* data also suggests that among the ever-married women, 78.2 per cent consume green, leafy vegetables daily, but the percentages of women who do not consume milk and curd is as high as 42. Although age does not play a very important role in women's food consumption pattern, illiterate women have poorer and less varied diets than literate women, and the differences are particularly sharp in the case of fruits, eggs, pulses and beans. The household's standard of living has a strong negative effect on the consumption of nutritious food; the percentage of women who consume milk or curd, fruit, egg and meat at least once a week is much less among households with a low status of living, compared to that among women enjoying a better standard of living.

The percentage of women with a body-mass-index (BMI) below 18.5 kg/m^2 is the lowest in Arunachal Pradesh among all northeastern states. As expected, nutritional deficiency is relatively higher among illiterate women and also among those whose standards of living are low. As per the *NFHS-II* survey, 62.5 per cent of ever-married women were anaemic, 50.6 per cent had mild-anaemia and 11.3 per cent moderate anaemia. Barring Meghalaya, the percentage of women with any anaemia was highest in Arunachal Pradesh among all the hill states of northeast India.

According to *NFHS-II*, 22.1 per cent of girl children under three years of age are underweight, 25.7 per cent are stunted and 4.7 per cent are wasted. Significantly, in terms of the anthropometric measures, girls have better nutritional status than boys.

12. In Arunachal Pradesh, the Panchayat Raj and the establishment of a Legislative Assembly preceded the introduction of universal adult franchise. A three-tier Panchayat Raj system, namely Gram Panchayat at the village level, Anchal Samiti at the block level and Zila Parishad at the district level, came into existence in 1969 in accordance with the provision of the North-East

Frontier Agency Panchayat Raj Regulation, 1967. An Agency Council was also created as an apex body in the whole territory. The Agency Council was converted into a Legislative Assembly in 1975 and a five-member ministry was formed under the chief ministership of P.K. Thungan without elections to the Legislative Assembly being held. The first assembly election was held in 1978. The introduction of the Panchayat Raj brought about a significant change in the traditional village council of Arunachal Pradesh. It gave a new orientation to politics in the state and helped the formation of an Arunachal civil society instead of a group of fragmented tribes and communities. It has also changed the outlook and broadened the political horizon of the people. It was in 1978 that electoral politics was first introduced in the state and the assembly elections paved the way for the introduction of a modern participatory and representative government.

13. The figures exclude Tirap district, where elections were not held.

14. Human security refers to freedom from hunger, torture and imprisonment without a free and fair trial, discrimination against minorities and women, and domestic violence. The basic freedom from all these diverse forms of violence, along with the positive freedoms that allow each human being to enjoy life to the fullest without imposing constraints upon others engaged in the same pursuit, have to be guaranteed to all sections of society (Upadhyay 2002a).

15. The tribal societies of Arunachal Pradesh have a strong tradition of self-governing institutions. Among all its 26 major tribes and more than 100 sub-tribes, some form of traditional self-regulating institution exists. The most prominent among them are the Kebang of the Adis, the Builiang of the Apatanis, the Nyele of the Nishings, the Mele of the Hrussos, the Tsorgan system of the Monpas, the Jung of the Sherdukpens, the Abbala of the Idu Mishmis, the Pharai of the Kaman Mishmis, the Mockchup of the Khamtis, the Ngojowa of the Wanchos, and the Mungphong or Nockthung of the Tangsas. Although common descent, kinship and blood relations generally form the basis of political union among the tribal people, territorial compactness appears to be the dominating factor of political union among the tribes of Arunachal Pradesh. Some of them are monarchial, while others are republics, some are democracies of a direct type, and others function through a chieftain or a small representative body. A few bodies are oligarchic in nature, limiting the choice of membership of the council to certain houses or clans (Pandey et al. 1999; Roy Burman 2002; Talukdar 2002).

16. Our assertions are based on the narration of a few women students belonging to these districts.

17. Baruah argues that 'the time has come to consider ways of breaking away from the ethnic discourse of the existing protective discrimination regime that, in effect, involves the state forever categorizing groups of people in ethnic terms and making descendents of immigrants into perpetual outsiders' (2003: 1626).

18. It is important to note that even the membership of this organisation is restricted to women belonging to Arunachal Pradesh Scheduled Tribes. Non-tribal women, who constitute a significant proportion of the female population, are not members of this organisation.

19. During the run up to the last Lok Sabha elections, the All Arunachal Pradesh Women Welfare Society organised an all-party meeting and asked the candidates and their representatives to put forth their views on rights of those women who were married to persons belonging to the Arunachalee tribes and those Arunachalee women who were married to non-Arunachalees. Almost all were against granting any rights to those women who were married to non-Arunachalees, but some were not adverse to granting some rights to women married to Arunachalee males, and at least one of them candidly said that women should not make demands which were against the 'interests of the community'.

20. For a discussion on some aspects of the changing agrarian relations and its impact on gender relations in the state, see Mishra 2003b.

21. Environmental entitlements refer to 'alternative sets of utilities derived from environmental goods and services over which social actors have legitimate effective demand and which are instrumental in achieving well-being' (Gasper 1993). 'The alternative set of utilities that comprise environmental entitlements may include any or all of the following: direct uses in the form of commodities, such as food, water or fuel; and the utilities derived from environmental services, such as pollution sinks or properties of the hydrological cycles' (Leach et al. 1999: 233). These environmental entitlements play a crucial role in different aspects of livelihood security at the household level, viz., economic security, food security, health security, and empowerment, particularly in fragile ecological contexts (Jodha 2001).

22. West Kameng district is characterised by a medium per capita district domestic product, a higher degree of occupational diversification of the workforce, a relatively higher share of in-migrants in the total population, a lower cropping intensity and a lower yield rate for most crops in comparison with state averages. For details, see Mishra 2003a.

23. Among all the sample households, around 16 per cent derive less than 5 per cent of their total income from forest resources, nearly 53 per cent have a

forest dependency of 5–20 per cent and more than one-fourth households have a forest dependency higher than 20 per cent.

24. For a discussion on the emerging challenges before the micro-level institutional arrangements for natural resource management, see Mishra 2002b, 2004.

REFERENCES

Barbora, Sanjay. 2002. 'Ethnic Politics and Land Use: Genesis of Conflicts in India's North East', *Economic and Political Weekly*, 37(13): 1285–92.

Baruah, Sanjib. 2003. 'Protective Discrimination and Crisis of Citizenship in North-East India', *Economic and Political Weekly*, 38(17): 1624–26

———. 2004a. 'Citizens and Denizens: Ethnicity, homelands and crisis of displacement in North East India', *Social Change and Development*, 2(1): 105–30.

———. 2004b. 'Historicizing Ethnic Politics in North East India', Keynote Address, Seminar on 'Inter-ethnic Conflict and Ethnic Crisis in North East India', Department of Political Science, Dibrugarh University, 16–17 February 2004 (unpublished).

Bates, Robert H. 1998. 'Comment on "Structure and Strategy in Ethnic Conflict" by Donald L. Horowitz', in Boris Bleskovic and Joseph E. Stiglitz (eds), *Annual World Bank Conference on Development Economics*, pp. 371–76. Washington: World Bank.

Bezbaruah, M.P. and M.K. Dutta. 2001. 'Economic Transition in the North-Eastern Region Before and After Liberalisation', *Assam Economic Journal*, 14: 17–31.

Collier, Paul. 1998. 'The Political Economy of Ethnicity', in Boris Bleskovic and Joseph E. Stiglitz (eds), *Annual World Bank Conference on Development Economics*, pp. 387–99. Washington: World Bank.

Dasgupta, Jyotirindra. 1991. 'Ethnicity, Democracy and Development in India: Assam in a General Perspective', in Atul Kohli (ed.), *India's Democracy: An Analysis of Changing State-Society Relations*. Hyderabad: Orient Longman.

Department of Women and Child Development, Ministry of Human Resource Development, Government of India. 1998. *India Nutrition Profile: 1998*, New Delhi.

Dreze Jean and Amartya Sen. 1995. *India: Economic Development and Social Opportunity*. New Delhi: Oxford University Press.

Edwards, Michael. 2000. 'Civil Society and Global Governance', in Ramesh Thakur and Edward Newman (eds), *New Millennium, New Perspective: The United Nations, Security and Governance*. USA: UNUP.

Elwin, V. 1957. *A Pholisophy for NEFA (Arunachal Pradesh)*. Reprint. 1999. Itanagar: Directorate of Research, Government of Arunachal Pradesh.

Fernandes, Walter. 1999. 'Conflict in North-East: A Historical Perspective', *Economic and Political Weekly*, 34(51): 3579–82.

Gasper, D. 1993. 'Entitlement Analysis: Relating Concepts and Contexts', *Development and Change*, 24: 679–718.

Gohain, Hiren. 1996. 'Extremist Challenge and Indian State: Case of Assam', *Economic and Political Weekly*, 31(31): 2066–68.

Government of Arunachal Pradesh (GoAP). 2006. *Arunachal Pradesh Human Development Report 2005*. Itanagar.

Gupta, Dipankar. 1999. 'Survivors or Survivals: Reconciling Citizenship and Cultural Particularisms', *Economic and Political Weekly*, 34(33): 2313–23.

Hirway, I. and D. Mahadevia. 1996. 'Critique of Gender Development Index: Towards an Alternative', *Economic and Political Weekly*, 31(43): ws87–ws96.

Horowitz, Donald L. 1998. 'Structure and Strategy in Ethnic Conflict: A few Steps Towards Synthesis', in Boris Bleskovic and Joseph E. Stiglitz (eds), *Annual World Bank Conference on Development Economics*, pp. 345–70. Washington: World Bank.

International Institute for Population Sciences (IIPS) and ORC Macro. 2002. *National Family Health Survey (NFHS-II), India, 1998–99: Northeastern States*. Mumbai: IIPS.

Jayal, Nirja Gopal. 1997. 'The Governance Agenda: Making Democratic Development Dispensable', *Economic and Political Weekly*, 32(8): 407–12.

Jodha, N.S. 2001. *Life on the Edge: Sustaining Agriculture and Community Resources in Fragile Environments*. New Delhi: Oxford University Press.

Krishna, Sumi. 2001. 'Gender, Tribe and Community Control of Natural Resources in North East India', *Indian Journal of Gender Studies*, 8(1).

Kymlicka, Will. 1989. *Liberalism, Community and Culture*. Oxford: Clarendon Press.

Leach, Melissa, Robin Mearns and Ian Scoones. 1999. 'Environmental Entitlements: Dynamics and Institutions in Community-based Natural Resource Management', *World Development*, 27(2): 225–47.

Madhab, Jayant. 1999. 'North-East: Crisis of Identity, Security and Underdevelopment', *Economic and Political Weekly*, 34(6): 320–22.

Mishra, Deepak K. 2001. 'Political Economy of Agrarian Change in Arunachal', *Man and Development*, 23(3): 40–50.

———. 2002a. 'Agrarian Structure and Labour-Use Patterns in Rural Arunachal Pradesh: A Case Study', *Arunachal University Research Journal*, 5(2): 31–56.

———. 2002b. 'Institutional Arrangements and Agrarian Structure during Periods of Transition: Evidences from Rural Arunachal Pradesh', in S.S. Acharya,

Surjit Singh and V. Sagar (eds), *Sustainable Agriculture, Poverty and Food Security*, Vol. II, pp. 891–902. Jaipur: Rawat Publications.

————. 2003a. 'Environmental Degradation and Changing Livelihood Strategies in Rural Arunachal Pradesh', Paper presented at the 45th Annual Conference of the Indian Society of Labour Economics, Kolkata, 15–17 December.

————. 2003b. 'Gender and Agrarian Relations in Arunachal Pradesh: A Study on West Kameng District', *Assam Economic Journal*, 16: 71–81.

————. 2004. 'Institutional Sustainability in Natural Resource Management: A Study on Arunachal Pradesh, India', *Asian Profile*, 32(6): 583–94.

Mishra, Deepak K. and Vandana Upadhyay. 2004. 'Governance and Development in Arunachal Pradesh: The Emerging Challenges', *Dialogue Quarterly*, 5(4): 73–96.

Pandey, B.B., D.K. Duarah and N. Sarkar (eds). 1999. *Tribal Village Councils of Arunachal Pradesh*. Itanagar: Directorate of Research, Government of Arunachal Pradesh.

Pandey, B.B. (ed.). 1997. *Status of Women in Tribal Society: Arunachal Pradesh*. Itanagar: Directorate of Research, Government of Arunachal Pradesh.

Peters, Pauline E. 1998. 'Comment on "The Political Economy of Ethnicity" by Paul Collier', in Boris Bleskovic and Joseph E. Stiglitz (eds), *Annual World Bank Conference on Development Economics*, pp. 400–405. Washington: World Bank.

Planning Commission. 2002. *The National Human Development Report: 2001*. New Delhi: Planning Commission, Government of India.

Rama Rao, G.L. Ladusingh and R. Pritamjit. 2004. 'Nutritional Status of Children in North East India', *Asia-Pacific Population Journal*, 19(3).

Roy Burman, B.K. 2002. 'Traditional Self-Governing Institutions among the Hill Tribal Population Groups of North East India', in Atul Goswami (ed.), *Traditional Self-Governing Institutions among the Hill Tribes of North East India*. New Delhi: Akansha.

Rustagi, Preet. 2000. 'Identifying Gender Backward Districts Using Selected Indicators', *Economic and Political Weekly*, 35(48): 4276–86.

Sachdeva, Gulshan. 2000. *Economy of the North-East: Policy, Present Conditions and Future Possibilities*. New Delhi: Konark Publishers.

Talukdar, A.C. 2002. 'Traditional Self-Governing Institutions among the Tribes of Arunachal Pradesh', in Atul Goswami (ed.), *Traditional Self-Governing Institutions among the Hill Tribes of North East India*. New Delhi: Akansha.

Mahbul ul Haq Human Development Centre. 1999. *Human Development in South Asia 1999: The Crisis of Governance*. Oxford: Oxford University Press.

United Nations Development Programme. 1995. *Human Development Report, 1995: Gender and Human Development*. Oxford: Oxford University Press.

Upadhyay, Vandana and Deepak K. Mishra. 2005. *A Situational Analysis of Women and Girls in Arunachal Pradesh*. New Delhi: National Commission of Women.

Upadhyay, Vandana. 2002a. 'Violence and Development', *Social Change and Development*, 1(1): 36–43.

———. 2002b. 'Labour Migration in Arunachal Pradesh: The Gender Dimension', *Arunachal University Research Journal*, 5(1): 77–86.

———. 2005. 'Women as Micro-Entrepreneurs: Towards an Alternative Strategy of Poverty Reduction in Arunachal Pradesh', *Rajiv Gandhi University Research Journal*, 8(2).

9

The Reinforcement of Gender Stereotypes through Modern Education
The Case of Mizoram

B. Lakshmi

INTRODUCTION

Among the geographical regions in India with a concentration of tribal populations, the states of the northeastern region present a distinct picture. The tongue-shaped state of Mizoram, tucked between the international boundaries of Bangladesh and Myanmar, is one of the last frontiers of India. Formerly the Lushai Hills district of Assam, it later became the Union Territory of Mizoram directly administered by the central government, and in 1987 it became a state. It is inhabited by over 15 tribal communities, including the larger groups of the Mizos and the Hmars, and numerically smaller groups such as the Paite, Ralte, Lai, Mara, Reang, et cetera. The Chakmas are a non-Mizo (Arakan) tribe. Each of the groups had their own dialects/languages (of the Tibeto-Burmese group), but that of the Lushai/Mizo, originally known as the Duhlian dialect, became the *lingua franca*. The state includes Autonomous District Councils of the Mara (formerly Lakher), Lai and Chakma (see also Nag 1994; Sangkima 1994). Its population, according to the 2001 Census, is 890,000; the majority of the people, 87 per cent, profess Christianity (mainly Presbyterian and Baptist) as their religion; and nearly 89 per cent are literate. At over 86 per cent, female literacy in Mizoram is only second to Kerala's 88 per cent.

After India attained independence, an important role was assigned to education as an agent of social change, along with law, science and technology. Assuming the significance of education in social transformation and socialisation, that is, the training of the young, this chapter examines the gender dimensions of education both in terms of the educational knowledge that the school transmits, and the process and experience of schooling. In the sociology of education, it is being increasingly emphasised that we need to pay attention not only to structures but also to micro-level school processes and curriculum. Further, schools have come to be seen not merely as social sites, but as cultural sites too, where significant battles of ideology, culture and politics are fought in the everyday context of the classroom.

The material for this chapter has been gathered using the technique of participant observation of a government school and textual analysis of the *Zoram Bharti* (Lakshmi 2005). The school is located in Chhimtuipui district (now Saiha district) in the southeastern corner of Mizoram, bordering Myanmar. *Zoram Bharti* is a Hindi textbook series for Classes V–VIII prescribed by the state government's Mizoram Board of School Education at Aizawl, the state capital. The choice of a government school and the officially prescribed school textbooks was guided, first, by the realisation that this would enable me to see the translation of official policies into practice and to decipher the role of the state in education, which is as yet an unresearched and hence unfathomed area. Second, it is necessary to understand the status of Hindi learning in Mizoram. Hindi is a compulsory subject in Mizoram through the middle years of schooling, from Class V to Class VIII. This is in consonance with the central government's National Policy on Education (NPE), 1986 which emphasises the need for a strong and united nation, which in turn is considered an essential pre-condition for progress (Government of India: 1992). It is believed that, among other things, the teaching of Hindi in schools would play a key role in achieving these goals.[1]

WOMEN'S POSITION IN MIZORAM

The tribal women's position in the household is considered supreme, but they are usually much busier than men. A typical Mizo woman's day starts at dawn, when she is woken up by the din created by the domestic livestock. She begins her day by pounding and winnowing rice, after which the food has to be cooked and the water drawn from the *tuikhur* (water point). During the course of the day, a Mizo woman collects firewood and weaves cloth. Evening is once again time to draw water, feed the pigs and spin. During the cultivating season, both men and women are extremely busy; in *jhum* fields (swidden, that is, slash-and-burn or shifting cultivation), the men cut the vegetation and may help in the harvest, but all other farming tasks are carried out almost entirely by women, especially weeding (see Krishna 1998). Men construct and repair houses, do basket work and lay traps for birds and beasts. The tasks performed by women, such as cooking, collecting firewood and water, washing clothes and playing an active role in agriculture, are extremely strenuous and exacting in the difficult terrain of the mountains.

Several scholars such as Verrier Elwin, C. Von-Furer Haimendorf and more recently, Zehol (1998 on Nagaland), have almost ecstatically stated that tribal women generally have a high and honourable position compared to women in caste society. In recent times, it is being argued that rather than talking about the low status of women in the context of tribal societies, it is more appropriate to treat it as gender inequality (Xaxa 2004). According to Xaxa, the division of labour in tribal society is based on gender and age and not on hierarchy and occupation. Exactly when these differences began to be graded is not precisely known. Nongbri (1994 on Meghalaya), too, has argued that gender inequality is not alien to tribal societies, but is obscured by their poverty, which compels men and women to cooperate in joint economic activities. (This is not to undermine the significance of tribal moral codes and ethics that govern behaviour.)

The position of women in Mizo society, though not as low as their counterparts in the plains, is still inferior to that of men. However, what is striking in the case of Mizoram is the visibility of women and the easy companionship that exists between men and women. It is easy to see that the values enshrined in the school curriculum are in consonance with the gender stereotypes prevalent in society. These findings are similar to those arrived at by researchers elsewhere, which indicate that school textbooks embody the dominant ideologies of the social and the public domain, and thereby reflect the relations of domination and control that are inherent in society.[2] Indeed, gender equality is a myth, as has been amply demonstrated by Sarkar and Karlekar (1991) and Nongbri (1994) in their examination of the tribal customary laws in Mizoram and Meghalaya respectively. Sumi Krishna (2005), too, states that despite the Mizo women's rich farming experience, adages ridicule women. The grip of these adages on the Mizo mind is still strong despite the conversion to Christianity, which emphasises equality between men and women. Consider some of these sayings:

Hmeichhe finin tuikhur ral a kai lo.	Women's wit does not go beyond the water point, which is just outside the village.
Hmeichhia leh pal chhia chu thlak theih an ni.	A wife and an old fence can be changed any time.
Hmeichhia leh chakaiin sakhua an nei lo.	Women and crabs have no religion.
Nupui vau loh leh vau sam loh chu an pawng tual tual.	An unthreatened wife and weeds of the field not properly cut are both unbearable.
Chakai sa sa ni suh, hmeichhe thu thu ni suh.	Just as crab meat is not considered meat, women's word is not regarded as word.

Landscapes and natural resources too are gendered in common speech (Krishna 2005). Ann Oakley (1972) has argued that feminine social roles are not an inevitable product of female biology. It is the culture of a society that determines the behaviour of sexes within it. Oakley (1974) shows how the process of socialisation shapes the behaviour of girls and boys from an early age. She states that there are four ways of socialisation: canalisation, which involves directing boys and girls towards different objects; use of verbal appellations, which lead children to identify with their gender; manipulation, which involves influencing the child's self-concept; and finally, exposure to different activities.

GENDER BIAS IN EDUCATIONAL KNOWLEDGE AND VALUES

Let us now turn our attention to the values being transmitted by the educational knowledge, especially from a gender perspective. In 'Work Education', a subject in the school curriculum, crafts are gendered as in society: girl students are required to take up weaving and tailoring, while boys opt for basketry, carpentry and such like. The curriculum reinforces the gendered performance of tasks by women as well as the qualities of obedience, docility and diligence for girls and women, while the qualities emphasised for boys and men are bravery, an outgoing nature, sportsmanship and leadership in socio-cultural affairs.

Of a total of 21 chapters in *Zoram Bharti* for Class VI, almost 10 deal with gendered subjects. The book opens with a prayer, where both a girl and a boy are shown praying. However, throughout the book, boys are shown in active roles such as studying, going to school and playing football and hockey, whereas girls are shown as passive onlookers. Sample this:

Lalfela achha ladka hai.	Lalfela is a good boy.
Uska haath saaf hai.	His hands are clean.
Veh lifebuoy sabun se nahata hai.	He bathes with Lifebuoy soap.
Veh Vairengte mein school jaata hai.	He goes to school in Vairengte.
Veh office mein nahin jaata.	He does not go to office.
Veh football bhi khelta hai.	He also plays football.
Mein bhi hockey khel sakta hoon.	I can also play hockey.
Vanzama gadi chalata hai.	Vanzama drives a car.
Veh Shillong mein jayega	He will go to Shillong.
Chhatra kaksha mein baithte hain.	The students sit in the class.
Veh path padte hain.	They read the lesson.

Women are depicted in gender-stereotypical roles focusing on nurturing, such as waking up the child for school and cooking. In a chapter titled *Hamara Parivar* (Our Family), the stereotypes find expression thus:

Mere pitaji ghar ke malik hain.	My father is the head of the household.
Mere dada boodhe ho gaye hain.	My grandfather has grown old.
Pitaji adhyapak hain.	Father is a teacher.
Veh angrezi padhate hai.	He teaches English.
Meri maa hamare liye khana banati hain.	My mother cooks food for us.
Veh kabhi-kabhi bagiche mein kaam karti hain.	She sometimes works in the garden.

Barely one poem, titled *Veer Nari* (Brave Woman), depicts a woman named Zaidiki as brave, as against seven male-centric selections of prose and poetry.

In *Zoram Bharti*: Book 7, while girls are depicted six times, the boys are depicted as many as 13 times. In the poem *Kaisa Jeevan Hamara* (How is Our Life), three girls along with a boy are shown in a garden, carrying the message of togetherness. In another chapter titled *Cherawlam* (a Mizo dance form), a group of eight girls is depicted dancing the bamboo-dance. In a chapter, *Sabun Ki Upyogita* (The Utility of Soap), a woman is depicted washing clothes, while the male figure bathes. In a poem, *Dharti Pukar Rahi Hai Sabko* (The Earth is Calling All), two women are depicted gathering the harvest, while a boy stands. Just one girl is shown amidst two boys, all buying books from a man. Generally, boys are shown as going to school to study, helping the elderly, dancing at *Mimkut* (a Mizo festival), hunting, working in a laboratory, or playing football and cricket. In *Zoram Bharti*: Book 8, not only are men and boys depicted more often than girls and women, but they are also shown in more active roles like participating in a march past, as being more aware of national duties, studying, climbing trees and wielding the hoe. Girls are only shown studying, selling vegetables and dancing at *Chapcharkut* (a Mizo festival).

An analysis of the educational knowledge as embodied in *Zoram Bharti* exemplifies that education is nowhere near the ideals and goals with which it was envisaged in the post-Independence era and after. The NPE, 1986 (Government of India: 1992) announced two decades earlier, and the subsequent Programme of Action, 1992, emphasised that

> Education will be used as an agent of basic change in the status of women and in order to neutralise the accumulated distortions of the past, there will be a well conceived edge in favour of women. The National Education System will play a positive interventionist role in the empowerment of women.

In actual practice, however, the policy reinforces the gender stereotypes prevalent in the society. A casual visitor to the hilly landscapes of Mizoram is bound to be impressed by the camaraderie between men and women, and the visibility of women in all spheres of life—agriculture, vegetable stalls, Church, Sunday school, et cetera. However, this visibility masks the underlying power structures that govern the lives of women. The gender values being transmitted in the curriculum and also by the school ethos are in consonance with the societal values pertaining to gender.

SCHOOL EDUCATION HIDES PATRIARCHAL POWER STRUCTURE

As mentioned earlier, one can see the subtle and micro processes of socialisation in modern school education in Mizoram, which, instead of mitigating the gender inequities prevalent in society, reinforce and strengthen them. Also worth noting is the role of the state, which, as is being argued in recent times, is far from neutral and benign. In this sense, modern education in Mizoram is 'la violence symbolique' (Bourdieu and Passeron 1977), that is, the imposition and inculcation of a 'cultural arbitrary' by an 'arbitrary power'. Though Bourdieu and Passeron are referring to class societies, their theory is also broadly applicable to tribal society. Bourdieu argues that the education system perpetrates 'symbolic violence' in the guise of fairness and equality. The effectiveness of the education system lies in the recognition of its legitimacy. This is done by concealing or '*meconnaisance*' (misrecognition) of the real, unequal power relations on which it rests. Bourdieu and Passeron write:

> Indeed, among all the solutions put forward throughout history to the problem of transmission of power and privileges, there surely does not exist, one that is better concealed, and therefore better adapted to societies which tend to refuse the most patent forms of the transmission of power and privileges, than that solution which the educational system provides. (ibid.: 88)

Viewed from a gender perspective, school education in Mizoram, in the guise of providing equal education to girls and boys, hides the patriarchal power structure of Mizo society, as far as the content of education is concerned. This curricular knowledge makes a deep impact on society and societal values as it is recognised as legitimate. But is the educational experience a modernising one?

Education in Mizoram has generally been geared towards transformation and change. Historically, the Christian missions furthered the education of both girls and boys. In comparison, in certain other tribal societies, including Arunachal Pradesh in northeastern India, the number of girls not entering the portals of school at all is alarmingly high.[3] The lofty ideal of modern education in Mizoram has resulted in a rapid expansion of schools all over the state, both private and government. What went on inside the 'black box' of the school was a mystery till scholars such as Michael F.D. Young and Karl Mannheim brought to our notice that there is no objective way of evaluating knowledge. If any knowledge is considered superior and worthy of being transmitted, it is primarily because those with power have defined it as such and have imposed it on the society, in a way in which the latter considers legitimate. Education, in the hands of the dominant middle-class Mizo elite and, shall we say, 'patriarchal elite', serves to impose and inculcate the 'cultural arbitrary' of gender stereotypes on the young generation that attends school. Although modern education in Mizoram is ensconced in ideas suffused with secularism and equality, in reality the school does not operate on an empty canvas. Rather, it functions as a microcosm of society. Those who come to school bring with them the stereotypes, including the gender stereo-types, inculcated through primary socialisation in the context of the family, the neighbourhood and the community. In turn, by valorising women's traditional domestic and nurturant roles of cooking, washing, cleaning, childcare as so on, school knowledge aims to socialise girls in a way that prepares them for their adult roles. Moreover, by emphasising the virtues of docility and obedience for girls, the school attempts to social-ise girls through 'canalisation', 'manipulation', 'verbal appellations', and also through different activities. Therefore, the school itself builds on the primary 'habitus', to use Bourdieu's term, even though it may deny this in principle and practice by making the 'school career a history with no pre-history'. Bourdieu observes that '... the habitus acquired in the family underlies the structuring of school experiences ... and the habitus transformed by schooling, in turn, underlies the structuring of all sub-sequent experience' (1977: 87). The school, thus, not only reinforces the existing stereotypes, but also adds its own force to them by virtue of its durability and legitimacy. Despite women's dominant role in farming and their responsibility for food production, the school system in Mizoram nourishes and nurtures different qualities for boys and girls in consonance with the perceived differential roles they are expected to play in their adult lives. Boys are encouraged to be brave and adventurous to fulfil their key role in the community and politics in later life, while girls are encouraged to be passive, docile, demure and selfless in order to prepare them for the roles of child-bearing, child-rearing, nurturance and house-keeping, which are seen to be in conformity with their primary tasks.

Ortner (1974) has argued that since women's tasks are considered closer to nature and men's tasks closer to culture, and because culture is assigned a higher value than nature, women are considered to have an inferior status as compared to men and that this is the main reason for women's de-valuation. School knowledge, legitimated by the state, is passed on to future generations in an institutionalised context. Rubina Saigol provides evidence from Pakistan to argue that the state strongly controls education and that from the beginning, the child internalises the hierarchy, includ-ing gender hierarchy. The image of the state as 'benign' is far from true, as Saigol (1995) and Krishna Kumar (2002) have shown. The school is an extremely potent ideological apparatus of the state, as it conveys strong gender stereotypical messages under the garb of a fair and just system.

INTERACTIONS IN THE CLASSROOM

The micro-level processes of interaction in the context of the school envir-onment and the classroom offer us another site to examine gender perspectives in pupil culture. Pupil culture has been described as being 'made up of the pupil and his private world in interaction with the school environment in its manifold character including people, events and situ-ations of the pedagogic process' (Thapan 2006 [1991]: 117). It is affected by the backgrounds, attitudes and experiences of students, their expect-ations from the school, their interactions with fellow students and their hopes and fears for the future. In this section, an attempt is made to de-scribe some dimensions of 'pupil culture'. The responses have been elicited through discussions with students about their views, attitudes and anxieties. Though the classroom is a 'front-region', in Goffman's (1973) terms, what is described here from my field notes is its picture as a 'back-region', primarily due to the fact that the teacher has not yet arrived in the classroom. In the absence of the teaching-learning process, when the pupils are casually sitting and interacting, the classroom can be treated as a back-region. An informal and casual air pervades the atmosphere.

Girls and boys sit separately. Three girls sit together in each row of the middle segment. The boys sit in one of the two side rows, the other row is occupied by the girls. I start my conversation with J. Her mother is a Mara (an ethnic minority in Mizoram), while her father is a Bengali (a migrant). She says that she is not accepted as a Mara as she does not know the Mara language:

> When I was in Class I and II, they [the Mizo and Lai pupils] looked at us like tigers do and teased me that I am an English lady from London and that my nose is pointed like a parrot.
>
> They would be very good to us, if we behave the way they want us to behave. For instance, if they tell me, 'Go and sit there' and I obey what they say. But we are not their slaves. I remain calm because my Mummy told me to remain quiet as I have to study here till Class X.
>
> There was a science seminar in February. I performed well but my name was not there. I have decided that I will not participate in any competition now.

Another Mara girl, S, says,

> They [the Mizo and Lai boys] knock our bags, we scold them and they go back. If we do not say anything to them, they will do everything with us that they do with Mizo girls. If a girl is absent, some boy will come and sit in the middle. They behave like married people do ... they can do it with any girl.
>
> If we get good marks, the Mizo look down upon us. They have a feeling of being separate.

Thapan (2006 [1991]) has observed that friendships among pupils are central to their life at school and these are expressed through being together, talking and doing things together. The most important bases of friendship are similar attitudes towards life and people, and common interests. In my fieldwork in Chhimtupui district, I found that friendship is governed by sex and ethnic background more than anything else. For instance, J said: 'I am only on talking terms with the Mizo students and not on friendship terms. They always come and fight with us but we keep quiet. But the situation is still better here than in Aizawl.' On a similar note, S observed, 'Outwardly they like, but inwardly they do not like, to make friends with us. Today, they may talk nicely but tomorrow they will talk badly with us.'

The insularity of friendship on the basis of ethnic differences is much more pronounced among girls as compared to boys. The classroom situation described above exhibits the fact that sex and ethnicity cross-cut each other. Classrooms are gendered spaces where self-identity is created and recreated, as well as contested and questioned. The gender inequity expressed in the context of the classroom is much more pronounced in the case of female students from the minority tribes vis-à-vis those from the majority tribes, as is exemplified in the case of the two Mara girls. However, the contestation of the situation by the two students and their self-reflexivity also point to the role of human agency.

INTERSECTIONS WITH POVERTY AND RURAL-URBAN RESIDENCE

Gender, poverty and rural-urban residence intersect with school education in Mizoram. Through case studies I examine this intersection.

Case Study: 1

E is a student of Class XI at a government higher secondary school in Saiha, the district headquarters of Chhimtuipui. She belongs to a clan of the Maras, and hails from a village in the Mara Autonomous District Council Area (which is in Chhimtuipui, now known as Saiha district). In Saiha, E lives with a politician from the same clan. E's father, who had studied till Class IX and was a *lo-siam mi*, a cultivator, died when she was very young. E's mother has studied till Class III and is also a cultivator. E is the youngest of five siblings, two brothers and three sisters. The eldest, a brother, is a lo-siam mi who dropped out of school after Class VII. The next brother studied till Class X and is a primary school teacher. E's two sisters are both illiterate. E came to Saiha as there was no high school in her village. Besides E, six other students stay with the politician, two girls and four boys. The politician has four children who attend a private school; the eldest has completed his schooling and is now at college in Saiha.

After school, E helps with the household chores, as do the other two girl boarders. The boys have to be taken care of and do not extend any help in the household. In the evening, the girls are visited by the boys according to the custom of *laisacharei* (courting of girls). The politician's wife says, 'When young boys come, I and my husband sit there itself and we switch on the TV. This is how we discourage them. Since the girls are in our custody, we have to take care that they study. After the household work and studies are over, I do not mind their having laisacharei.'

E did her primary schooling with Mara as the medium of instruction in her own village and got a third division (grade). She completed middle school also in the village, but with Mizo as the medium, and got a second division. In Saiha, E's friends are only from her own village. She says, 'Girls from the town do not want to make friends with us.' In the classroom, too, E sits in the second last row along with other girls from the villages. She aspires to be a nurse. Her own family provides her with only her school uniform. For all her other needs, she is dependent on the family with whom she stays. Her family does not visit her frequently, nor does she talk about her family. E wishes to take tuitions, but feels shy to ask for money from her hosts.

E's case reflects the solidarity among the Mara clans. In times of distress, a person is morally bound to help their fellows. Because E's father is dead, her mother does not have the resources to educate her and there is no high school in her village; E has found succour in the politician's house in Saiha. She does not possess either cultural or economic capital. She does not have much motivation or enthusiasm, and the little that she has is dampened by her circumstances. Though clan members are bound by tribal custom to help one another in distress, other's children do not have the same status as one's own children. E has to labour in return for the food, lodging and education that she is provided with. In a politician's house, where innumerable visitors are common, additional working hands are an asset. Clan solidarity, though an appreciable facet of the society, cannot compensate adequately for the inputs that parents generally make for their children, particularly the investment of time. The custom of laisacharei also distracts girl students sometimes. E's family accepts the ends of schooling, but cannot provide the appropriate means for it.[4]

Case Study: II

R belongs to the Lai tribal community and hails from a village in the Lai Autonomous District Council Area in Lawngtlai District (earlier part of

Chhimtuipui District). She is a student of Class VIII at the government higher secondary school at Saiha and stays with a cousin, her father's brother's daughter. Her father has passed the High School Leaving Certificate (HSLC) and is a middle school teacher in their village. Her mother is literate and practices lo-siam mi (farming). R's family of nine includes a grandparent (father's mother), her parents and five siblings (three sisters and two brothers). The eldest sister, studying in Class X, stays with their father's brother at another place. The other children study in the village itself.

R speaks Mizo at home and attends the services of the *Isua Krista Kohhran* (IKK) church. Her cousin and host earns a living by making beedis and *kuhva* (betel). The cousin's husband, who earlier worked as a bus conductor and then as a tailor, is presently unemployed. Both have passed the HSLC. They have two daughters. The family has some savings but no steady source of income, but have rented out a room for Rs 300 per month.

R has all along been a good student. She did her primary and middle school in the village with Mizo as the medium and secured a first division. In her free time, R helps her cousin with all household chores, such as cleaning, washing and cooking. She is a quiet girl and spends the rest of her time with her studies. She is also very regular in attending the services and the Sunday School at the church. She gets emotional support from her cousin.

R's is a interesting case because her father motivates and encourages both his daughters, R and her eldest sister, who are studying away from home. R has deeply incorporated the culture and the ethos (*bildung*), which have almost become her second nature. Though her mother is just literate, her father has more than compensated for it. Highly motivated, unlike other pupils from rural areas, she has overcome the disadvantages of the place of her birth and upbringing primarily due to hard work, determination and a single-minded pursuit of education. R's cousin, too, has motivated her to do better. As her father is himself in the teaching profession, the family endorses and understands the school processes.

The two case studies throw some light on certain aspects of school education in Mizoram. Gender, class, minority ethnic status and rural-urban residence interact meaningfully and in substantial ways. Students such as E suffer from the burden of gender, poverty, rural origin and minority ethnic identity. The school does not mitigate these inequities; rather, it strengthens them. The case study of R, however, exemplifies the role of 'cultural capital', human initiative and hard work, which can successfully overcome the structural constraints. The resistance offered by S and J to the monolithic messages in the classroom on the one hand and the initiatives of students such as R on the other are significant pointers to the role of human agency in overcoming gender stereotypes in education. It is in examples such as these that a 'discourse of possibility' (McLaren and Giroux 1997) must be found.

CONCLUSION

The major challenge for democratic governance in the twenty-first century is participation and inclusion as safeguards against exclusion. Perhaps the answers are to be found in Amartya Sen's theory of 'social choice' and the 'capabilities approach' (see Nussbawm 2006). A broad view of social choice can shift our focus from problems of aggregating individual preferences to participation and inclusion in democratic decision-making, including educational decisions. With regard to policy making in the realm of education, this means taking women's evaluations as situated agents seriously and enhancing their participation in policy discourse (Peter 2006). The capabilities approach can ensure gender justice, provided those capabilities are clearly specified; this is especially significant for social justice in the case of women. The need is to define democracy and development in a different way. A rethinking about participation and inclusion in educational decision-making calls for fair procedures and for giving women a chance to be heard and be involved in collective evaluations and decisions. In order to have an active and a 'sex-equal citizenship', women need to be empowered and included in the public sphere through communication, speech and action (see Mouffe 1992).

The reinforcement of gender stereotypes through modern education in Mizoram can be tackled head on by ensuring 'thick citizenship' for its women, the essence of which is a sense of belonging, horizontal camaraderie and the treatment of women as equals. In the tribal society of Mizoram, where kinship and community ties have traditionally been strong, the shift in thinking about a woman as a member of the community to woman as an individual and citizen is undoubtedly difficult and challenging.

NOTES

1. According to the Constitution of India, all the languages in the Eighth Schedule and the other languages that are not listed in the Schedule are equally 'national' languages. Both Hindi and English are the administrative languages of the Indian Union, that is, 'official' languages. State governments may adopt their own regional languages as 'official' languages for administrative purposes. The 1964 Education Commission put forth a 'three-language formula' for schools: (*i*) the mother tongue or the regional language; (*ii*) the official language of the Union, that is, Hindi, or the associate official language, that is, English; and (*iii*) a modern Indian or foreign language. This policy was reversed in 1988 by the new National Policy on Education, which made the study of both Hindi and English compulsory. Mizoram's Autonomous District Councils control primary education, but education at the middle and higher levels are within the purview of the Mizoram state administration (see Krishna 1991).

2. See, for instance, the studies by Nischol (1976), Kalia (1986) and Scrase (1993).

3. Among many tribal societies in India, the number of girls not entering the portals of school at all is alarmingly high, as is the drop-out rate for girls due to sibling care and other household responsibilities. In patriarchal caste societies, as in rural Rajasthan, the practice of sending girls to school is constricted by considerations of *izzat*, social honour. Investment in girls' education is also seen as being without potential gains (Gold 2002). Nita Kumar (2000) suggests that modernising necessarily means to question existing practices and beliefs. In the case of Rajasthan, education as a modern influence is pitted against family, home and tradition. The essence is that those who attend school must forget everything they had on their minds before arriving at school. The role envisaged for education is therefore that of a catalyst in modernisation, and as breaking free from the shackles of tradition. The actual experience of it is, however, far from this lofty ideal. The very notion of girls' education in Rajasthan is united with that of good health, good housekeeping and jobs for literate women (Gold 2002).

4. See Bernstein on the interrelationship between pedagogic practice and social class (1977, and his later work).

REFERENCES

Bernstein, B. 1977. *Class, Codes and Control*, Vol III. London: Routledge and Kegan Paul.

Bourdieu, P. and J-C. Passeron. 1990 [1977]. *Reproduction in Education, Society and Culture (Book 1)*. London: Sage Publications.

Goffman, E. 1973. *The Presentation of Self in Everyday Life*. New York: The Overlook Press.

Gold, A. Grodzins. 2002. 'Schooling Girls in Rural North India', in Diana P. Mines and S. Lamb(eds), *Everyday Life in South Asia*. London: Bloomington.

Kalia, N.N.1986. *From Sexism to Equality*. Delhi: New India Publications.

Kumar, Krishna. 2002. *Prejudice and Pride*. New Delhi: Viking.

Kumar, Nita. 2000. *Lessons from Schools: The History of Education in Banaras*. New Delhi: Sage Publications.

Krishna, Sumi. 1991. *India's Living Languages: The Critical Issues*. New Delhi: Allied Publishers.

———. 1998. 'Mizoram', in M.S. Swaminathan (ed.), *Gender Dimensions in Biodiversity Management*. New Delhi: Konark.

———. 2005. 'Gendered Price of Rice in North-East India', *Economic and Political Weekly*, XI(25), 18 June.

Lakshmi, B. 2005. 'Education and Society: A Sociological Study in Chhimtuipui District of Mizoram'. Unpublished Ph.D. Thesis. Department of Sociology, Delhi School of Economics, University of Delhi.

McLaren, P. and S. Giroux. 1997. 'Multiculturalism and the Post-Modern Critique: Towards a Pedagogy of Resistance and Transformation', in A.H. Halsey, H. Lauder, P. Brown and A. Stuart Wells (eds), *Education: Culture, Economy and Society*. Oxford: Oxford University Press.

Mizoram Board of School Education. *Zoram Bharti*: Text Books of Hindi for Classes V–VIII. Aizawl.

Mouffe, C. 1992. 'Democratic Citizenship and the Political Community', in Chantal Mouffe (ed.), *Dimensions of Radical Democracy*. London: Verso.

Nag, C.R. 1994. *Mizo Society in Transition*. Guwahati: Spectrum.

Nischol, K. 1976. *Women and Girls as Portrayed in Hindi Textbooks*. New Delhi: NCERT.

Nongbri, T. 1994. 'Gender Relations in Matrilineal Societies', *Lokayan Bulletin*, 10(5/6): 79–90.

Nussbawm, M. 2006. 'Capabilities as Fundamental Entitlements: Sen and Social Justice', in B. Agarwal, J. Humphries and I. Robeyns (eds), *Capabilities, Freedom and Equality: Amartya Sen's Work from a Gender Perspective*, pp. 39–69. Delhi: Oxford University Press.

Oakley, A. 1972. *Sex, Gender and Society.* London: Temple Smith.

————. 1974. *The Sociology of Housework.* Oxford: Martin Robertson.

Ortner, S.B. 1974. 'Is Female to Male as Nature is to Culture?', in M.Z. Rosaldo and L. Lamphere (eds), *Women, Culture and Society.* Stanford: Stanford University Press.

Peter, F. 2006. 'Gender and Foundations of Social Choice: The Role of Situated Agency', in B. Agarwal, J. Humphries and I. Robeyns (eds), *Capabilities, Freedom and Eqality: Amartya Sen's Work from a Gender Perspective.* New Delhi: Oxford University Press.

Saigol, R. 1995. *Knowledge and Identity: Articulation of Gender in Educational Discourse in Pakistan.* Lahore: SAHE.

Sangkima, B. 1994. *Mizos: Society and Social Change.* Guwahati: Spectrum.

Sarkar, L. and M. Karlekar. 1991. 'Mizo Customary Law: Marked Bias Against Women', *The Indian Express,* 23 May.

Scrase, T.J. 1993. *Image, Ideology and Inequality: Cultural Domination, Hegemony and Schooling in India.* New Delhi: Sage Publications.

Thapan, M. 2006 [1991]. *Life at School: An Ethnographic Study.* Delhi: Oxford University Press.

Xaxa, V. 2004. 'Women and Gender in the Study of Tribes in India', *Indian Journal of Gender Studies,* 11(3).

Zehol, L. 1998. *Women in Naga Society.* New Delhi: Regency Publishers.

IV

Restructuring Institutional Systems

10

Mainstreaming Gender in Agricultural Research and Extension
How Do We Move beyond Efficiency Arguments?

Meghana Kelkar

INTRODUCTION

Social research on agricultural technologies, especially in the context of the Green Revolution, has pointed to the socially biased outcomes favouring certain groups and locations in society. The literature pertaining to women and technological change in agriculture suggests that the Green Revolution package not only had a class bias but also a gender bias, reinforcing women's subordinate positions both in the household and wider society. This raises the issue of critiquing the gender sensitivity of the formal agricultural network in India. In this chapter, I try to present an analysis based on my three-fold experience, first as an alumni of one of the agricultural universities in India, second as a Class I officer at the Department of Agriculture, Maharashtra, and third as a Ph.D. research scholar working on similar issues. My observations are largely in the context of the agricultural network in the state of Maharashtra, which reflects the national picture on a smaller scale.

First, I summarise the functioning of the formal agricultural network, including a brief historical account and details regarding the three-fold functions of research, extension and education. Then, I review the gender mainstreaming efforts in the agricultural network in Maharashtra. I find that the current approach of mainstreaming, which is largely based on efficiency arguments, is perhaps strategic pragmatism and is a welcome departure from the paternalistic welfare approach that was observed earlier in Maharashtra. However, I point to the likely pitfalls of the sole focus being on 'women' as a homogeneous group and of the instrumental benefits of gender mainstreaming. I then discuss alternative strategies based on equity considerations. A critical review of the objectives, methods and methodological foundations on which agricultural research and extension rest points to the intrinsic problems of integrating equity concerns based on well-founded feminist principles. Finally, I conclude that the mainstreaming of gender concerns in the agricultural network requires politicised strategic efforts with a two-pronged strategy: first, strong advocacy efforts at the policy levels to keep the issue on the anvil and second, a constant re-enforcement of these efforts through explicit feminist research.

AGRICULTURAL NETWORK IN MAHARASHTRA

In Maharashtra, agricultural research and extension of technologies is largely the prerogative of state agricultural universities, state departments of agriculture and various regional organisations such as the Krishi Vigyan Kendras (Agricultural Science Centres) and zonal research stations, which are either central and/or state government agencies. These organisations, along with the policy-making secretariats, formulate a complex agricultural network in the state.

The roots of state-induced intervention in agricultural research, extension and education can be traced back to colonial days. The Department of Agriculture established in Maharashtra in 1883, largely to combat recurrent famine situations. Soon after independence, the Report of the University Education Commission recommended a system of rural agricultural universities patterned after the US land grant systems (Easter et al. 1989). As per this pattern, professional training in the western sciences of agriculture was seen to be a major vehicle for producing a team of agricultural scientists, who would then bring about a radical modernisation of Indian agriculture. Thus, specialised scientific education was seen to be an emerging need, which would be catered for by special agricultural universities isolated from the mainstream educational system. Accordingly, the Maharashtra legislature passed the Maharashtra Krishi

Vidyapeeth Act, 1967, which was followed by the establishment of the Maharashtra Agricultural University in 1968 (Mahatma Phule Krishi Vidyapeeth 2006). Later, regional political compulsions led to this single university being split into four agricultural universities, located at Rahuri, Parbhani, Dapoli and Akola. Recently, the disciplines of animal husbandry, veterinary sciences and fisheries have been transferred to a separate Maharashtra Animal and Fisheries Sciences University at Nagpur.

The functions of agricultural research and education were exclusively transferred to the agricultural universities, whereas agricultural extension remained a joint activity of the agriculture department and the universities.

Agricultural Research

The primary objective of agricultural research, especially during the Green Revolution decades (1960s and 1970s) and into the present, has been 'increasing productivity in order to feed the burgeoning population'. In recent decades, the issue of conservation and sustainable use of natural resources has also gained significance in research priorities. The outcome of research influences state policies as well as the state-funded extension programmes.

Agricultural Extension

Another major outcome of research is the 'generation of technologies', which can then be transferred to the farmers for adoption via the extension machinery. This kind of organised agricultural extension has been through various phases of change since independence. The first phase began with the 'Grow More Food' campaign of 1948 and the 'Community Development Programme' of 1952. The second phase, the 'Training and Visit System' (popularly known as the T&V system) sponsored by the World Bank, was initiated in Maharashtra in 1981. The National Agricultural Technology Project launched in 1998 can be considered the latest phase of agricultural extension in the state. The 'transfer of technology model', however, remains the 'soul' of all these phases (Raina 2003). Apart from the organised extension programmes, the Department of Agriculture functions in a subsidy-based programme mode. It implements various state and centrally sponsored programmes for crop production, horticultural promotion, watershed development, soil conservation and agricultural inputs (seeds, fertilisers and agro-chemicals).

Agricultural Education

To impart scientific education in agriculture, the agricultural universities in Maharashtra offer various diploma/certificate, graduate and post-graduate courses. One of the universities also has a separate college of home science affiliated to it. Recently, Maharashtra has legalised the establishment of private colleges offering agricultural education, affiliated to the state agricultural universities. Unlike mainstream universities, agricultural universities in India do not have a national regulatory authority along the lines of the University Grants Commission (UGC) and the All India Council of Technical Education (AICTE). The Indian Council of Agricultural Research (ICAR) supports the state universities by developing model course curricula, uniform guidelines and norms for the management of academics (National Academy of Agricultural Sciences 2004). In 1983, Maharashtra constituted an autonomous statutory Maharashtra Council for Agricultural Education and Research (MCAER) to coordinate the functioning of the four agricultural universities in the state.

MAINSTREAMING GENDER IN THE AGRICULTURAL NETWORK

The official and grey literature in the agricultural network, that is, the agricultural policy, government resolutions, research mandates and extension programme guidelines, rarely use gender terminology. Instead, the phrase 'women in agriculture' is used more often. In 2002, the Government of Maharashtra appointed a high-level committee to prepare an action plan for agriculture for the next 25 yeas (Government of Maharashtra 2002). This committee included agricultural scientists, administrators, representatives of private-sector agricultural firms, NGO representatives and political leaders. The committee functioned through subgroups that examined various topics related to agricultural prosperity in Maharashtra. The issue of 'strengthening the role of women in agriculture in Maharashtra' was initially not under consideration, and was later added on the recommendation of Dr M.S. Swaminathan, Chairperson of the committee. I served as coordinator of this sub-group because, being a woman officer, I was considered most suitable for the job. I presented the report to the committee meeting after perusing the available literature and holding informal deliberations with various authorities and agricultural scientists. The following section recapitulates the findings of this report and also the progress thereafter.

In 1994, Maharashtra was the first state to formulate a policy for women, which was revised in 2001. The policy recognises the key role played by women in various activities. The policy states:

> Women play a key role in various activities in the rural areas. *Their empowerment can sharply increase productivity and incomes, generate employment and promote rural regeneration.* For this purpose research and extension efforts shall fully reflect the concerns of women. 50 per cent of the extension efforts shall be focussed on women. Women groups shall be assisted in taking up various activities of contract farming, farm services and processing and marketing of farm products. They shall be encouraged to start dairy and poultry co-operative societies. The relevant land legislation shall be suitably amended, if necessary, to promote contract farming and farm services. (GoM 2001: 15; emphasis added).

The policy envisages various other measures to mainstream women in all developmental activities. Subsequent to the announcement of this policy, the state announced a 33 per cent reservation for women candidates in all streams of agricultural education and for all positions of direct recruitment to agricultural services in Maharashtra. Agricultural universities that were ill-equipped to host the surge of newly admitted girl students took the lead by establishing agricultural schools especially for girls and by strengthening girls' hostels in agricultural colleges.

Since 1995, the Department of Agriculture has recognised the role of women in agriculture by the Jeejamata Krishi Bhushan award that is being given to exemplary women farmers. Women 'beneficiaries' were identified in a few horticultural schemes such as the National Watershed Development Programme and the National Agricultural Technology Project. The central sector scheme, 'Women in Agriculture', was being implemented in Thane district on a pilot basis since 1994–95.

The sub-group reviewed these efforts with the comment that they were woefully inadequate in view of the magnitude of the issue of women's empowerment. The report pointed to the discouraging down trend of sex ratio in rural Maharashtra, especially in the agriculturally advanced western regions. The report emphatically drew the attention of the rest of the committee members (mostly men) towards the gender dimensions of agriculture:

> India has achieved self sufficiency in food production. However, sustainability of food supply is a great challenge of the decade. The national agriculture policy has targeted 4 per cent annual growth in agriculture sector and at least 8 per cent growth in each of the sub sectors viz. horticulture, livestock products and fisheries. For achieving this kind of target it would be highly essential to tap the tremendous potential of women in food security, production efficiency and quality revolution. (GoM 2002: 201)

The report highlighted the fact that no agricultural university had gender issues on their research agenda and that there was an overall lack of attention vis-à-vis gender issues in the fields of agricultural research and extension in the state. Moreover, the statistical data related to women in agricultural communities and gender analysis of the agricultural sector was severely lacking. Research on technological advancement and skill upgradation of women workers was also not prioritised. The committee suggested a range of action points: information and data collection on rural women; gender sensitisation and institutionalisation at all levels in the department and universities; formulation of research strategies for mainstreaming women in agriculture on the part of agricultural universities; development of strategies for improving extension services for women in agriculture; involvement of the private sector and NGOs wherever possible for ensuring a holistic approach; and credit linkage of women's Self-Help Groups involved in agricultural activities (see GoM 2002).

After the report was submitted, the state government launched an ambitious programme called the Krishi Saptak Yojana, which aimed to improve the participation of women in agriculture (GoM n.d.). The 'women in agriculture' scheme was expanded to all the districts, covering at least one tehsil per district as a pilot project. An impressive outlay of Rs 80 million was sanctioned for 2003–04, the first year of state-wide implementation. Gender sensitisation workshops were organised at the apex training institute and also at the regional satellite training institutes. Scheme guidelines were altered, and field functionaries were directed to encourage women and include at least 30 per cent women 'beneficiaries' in all the schemes implemented by the Agriculture Department. The emphasis was on increasing the number of women in all training programmes, field trips, study tours and agricultural exhibitions. Agricultural universities increased the number of technology and skill trainings for women[1].

These efforts to 'mainstream' gender concerns into the agricultural network in Maharashtra are a welcome departure from the earlier welfarist approach. The current approach recognises the productive role of women and encourages their economic participation in development. It accords 'visibility' to women farmers, something that was denied hitherto, and sees them as actors in agrarian development. As envisaged in the Committee Report, the agricultural network seems to have initiated efforts towards the addition of economic value to women's time and labour, and to providing the required support services such as credit and technical skills. The policy of positive discrimination for women in agricultural education and services is also a step ahead towards equity of opportunities. This is all the more commendable given the fact that earlier, there had been only a scant proportion of women opting for agriculture as a stream of education as well as a career.

As agricultural growth in Maharashtra had reached a plateau, the state searched for new avenues that could perhaps improve the situation. The line of argument in the state women's policy was reiterated in the Committee Report: that women farmers deserve better attention as they are active players in the processes of agricultural production and food security, and that there was a need to further improve their efficiency to increase the pace of these processes. This was a powerful argument strategically pitched at an appropriate time, resulting in an immediate policy change. This shows that mainstreaming efforts, based on an efficiency approach, have the potential to open varied opportunities for women in rural Maharashtra. Critical hindsight, however, points to various problems that I will discuss in the following section.

PROBLEMS OF 'MAINSTREAMING'

'Women in agriculture', as a homogeneous category so often observed in the grey literature in Maharashtra, is a problematic concept in itself. This categorisation puts all rural women into a single group, regardless of caste, class, religion and varied livelihood contexts. Thus, instead of problematising the unequal gender relations that are a major reason for the subordination of women, 'women' themselves are likely to be identified as a problem zone. Further, the efficiency approach rests on the hope of strengthening the role of women in agriculture to simultaneously achieve the instrumental goals of increasing productivity and food security. If women fail to live up to these expectations, they are likely to be blamed as 'laggards' in the adoption of technology and its subsequent economic application, without considering the economic, social and cultural constraints that women face due to their gendered position within the household and the wider society. The narration of my field experience in Box 10.1 demonstrates how social perceptions about a woman, which result from her gendered position within the household and the society, shape access to public extension services.

Box 10.1
'Oh, I think I have Just Missed the Women, Totally!'

This is the experience that I gained, while I was visiting a few villages in Satara district as a pilot exercise for my Ph.D. fieldwork. Mr Jadhav,* agricultural assistant, took me to village Kathapur in Koregaon tehsil. He had organised an informal meeting with members of the women's self-help group. Most of the women who had gathered for the meeting belonged to farming households of the Maratha caste. In the same village, Mr Jadhav had recently held a Farmer's Field School (FFS) on Integrated Pest Management (IPM) for gram in the same village. Being a dedicated fieldworker, his field school had received a very good response and participation from the village.

Against this backdrop, when I started talking to the women, they were initially very reluctant to start any discussion. They kept asking me to complete my 'talk' so that they could proceed for their work.

(Box 10.1 continued)

(*Box 10.1 continued*)

I sent Mr Jadhav and his male colleague outside the house where we had gathered. This strategy worked, and slowly the women started talking to me openly. I asked if any of them knew anything about agriculture and whether they worked in their fields.

This question annoyed middle-aged Meerabai,* who retorted,

All you people are just alike. What do you mean by this question? Of course, we work in the fields; we do everything—weeding, plucking, harvesting, watering, winnowing and threshing. We work day and night, and anyway what do the men folk know? This man (Mr Jadhav) organised this school in the village. He taught everything to them (men). I was so curious to know what he taught; it was so interesting, this 'friendly insects' (predators) and 'enemy insects' (parasites) and all that. I used to linger around in the field, so that I could overhear something of their discussions. But he never called me to participate. Also, my husband would have got annoyed had I lingered longer around the men. But I know everything. What do you think? We always plant *javas* (linseed) as an intercrop with gram. I use the seeds to make dry chutney. But now, he (Mr. Jadhav) tells us that javas also attracts friendly insects that eat the worms on gram. I didn't know that. He should have told us all this. He just felt, what would these ignorant women know anyway?

Later on, I related this experience to Mr Jadhav, who was extremely surprised and exclaimed, 'No Madam, this was not intentional. I just didn't think about them (women). I never thought they would be so much interested. Did they really talk about pests and predators? Oh, this is so interesting, and how proud I was about my technical and field effectiveness. Oh, I think I have just missed the women, totally!'

* Names changed.

Thus, it is necessary to move beyond 'adding women' and rethink agricultural development concepts and practices as a whole, from a gender perspective (Jackson 1998, modification mine). The question that persists is: will the agricultural research and extension network move in this direction, and how?

A critical review of the objectives, methods and methodological foundations of agricultural research and extension points to the intrinsic problems in the system that make this a difficult proposition[2].

Unidisciplinary Research

Agricultural research in India is largely conducted within rigid disciplinary principles. As the research is concentrated within natural scientific enquiries, the conceptualisation of farming is limited to the biophysical realities surrounding the farming household. The influences of dynamic interactions with other institutions and socio-economic and politico-legal environments are glossed over. Although a range of technology is generated through this research, the perspective of research continues to be partial, and technology continues to be in the form of blanket recommendations. Due to the hegemony of natural sciences in the agricultural network, the social scientific enquiry remains weak and limited within a narrow, technology-oriented focus.

Transfer of Technology

A close examination of this model of extension indicates that preferences, perceptions and priorities of the end-users of technology do not form an integral part of the technological design. For example, the concerns of 'productivity', which may well be the concerns of the scientific community or the policy makers, may not necessarily be those of the farmers, women and men, who actually manage their land. Similarly, the constraints faced by the farmers also do not reach the designers of technology, or may reach them in an altered form. Technological constraints are still likely to find a space, but the non-technical ones, such as questions of land tenure, land rights or cultural beliefs, are accorded the position of 'barrier to adoption', or something that is to be overcome through 'education' and 'motivation'. The easiest solution is to neglect the non-adopter as illiterate and a 'laggard', making it easier to concentrate on the easy adopter, that is, 'the innovator', who would be a well-off farmer with irrigation and other facilities. The ethos of research thus alienates researchers from the field situation, leaving them unaware of the actual reality of farmers. Besides, wherever there is any account of actual land managers, they are lumped together into the facile categories of 'farmers', 'farming community', and 'farming households' or 'village folk'.

Conceptualisation of the 'Household'

Agricultural scientists and economists commonly use 'household' as a unit of analysis in agricultural research. However, deconstruction of farming households on the basis of caste, class, religion and gender is seldom done. Agricultural technology design and its dissemination have relied heavily on the farm-household model (Singh et al. 1986), which is based on the unitary household model. It considers the household an undifferentiated entity, with common resources and preferences, headed by an altruistic male patriarch. The model neglects the activities, preference and constraints of women in the farming household (Feldstein and Poats 1989). Also, the division of labour is 'naturalised' (Harris 1981: 136), and is assumed to be dependent on sex-attributed characteristics according to the principle of maximum efficiency, rather than the socialised gender identities of men and women in agricultural households. This misconceptualisation of a farming household in agricultural research obviously has a gender-biased outcome (as has been demonstrated by post-Green Revolution social studies, for example, Agarwal 1985; Chowdhury 1994; Whitehead 1985).

Epistemological Foundations of Mainstream Agricultural Research and Extension

The epistemological stance of mainstream agricultural research in India is positivist realism, wherein the ideas of socio-political neutrality and objectivity are seen to be deeply entrenched. The objectives and methods arising from this are obviously tailored to feed the realist positions. The dogmatic belief in the methods of science as being those yielding the ultimate truth is also deep-seated. The ideas of the social construction of reality and its multiple perceptions are not considered to hold good. Scientists and policy makers are accorded sole agency and space for action. Reflexivity in research, taking into account the subjectivity of researchers, seems to be absent. Questions about who decides the agenda and whose priorities get an upper hand are not enquired into, nor are they reflected upon. In the main, the local knowledges of people are deemed inferior and not worthy of consideration.

Institutional and Organisational Problems

National and state funding towards agricultural research and extension is increasingly becoming a constraint as agriculture is no longer a priority sector (Mruthyunjaya and Ranjitha 1998). There has been a major change in research priorities and an increasing push towards public-private partnership in agricultural research, extension and education under the regime of globalisation and the WTO (Easter et al.1989). Instead of institutional reforms involving a transformation of the rules/norms that govern agricultural policy, research and extension organisations, there have been cosmetic changes in the organisational structure (Raina 2003). These are some of the pertinent problems that are being faced by the agricultural network in India, and Maharashtra is no exception to this.

FUTURE DIRECTIONS AND WAYS FORWARD

Considering the institutional philosophy of the agricultural network, the integration of gender and equity concerns on well-founded feminist principles seems a daunting prospect. The expectation that the stimulus for 'integration' can be generated within the system solely by increasing the number of women in the network is ill-founded: 'Access is not enough to change the gender asymmetries, though it is clearly crucial to the process of change in the forms of education and in the uses of technology' (Bourque and Warren 1990: 10). In the absence of conscious efforts to infuse gender sensitivity as a core component in agricultural education, it is erroneous to assume that the neo-entrant women professionals would automatically be sensitive towards these issues.

Thus, as mentioned earlier, the mainstreaming of gender and equity concerns in the agricultural network requires politicised strategic efforts with a two-pronged strategy, the first being strong advocacy efforts at the policy levels to keep the issue on the anvil. These advocacy efforts should conceptualise women farmers as equal citizens with their own aspirations of and agendas for progress, as well as their right to access a gender-sensitive public network of agricultural research and extension. These advocacy efforts are to be constantly re-enforced by conducting explicit feminist research on these issues. The research agenda should not only include farmers as gendered subjects and farming systems as gendered systems, but also the agricultural network (research, extension and education) as a gendered institution. There is a need to analyse the institution, the organisations within the institution and the actors in the organisations from a gender perspective with a feminist research gaze. This is all the more urgent because the agricultural systems are undergoing a transition with market forces playing the dominant role and the agendas of the marginalised are getting increasingly left out.

NOTE

1. I have gathered the information on progress initiated after the submission of the committee report by talking to my colleagues at the Department of Agriculture and agriculture universities.

2. The critique of the rigidity of agricultural research within the natural science disciplines and the 'transfer of technology' model of extension is based on my paper, 'Soil management and Scientific enquiry: A critique', which is part of the pre-doctoral thesis submitted to the Tata Institute of Social Sciences, Mumbai, in 2005.

REFERENCES

Agarwal, B. 1985. 'Women and Technological Change in Agriculture: The Asian and African Experience', in I. Ahmed (ed.), *Technology and Rural Women: Conceptual and Empirical Issues*. A study prepared for the International Labour Office within the framework of the World Employment Programme, pp. 67–111. London: Allen & Unwin.

Bourque, Susan C. and Kay B. Warren. 1990. 'Access is not Enough: Gender Perspectives on Technology and Education', in I. Tinker (ed.), *Persistent Inequalities: Women and World Development*. New York, London: Oxford University Press.

Chowdhury, Prem. 1994. *The Veiled Women: Shifting Gender Equations in Rural Haryana 1880–1990*. New Delhi: Oxford University Press.

Easter, K. William, S. Bisaliah and John O. Dunbar. 1989. 'After Twenty Five Years of Institution Building, the State Agricultural Universities in India Face New Challenges', *American Journal of Agricultural Economics*, 71(5): 1200–05.

Feldstein, Hilary Sims and Susan V. Poats. 1989. 'Conceptual Framework for Gender Analysis in Farming System Research and Extension', in H.S. Feldstein and S.V. Poats (eds), *Working Together: Gender Analysis in Agriculture*. West Hartford, Conn.: Kumarian Press.

Government of India. 1992. 'National Policy on Education, 1986 (As modified in 1992)'. New Delhi: Government of India, http://education.nic.in/policy/npe86-mod92.pdf.

Government of Maharashtra. 2001. 'Women's Policy'. Government of Maharashtra: Department of Women and Child Development.

———. 2002. 'Report of the High Level Committee to Prepare an Action Plan for Agriculture for Coming Twenty-Five Years', Vol. 2. Pune: Commissionerate of Agriculture, Maharashtra.

———. n.d. *Krishi Saptak Karyakram*. Pune: Commissionerate of Agriculture, Maharashtra.

Harris, O. 1981. 'Households as Natural Units', in K. Young, C. Wolkowitz and R. McCullagh (eds), *Of Marriage and the Market: Women's Subordination Internationally and it's Lessons*. London and New York: Routledge.

Jackson, C. 1998. 'Rescuing Gender from the Poverty Trap,' in C. Jackson and R. Pearson (eds), *Feminist Visions of Development: Gender, Analysis and Policy*. London: Routledge.

Mahatma Phule Krishi Vidyapeeth. 2006. 'Formation of Agricultural Universities'. Available online at http:/mpkv.mah.nic.in/formantuniver.htm (Accessed on 7/03/2006).

Mruthyunjaya and P. Ranjitha. 1998. 'The Indian Agricultural Research System: Structure, Current Policy Issues and Future Orientation', *World Development*, 26(6): 1089–1101.

National Academy of Agricultural Sciences. 2004. *Stake holder's perceptions on employment oriented agricultural education*. New Delhi: National Academy of Agricultural Sciences.

Raina, R.S. 2003. 'Institutions and Organisations: Enabling Reforms in Indian Agricultural Research and Policy.' *International Journal of Technology Management and Sustainable Development*, 2(2): 97–116.

Singh, I., L. Squire and J. Strauss (eds).1986. *Agricultural Household Models Extensions, Applications, and Policy*. Introduction and Chapter 1. Baltimore, MD, London, John Hopkins University Press.

Whitehead, A. 1985. 'Effects of Technological Change on Rural Women: A Review of Analysis and Concepts', in I. Ahmed (ed.), *Technology and Rural Women: Conceptual and Empirical Issues*. A study prepared for the International Labour Office within the framework of the World Employment Programme. London: Allen and Unwin.

11

Women and Water Policy
Issues and Alternatives

Seema Kulkarni

INTRODUCTION

In recent years, there has been a global recognition of the crisis in the water sector. Different national and international fora are now voicing their concern about the challenge of meeting the growing demands for water while maintaining the sustainability of the environment. Increasing conflicts over water have now reached alarming levels due to scarcity, pollution and the priority accorded to industrial as against agricultural use.

Fragmentation in water resource planning is an important factor responsible for the crisis. In the first two or three decades after independence, the thinking that dominated the irrigation sector in India was largely that of making water available for increasing agricultural production to overcome food shortages. This led to massive investments in large dams, storage structures and canal networks. The post-1970s period saw a spurt in groundwater resource development. The number of borewells and dug wells grew, and so did the extraction of groundwater for irrigation. Today, about 60 per cent of the irrigated area is fed by groundwater. Though the expansion of irrigation has undoubtedly been rewarding, it has also brought to the fore the issues of sustainable and equitable use of water.

For example, overemphasis on large storages has led to problems of displacement and environmental sustainability. Overdrawing of groundwater has led to the depletion of the water source and problems of salinisation, and an increase in the arsenic and fluoride levels in the water, rising energy costs and, finally, drying up of the sources. This has affected the availability of drinking water. The lack of effective governance in the groundwater sector has deepened the drinking water crisis in rural areas, the impact of which is largely borne by rural women.

The overriding concern in the water sector today is to ensure adequate, assured and accessible and supplies of potable water for livelihood security, particularly for the poor and marginalised groups.

HOW DOES THIS RELATE TO THE QUESTION OF GENDER?

In arguing for a radical potential for a link between gender and water, we are not claiming that women somehow share a natural affinity with water, but rather that it is not possible to understand the various dimensions of the crisis in the water sector completely in the absence of a gendered understanding of access to resources and their use. In this context, to focus on the inequality based on gender is not to imply that an analysis with class, caste, racism and/or ethnicity as its starting point would be any less important or relevant. Neither does it try to undermine the enormity of the problems with which the water sector itself is besieged. The attempt here is to show how all of this is in fact organically linked together. This is explored in the context of the new water policy.

NEW WATER POLICY ENVIRONMENT

The new policy environment seeks solutions in institutional reforms, incentive structures and through a shift in approach from supply-side to demand-side management to come out of this crisis. This brings in a whole new set of implications regarding the questions of equity and sustainability. This shift has also meant a slow but definite withdrawal of the state, which now sees itself more as a promoter of water systems and services than as a provider. This has opened the door for private interests in water, especially in the drinking water and sanitation sector. Particularly in urban areas, privatisation of drinking water has now become the norm rather than an exception. Cities like Delhi, Bangalore and many others have already signed contracts with large water companies like the French Vivendi, Suez and Thames Water for drinking water and sanitation facilities. Examples outside of India, like the famous Cochabamba case in Bolivia, have shown the disastrous results that ensue when private interests take over water provisioning. This has serious implications for a large section of the poor, who may not be able to afford drinking water in the new scenario.

The new policy approach perceives the problem as primarily one of scarcity—of finances and of water resources. What then follows as a logical outcome is the emergence of policies geared towards managing demand rather than extending supply. Therefore, a new set of directives falls into place, which treat water as an economic good that has to recover the costs incurred (on its development and management) through its use. This new thinking has its roots in the early 1990s, when the economies of most countries were stagnant and there was a general reconsideration of the role of the state in the economy. This was also the period when most countries were in the process of introducing a structural reform agenda.

In the water sector, a natural fallout of this thinking was the changing role of the government from a provider to a promoter and facilitator, the involvement of the private sector, NGOs and communities as service providers, and the need for strong institutions (Ballabh 2004; Cleaver 1995; van Koppen 1999; Zwarteveen 1998). Much of this policy discourse is largely relevant to public-sector irrigation and keeps groundwater almost entirely out of its purview. This chapter, therefore, largely focuses on public-sector irrigation and the gender issues within it.

HOW SCARCE IS WATER?

Posing scarcity as the only problem forces water-deprived poor women and men to not stake any claims on water. The conflict between men of different groups, which is already severe, deepens further when women want to stake independent claims over water. Better and more revenue generating options are preferred, and this is reflected in the present water policies where industrial water use gains priority over water for agriculture. Any new investments that could take water schemes to the remote areas are thus thwarted on the grounds of scarcity of both funds and water. Typically, then, equity gets the first cut as equity would come at an additional cost. Taking water to diverse social groups of women and men, and to remote and high altitude areas (such as those inhabited by adivasis), requires more investments and also specific allocations of water.

Project-level experiences show that abundance or scarcity of water cannot be judged without considering the various competing claims and demands on water, and understanding how the resource is being currently used. Various studies (see, for example, Vaidyanathan 2003) have shown that while scarcity of water is a critical issue, the problem is usually more complex; and this needs to be understood before policy prescriptions are made. Indeed, studies point out that inequitable distribution of water and gaps in water resource management are more often the reason for the present crisis.

However, because the present discourse around water is centred on water scarcity as the central concern, this acquires a value that needs to be quantified in economic terms. With such an understanding, a new set of reforms have found space, which will have a long-standing impact on the water sector and the users.

GENDER CONCERNS AND THE NEW IRRIGATION THINKING

The role of irrigation in improving agricultural production hardly needs any special mention. In the last few decades, most of the increased yields have been possible largely due to irrigation. The productivity of non-irrigated lands has mostly been stagnant. Before the 1990s, the emphasis of irrigation policy makers was on planning for the provisioning of water through improving infrastructure, identification of sites, and the design, appraisal and implementation of projects (Vaidyanathan 2003; Zwarteveen 1998). Large-scale investments were made in the irrigation sector, with a focus on augmenting the water supply through the construction of large storages and developing a canal network. This agenda was pursued with vigour both due to an ever-increasing demand for food supplies and water, and of course the commensurate technological advances in this direction. The driving force behind this thinking was a strong production agenda. Improved irrigation facilities, along with other agricultural inputs, have had a phenomenal impact on the overall development in agriculture. However, the many benefits are also accompanied by water insecurity for a large number of poor women and men. Expansion of irrigation to meet the livelihood requirements of the poor has rarely been on the irrigation agenda.

The present policy thrust is focused on the pricing of water, recovery of capital costs, and decentralised management of the resource. In the following section we look at the impact this has on water-deprived groups, particularly women (see Kulkarni 2005).

PRICING AND COST RECOVERY

With the policy thrust on treating water as an economic good, debates around water pricing and full cost recovery are now gaining ground. The irrigation sector has been recognised as a loss-making one, and the state therefore wants to rid itself of the responsibility of managing it. One of the solutions to recovering the costs of operation and management is seen in the *user pays principle*. Although fine in theory as far as the productive use of water is concerned, in plain terms it simply implies that only those who are ready, willing and have the ability to pay will have access to water. No distinction is made in pricing policies for water for livelihood needs and water requirements beyond that.

This has two kinds of implications: the first is the priority given to industrial water use over irrigation for agriculture. Since the simple rule of economics says that allocation is to be accorded to wherever the returns are the highest, water for industry becomes the more favoured option. The second implication is vis-à-vis cropping preferences within irrigated areas. As men increasingly come to see greater advantages in either selling or using the available water to generate cash incomes, there is the possibility that access to water for non-marketable produce or survival tasks will be restricted (Green and Baden 1995). In such a scenario, it is usually the 'paying' crops that get preference over the 'non-paying' food crops largely cultivated by women. Women have often informally used irrigation water for micro-enterprises concerning small-scale activities, such as goat rearing, cattle rearing, brick moulding and vegetable growing, that are crucial from the point of view of household consumption. In all these enterprises, the economic benefits are not very high, thereby forcing women out of irrigation usage (Cleaver and Elson 1995).

The economic criterion also raises some very critical issues regarding what is really economically affordable for women. Most studies and experiences indicate that women rarely have control over their own or the household income. In many of the drinking water schemes, guaranteeing assured supplies has prompted women to agree to the 'user pays' principle. However, willingness to pay cannot be equated with the ability to pay. This leads to critical questions: how does one arrive at what the necessary quantum of water for meeting livelihood needs is? And how can this become affordable? Water also has other social and cultural dimensions; given the nature of the resource and the socio-cultural value that it commands; treating water purely as an economic good may not be a very viable option.

Cost recovery is the other principle that is seen as critical for reforming the water sector. Although this is happening rapidly in the drinking water and sanitation sector, the irrigation sector too is not far behind. An example is the recently formulated scheme of the Minor Irrigation Department of the Maharashtra government supported by the KfW (the German development bank), which promises to involve the beneficiaries from the resource development stage itself. The new terminology is Participatory Irrigation Development and Management (PIDM). The scheme is designed in such a way that the beneficiaries themselves bear a large part (60 per cent) of the distribution costs. This would be done through a combination of contributions in the form of labour, cash and bank loans. Here, it was found that a large part of the labour contribution came from the women of the beneficiary households. Experiences from across the world also show that the labour inputs for capital cost recovery and for recovery of the operation and maintenance costs of the irrigation schemes are largely borne by the women of the households. Thus, a gender analysis of the implied cost savings from decentralised management systems with appropriate cost recovery and pricing mechanisms may reflect hidden costs in terms of the increased labour for women at the community level (Green and Baden 1995).

IMPROVED PRODUCTIVITY AND EFFICIENCY

Irrigation efficiency at both the project and the farm levels has been one of the important goals of the irrigation sector. However, improved productivity has hardly been seen in the context of the regenerative and sustainable use of the water resources. This myopic view has limited the expansion of the total irrigated area to the pre-defined command area. High productivity at the level of the irrigation system does not automatically mean that all the households benefit from their involvement in irrigation, or that they benefit to the same extent. Nor does a high productivity or income at the household level always imply that all household members have contributed equally to this income and have also shared it equally.

Women's use of irrigation water is seen in uses other than irrigating the 'main' crops. Indeed, informal withdrawal of water for small patches of vegetables or for domestic uses by women is not uncommon. However, from the conventional analyses of the irrigation efficiency model, this distraction from irrigating the main crops would very likely be seen as wastage. In most irrigated areas, it is evident that the obverse of improved productivity and irrigation efficiency is increased labour for women. Although there is a positive aspect to improved labour opportunities, often the increased burden of work for women does not substantially improve their status or relieve them of their domestic workloads (SOPPECOM 2002; Vasavada 2005; Ahmed 2005; Zwarteveen 1998).

DECENTRALISED MANAGEMENT: TRANSFER OF POWER TO THE PEOPLE OR TRANSFER OF A SICK SECTOR

In the present paradigm, decentralised management is often viewed as the acceptable side of economic efficiency. It is considered a human investment in recovering costs on the physical structure. The state is rolling back, and has been promoting the idea of decentralised water users associations (WUAs), which it is hoped would manage the resource better (see Box 11.1). However, decentralised management is often limited to

---

Box 11.1
Water Users Associations

Water users associations (WUAs) are typically formed for surface irrigation systems. Farmers who fall within the 'beneficiary' area of the irrigation dam concerned can come together at the minor canal level to form a WUA. The 'beneficiaries' may belong to different village units.

Until recently in Maharashtra, such a WUA would be registered under the Cooperative Societies Registration Act. At least 51 per cent of the beneficiary farmers would have to become members for the society to be registered. The WUA is a legal entity recognised by the Irrigation Department, which signs an agreement with the WUA on issues related to water quotas and its management. A typical WUA has a general body and an executive body, which take decisions for it. WUAs have no organic relationships with the gram panchayat and have to directly deal with the Irrigation Department.

These societies only allow farmers with a landholding in the beneficiary area, or what is called the 'command' area, to become members. Typically, these are men from better-off classes and castes. This norm excludes women from membership. Therefore, women are neither in the decision-making bodies, nor do they receive a share of water for themselves.

Maharashtra has recently passed a legislation that makes it mandatory for the Irrigation Department to set up WUAs, in the absence of which water would not be released. However, there are very few changes in the policy to allow for space for women and the landless.

---

being a mechanism for recovering costs and improving irrigation. It has not really redefined rights, which would make it more inclusive of various other hitherto deprived stakeholders.

Notions of a Decentralised Community

Decentralisation almost always translates into community participation, but the notion of the community as a homogeneous unit often ignores the social and economic differentiations within it. Decentralisation also brings with it a promise to improve the participation of women and other resource-poor groups; however, decentralised planning does not guarantee that women would be allowed membership to WUAs or a role in the decision-making processes. In this male-dominated society, it is no wonder that caste/class and gender assumptions are reflected in the approach and conceptualisation of the WUAs. The typical arguments used are that women do not own land; women are unable to attend meetings; women have never been traditionally involved in irrigation management and hence need not be involved. The efforts to organise WUAs often continue to suffer from the already criticised narrow conception of farmers as male heads of the household. The result is that only the male member is considered the representative to the WUA.

In fact, what was earlier the domain of the male-dominated irrigation department has now become the domain of the upper-caste/class male-dominated WUAs. From the point of view of women, therefore, control by the Irrigation Department has now been replaced by that of the WUAs, represented by upper-caste/class men. The one household, one representative rule is still largely applicable in membership criteria for WUAs. It therefore eliminates what little possibility women would have had in participating in decision-making processes in the water sector. For women who are already constrained by socio-cultural roles, participation becomes even more difficult when formal rules restrict their presence in the WUAs. Thus, unless conscious efforts are made to recognise these differences and involve women, Dalits and other resource-poor groups, there is little likelihood that such institutional reforms will guarantee rights to women, or for that matter to other resource-poor groups.

Other related issues that have come up from a few studies show that women are much more attuned to participating and sharing their views in informal networks rather than the formal set-ups that are seen as legitimate fora by the experts. The rigid rule-making procedure and 'boundedness' of the formal association often restricts women's participation (Cleaver 1998).

A GENDERED FRAMEWORK FOR WATER SECTOR RESTRUCTURING

That brings us to the most vexed question: what, then, is the alternative framework that gives us a gendered understanding of the water sector and advances its restructuring? The following are the main elements of such a framework.

Reconceptualising Women

One of the first things that we propose in the alternative framework is the need to change the ways in which we understand women. This is a question of changing the entire worldview surrounding women, their interests, their perceptions, their ways of negotiating for access and so on.

Perceiving Women as Independent Members of the Household

Despite two decades of women's studies pointing to gender biases in intra-household differences in incomes, access to productive resources and health care, the household is still treated as a coherent unit with the male head representing the common interests of all. Women are still not recognised as active, thinking members of the household, and their interests, needs and opinions are merged with those of the male members. The dominant idea today is that water for irrigation lies in the male domain. Water users are seen as the male heads of households, and therefore it is presumed that women do not require independent entitlements over water. This is also very much in line with the assumption that the household is a unit with congruent interests, among whom the benefits of available resources are shared equitably (Agarwal 1994).

The fear, or rather the unwillingness, of policy makers and planners to openly interfere within the private sphere of families is as evident in the water sector as it is anywhere else. The socio-cultural barriers to granting women independent rights over resources holds true in the case of water too. Rights to water and land usually translate into security and better bargaining power, both within the household as well as outside. Improving women's access to this resource would lead to improved bargaining power for women within the household, but this is usually perceived as a threat to the current patriarchal order. While recognising that the household is a site of both cooperation and conflict between members, there is a need to see women as active and independent members with their own ideas and interests. Unless this perception becomes part of mainstream thinking, it might be difficult to forge the agenda of gender equity in irrigation.

Understanding Differences among Women

Grouping women as a category is a fallacy that needs to be tackled. It is important to understand that women are not an abstract, homogeneous category, and come with large differences across class, caste and tribe in the Indian context. Women from oppressed castes and tribes face a dual oppression—as both women and members of the caste/tribe to which they belong (Joy and Paranjape 2005; Kulkarni and Rao 2002). These differences in social relations amongst women undermine any notion of groups formed through a homogeneity of common interests as women. While the notion of homogeneity has its relevance in the broader context of addressing patriarchy, various experiences indicate that grouping women as a category vis-à-vis their relationship to water or other natural resources has only been counterproductive.

Once this difference is understood, we will see that water needs vary across caste, class and tribe. Defining equity thus becomes a complex process. It calls for the unpacking of women as a category. For Dalit women, for example, social taboos prevent access to drinking water. The needs of women farm owners are considerably different from those of women wage labourers, or those from landowning households deriving water rights through their husbands. For non-land owning Dalit and adivasi women, water needs could revolve around water-based enterprises like fishing or share-cropping.

Gender Division of Tasks is not Static

Until recently, much of the gender planning around natural resources has been placed in the context of women's current tasks of collecting fuel, fodder, water and related survival tasks. Gender planning undertaken through these conceptual frameworks has largely focused on reducing the time spent by women on these survival tasks. In the water sector, women are thus seen as spending hours collecting water for domestic use. Various studies (for example, Swaminathan 1997) do point to how women's tasks revolve around the collection of water and the impact that this has on their health and livelihoods. Time spent on collecting water for domestic use has meant reduced opportunities for women to participate in 'productive' activities. This static notion of women's roles in survival tasks has translated into policy prescriptions that perpetuate the existing gender roles. In the case of water, a natural fallout of the above assumption is the creation of two separate spheres, the 'domestic' represented by women and the 'productive' represented by men (van Koppen 1999; Zwartveen 1998).

RESTRUCTURING THE WATER SECTOR

The second important aspect is the need to address macro-level issues in the context of the water sector. Here, we outline the main approach to water-sector restructuring, which is based on SOPPECOM's approach to water-sector reform, emphasising equity as the organising principle for change.

Equity in Water Entitlements: The Foundation of a Gender-Sensitive Water Sector Reform

We propose that all households should have equitable access to a basic quantum of water that is essential for meeting livelihood needs. This will vary across regions. Within the household entitlement, at least half the share should be earmarked for the women of the household. While the practical possibilities of doing this may not be easy, accepting in principle a separate dedicated allocation for women is critical. Women could either use it on their own lands in a manner they deem appropriate, or they could use it collectively for different water-related enterprises.

Minimum Water Assurance for Livelihood Security

Water has always been acknowledged as an important resource that changes and enhances the value of land manifold. However, almost all conventionally accepted norms have looked at water rights as being linked to landholding rights. It is only recently that the dissociation of water and land rights has begun to be viewed as a serious possibility with substantial potential for creating equitable access. The right to water, therefore, should be understood as a matter of minimum assurance for all the water required for livelihood needs, irrespective of the ownership of assets. Disconnecting land rights from water rights provides a space for the landless and resource-poor women to gain access to water, as well as to decision-making mechanisms related to water. There are various interpretations of such delinking of water rights from land rights, the most prominent being that water now becomes a tradable commodity, which can be tapped by those willing to accord it the highest price. However, tradability of water rights will have to be opposed at all costs as it would further marginalise the water-deprived sections, especially the women and the landless. Equity in access to water has to be seen as an important component of the water-sector reform strategy, although there are differences in the ways in which equity could be achieved and the extent to which this could be done.

Significance of Independent Water Rights

The principle of independent water rights has important implications so far as access to livelihood resources is concerned. This creates an opportunity for women, the poor and the landless to sell their annual allocation, or at least part of it, thereby generating supplementary income. But more preferably, they could use their share to lease in land, on which they could utilise their share of water. In India, groups like the Pani Panchayat and Mukti Sangharsh Chalwal[2] in Maharashtra have worked towards independent entitlements over water. Such a standpoint opens up the space to further the agenda for equitable access to water for women and other landless people. These sections would have the option of either trading their water rights or, preferably, using these water rights on leased lands or commons for meeting their livelihood needs. This was demonstrated by the experience in Khudawadi[3] village in Osmanabad district of Maharashtra, where a WUA situated at the tail end of a distributary resolved to allocate 15 per cent of the water quota they received from the Irrigation Department to the landless and women's groups in the village. The women then organised to plant trees and cultivate fodder on barren lands, using this water to meet their livelihood needs. Independent rights could also be used for micro-enterprises like brick kilns, small plot cultivation, kitchen gardens, fishing and livestock.

Like the resource, equity too cannot be a static concept and will vary in time and space. What is considered optimum use today may not be so tomorrow. It is for this reason that equitable rights are to be considered provisional rights subject to later study and negotiation, rather than fixed rights that are likely to perpetuate monopolies.

Need for Associated Rights

Greater control over water will be meaningful only if it is accompanied by a greater control over rights to land, greater voice in farm decisions, or greater control over the produce. The legal possibility of drawing water is meaningless without the associated technology to subtract water from a source and convey it to irrigated fields. Thus, it is also the means to operate and maintain the technology and convert it into livelihood outcomes that are important if rights are to be transformed into livelihood opportunities. Right to water, therefore, will have to include the right to infrastructure, skills and knowledge base so as to use the infrastructure and entitlements for positive livelihood gains.

EQUITY IN VOICE: NEED FOR EXPANDING THE DEFINITION OF WUAs

In the present irrigation context, the WUA is considered the unit for decision-making. This is a formally registered body that manages the irrigation system. Typically, it comprises landholders and owners in the designated command or beneficiary areas of a particular canal. Such a limited membership of a resource that is so communal in nature eliminates the possibility of involving women from the beneficiary families, as well as women and men from the non-beneficiary households.

There are two issues involved here. The first is related to the lack of legal space for women to participate in the decision-making process, and the second is related to the cultural barrier that formal organisations present to women. So, unless legal space is created for women and other water-deprived people by expanding the scope of WUAs, these sections will never become part of the planning and decision-making processes that are envisaged through the WUAs. Importantly, it raises questions about the democratic processes themselves. If water is to be seen as a common property resource, why are decisions taken by only one section of users? Decision-making should be based on citizenship rather than membership. An effort is being made in Maharashtra by the Shramik Mukti Dal,[4] an organisation working in western Maharashtra, on the question of water management, and SOPPECOM has tried to introduce such changes in the draft legislation on Participatory Irrigation Management (PIM).

The second issue is related to the nature of the organisation. Participation in formal organisations requires spending time in meetings. Women weigh the benefits and costs involved in such participation. They are not able to spend that kind of time as there is often no one to share the reproductive tasks that women are involved in at present. Moreover, many of these meetings are not held at times that are suitable for women. Women would also have to challenge the prevailing norms in the society, as irrigation is not traditionally considered to be in the female domain.

It is not enough to fight for a legal space for women, or for those who have been conventionally on the margins of irrigation thinking. For women, formal organisations represent the domain of the male. As mentioned earlier, it has been observed that women are at their best in informal situations and share their insights, negotiate for rights, et cetera, in informal networks. A well-structured formal set-up may be a barrier to the participation of resource-poor women. (Meinzen-Dick and Zwarteveen 1998).

Therefore, we propose (*i*) the expansion of the WUA to include all adult members of the particular hamlet/village/water unit, and that decisions be made in the presence of every citizen residing in the redefined area of the irrigation project; and (*ii*) that (recognising that formal structures cannot be done away with) the insights and suggestions emerging from women's informal networks should find a hearing at the jointly held meetings in the formal set-ups.

INTEGRATION OF VARIOUS KINDS OF WATER RESOURCES

Planning in the water sector has failed to understand the common pool character of water. Water has often been compartmentalised as surface water, groundwater, local and exogenous water. Each of these is handled by independent departments that have little or no interaction with one another. This lack of integration is cited as one of the most important reasons for the crisis in the water sector, leading to over-extraction of groundwater and also to increased seepage and wastage of surface water. If planned in an integrated manner, the resource can be extended to a larger number of people with a closer control over the quantum of assured supply available at an appropriate time. Integration of local and exogenous resources has the potential to overcome the limitations of both kinds of sources. If local water harvesting efforts are inadequate for meeting the livelihood needs of the local population, these can be supplemented by the exogenous water. The underlying assumption here is that it is the local system, rather than an individual irrigator from a designated command area, that actually receives the water supplement from the exogenous system. This creates a space for women and men, landless and landed, to participate in the process as users of the water resource.

PRICING OF WATER SERVICE AND RECOVERY OF CAPITAL COSTS

Pricing of water and the recovery of capital costs are among the most critical issues in the water sector today. Debates cover the whole spectrum, from full assistance to full cost recovery. The concept of what is affordable is vitiated by the very low rates that prevail in the canal irrigation command areas, and simultaneously by the very high rates of the water service outside canal command areas. Though there are differing views, it appears that people would be willing to pay a price for irrigation water service if it is sufficiently reliable and offers reasonable control over timing and application. The underlying principle here is the reliability of the water service for the poor. Without this, economic mechanisms of pricing and cost recovery would not work.

For women, the economic disadvantage that they face within the household as well as in the community at large has already been discussed. The question, however, is: what would constitute affordable use for the poor? How much of the expenditure should be considered assistance and how much a recoverable component? In such a context, there has to be a

greater focus on introducing measures that have a bearing on this disadvantage. The alternative would therefore have to base itself on a distinction between basic service for livelihood needs, and extra or economic
service.

> The concept of the minimum assurance of water for livelihood needs
> is closely tied to the concept of a basic water service that should be pro-
> vided to everyone at an affordable cost and as a matter of right. Any extra
> service above such basic service would conceptually be extra service and
> should be tied much more closely to achieving economic efficiency.
> (SOPPECOM 2002)

In the case of water entitlements for single or deserted women, or
women household heads, it might in the initial stages be necessary for an
enabling policy support to create a 'level playing field'. This could come
in the form of initial credit and skills support with a specific policy of
withdrawal in place. Taking water to the poor people living in remote
areas implies a heavy cost of lifting the water, or taking it across longer
distances. Do the poor, adivasi women and men pay for this recurring
cost of energy while those in the more favourable locations get away with
it? Here it is important to stress that pricing for basic services has to be
affordable to all, regardless of whether they live at high altitudes or in
the plains.

The other contentious issue is the recovery of costs incurred on resource development. Part of this recovery should come from the pricing
of economic services. Another suggested method of easing the cost recovery burden of basic services is that of recovery in kind. A portion of the
cost recovery can be tied to recovery in kind. This could ease the pressure
on women and those who would use their water right essentially for
meeting livelihood needs (SOPPECOM 2002). The main issue here is
adjusting recovery through differential pricing for basic and economic
services. The key principle to be followed is that, whereas the operation
and management charges are shared equally by all, the capital costs are to
be recovered through differential pricing. Concessions need to be given
in the form of provisions for recovery in kind for various disadvantaged
groups.

In conclusion, one can say that the task of feminists in this sector has
been to struggle at different ends. One of these has been to systematically

link up to the design of restructuring the water sector, as opposed to drawing up a list of demands within the current mainstream water resource development paradigm within a coherent framework. There has been a tendency to highlight the relevance of gender issues in a language that is familiar to the policy makers within the water sector. There has also been a compelling need to link gender equity goals to the 'legitimate' goals of water-sector reform in order to be heard. The arguments that have taken up a large amount of space have been on proving that, given an opportunity, women can manage the resource efficiently. The positions that have so far been taken are those that are likely to face least resistance— a process of negotiation for the least adverse scenario rather than one that is based on changing power equations within the sector. However, the real challenge is to demand a space that can challenge the structures of patriarchy. In this context, the question of entitlements and decision-making becomes very important.

NOTES

1. This chapter largely draws on 'Gender Concerns in the Water Sector: Issues and Alternative', Women and Water Network, India, 2005.

2. Pani Panchayat in a way pioneered the idea of equity in access to water irrespective of landholding in Maharashtra. Pani Panchayat work started on small lift irrigation societies with an understanding that water allocation would be done with a maximum ceiling on water quantum, enough to irrigate two acres of land for each household. The rules laid down by Pani Panchayat clearly stated a crop code, whereby water-intensive crops like sugarcane would not be cultivated unless minimum water for all was assured. Through their experiments, they paved the way for a dynamic movement on this issue.

3. SOPPECOM initiated a pilot project in Khudawadi village, where on one of the WUAs on a minor canal, water sharing was extended to women and the landless in the village. This experience was considered one of the first of its kind in India.

4. Shramik Mukti Dal, an organisation in western Maharashtra, has been actively working on the question of equitable access to water since the 1980s. They have proposed changes to irrigation thinking as a whole, particularly in the context of the redefinition of water rights and expansion of WUAs to include women, the landless and the non-command area households. Similarly,

SOPPECOM had taken an initiative in Maharashtra to reformulate the legislation on PIM to make it more inclusive of women, the landless and those outside the designated command areas. SOPPECOM also held a public meeting to discuss the draft suggestions that were later developed as a consensus and sent to the state government.

REFERENCES

Agarwal, B. 1994. *A Field of One's Own: Gender and Land Rights in South Asia*. Cambridge: Cambridge University Press.

Ahmed, S. 2005. 'Why is gender equity a concern for water management?', in S. Ahmed (ed.), *Flowing Upstream: Empowering Women through Water Management Initiatives in India*. New Delhi: Foundation India Books and Ahmedabad: Centre for Environment Education.

Ballabh, Vishwa. 2004. 'Governance in Water Sector', Draft theme paper for the workshop on 'Governance Issues in Water Sector', to be organised by IRMA to commemorate 25 years of its existence.

Cleaver, F. 1995. 'Approaches to Water Development', in *Development Projects: Issues for the 1990s*. 25 Anniversary Conference Papers, Development and Project Planning Centre, University of Bradford.

Cleaver, Frances. 1998. 'Incentives and Informal Institutions: Gender and the Management of Water', *Agriculture and Human Values*, 15: 347–60.

Cleaver Frances and Diane Elson. 1995. *Women and Water Resources: Continued Marginalisation and New Policies*. GATEKEEPER Series No. 49, Sustainable Agriculture and Rural Livelihoods Programme, London: International Institute of Environment and Development.

Green, Cathy and Sally Baden. 1995. *Integrated Water Resources Management: A Gender Perspective*. Institute of Development Studies Bulletin, 26 (1).

Joy, K. and S. Paranjape. 2005. 'Women and Water: Relationships, Issues, Experiences, Approaches', in B. Ray (ed.), *Women of India: Colonial and Post-Colonial Periods*. New Delhi: PHISPC and Sage Publications.

Kulkarni, S. 2005. 'Looking Back, Thinking Forward: The Khudawadi Experience with Access to Irrigation for Women and the Landless', in S. Ahmed (ed.), *Flowing Upstream: Empowering Women through Water Management Initiatives in India*, pp. 179–210. New Delhi: Foundation India Books and Ahmedabad: Centre for Environment Education.

Kulkarni, Seema and Nagmani Rao. 2002. 'Gender and Drought in South Asia: Dominant Constructions and Alternate Propositions', Paper presented at a workshop in Islamabad, Pakistan, on Droughts in South Asia, (October 2002, organised by SaciWaters).

Meinzen-Dick, Ruth and Margreet Zwarteveen. 1998. 'Gendered Participation in Water Management: Issues and Illustrations from Water Users' Associations in South Asia', *Agriculture and Human Values*, 15: 337–45.

SOPPECOM. 2002. 'Restructuring the Water Sector: A Framework for Restructuring of Water Sector in Sustainable, Equitable and Participatory Lines'. Unpublished Internal Report. Pune: Soppecom..

Swaminathan, Padmini. 1997. 'A Hobson's Choice for Indian Women?', *Economic and Political Weekly*, 25–31 October.

Vaidyanathan A. 2003. 'Water Resource Development: Scarcity and Conflict', in Ramprasad Sengupta and Anup K. Sinha (eds),. *Challenge of Sustainable Development: The Indian Dynamics*. Kolkata: Indian Institute of Management Calcutta.

van Koppen, Barbara. 1998. 'Water Rights, Gender, and Poverty Alleviation. Inclusion and Exclusion of Women and Men Smallholders in Public Irrigation Infrastructure Development', *Agriculture and Human Values*, 15: 361–74.

———. 1999. Sharing the Last Drop: Water Scarcity, Irrigation and Gendered Poverty Eradication. Colombo: IWMI Tata.

Vasavada, S. 2005. 'Mainstreaming gender concerns in participatory irrigation management: The role of AKRSP (I) in South Gujarat', in S. Ahmed (ed.), *Flowing Upstream: Empowering Women through Water Management Initiatives in India*, pp. 123–52. New Delhi: Foundation India Books and Ahmedabad: Centre for Environment Education.

Zwarteveen, Margreet Z. 1998. 'Identifying Gender Aspects of New Irrigation Management Policies', *Agriculture and Human Values*, 15(4): 301–312.

12

Do Property Rights in Land Ensure Greater Participation of Women in Resource Management? Notes from a Study in Rural Karnataka

M. Indira

According to the 2001 Census, women constitute around 50 per cent of the total population in Karnataka. However, their participation in decision-making both at the macro and micro levels is very low. The 73rd and 74th Constitutional Amendments are a landmark in the efforts towards engendering governance. These amendments gave women an opportunity to enter the decision-making process at the local and district levels. However, field-level studies reveal mixed results about the effective participation of women in decision-making and several causative factors were identified, like poor literacy among women, patriarchal norms of society and insensitive political parties. Similarly, women's participation in decision-making at the household level has been analysed, and the reasons for the differential performance have been explained in terms of earning power, literacy, social and economic background, et cetera. Agarwal (1994) argued that denial of property rights to women is an important factor affecting their empowerment. After persistent campaigns, the Hindu Succession Amendment Act has also been passed by the Parliament (see Box 12.1).

In the present chapter, an attempt is made to analyse the pattern of property rights over land in selected villages of Karnataka, and to explore the relationship between women's property rights over land and participation in decision-making. The chapter first briefly reviews the existing literature on issues of women's participation in decision-making at the

---

Box 12.1
The Hindu Succession Amendment Act, 2005

Recognising that sons and daughters are equal members of their natal family, this Amendment provides for legal equality with respect to land rights in joint family property for Hindu women and men across all states. Formerly, the inheritance of agricultural land was governed by tenurial laws at the state-level. In Delhi, Haryana, Punjab, Uttar Pradesh, Himachal Pradesh and Jammu and Kashmir, these laws were markedly un-egalitarian. However, other states had already made changes in the civil law governing joint family property. Kerala had abolished joint family property and gave sons and daughters equal inheritance rights for land and other property. Maharashtra, Karnataka, Tamil Nadu and Andhra Pradesh retained the joint family property (the *mitakshara* 'coparcenary') system, but unmarried daughters were considered partners ('coparceners') in the property. Agricultural land, however, was not covered. The 2005 Amendment to the Hindu Succession Act provides for daughters (including married daughters) to be treated as partners in joint family property. What this means is that Hindu women in all states now have a 'birth right' in joint family property, which cannot be willed away by their fathers.

---

household level and in relation to farming; it then gives an account of the methodology followed in this study. The last section deals with the analysis of data collected through field survey, the results and recommendations.

DECISION-MAKING IN THE HOUSEHOLD

There are a few studies relating to the participation of women in decision-making within the household. The National Family Health Survey 1998–99 included some questions about household decision-making, which throw light on this issue. The survey reveals that women's participation is restricted only to daily decisions about what to cook. Decisions about obtaining personal health care, spending the money that she earns, purchase of jewellery and so on, are taken by the husband alone in the majority of the cases. The following Table 12.1 summarises women's participation in decision-making.

Table 12.1
Percentage of Women Who Answered 'Yes'

Household decision	Women alone Rural Urban		Husband alone Rural Urban		Wives & husbands in consultation Rural Urban		Others in the household Rural Urban	
What to cook	85.4	.3	3.5	3.8	1.1	1.8	8.4	7.1
Health care of herself	21.7	32.9	45.5	38.0	22.0	19.7	8.6	6.4
Purchase of jewellery	10.0	13.6	43.6	37.1	29.2	36.7	12.9	8.6
Visit to parents	13.0	17.8	47.4	41.8	24.5	29.7	11.4	7.5
Spending money she earned	35.9	54.4	36.9	19.1	19.3	22.3	5.5	2.5

Source: National Family Health Survey, 1998–99.

The results show that participation levels are low in rural areas compared to urban areas. Only 34 per cent of rural women can take decisions by themselves about spending money that they have earned. In the case of urban women, 54 per cent can take decisions independently. Similarly, in obtaining personal health care, it is the husband alone who decides in the case of 45 per cent of rural women. Only 34 per cent of women in rural areas have a definite say in spending the income that they have earned; in the case of 37 per cent of the women, the husband alone decides.

DECISION-MAKING RELATED TO FARMING

During the last few decades, there has been an increase in the number of women joining the agricultural workforce as labourers as compared to cultivators; this has been termed the 'feminisation of agriculture'. In India, the 'feminisation of agriculture' indicates both an increasing proportion of women in agricultural labour and the deteriorating conditions of such labour, due to the casualisation of work and distress migration in a context where farming is itself becoming unprofitable. Low female wage rates and women's social inferiority result in their being increasingly concentrated in low-paid casual agricultural labour. Such feminisation marginalises women and does not enhance their position in the household (see also Ghosh 2004).

According to the 2001 Census, the share of cultivators among rural women has decreased from 42.74 per cent in 1991 to 32.32 per cent in 2001. Table 12.2 gives the changing work composition of rural women.

Table 12.2

Trends in the Composition of Rural Workers

Category	Men	%	Women	%	Total	%
		2001 Census				
Main workers	167,812,785	44.57	60,060,841	16.86	227,873,626	31.10
Marginal workers	29,457,579	7.82	50,454,815	14.17	79,912,394	10.91
Non-workers	179,241,984	47.61	245,662,759	68.97	424,904,743	57.99
Total workers	197,270,364	52.39	110,515,656	31.03	307,786,020	42.01
Total Population	376,512,348	100.00	356,178,415	100.00	732,690,763	100.00
		1991 Census				
Main workers	166,067,847	51.76	55,926,401	18.57	221,994,248	35.69
Marginal workers	2,302,866	0.72	24,392,740	8.10	26,695,606	4.29
Non-workers	152,460,213	47.52	220,771,607	73.32	373,231,820	60.01
Total workers	168,370,713	52.48	80,319,141	26.68	248,689,854	39.99
Total Population	320,839,126	100.00	301,098,600	100.00	621,937,726	100.00

Source: http://www.censusindia.net/results/2001_census_Prov_Workers_Table1.xls.

The number of rural female marginal workers had doubled from nearly 24 million to 50 million between 1991 and 2001. Increased competition in the product market forced producers to reduce on production costs, and since women's labour is cheaper than men's (the wages paid to women labourers are less than those paid to men), more women are employed as agricultural labourers. Women became the disposable factor of production in Indian agriculture (Muller and Patel 2005). The share of non-workers among women has declined from 73.32 to 68.97 per cent.

The greater participation of women in the agricultural workforce increases their contribution to household expenditure. In recent decades, while rural male labour has tended to move away from agricultural to rural non-agricultural labour, rural female labour has remained largely confined to agriculture (see Kapadia 1999). Earlier studies in south India indicate that among casual labour households, women bear the bulk of household expenditures (Kapadia 1996; Mencher 1985, 1988; Mencher and Saradamoni 1982).

However, in order to understand whether this work participation has translated into empowerment, women's position in the household has to be understood because that is what determines her empowerment. It has been observed that participation in agricultural work does not in itself give women the power to take decisions (Sharma 1980), and that economic contribution itself does not necessarily empower women (Kabeer 1994).

Participation in the workforce and contribution to household expenditure is a necessary but not sufficient condition for empowerment. It has also been demonstrated that in Punjab, the size of the land that the family owns has no bearing on either the extent of women's 'say', or the factors that enable women to have a greater voice in decisions regarding crop production, purchase of livestock, sale of milk, schooling of children, political participation and religious ceremonies. These are mainly determined by cultural factors (Singh and Kaur 2004).

There are regional differences in women's participation. For example, in Assam women have no say in financial matters, but have a considerable say in crop production decisions (Saikia 2004). But in Punjab, it was observed that women have a greater say in financial matters than in decisions relating to crop production (Singh and Kaur 2004). In another study from Andhra Pradesh, it was observed that major decisions regarding the selection of crops, seed and variety, fertiliser use, sale of produce, dairying, and so on, were taken by men and women together with mutual consultation. Greater participation of women has been observed more in villages where extension efforts were made rather than in those villages that were not covered, suggesting the need for better extension services for greater participation of women in decision-making. The study by Singh and Kaur (ibid.) revealed that working status and education are the most important correlates in explaining women's participation in decision-making in farm-related activities in Punjab. Women with higher education, and those who work outside, have a greater say in decision-making.

OBJECTIVES AND METHODOLOGY

The objectives of this chapter are four-fold: (*i*) to analyse women's property rights over land in selected villages of Karnataka; (*ii*) to analyse the participation of women in decision-making relating to agricultural and household management activities; (*iii*) to establish the linkages between property rights and participation in decision-making; (*iv*) to identify factors responsible for differential participation.

The landownership patterns are derived on the basis of a survey of 20 villages spread over five districts of Karnataka, namely, Tumkur, Dharwad, Kolar, Hassan and Mysore. These villages were selected for a study on the Watershed Development Programme implemented by Action for Food Production (AFPRO) as a network programme, which in its turn was implemented by 10 NGOs in Karnataka. One of the objectives was the involvement of women in watershed management, and a benchmark study was undertaken to identify the existing participation levels. The survey data presented here was part of the larger study. While landownership and participation in decision-making were analysed for all 20 villages, three villages were selected for analysing the factors responsible for the differential participation of women in decision-making. Data was collected through questionnaires from 233 women of these villages.

Women's participation in land-related activities is identified with participation in decisions relating to cropping patterns, participation in the marketing of crops, and the purchase and sale of land. Similarly, participation in household management decisions is identified with participation in decisions relating to children's education, children's marriage and purchase of clothes. The responses were recorded by asking each woman in the survey whether she was consulted while taking decisions, and if so, how often she was consulted. A composite graded scale was developed.[1] In order to understand what variables, apart from ownership of land, influences women's participation in decision-making, the education level, occupation and age are considered explanatory variables, and the variable measuring her participation was regressed on each of the three independent variables. Correlations and regression analysis were carried out.

ANALYSIS AND RESULTS

The analysis of primary data and results obtained, along with recommendations, are presented in this section.

Landownership in Selected Villages of Karnataka

Landownership is skewed against women. Among the landowning households, very few women have land in their name. Table 12.3 gives the extent of land in the name of women in 20 villages from five districts of Karnataka. It clearly shows that only in the case of four villages, namely,

Table 12.3
Percentage of Women Owning Land in Their Names

Village	% Women Who Own Land in their Names
Tumkur district	
Gadigunta	17.00
Pendlijeevi	5.63
Garani	21.51
TN Halli	2.99
Thimmasandra	35.11
Huluvangala	17.36
Pathaganahalli	6.70
Dharwad district	
Hunsekatte	3.13
Singanahalli	4.85
Kolar district	
Hakki-pikki	44.00
CB Ghatta	24.39
DB Ghatta	15.38
Poolakuntahalli	1.96
Hassan district	
Honavalli	28.17
Nelamane	11.71
Kellur	4.95
Mysore district	
Kamarahalli	9.50

Source: Survey data from author's study.

Thimmasandra (Tumkur district), Hakki-pikki (Kolar district), Honavalli (Hassan district) and CB Ghatta (Kolar), more than 20 per cent of women have land in their names. In Poolakuntahalli village, Kolar district, less than 2 per cent of women have land in their names. In Tumkur district, while 35 per cent of women in Thimmasandra village own land, only 3 per cent do so in TN Halli. Women's landownership is better in Hakki-pikki, a small village inhabited by the Hakki-pikki tribe.

Participation of Women in Land-Related Decisions

The choice of crops depends on the suitability of the soil and the availability of irrigation. Within the feasible choices, what is to be grown is an important decision that will influence the food security of the family.

Ultimately, the burden is on the woman, who manages food distribution within the household. Therefore, women need to be involved in decision-making regarding cropping patterns. Similarly, marketing decisions regarding where to sell, how much to sell, et cetera, will influence the returns from crop and access to income. Buying and selling of land is another important decision because land is an important source of livelihood for rural households. Table 12.4 gives an account of women's participation across the selected villages. The results indicate differential participation across the villages. While in Hakki-pikki (Kolar district) 80 per cent of decisions regarding the cropping pattern are taken by men alone, in Garani (Tumkur district) 91 per cent are taken in consultation with women.

Table 12.4
The Extent of Women's Participation in Land-related Decisions

	Cropping Pattern		Marketing Crops		Land Purchase/sale	
Village	Men alone	Women & Men in Consultation	Men alone	Women & Men in Consultation	Men alone	Women & Men in Consultation
Tumkur district						
Gadigunta	20.14	65.47	24.46	65.47	10.79	74.10
Pendlijeevi	36.88	60.63	31.88	43.13	–	–
Garani	0.29	91.25	4.08	74.64	2.33	74.93
TN Halli	–	95.52	–	94.03	–	95.52
Thimmasandra	8.60	39.78	17.20	56.99	4.35	68.48
Huluvangala	15.70	38.02	43.80	15.70	14.05	52.49
Pathaganahalli	9.62	43.27	15.94	74.88	17.39	80.68
Dharwad district						
Hunsekatte	37.50	10.94	12.50	45.31	96.88	2.08
Singanahalli	46.60	45.63	45.63	38.83	46.60	39.81
Kolar district						
Hakki-pikki	80.00	16.00	52.00	16.00	56.00	16.00
CB Ghatta	2.50	85.00	5.00	80.00	2.50	82.50
DB Ghatta	8.00	88.00	4.35	95.65	4.35	95.65
Poolakuntahalli	16.00	84.00	15.56	73.33	16.28	83.72
Hassan district						
Honavalli	5.63	80.21	5.63	92.96	11.27	87.32
Nelamane	1.00	99.00	2.54	97.46	2.50	97.50
Kellur	40.00	40.00	66.67	33.33	58.16	41.84
Mysore district						
Kamarahalli	12.06	66.83	8.50	86.9	0.50	99.0

Source: Survey data from author's study.

So, too, in the case of marketing of crops 94 per cent of women in TN Halli (Tumkur) are consulted in decision-making, but only 16 per cent of women in Huluvangala (also Tumkur) are consulted. More women were consulted in decisions relating to purchase and sale of land in all the villages except in Hunsekatte (Dharwad), where only 2 per cent of women were consulted.

Participation of Women in Decisions Relating to Household Management

Several decisions are to be made by poor households to maximise the returns from the limited resources they possess. Decisions regarding sending children to school or to work, marriage of the daughter, purchase of clothes, et cetera, influence the availability of resources for other purposes. But even in these matters, men have a better say compared to women. Women's participation in these decisions is low in some of the villages (see Table 12.5). In the case of Hakki-pikki, only 16 per cent of women reported that they were consulted in decision-making about the children's

Table 12.5
The Extent of Participation of Women in Household-related Decisions

| | Children's Education | | Children's Marriage | | Purchase of Clothes | |
| | *Men alone* | *Women & Men in Consultation* | *Men alone* | *Women & Men in Consultation* | *Men alone* | *Women & Men in Consultation* |
Village						
Tumkur district						
Gadigunta	20.14	64.75	19.42	65.47	10.79	74.10
Pendlijeevi	31.88	43.13	31.88	41.88	–	–
Garani	5.83	74.05	3.79	74.64	6.12	74.93
TN Halli	–	95.52	–	95.52	–	95.52
Thimmasandra	9.68	81.72	5.38	87.10	9.68	82.80
Huluvangala	21.49	30.58	8.26	52.07	14.05	52.89
Pathaganahalli	17.87	80.19	17.39	80.68	17.87	80.19
Dharwad district						
Hunsekatte	3.65	92.19	0.52	95.83	9.38	87.50
Singanahalli	46.60	36.89	46.60	38.83	46.60	38.83
Kolar district						
Hakki-pikki	52.00	16.00	52.00	16.00	44.00	24.00
CB Ghatta	12.50	62.50	2.50	65.00	–	82.50

(*Table 12.5 continued*)

(*Table 12.5 continued*)

Village	Children's Education		Children's Marriage		Purchase of Clothes	
	Men alone	Women & Men in Consultation	Men alone	Women & Men in Consultation	Men alone	Women & Men in Consultation
DB Ghatta	4.35	91.30	4.35	78.26	4.35	95.65
Poolakuntahalli	15.56	77.78	15.56	75.56	16.28	83.72
Hassan district						
Honavalli	7.04	91.55	7.04	91.55	7.04	91.55
Nelamane	3.31	96.69	2.50	95.50	4.31	96.69
Kellur	17.53	82.47	42.68	57.14	22.45	77.55
Mysore district						
Kamarahalli	2.50	96.0	3.0	95.5	0.5	99.0

Source: Survey data from author's study.

education and marriage; only 24 per cent of women were consulted in the purchase of clothes for the family members. Greater participation is observed in villages where more women are literate.

Factors Influencing Participation in Decision-Making

Participation in decision-making at the household level depends on several factors. Here, the attempt is to understand if there is any relationship between property rights over land and participation. It has been hypothesised that women owning land have a greater say in decision-making vis-à-vis farm-related decisions. A positive relationship is expected between ownership of land and participation score. The other factors identified are education, occupation and age. Education is expected to have a positive impact on participation levels because educated/literate women are consulted more in decisions. Similarly, occupation is expected to have a positive influence because if the woman is working outside her home and contributing to the family income, she would be consulted more than the ones who are not contributing directly. Age is considered in order to observe whether the younger generation has better participation. The correlation between these variables is presented in Table 12.6.

The results do not indicate any significant relationship between ownership of land and participation in decision-making related to agriculture. However, in the case of household-related decisions, land appears to have a *negative* influence, indicating that women who do not

Table 12.6
Correlation Between the Extent of Participation and Influencing Factors

	Children's Education	*Children's Marriage*	*Purchase of Clothes*
Household Decisions			
Landownership	−0.153*	−0.173*	−0.151*
Age	0.046	0.066	0.035
Education	0.14*	0.109	0.098
Occupation	−0.217**	−0.181**	−0.025
Land-related Decisions			
	Cropping	*Marketing*	*Buying/Selling Land*
Landownership	−0.029	−0.147*	−0.187
Age	0.065**	0.109**	0.055**
Education	0.205**	0.176**	0.105
Occupation	0.283**	0.241**	0.126

Source: Calculated based on the survey data.
Notes: * Significant at 5 per cent level.
   ** Significant at 10 per cent level.

own land in their names are participating more in these decisions. Age is not a significant factor in household decisions, but in farm-related decisions it is significant, indicating that older women are consulted in matters of farming. The educational status of women appears to be a factor influencing decisions relating to children's education, cropping patterns, as well as marketing. This shows that regardless of whether the women own land, educated women have better participation in all decisions. On the other hand, occupation also showed a positive and significant correlation. Caste-wise responses show that women belonging to the Scheduled Castes participated more in both household and farm-related decisions than women from 'forward' and 'Backward caste' categories. This can be attributed to a more rigid patriarchal control among the better-off castes. More information is needed to identify the influence of social/family background, which was beyond the scope of this study.

As the majority of the sample respondents are working as agricultural labourers (48 per cent), earning from outside and contributing to the household expenditure has a significant correlation with women's participation in land-related decisions. However, the correlation between the score of participation in household and farm-related decisions is 0.825, and this is significant at 1 per cent level, indicating that the women who are participating in land-related decisions are also participating in household decisions, and those who are not participating are not taking part in any decisions. The results of the regression analysis that attempts to quantify the correlates of women's participation in decision-making in land-related and household-related activities are presented in Table 12.7.

Table 12.7
Results of Regression Analysis

	Land-related Decisions	Household-related Decisions
Sample size	233	233
Land	−0.012	−0.021
Occupation	0.166*	0.13*
Education	0.285*	0.28*
R²	0.891	0.862

Source: Calculated based on the survey data.
Notes: Dependent variable 1 = Land related integrated score.
Dependent variable 2 = Household related integrated score.
* significant at 1 per cent level.

The results show that a woman's education and earnings from outside are influential factors in her participation in decision-making. Owning land is not a significant variable. On the other hand, women who are literate and who work outside participate more in decisions relating to both land and household. Age is another important factor which has a positive impact. The results indicate that older women are consulted more than younger women in all matters.

CONCLUSIONS

Women's participation in decision-making has been studied by several researchers, and attempts were also made to characterise the factors responsible for it. The main contribution of this chapter is that it tries to understand whether the ownership of land has any influence on women's participation in decision-making at both the farm level and in household management. This variable was not considered by earlier researchers. This gains significance in the context of the property registration concessions extended to women in the 2005–06 central budget. In this chapter, my attempt has been to see how land ownership influences women's participation in decision-making. The results show that property rights over land are not influential in the specific local context of the study. The influential factors are literacy and occupation. Literate women are participating better because they are consulted. Similarly, women's unpaid work in the household and on the family farm is not valued. But if a woman works outside and contributes cash income to the family, she is consulted. This clearly shows the influence of paid and unpaid work on women's participation in decision-making. As far as age is concerned, it has a positive impact, indicating that older women are consulted more. The logical conclusion of these results is that efforts towards the empowerment of women should concentrate on improving the literacy levels of rural women and improving employment opportunities.

NOTE

1. The composite scale was based on the following grading:
   If the husband alone takes the decision, the rank is 1.
   If the wife is consulted occasionally, the rank is 2.
   If the wife is always consulted, the rank is 3.
   The greater the rank, greater her participation.
   The composite index, across various decisions under the above two categories, measures aggregate say of the ith women.

   $$Y_i = \sum_{J=1}^{3} \sum_{k=0}^{3} \sum_{l=0}^{3} R_{ijk}$$

   Aggregate score

   R_{ijkl} = the decision score of the ith woman.

REFERENCES

Agarwal, Bina. 1994. *A Field of One's Own: Gender and Land Rights in South Asia.* Cambridge and New York: Cambridge University Press.

Census of India. http://www.censusindia.net/results/2001_census_Prov_ Workers_Tables.xlx

Ghosh, Jayati. 2004. 'Informalization and Women's Workforce Participation: A Consideration of Recent Trends in Asia', National Seminar on Globalization and Women's Work, 25–26 March. Seminar Papers Volume 1. NOIDA: V.V. Giri National Labour Institute.

Kabeer, Naila. 1994. *Reversed Realities: Gender Hierarchies in Development Theory.* London and New York: Verso.

Kapadia, Karin. 1996. *Siva and Her Sisters: Gender, Caste and Class in Rural South India*. New Delhi: Oxford University Press.

———— (ed.). 1999. *Rural Labour Relations in India*. UK: Routledge.

Mencher, J.P. 1985. 'Women in Rice Farming', Proceedings of a conference on Women in Rice Farming Systems held at IRRI, Manila, Philippines, 26–30 Sept. 1983, pp. 351–71. Aldershot, England: Gower Publishing Co.

————. 1988. 'Women Work and Poverty: Women's Contribution to Household Maintenance in South India', in D. Dwyer and J. Bruce (eds), *A Home Divided: Women and Income in the Third World*. Stanford: Stanford University Press.

Mencher, J.P. and K. Saradamoni. 1982. 'Muddy Feet, Dirty Hands', *Economic and Political Weekly*, 17(52).

Muller. R.A. and R. Patel. 2005. 'Shining India? Economic Liberalization and Rural Poverty in 1990s', available at http://www.foodfirst.org/pubs/policy/pb10.pdf.

National Family Health Survey India 1998–99, Karnataka (2001) Mumbai: International Institute for Population Sciences.

Saikia, Anuva. 2004. 'Employment Patterns of Rural Women and Their Involvement in Decision Making: A Study in Jorhat District of Assam', *Women in Agriculture and Rural Development*, Supplement to the *Indian Journal of Agriculture Economics*, 59(1).

Sharma, Ursula. 1980. *Women, Work and Property in North-West India*. London: Tavistock Publications.

Singh, Bant and Kaur, Lavleen. 2004. 'Quantifying the Extent and Determinants of Women's Say in Decision Making: A Study in Amritsar District, Punjab', *Women in Agriculture and Rural Development*, Supplement to the *Indian Journal of Agriculture Economics*, 59(1).

13

'Just' Laws are not Enough

A Note on the Common Civil Code, Marriage and Inheritance in Goa*

Shaila Desouza

INTRODUCTION

The relationship between law and society is today a prime juristic as well as a sociological concern. The common argument is that the law positively affects social status, and that gender-just laws in particular can greatly transform and improve women's position in society. However, field experience tells a different story. This chapter debates the role that law plays in bringing about social equality and justice, and the ability of the law to effect social control and change. This is done by highlighting a few features of the civil law in the Indian state of Goa, namely, the Portuguese Civil Code which has been in effect for over a century, and by contrasting the existing law with some of the field realities. This chapter argues that though the law may seem to be pro-women, it alone cannot bring about an improvement in the status of women in that society. The law has to go hand in hand with appropriate dissemination, social movements and social action, as well as programmes to deal with the consequences of

---

* This chapter critiques the Civil Code in Goa, India, but in no way seeks to suggest that the Civil Code be replaced by the personal laws that govern the rest of the country. The author also does not claim that the chapter is exhaustive, as only a few aspects of the law have been discussed.

changes that are either prescribed by the law, or necessary for the law to be assimilated into the lives of the people governed by that law.

Article 44 of the Indian Constitution provides a Directive Principle that 'The State shall endeavour to secure for the citizens a uniform civil code throughout the territory of India'. In the last five decades since then, there has been much debate in India about the institution of a Uniform Civil Code (UCC) in the country. One of the arguments against the UCC is that it goes against one's Fundamental Right, which is to be governed by one's religious personal law. Several religious fundamentalists, political parties and others have argued in favour of the retention of separate religious personal laws. While the rest of the country discusses the pros and cons of a Uniform Civil Code, few are even aware that in Goa, a small state situated on the west coast of India, which was under Portuguese rule for 450-odd years (1510–1961), a Common Civil Code instituted in 1867 exists even today. Those aware of this law have often argued that the unique law in this state is responsible for the seemingly high social status of women in Goa. While this may be true with respect to certain aspects of women's lives, such as health status, education, et cetera, there remains much to be desired before we can talk of equality of sexes in Goa (Desouza 2004). The credit given to the law is debatable. Besides, we have had the Common Civil Code for 450 years, while the changes we have noticed in Goan society are much more recent. Credit is due to the women's movement in Goa, which is largely responsible for creating an awareness about women's rights. The proclaimed advantages of the law really contribute only marginally to women's advancement in society. We will discuss this by looking at a few provisions of the Civil Code regarding 'marriage', and some of the laws regarding succession and inheritance.

Goa comprises approximately 64 per cent Hindus, 31 per cent Christians, 4 per cent Muslims and 1 per cent other communities. Goa was a Portuguese colony for over four centuries. The 'Codigo Civil Portugues' or the Portuguese Civil Code of 1867, which is often referred to as the Common Civil Code and is based on the French Civil Code (Code Napoleon), has been in effect in Goa since 1870, and continues to exist with some modifications over the years. The title Common Civil Code has been earned because the code applies to all communities in Goa. Here, the personal laws are not applicable.

REGISTRATION OF MARRIAGE

Under the Civil Code registration is mandatory, registration not only of births and deaths, but of all marriages too. This proof or recognition of marriage is meant to ensure a certain amount of security to a married woman, as the law also assures a married woman of a share in her husband's assets.

Although registration is mandatory for all communities in Goa, the implementation differs from community to community. The procedures for registration are as follows: the two parties entering into the contract of marriage have to first declare their intention to marry before the office of the Civil Registrar by signing the declaration in the presence of two witnesses. A period of two to three weeks is then sought by the Civil Registrar, who has to post this intent on the door of the office to invite objections, if any, to the marriage. Objections are referred to the civil court for examination before a decision is taken. If there are no objections, the couple must appear before the Civil Registrar after the stipulated period to confirm their intention and to sign the Book of Registration, again in the presence of two witnesses. For Catholics wishing to marry in a church, the procedure is different. After declaring their intent to marry at the Civil Registry, a no objection certificate is obtained from the Civil Registrar, which is handed over to the church. The officiating priest is granted the power of a Civil Registry. This was given under the treaty signed in 1946 between the Roman Catholic Church at the Vatican and the Portuguese government under Antonio de Oliveira Salazar. At the church, after the marriage rites have been performed, the couple sign a register in front of witnesses, and an extract of the church register is then sent to the office of the Civil Registrar, who prepares the civil marriage certificate.

Problems with this System of Registration

The flaws in this system are numerous, not least among them being that the procedures are too complicated, cumbersome and do not apply uniformly to all communities. Very often the declaration of intent to marry has been mistaken by women as the civil marriage itself, resulting in several cases where women have believed themselves to be married when they are actually not married in the eyes of the law. If the intent is not confirmed within a year, the declaration ceases to be valid. Women's organisations in Goa have found several such cases, which came to light especially when women wished to take legal recourse for marital problems. A religious marriage alone is not a valid marriage in the eyes of the law, leaving many ignorant women in more vulnerable positions.

Then, unlike Sections 405 and 406 of the Indian Penal Code where a denial of *stridhan* (the wife's personal property under Hindu law) is considered a criminal offence, under the Civil Code a woman cannot immediately claim any of her belongings from her husband without going through the court to retrieve them. So, if a woman has been thrown out of her marital home, she cannot even take her clothes and personal effects with her, leave alone her rightful share in the family assets, without applying for the same through the court. There is no distinction between personal property and communion of assets. Then, for Hindus and Muslims, it is taken for granted that the people are aware of the compulsions of registration, so the marriages of persons who are oblivious of this mandate and are married by religious rites are considered invalid.

Another problem with the system is that there are civil registries only in the talukas (administrative headquarters) and not in the village panchayats. Then there is an additional problem as these offices are not yet computerised. Therefore, it is very difficult for the offices to check if the partners seeking to marry have in fact been married before or not. And in cities there is now so much of anonymity that it is not uncommon for a person to register, in the same office, marriages to two different women.

People Aware of Mandatory Registration of Marriage

A study conducted by the Centre for Women's Studies, Goa University, showed that although women were not aware of the actual procedures of registration, the awareness of the need to register marriages was fairly high, particularly among Muslim women. The provisions in the Civil Code are quite contrary to the Muslim personal law, which might be an explanation for the high degree of awareness among people in this community.

Another contributing factor to the general awareness of this need to register marriages is the tax benefit that is made available on the registration of marriage. Income from all other sources is considered joint property and taxed likewise, that is, each partner is taxed on only half the total amount of assets owned.

MARRIAGE IN GOA

Law views marriage as a contract, and according to the Civil Code there are four systems by which a marriage can be contracted. Therefore, before the civil registration, an Ante Nuptial agreement is to be signed by the two partners entering into marriage, stating clearly how the properties of each party are to be held. If no agreement is signed prior to the marriage, the marriage is considered contracted under the first type of marriage system, that is,

(i) Communion of Assets: All wealth and properties here, regardless of the source, owned by both partners are considered joint family assets, and both partners own equal shares. It might be interesting to note here that the husband cannot sell or do away with his property without the consent of his wife. Even in the event of non-payment of a loan taken by the husband alone, the half share of the property belonging to the wife cannot be attached. In other cases, however, the division of properties cannot be done during the subsistence of the marriage. The collective property can be partitioned only on the dissolution of the marriage, that is, in the event of death or divorce. The main drawback of this system is that the administration of common assets rests solely with the husband. If there are children, the family assets are further shared between sons and daughters equally.

(ii) The second system is that of a total separation of properties or no communion at all, which is a very rare agreement signed before marriage as it is not in keeping with the sentiment surrounding marriage. Here the partners hold all their properties independently.

(iii) The third is where there is total separation of the properties and assets owned prior to the marriage, and a communion of those assets and properties acquired subsequently. This type of agreement was not very common until very recently, when it started becoming increasingly common. This might reflect the nature of marriages today.

(*iv*) The fourth system is the one often mistaken for dowry. It is the Dotal Regime. The bride is given a certain share of her father's property and assets, which are handed over to her husband at the time of marriage. The husband is bound to restore to his partner all the property and assets, should the marriage be dissolved. It is not a consideration for marriage, but a 'trust' in the hands of the husband. In the case of his death, his heirs are liable to pay the wife the corpus of the amount.

Regardless of the system of marriage, all children have a share in the family property, and sons and daughters are treated alike. It is, therefore, next to impossible for parents to disinherit their children, as only half of their share of the property can be disposed of according to their wishes. In the absence of descendants, ascendants are entitled to the share and in their absence, brothers and sisters and their descendants are entitled to equal shares.

The Reality is Something Different

Very often daughters get a certain amount of gold at the time of their marriage and are asked to sign off their rights to the family property. It is not common for daughters to fight for their share of the parental property and if there are such cases, it is invariably because of the informed son-in-law, who wishes to claim his share. It may also be because of the land prices today and the known wealth that the construction industry can bring. Regarding awareness in Goa about the inheritance and succession laws, there is awareness of the fact that by law the spouses are equal partners to family assets, but awareness of the other provisions of the Ante Nuptial agreement is not very high.

A problem that has been noted by women's organisations in Goa is that invariably, it is the husband's name that is recorded in the land records unless the wife insists that her name be included too, which is very rare. Therefore, a man wishing to dispose of his property and disinherit his wife can do so by concealing the fact that he is married.

In Article 1204, which talks of the separation of persons and properties, adultery committed by the wife is a ground for separation. However, for the husband, only adultery accompanied by public scandal, or a complete abandonment of the wife, or keeping a mistress in the conjugal domicile are grounds for separation (this is apart from ill-treatment and serious injuries, and conviction to life imprisonment, which are applicable to both spouses).

Bigamy in Goa

Bigamy is not uncommon in Goa. Women's organisations have been discussing this issue and have noted that bigamy is very high in the state. Some might reason that this is the practice, as there is a provision for polygamy under Articles 3 and 4 of the section on 'Usages and Customs of Gentile Hindus of Goa' in the family laws. However, polygamy is permitted only under certain conditions:

 (i) Absolute absence of issues by the wife from the previous marriage until she attains the age of 25 years (with the consent of the wife from the previous marriage).

 (ii) Absolute absence of male issue, the wife from the previous marriage having completed 30 years of age; and being of lower age, 10 years having elapsed from the last pregnancy (with consent of wife from the previous marriage).

 (iii) Separation on any legal grounds, when proceeding from the wife, and when there is no male issue.

 (iv) Dissolution of the previous marriage as provided under Article 6 of Usages and Customs, that is (a) impotency of spouses, duly proved; (b) adultery by the wife; (c) ill-treatment and serious injuries; (d) change of religion.

Interestingly, however, bigamy is prevalent in all Hindu, Catholic and Muslim communities. This is despite the fact that Section 494 of the Indian Penal Code considers bigamy an offence. It may be interesting to note that prior to 1955, in the eyes of law there was no such thing as a monogamous marriage as there was no mention of polygamy as an offence. Divorce laws also did not exist.

LAW AND SOCIETY

An important aspect of the relationship between law and society is the process of assimilation of the law into the lifestyle of the people, as only then will the law be consciously used as a vehicle of social transformation.

With the entry of modern influences on education, political ideology and socio-cultural values, such as ideas of democracy and equality, which have led to a serious questioning and rethinking of traditional values, the desired position or status of women in society has undergone a fair change. The law, likewise, also has to be updated vis-à-vis the needs of the society. According to the Civil Code (Chapter V, Article 39), 'The conjugal union is based on liberty and equality, the husband being duty bound, especially, to defend the person and the properties of the wife and of the children, and the wife having the duty mainly of domestic management and moral assistance to the strengthening and improvement of the family unit'.

'Development' is indeed a primary goal today, and the question of women's status and the creation of an environment that will enhance their social functioning are incorporated in the agenda. Law is believed to be one way by which societies provide protection to individuals, maximise civil liberties and promote equality; however, it is often the law that has to be transformed if development is to be achieved, especially those laws that delay or distort development efforts rather than help realise them—gender-biased laws, for instance. But just laws are not enough. The law has not helped to improve women's access to economic resources, incomes and employment, nor has it helped to improve women's health, nutritional and educational status. In reality, women have been unable to exercise their rights, and neither do they have freedom from and protection against violence, as the number of reported cases of violence has been on the increase.

The various movements for reform and revival in earlier times were all usually accompanied by a social service counterpart. If change is desired, it has to be the 'felt need' of the society, for it has also to be accepted and assimilated. Social sanction for the law and an informed society are vital. Not only is social awareness necessary, but the society also requires supportive services to help it 'adjust' to the consequences of any change. Social reform and legal reform should be linked, and be considered synonymous with development as both essentially aim at change—a change sometimes involving the values of a society. But this is easier said than done.

Traditional Indian society has only in the last century been exposed to modern ideas of democracy and equality, and it is therefore still too soon for these new ideas to be completely assimilated by the people who have for centuries been living with different values. There is also an underlying belief that anything that has earned itself the name 'tradition', and has stood the test of time, should have some merits to account for its continued existence. Thus in our society, we have even today both defensive and assimilative reactions to law, and more particularly to law reform. Legal reform and social reform, as stated earlier, should go hand in hand. Even social transformation is meaningless without an adequate legal system to sustain it. This can be exemplified by past social movements.

CONCLUSION

It is true that the well-being and development of the individual and equal recognition of the dignity of every individual, are indicators of social progress. However, there is one major problem with regard to human rights, and that is the conflict that often arises between individual good and social good. This conflict is often overlooked by law, which tends to view things more in terms of black and white, and wrong and right. The reality in society is not that simple. These complexities have to be understood and dealt with before we can even hope that the law will determine or improve society, particularly women's status within it. The law-enforcing agencies should therefore go beyond the 'institutional' and also include the 'social'.

REFERENCES

Desouza, Shaila. 2004. *Situational Analysis of Women in Goa*. Delhi: National Commission for Women.

Usgaonkar, M.S. 1988. *Family Laws of Goa, Daman and Diu*, Vols. I and II (English translation of laws). Goa: Vela Associates.

V

Women's Collective Agency, Development and Citizenship

14

The Sangha Mané
*The Translation of an Internal Need into a Physical Space**

Vinalini Mathrani and Vani Periodi

AN OVERVIEW

The sangha mané, the hut or home of the 'sangha' (women's group) in the Mahila Samakhya Karnataka (MSK) programme, is a space where the women conduct meetings, develop action plans, implement income-generation programmes and even take refuge. The sangha mané is a symbol of time and space that women have carved out for themselves. It signifies their newly acquired access to community resources, and their ability to bring their views to the process of decision-making in the panchayat. The structure assumes added relevance due to the fact that it is a public declaration of an association of women who have been marginalised for generations.

The Mahila Samakhya (MS) programme was initiated in 1987–89 in nine states of India to translate the goals of the National Education Policy (1986) into a concrete programme for the education and empowerment of women in rural areas. Special focus has been given to the socially and economically marginalised women. The foundation for empowerment was laid with the organisation of cohesive '*mahila sanghas*' (women's groups). In Karnataka, a belief in self-determination has enabled the programme to assume varying forms in different districts.

* A version of this Chapter has also appeared in the *Indian Journal of Gender Studies*, Vol. 13, No. 3, 317–42, 2006.

The existence of such a collective space (sangha mané) can contribute
to women's empowerment. Empowering processes assume multiple
expressions, which have a varying impact depending on the local situation
and the aspirations of the people involved. Feminist theorists have posited
various definitions of empowerment. The idea of power is at the root of
empowerment. Therefore, there is power 'to', wherein power relates to
possessing decision-making authority; power 'with' involves people
getting organised with a common purpose or understanding to achieve
collective goals; and power 'within', which refers to self-confidence, self-
awareness and assertiveness. The feminist movement has emphasised
collective organisation (power with) and has been influential in developing ideas about power within. Thus, power works at different levels:
the institutional, the household and the individual. Empowerment
becomes a process by which women freely analyse, develop, and voice
their needs and interests (Oxal and Baden 1997).

Gender is configured within a range of socio-economic and cultural
constraints. Gender identity starts out with the knowledge and awareness,
whether conscious or unconscious, that one belongs to one sex and not
the other. As one develops, gender identity becomes more complicated.
Exclusive gender identity is a suppression of natural similarities between
men and women. It requires the repression of the 'local version' of
feminine traits in men and masculine traits in women. Therefore, the
gender role that one plays out before others may offer little clue as to who
one really feels oneself to be. This indicates that one's inner and outer life
may be deeply conflicted, or fail to coincide (Glover and Kaplan 2000).
This study examines whether the *processes* surrounding the *construction
and the use of the* sangha manés (houses/huts/offices) in the MSK field
area enable women to reduce this inner discord. It attempts to see whether
these have provided women with the opportunity to delve into their gender identity and role. In doing so, have women become empowered, and
has this empowerment engendered effective citizenship?

In this chapter, the *notion of citizenship* is seen as membership in a
political community, and carries with it *rights* to political participation.
It implies working towards the betterment of oneself and one's community
through participation and volunteer work. In general, the practice of citizenship is largely seen within the political context. In the current climate,
vulnerable groups are finding it difficult to exercise citizenship for a variety

of reasons. The state is either withdrawing, leaving these groups exposed to the forces of privatisation, or it is becoming increasingly coercive. Therefore, there is a need to dwell on the notion of 'emancipatory and potential citizenship'. Is there a possibility for people to engage in certain activities, which will empower them, enable them to exercise their civil rights and thus enable citizenship? This chapter unveils images, which are attempts at constructing 'stepping stones' that will lead on to an effective citizenship. Hence, reflection on gender role and identity, empowerment and citizenship are seen as synergistic processes, feeding into one another (Figure 14.1).

Figure 14.1

Synergies between Gender, Role and Identity;
Empowerment; and Citizenship

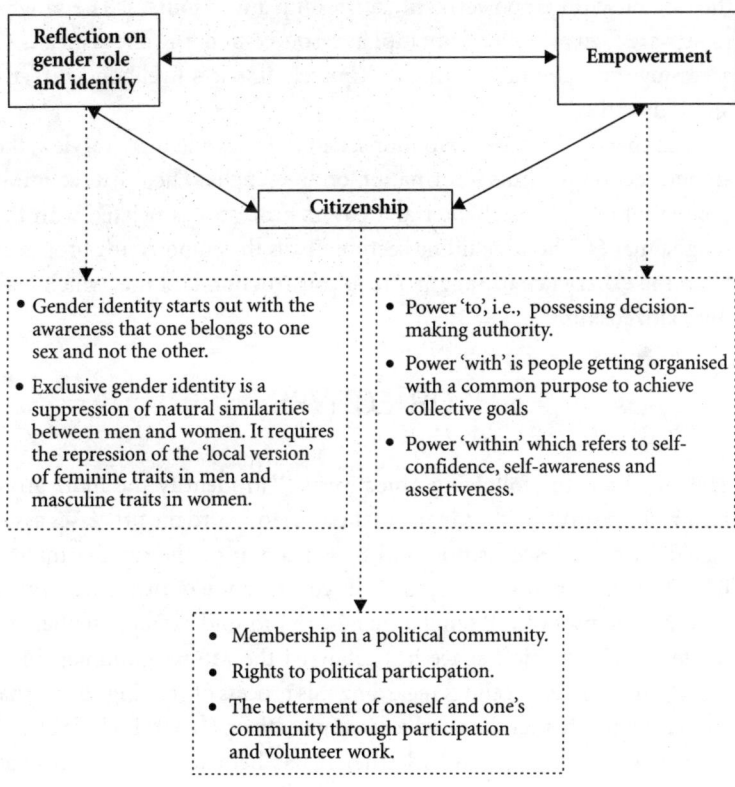

- Gender identity starts out with the awareness that one belongs to one sex and not the other.
- Exclusive gender identity is a suppression of natural similarities between men and women. It requires the repression of the 'local version' of feminine traits in men and masculine traits in women.

- Power 'to', i.e., possessing decision-making authority.
- Power 'with' is people getting organised with a common purpose to achieve collective goals
- Power 'within' which refers to self-confidence, self-awareness and assertiveness.

- Membership in a political community.
- Rights to political participation.
- The betterment of oneself and one's community through participation and volunteer work.

We will examine these processes in the context of the MS programme, which is running in 1,400 villages located in 33 talukas of seven districts of Karnataka, and has instituted 1,082 mahila sanghas (December 2002). In each location, the sanghas identify critical issues, devise strategies to address them and implement their localised plans. As part of the feminist movement, this programme is rooted in the belief that the process of empowerment itself constitutes a goal. The present study is an attempt at documenting one such process by examining the philosophy, structure and system behind the sangha mané.

In December 2002, there were 281 sangha manés. Most of the other sanghas were either thinking of building sangha manés, or are in the process of doing so. This indicates that women regard it as a critical component of their empowerment. Therefore, documenting the processes associated with the institution and maintenance of the sangha manés contributes to the discourse on empowerment, citizenship and resources. The sangha manés are seen as both an attempt at resource-building and a means of accessing local resources, which ultimately impacts livelihood directly and indirectly.

This chapter is divided into four sections. Following this overview, the second section presents information on the sangha. The third section is the main body of the chapter and covers processes associated with the sangha manés. The concluding section distils the empowering processes from the experience of sangha mané construction and use, which lead onto citizenship.

OBJECTIVES

The study has the following objectives: (*i*) to identify the motivating factors for instituting the sangha manés; (*ii*) to record the processes associated with land acquisition and construction of the sangha manés, including the expenses incurred in the construction of this space; (*iii*) to describe the uses of the sangha manés; (*iv*) to understand whether the existence of a physical space has catalysed the MS programme; (*v*) to capture the women's feelings regarding this process of creating an external space, that is, whether the sangha mané gives them an ontological validity (a new way of being), and whether it has helped women transcend restrictive socially prescribed gender roles; (*vi*) to distil the empowering aspects associated with the process of constructing and using the sangha mané, whether possessing a 'space of one's own' is empowering; (*vii*) to reflect upon whether these processes have helped engender citizenship.

METHODOLOGY AND LOCATION

This study is an outcome of two felt needs expressed by the field staff, the sahyoginis (fieldworkers) of MSK: 'First, we feel that the sangha manés are a key component in the empowering processes of the MS programme, but we would like a clearer picture on the actual role. Second, we have spent long years in setting up sanghas, conducting training programmes, supporting activities, we now want to develop the skill to effectively research and document our work.' The response was a series of training workshops, which would enable the sahyoginis to collect and analyse data.

A decision was taken to actually undertake a study rather than merely provide inputs, which may or may not be utilised. In choosing the sangha manés, the following selection criteria were adopted: new/old sangha, multi-caste/unicaste sangha, problematic/smooth processes associated with sangha mané construction, medium-sized/large village, and exterior/interior village. Based on this, the following villages were selected: Tuppanakhanahalli (Bellary district), Marakunda (Bidar district), Agasanahalli (Bijapur district), Kudli (Gulbarga district), Kurukunda (Raichur district), Dotihalla (Koppal district) and Banikuppe (Mysore district).

A qualitative study was proposed as the focus was on processes. This would yield insights, rather than statistical data. This chapter is largely based on primary data, which the sahyoginis directly collected from the women involved in the process. The main technique was focus group discussions with the sangha women; the tool was a detailed guideline.

THE CONTEXT: THE SANGHAS

A brief introduction to the mahila sanghas will help contextualise the processes associated with the construction and use of the sangha manés.

Table 14.1 reveals that these sanghas have been functioning for between three and 13 years. There is a similarity in the average age profile (32 to 45 years). Most sanghas have 15 to 17 members. This seems to be the appropriate size.

Sangha Formation Processes

In most of the study villages (except for Kurukunda and Banikuppe), the motivation for forming the sangha came from the MS team. The sahyoginis and other field staff paid numerous visits to the villages for four to six months before the sanghas were instituted. The women were unaware of the potential of such a collective, hence their resistance. In Marakunda, there was tremendous opposition from the village. During the initial meetings, the village youth and men would throw stones at the women. They maintained that the sahyogini was of loose character, and would sell the village women into prostitution. In these five villages, the sahyogini's perseverance enabled sangha formation. In Kurukunda, the women would go to Siruvaru village (12 km away) to sell their ware (broomsticks). During their visits, they met women from Nugudoni and Chincharaki villages where sanghas had been instituted. These women wanted to run similar programmes and access schemes, as they felt that this was an opportunity for them to change their life situation. They invited the sahyogini to help them set up a sangha. A similar situation prevailed in Banikupppe, where a sangha from the neighbouring village inspired them.

In the other five villages, once the MSK staff convinced the women, the latter realised that:

> We could run savings schemes through the sangha. We will be able to access knowledge from different realms. We will gain the confidence and courage to go out. Before, we were too scared to go out for anything but work. We did not have the ability to think logically so we feared everything. The sangha can help us mainstream ourselves. We realised that we are very backward, so a collective will strengthen us. We can ensure the accountability of teachers, medical staff and political representatives. We can learn to read and write and take decisions based on information.

Thus, it is evident that the women felt the sangha would help them move from a subservient position to one of questioning and demanding

Table 14.1
Sangha Details

Sangha, Village, District	Date of Inception	Age Profile/Number of Members	Caste Profile
Durgambika Mahila Sangha, Tuppanakhanahalli Bellary district	December 1998.	28 to 40 years (average: 34 years).15 members.	Multi-caste sangha: 8 Scheduled Tribes (STs), 4 Jungamaru and 3 Gollaru.
Ramabai Ambedkar Mahila Sangha, Marakunda, Bidar district	1990.	30 to 60 years (average: 45 years). There were 30 members in 1990, but in 2002 the membership was 15.	Unicaste sangha: Holeya members. Other SC groups have not been represented.
Rukamabai Mahila Sangha, Agasanahalli, Bijapur district	1990.	21 to 45 years (average: 32 years). 17 members.	Multi-caste sangha with the Lingayats, Kurubararu, Malagaru, Muslims, Hoogararu, Agasararu and Kamararu almost equally represented. The SCs have not joined this sangha.
Lakshmibai Mahila Sangha, Kudli, Gulbarga district	March 1995.	30 to 60 years (average: 45 years). 17 members.	Unicaste sangha: SCs (Holeyaru).
Durgadevi Mahila Sangha Kurukunda, Raichur district	October 1999, registered in March 2001.	28 to 50 years (average: 40 years). 29 members.	Multi-caste sangha, but all belong to the socio-economically depressed category (SCs: 15, STs: 1, Others: 13).
Chaitanya Mahila Sangha, Dotihalla, Koppal district	October 1992, registered in June 1994.	25 to 50 years (average: 37 years). 15 members.	Multi-caste sangha, but the membership is dominated by the SCs and STs (14).
Channamma Mahila Sangha, Bannamma Mahila Sangha, Banikuppe, Mysore district	1990.	25 to 65 years (average: 45 years). 40 women became members, which made it unwieldy for running the savings programme. Hence, the group broke into two: Channamma Mahila Sangha: 18 members; and Bannamma Mahila Sangha: 19 members. Total membership now amounts to 37.	Unicaste sangha Madigaru (SCs).

Source: Based on primary data collected by sahyoginis.

accountability from public officials. The activities adopted by the sanghas reflect their interest areas and prioritisation.

Sangha Activities

The women from different sanghas have taken up a range of activities. It is clear that a high premium is set on economic control, independence and mobility. There are some common activities in which all the sanghas are engaged:

- The women are running thrift and savings activity. They contribute Rs 5 to Rs 10 per week. The money is deposited in a bank account on which interest is generated. This money is used for issuing loans at an interest rate of 3–5 per cent per month. It is also used for tiding over lean financial periods.
- Meetings are held once a week. The women are divided into six issue-based committees: Education, Health, Panchayati Raj, Legal Literacy, Sangha Self-Reliance, and Economic Development Programmes (EDP). Committee-wise meetings are also held, and each committee shares information with the other sangha women.
- The women visit the panchayat to access different government schemes like Ashraya housing, Bhagyajyothi and Astra Chulah. They attend all the gram sabhas.
- A number of sanghas run adult literacy classes. Most of them have focused on enrolment of school drop-outs.
- They visit the PHC to ensure that the staff members execute their responsibilities.
- They go to the police station when required.
- They attend *ghataka* (cluster), taluka and district-level programmes.

There is also a range of other activities that the sanghas have adopted, based on local issues. In Tuppanakhanahalli, Agasanahalli and Dotihalla, the women have protested against child marriage and the Devadasi tradition. In Marakunda, there has been a focus on EDP activities like sheep and buffalo rearing and poultry. The women have bought large vessels from their savings, which are rented out and the proceeds shared. In Agasanahalli, they have helped update voter lists, and have undertaken a shramdan (voluntary labour) to clean the village. They run a crèche, participate in medical camps, and awareness camps on dowry, rape, alcoholism and widow remarriage. In Agasanahalli and Kurukunda, they ensure that the *anganwadi* programme is running efficiently. (This initiative under the Integrated Child Development Scheme provides nutrition to pregnant women, lactating mothers and preschool children, and educational and socialisation inputs for the children.) In Kurukunda, they have created a *nari adalat* (women's court) programme. In Dotihalla, they run Non-Formal Education (NFE) classes. They rear sheep and grow mushrooms. In Banikuppe, the women have helped set up an *okutta* (federation) office in Hunsur. The health committee is involved in keeping the borewell surroundings clean.

All the sanghas felt the need for a space to run these programmes efficiently. Therefore, it becomes relevant to examine the different reasons for building the sangha manés.

Reasons for Building a Sangha Mané

Almost uniformly, women from all the sanghas declared, 'We had no space to conduct our meetings'. The women would conduct their meetings in public places, that is, the Samudaya Bhavan, temples, in a sangha woman's house, schools, and sometimes even on the roadside or near the garbage dump. All these locations were open to the public, and hence did not provide them with any privacy. The men would hang around, smoke beedis, drink, and even throw stones at the women. They would taunt the women and cast aspersions on their character. Further, some of these places did not have a roof, so during the rainy seasons their meetings would get disrupted. The women would move from place to place, seeking some measure of privacy. Given all these factors, even the MSK team found it difficult to conduct meetings. This left the women highly frustrated, as they felt that the existence of the sangha was in jeopardy. Apart from not being able to hold meetings, the women wanted their own space to run the other activities. This indicates that the women felt the sanghas could not be sustained without a private and independent space of their own.

Sangha manés, therefore, feature in the realm of felt needs, as the women themselves articulated this requirement. A series of complex processes unfolded once the decision to build a 'space of one's own' was taken.

Initially, we thought of highlighting the main trends across all the villages, but after we collected the data we realised that each of these apparently innocuous looking structures conceal distinct tales of intrigue, perseverance, despair, hope and success. Hence, each story has been recounted. It is also useful to look at acquisition and construction processes separately, as in some cases construction has not begun and in others construction proceeded smoothly while land acquisition was fraught with problems, and vice versa.

SANGHA MANÉ PROCESSES

Land Acquisition

Tuppanakhanahalli, Bellary district: The process of land acquisition was initiated in December 2000. The women approached the secretary of the gram panchayat (GP), who maintained that first, they had to get their sangha registered. The women had to go to the MLA five to six times before the sangha was registered in February 2001. Both the traditional village head (Gowda) and the secretary of the gram panchayat accepted the women's application, and showed them a site for the sangha mané. The women went to the gram panchayat (GP) four times, but the title deed was not issued. They then contacted the MLA in Kudligi twice and Badalaku once, to recount all their problems. The MLA asked a Congress member to help the women. Six women went to the GP again, where the Congress member requested GP members to issue the title deed. Finally, in October 2001, the sangha became the owner of the allotted site.

Marakunda, Bidar District: The sangha women submitted an application to the GP in 1991, asking for a plot of land. Till then, the women had been conducting their meetings in the temple. The GP informed the women that they were unaware of any free plots in the village, so the women would have to find a site for themselves. The women identified a plot, which had been used as a garbage dump, in the Kuruba (OBCs, shepherds) colony. The GP members verbally agreed to their request. Hence, the women proceeded to clean up the area. When they decided to conduct a ceremony before initiating construction, the Kurubaru intervened and showed them the title deeds to the same plot. The GP realised that the Kurubaru were the actual owners, so they revoked their permission for the sangha mané. They asked the women to identify another plot. The women were extremely unhappy at the turn of events, as all their efforts had come to naught. Meanwhile, they continued to conduct their meetings in front of the temple. They came to the conclusion that it may be possible to use the temple premises to build a sangha mané, and install the idol within the mané. In 1995, they put in an application for this place. The GP contacted the SC community, who were amenable to this, on condition that the idol was reinstalled. In 1996, the women received the title deeds.

Agasanahalli, Bijapur District: The women contacted the traditional village leader (Gowda) who was more powerful than the elected representatives. During the first few visits, he was unresponsive, but seeing their perseverance, he agreed, provided they were able to identify an appropriate plot. The women identified a piece of gaothan (community land owned by the GP), which was being used by the Kurubaru and the Malagaru (shepherds and OBCs) to store agricultural implements and produce. Both communities opposed this request, despite the fact that this sangha has members from these communities. This reaction can be attributed to the fact that the men did not want women to assert their identity in public. Nonetheless, the Gowda asked them to measure the plot. The women earmarked a plot of 60 by 40 feet. They also approached a taluka panchayat woman member who belonged to Agasanahalli. No help was forthcoming from this quarter, so they contacted the Gowda again who approached the GP. This issue was discussed in the gram sabha, and finally after six months, the title deeds were issued.

Kudli, Gulbarga District: The women approached the sahyogini for advice in October 1995. She told them to put in an application at the panchayat. Three sangha women accompanied the sahyogini to the panchayat. The panchayat president and secretary maintained that there was no suitable plot available. The women approached the GP again after 15 days. The members took them to a site 2 km from the SC colony, but the women felt that the plot was not conveniently located. The GP members showed them another site close by, which had a tank that had been constructed for drought relief. At that time, it was not being used. The women sold their crops to raise Rs 400 for registering the sangha. After three visits to the GP, they received the title deeds in December 1995. In the middle of December 1995, the sangha women and their husbands proceeded to break the tank. At this juncture, an SC schoolteacher filed a police complaint alleging that the women were destroying a public facility. In reality, he wanted to acquire the land for himself. A police constable and some other officials arrived at the site, and requested the women to stop breaking the tank till they verified the claims. They contacted the panchayat members who clarified that the women's claims were valid.

Kurukunda, Raichur District: The women contacted the sahyogini, who advised them to go to the GP. In September 2000, the women put in an application. At the same time, the MLA visited the village to canvass votes for the forthcoming election. All 30 sangha women agreed to vote for him on the condition that he help them construct their sangha mané. He agreed, provided they identified and acquired the land themselves. The women identified a plot on the grazing land of the village. They asked the MLA and the Gowda to assist them in getting it sanctioned. Two women from the Panchayati Raj Committee took the responsibility for getting the title deeds. In December 2000, two sangha women went to the panchayat meeting. A sangha woman was the panchayat *adhayksh* (head). She ensured that the plot was sanctioned. In February 2001, the GP secretary came to the village and marked out the sanctioned site.

Dotihalla, Koppal District: The process of land acquisition began in June 1995. A sangha woman was a member of the Panchayati Raj Committee in the mahila sangha. She contested for the gram panchayat elections and won, because she had the required experience and the support of the sangha women. The elections took place while the land acquisition process was underway. Hence, the two processes fed into each other. The women approached the GP for this purpose on numerous occasions. Their requests were rejected on the grounds that there was no land available. The women identified a plot in the SC colony, but the GP refused to consider this application as it was a part of the gaothan land. The women asked the GP secretary to issue a letter stating this. He refused. In the meantime, the sangha woman who had been elected to the panchayat went to Bangalore to attend a training programme. With the help of the Mahila Samakhya state office team, she got in touch with the chief secretary on this matter. He agreed to look into the case. Finally the GP issued the title deeds to the same plot in June 1996.

Banikuppe, Mysore District: The sangha women contacted the village Gowda in 1993. He in turn approached the men's sangha (Adi Jambava

Sangha). This group had a plot of land that was underused. The men felt that the women had proved themselves capable of good work. Without a hitch, they transferred the plot to the women's sangha within 40 days. The women did not incur any expenses except for a small registration cost.

It is relevant to reflect upon the *time taken in the land acquisition process.* The women of Marakunda took six years to acquire their plot. These women had to deal with an unsupportive gram panchayat and face opposition from the Kurubaru. In Kudli, the women got their plot within two months, despite a GP that was not supportive at the outset. The women's husbands extended both mental and physical support. Banikuppe is the exception, as the sangha women were able to acquire the land in 30 to 40 days. The men in this village were highly supportive of the sangha itself. This seems to be a key factor in expediting the matter. In the other villages, the time span ranged from five months to one year. The ability to sustain their efforts despite opposition from many quarters is creditable.

One can see a *range of strategies in operation.* In Agasanahalli and Banikuppe, the Gowdas seem to be more powerful than the elected representatives. The fact that the women chose to approach these traditional leaders before contacting the GP members is indicative of the women using information they have internalised through exposure to village politics and dynamics. The women also seemed to be imbued with sufficient confidence to approach the chief secretary and local MLAs to request, and even bargain with, them to promote their interests.

Sangha Mané Construction

Land acquisition was followed by the construction, which bought with it a range of other developments. In all the villages except for Tuppankhanahalli, the construction has been completed, and the sangha manés are in use.

Tuppanakhanahalli: In October 2001, the sangha women withdrew Rs 5,000 from their savings accounts. They gave this to the Congress member for starting the construction. Unfortunately, before the foundation stone could be laid, he was (allegedly) murdered, by a member from the opposition party. Distressed by this development, the women contacted the MLA at Hagaribomanhalli. He reassured them and agreed to assist them with the construction. In the meantime, a villager encroached upon the allotted site and started constructing a house on it. The women put in applications with the zilla parishad (ZP) executive officer and the tahsildar. Yet no action was taken. They finally contacted the police. A constable took the encroacher to the police station, but his relatives got him released. He then proceeded to complete building his house on a part of the plot. The women have currently abandoned construction. This has left them disheartened, and they are uncertain of the future of the sangha itself.

Marakunda: The women contacted MSK for seed money. MSK gave them Rs 15,000, and got Rs 10,000 sanctioned from the ZP. In 1999, the women hired a local mason to oversee the construction, and purchased all the raw materials themselves. They hired a local carpenter to make the doors and windows. Three women would engage in shramdan (voluntary labour) on a daily basis. The actual construction took 30 workdays, but this stretched over a period of one year because the mason gave this task very low priority. He failed to report to the site on numerous occasions, which slowed down the pace of work. The structure was finally ready in 2000.

Agasanahalli: The women approached the MSK for funds for construction in 1992. MSK sanctioned Rs 15,000. The sangha women and their husbands laid the foundation themselves. The village Gowda contributed two neem trees and one mango tree for timber. By 1993, the foundation was laid. Work proceeded on the site with voluntary labour till the structure reached door level. At this juncture, the sangha president went through a personal financial crisis, which brought construction to a halt. Finally, in 1997, she committed suicide. Subsequently, the sangha also collapsed. The timber got stolen. The MSK was also in a dilemma as to whether they should continue working in this village. Five women continued with the savings activity through all these adversities. The Kurubaru and the Malagaru began taunting the women, 'Now that your leader is dead, the rest of you can also go and jump in the well. You are not capable of achieving anything.' This spurred the five women into action. They motivated 10 more women (some old and some new members) to join the sangha. The GP and the Gowda supported them as they felt that a multi-caste sangha would promote the interests of the village in general. The women collected Rs 5,000 from the villagers and Rs 10,000 from MSK (honorarium). They also approached the GP, which refused to contribute in monetary terms as they claimed that they did not have the funds to build such a large structure. After repeated visits, the GP agreed to sanction Rs 35,000, which they wanted disbursed directly to the contractor. In 2001, construction resumed and the structure was built by August 2001.

Kudli: The women started construction in December 1995. In one day, 14 people (sangha women and their husbands) broke the water tank. On 13 January 1996, while construction was underway, the police arrived in the village to serve a court notice to two sangha members. One person who was interested in acquiring the land for himself had filed a complaint, stating that the construction was proceeding on disputed land. The hearing was scheduled for 8 February. At this stage, a sangha woman's son, who was a GP member, the president and secretary of the GP, supported and encouraged the women, as they were not guilty of any crime. The women approached some prominent village leaders to discuss the issue. As the women were in possession of the title deed, everyone reassured them.

On the appointed day, the women arrived at the court at 11:00 a.m. They waited till 5:30 p.m., but their case was not taken up. The women returned to the village and conducted a sangha meeting to devise a strategy. They decided that it would be worthwhile to appoint a lawyer to launch a counter-case. The sangha woman's son (GP member) took the responsibility to appoint a lawyer. This lawyer demanded Rs 5,000 as fees. The women contributed whatever they could, and the rest was raised by collecting donations. On 16 February, the women went to the court to meet the lawyer. They waited in vain, from 10:00 a.m. to 2:30 p.m. Finally, when he emerged from his lunch break, he claimed that he had not received their fees. The women called for a sangha meeting. At this stage, the sangha woman's son turned against them and maintained that the women were engaged in an illegal construction and would be put in the Bellary jail if they proceeded. The women were unnerved and felt it would be relevant to postpone the construction till the case was closed. They raised another Rs 10,000 by taking a loan at the rate of 4 per cent per month to pay the lawyer's fees. The women went to the court four to five times, but the case did not come up for hearing. They decided to proceed with the construction. The structure reached door level when the women got a stay order from the Assistant Commissioner (AC) of Sedam on 8 August 1996. The following day, 9 August, a similar letter came from the GP. After the women received four or five such letters, they decided to stop the construction.

The women raised Rs 100 each (travel expenses) to go to Gulbarga. They contacted the District Programme Coordinator (DPC), MSK, who advised them to contact the AC at Sedam. When they visited the AC, he agreed to look into the matter. On 20 December, the AC visited Kudli. He measured the plot in the presence of the GP. He declared that the complainant's claims were unfounded and gave the women permission to proceed with the construction. To formalise this declaration, the women and the DPC, MSK, went to Sedam to get a permission letter from the AC. Construction resumed by the end of January 1997.

This enraged the complainant greatly. He contacted a local thug to threaten the sangha woman's son who was a GP member, thinking he was a sangha supporter. The thug's men hunted for the GP member but could not locate him. The women and a few villagers then contacted the taluka panchayat member and asked him to intervene. He took the complainant to task, 'These women have not usurped your land or your fields, why are you troubling them. If the thug's men are seen lurking around, we will throw you out of this village.'

Three days after this incident, the GP member concerned returned to the village. When he heard about these developments, he got infuriated. He grabbed a knife and went looking for the complainant. When the villagers tried to reason with him, he claimed that he had nothing to do with the sangha women, so why should he be incriminated. The sangha women were disturbed by these developments. One of them went to the police station so that pre-emptive action could be taken. The official concerned was most unsupportive and berated her, 'Since you people have formed the sangha, there has been nothing but trouble. We will put all of you in the remand home' (where persons under trial are kept in protective custody). However, she did not get intimidated, 'If you lay a finger on me you will have to pay for your actions. If you are a responsible police officer, you will come to the village and investigate the matter.' He calmed down and agreed to go to Kudli. In February, the police called for a village meeting. All those concerned, the ZP and GP members, attended the gram sabha. The police made a public declaration that anybody engaging in any form of violence or threatening the women would be jailed.

By March 1997, the structure reached roof level. At this stage, the women needed more wood. They cut four trees. The process of drying the wood took four months. Then the women realised that they did not have enough money for plastering and flooring. They applied to the GP, requesting it to bear these costs. Initially the GP refused to help. After much persuasion, they showed these as repair and maintenance costs. In January 1998, the structure was completed.

Kurukunda: The allotted site was dirty and overgrown with wild shrubs. The sangha women, along with their husbands and children, laboured at cleaning the site. The construction began on 15 March 2001. The MLA played a key role in the construction as he contacted the Hyderabad-Karnataka Regional Development Board (HKRDB) to get a sum of Rs 1,50,000 sanctioned. The women were keen on constructing the structure themselves, but the MLA decided to contract the job out to the Junior Engineer (JE). (When the JE takes on the contract, he usually makes some money illegally.) The JE contacted the Bhoosena Nigam (land army). This body is responsible for construction on government land.

The first installment of Rs 50,000 was released on 15 March. The women worked along with the Bhoosena as hired labourers on the site. While the foundation was being laid, the women realised that poor quality bricks were being used. They immersed the bricks in water to find that these dissolved in 10 minutes. The women requested the JE to stop the construction. When he refused to pay any heed to them, they brought in a ZP member to pressurise him. Work on the site stopped for 45 days. The women went to the MLA's office three times before he agreed to meet them. He registered their complaint and ensured that superior quality bricks were purchased with the next instalment. The second instalment was released on 25 May and the third on 15 June. While the doors and windows were being installed, the women supervised the process closely. The MLA visited the construction site and suggested that the building should have a large verandah to seat up to 50 women. The construction was completed on 2 July 2001, three and a half months after it had begun.

Dotihalla: The women received the title deed on 14 June 1996. It took six months to get the money for construction sanctioned from the MSK. In December 1996, Rs 5,000 was released. In February 1997, the women appointed a local mason to supervise the construction. MSK sanctioned another Rs 10,000. The women bought raw material worth Rs 12,000, and paid the mason Rs 3,000 for paying the labourers and for supervision.

By April 1997, the foundation was laid. The structure reached roof level in May 1997 through the efforts of hired labourers. The women dipped into their savings and the MSK honorarium (Rs 2,000) to continue with the construction.

At this stage, a controversy arose regarding the roofing. One of the sangha women was keen on putting an RCC roof, while the others felt that sheet roofing was adequate. The women also ran out of funds. In November 1997, the women approached the GP for funds. The GP refused outright as they felt that the women could use the Samudaya Bhavan for their meetings. At this stage, the local butcher was using the Samudaya Bhavan as an abattoir. The women visited the GP a number of times to get the funds sanctioned. Finally, a resolution was passed, stating that some money should be released. During this time, three GP secretaries changed and the resolution got misplaced. In the interim, a JE visited the village. The women asked him to intervene. He advised them to go to the taluka panchayat.

Finally, after one year, the GP sanctioned an amount of Rs 32,669, which was released in 1998–99. The JE was appointed the contractor and he received the money directly from the GP. The women felt that they needed additional funds for doors and windows, so they put in a second application to the GP. In the meanwhile, one of the sangha women had become active in questioning corruption and had established herself as an important public figure. The GP members realised that she could publicise this matter, so in April 2000, they released Rs 25,336 without any problems. The women tapped the GP funds for SC welfare as well. The JE hired the women as labourers at the rate of Rs 20 per day. The husbands also helped in stone breaking and carrying. By the end of 2000, the structure was built.

Banikuppe: Construction began on 24 October 1993. The women put in their savings of Rs 35,000. They approached the MLA for tiles. He agreed to contribute 1,000 tiles. The MSK seed money of Rs 15, 000 and honorarium of Rs 4,600 were also used for the construction. The women procured the additional construction material from quarries and scoured the surrounding area for sand. The rest of the raw material was purchased. The men played a key role in the technical aspects of construction. The structure came into being entirely through 'shramdan'. Based on a roster system, two persons from the 40 sangha women's households contributed their labour. If anyone failed to report to the site on the allotted day, a penalty of Rs 50 was imposed. Construction came to a close on 11 October 1994.

With regard to the *time taken for construction*, there is a wide range from four months in Kurukunda to nine years in Agasanahalli. In Tuppankhanahalli, the construction began in 2001 but is still underway. In the other villages, it took between one and four years. The women have displayed a remarkably high level of *involvement in the different stages of construction*.

During this period, one can see a *range of strategies* at work.

(a) In Marakunda, the women deliberately chose to avoid confrontation with the Kurubaru. They took the matter to the community and the GP. They did not pressurise the GP into allotting a plot immediately, even though they had been dealt with unfairly. They continued with their meetings, indicating that sangha processes are their priority. They succeeded in creating a local support base within the Holeya (SC) community by creating a space for the idol within the sangha mané.

(b) In Agasanahalli, the women had the maturity to hand the construction over to the GP when they realised that they would be unable to proceed independently. The five women displayed their perseverance by keeping the sangha in existence despite all odds.

(c) In Kudli, the entire process was fraught with problems. The women dealt with the pressure of high direct and indirect expenses by raising money through personal contributions and donations from the community. Their determination made the authorities take them seriously enough to respond to their demands. The women did not get intimidated by any of the villagers or the police. In the past, the sangha leaders had proved themselves to be socially responsible women and had intervened to resolve a number of domestic crises. This helped to push their agenda for the sangha mané in the larger community.

(d) In Kurukunda, they were able to bargain effectively with the MLA and use the elections as an occasion to achieve their goals.

(e) In Dotihalla, the sangha president's membership in the GP played a key role in sangha mané construction. The women participated in the actual construction work and closely supervised the process.

(f) In Banikuppe, the women had built enough good-will in the community prior to the construction, which stood them in good stead during this period.

With regard to *handling finances*, it is relevant to examine how this aspect is dealt with, as traditionally it is located in the domain of male responsibility. This function assumes additional significance, as most of the sangha women are illiterate.

(a) In Tuppanakahnahalli, the women handled all financial matters themselves.

(b) In Marakunda, one sangha member was in overall charge, with her son providing assistance when required; another member maintained the vouchers.

(c) In Agasanahalli, the sangha member took the assistance of the MSK staff whenever required. After her death, four other sangha women took over and requested the sahyogini for help.

(d) In Kudli, the women asked the GP member whose mother belonged to the sangha to take over this function. The women themselves issued receipts for all contributions and maintained a receipt book. Two of the women maintained the records and shared expense details with the other women periodically.

(e) In Kurukunda, the women had no role to play in this aspect as the JE was paid directly.

(f) In Dotihalla, the women purchased the raw material. They paid Rs 2 per head per month to a sangha woman's son for maintaining accounts. The women could not get any accounts from the JE. They were unaware that the second instalment had been released till the sahyogini intervened. Some amount of money seems to have been siphoned off, as the amount expended on doors and windows is very high.

(g) In Banikuppe, one sangha member maintained the documents.

Thus, in all the villages, the women have played a large role in handling financial matters, thereby ensuring that this critical area remained within their control.

Expenses Associated with Land Acquisition and Construction

Table 14.2 provides information on the amount of money raised by the women from multiple sources, donations in kind, and the total expenses incurred in the process. The women maintained that in addition to this, they bore indirect costs through the loss of daily wages due to the time spent on this work. The data reveals a high degree of variation in terms of the amount expended and the sources from which funds and raw material have been accessed, except for the seed money that MSK has contributed to all the villages. It is evident that no prescribed blueprint has been adopted. Structures of differing sizes and varying durability represent the women's abilities, and their different visions for the sangha manés.

It is pertinent that there are no positive correlations between the multicaste status of the sangha, and the ability to raise large funds. The highest expenses were incurred in Kurukunda, where the majority of the sangha members belong to the lower castes. Accessing funds was easiest in Banikuppe where the sangha members are Madigaru (SCs).

Community Reactions

It remains undisputed that the larger community plays an important role in contouring the image of the sangha and what the sangha mané represents. This can be regarded as a critical factor in facilitating, hindering, and even spurring on the processes associated with land acquisition and construction.

- In Tuppanakahnahalli, very few villagers and sangha women's husbands extended support. Most villagers were openly derisive of the women's efforts. This can be one of the reasons why the structure remains unfinished.
- In Marakunda (with a unicaste sangha), the landed upper castes were openly scornful, 'These women attend meetings and visit the panchayat to get money. They are trying to usurp the position of the Gowda and take control over the village.' The Kurubaru displayed intense antagonism when the sangha women were granted their land.

Table 14.2

Sangha Mané Construction: Sources of Money and Quantum of Expenditure

Village	MSK – Rs	Sangha Savings – Rs	Zilla Parishad/ GP – Rs	Loan – Rs	Other Sources – Rs	Material donated	Total – Rs
Tuppana-khanahalli		5,000					
Marakunda	15,000; MSK honorarium: 10,000.	5,000, Sangha women's personal contribution: 1,600.	ZP: 10,000.				41,600
Agasanahalli	15,000.	15,000.	GP: 35,000.		5,000: Village contribution. 1,000.	Neem and mango tree trunks.	55,000
Kudli	15,000	18,450: Sangha savings and women's personal contributions.		Lawyer's fee 15,000 raised by loan of 10,000 @ 4% interest per month.	From rich villager For inauguration; 9,000: donations from the village.	Rich villager gave his tractor for use.	53,450
Kurukunda	15,000 (not used yet). Will be used later for building a kitchen.	630: Savings, along with Rs 40 each contribution by 29 Sangha women.			KHRDB fund through the MLA: Rs 1,50,000.	Sangha women gave 1.50 kg rice and 1.50. kg. jowar (millet) for the inauguration ceremony	1,51,790
Dotihalla	15,000; MSK honorarium: 1,000.	1,000	58,004: GP contribution				75,004
Banikuppe	15,000; MSK honorarium: 4,600.	35,000				1,000 tiles: MLA's contribution.	54,600

Source: Based on primary data collected by sahyoginis.

- In Agasanahalli, the Kurubaru and Malagaru gloated over the death of the sangha leader. They felt that the sangha women were being over-ambitious. This is a multi-caste sangha. The larger community was of the view that sangha formation is relevant only for the lower castes and that women from the upper castes were demeaning themselves by getting involved in this work. The village Gowda and the GP were supportive.
- In Kudli, the villagers seem to hold the women in high regard, given the nature of financial and physical support extended during construction and the inauguration.
- In Kurukunda, the villagers were initially scornful of the women's efforts. They felt vindicated when they discovered that poor quality bricks were being used. 'What kind of a structure have these women constructed? They are like monkeys, if we hit their home it will collapse.' This spurred the women on as they were determined to do something creditable, which would gain them accolades in the future.
- In Dotihalla, a few villagers did feel that the sangha women were being over-ambitious, but there was a general atmosphere of encouragement.
- In Banikuppe (unicaste sangha), the villagers had a fairly good opinion of the women and supported them during construction.

Thus, there is a direct correlation between the opinions of the larger society, the time taken on construction and the type of structure that finally emerged.

Usage and Maintenance of the Sangha Mané

It is apparent that the sangha mané has played a critical role in amplifying the sangha activities. The women have been able to continue with the existing programmes. In nearly all the villages, they have succeeded in expanding their activities. Table 14.3 focuses on the additional programmes that the women have been able to engage in due to the existence of the physical structure. Across the villages, there is a diversity of activities in the different sangha manés, and there are some activities that are common to all the villages. In all the villages, the women claimed that violence against women has decreased because the women threaten to walk out

Table 14.3
Usage of the Sangha Mané

Village	Usage
Marakunda	Storing musical instruments, bhajan sessions. Drying the harvest. Renting out during festivals. For adult and non-formal education (NFE) classes. Keeping Dr Ambedkar's pictures.
Agasanahalli	For NFE classes, crèche. As refuge for battered women. Renting to visitors. Storing cement. Conducting meetings (by the bank manager, ANM and *anganwadi* teachers).
Kudli	For night meetings of the sangha. Legal literacy assembly. For NFE classes and awareness camps.
Kurukunda	EDP programmes. For *kishori* camps, *nari adalat*s, ghataka and federation meetings. For weddings. As a shelter for women whose houses leak. For the Public Health Forum.
Dotihalla	For the ghataka sabhe, kishori sangha meetings, bhajan sessions, personal celebrations. For conducting meetings by PHC staff, bank managers, horticulture department conduct meetings GP posts circulars. Venue for pulse polio immunisation.
Bannikuppe	As a crèche, and for kishori sangha meetings. For literacy and music classes.

Source: Based on primary data collected by sahyoginis.

and stay in the sangha mané if their husbands harass them. The mere fact of possessing a space, regardless of whether the women use it or not, has had positive consequences. This is in consonance with the MS philosophy of enabling grassroots issues to come to the fore.

With regard to the maintenance, in all the villages the women take turns to sweep the sangha mané. The sangha women whitewash the structure usually once a year. They use their savings for this. In Kurukunda, they pay property tax of Rs 300 per annum. In Dotihalla, the walls are painted with gender-sensitive slogans and the structure is maintained very well. The women spent Rs 350 on a name board.

The varied uses of the sangha mané are particularly significant in the context of resource-building and accessing local resources. In some of the villages where EDP activities are being conducted, it is a direct source of livelihood.

The Future of the Sangha Mané

In all the villages, the women seemed to have a vision for the sangha mané. They are aware of the current utility. Hence, they were in a position to articulate a future. The women see the sanghas as evolving entities, where the sangha manés will play a critical role in lending these groups a measure of dynamism.

In Marakunda, they want to use the sangha mané as a shelter for women encountering domestic violence. The Agasanahalli women visualise a garden in front of the sangha mané, where they will grow herbal plants. They want to convert it into a proper office with a phone, desks, chairs and a TV. The sangha women want to see it being used as an *okutta* office, a counselling centre, a *nari adalat* and the *santvana* project office (helpline for women in distress). They claimed that this could be regarded as an 'ideal space' within the village. They see this as a legacy for their grand-children, who will later run the sangha. The Kurukunda women want to use it for running large okutta residential programmes. The Dotihalla women displayed sentiments similar to the Agasanahalli women with regard to converting it into a formal office. They felt that this image would empower them further. They want issue-wise programmes to be conducted here, thereby furthering the federation processes. The Banikuppe women were interested in promoting the kishori programme by giving them the freedom to use the sangha mané in a way they deemed fit. They also wanted to start a library for the Continuing Education Programme. 'All 40 of us have joined hands to create this mané. It is something we leave for the future generations.'

CONCLUSION

The narratives and the information presented in this chapter appear replete with variation. Yet, there are certain core elements that we need to dwell upon. Is the sangha mané a symbol of empowerment? Has it given women a new ontological validity by enabling them to transcend the restrictive, socially prescribed gender roles? Has it engendered citizenship? It is at this juncture that we seek to understand whether synergies have emerged.

It is relevant to first examine the *time taken in the land acquisition process and construction process*. The time taken in acquisition ranged from a month to six years. Construction time ranged from four months to nine years. The time taken seems to be an indicator of the extent of the problems the women encountered. The actual time required to construct these structures is not more than two months, if the work proceeds smoothly. This varying time schedule is indicative of multiple complex processes. *This structure does not have the mandate of all segments of society as it represents a shift in the status of women and disturbs the status quo, hence all the opposition.* It is evident that despite all this opposition, women have gone ahead with 'creating a space of their own'. This in itself represents women coming into their own, which implies getting empowered. It is also an indication of the premium placed on possessing such a structure.

The women have used *a range of strategies* to acquire the land and construct the sangha mané. In only two of the villages did they contact the sahyogini for advice on the procedures to be adopted. In all the other villages, the women seemed to posses the adequate know-how to approach the right people. Again, in all the villages the women have chosen the straight and narrow path, as there are no illegal acquisitions (despite their being put upon). This speaks volumes of their good citizenship. Due to this, the women have been successful in acquiring the plots as their claims have been vindicated. They have displayed tremendous perseverance and resilience despite all the hurdles. They have used their collective strength consistently. Hence, one can see how this has empowered them and enabled them to assume functions that would otherwise have been restricted to the male domain. An absence of unpleasantness on the part of the women is a feature that characterises the land acquisition and construction processes in all the villages. Any conflicts that emerged are a result of them asserting their rights. Thus, it is apparent that this process became an opportunity for them to draw upon their inner reserves, external contacts, and the legal information acquired through training programmes.

It also helped build upon the existing knowledge base. One sees the assertion of rights accompanied by the execution of responsibilities—a critical element of citizenship.

With regard to the *nature of involvement*, in the process of acquisition and construction the women have displayed an ability to play out roles traditionally restricted to the male domain with ease. They have raised funds, handled the finances, accessed raw material, supervised the carpenters and masons, physically laboured themselves, visited the courts and contacted government officials. Yet, interestingly, they do not attribute a great deal of importance to the transgression of socially prescribed gender roles. They said: 'Sangha mané construction is our responsibility; so we have to do everything that will make it a reality. Why should the men manage our affairs?' This has helped the women develop an enhanced sense of the self, which has reference to power 'within'.

It is also evident that the physical existence of the space has *consolidated the existing activities*. It has also enabled women to *take up new programmes*, which require space. The women claimed that after the sangha mané had been constructed, the groups have become more cohesive and the membership has not dwindled. A number of women who had left earlier have rejoined the sanghas. In Agasanahalli, especially, it is seen as a concrete symbol of a group, which was on the verge of breaking up. The next generation (*kishoris*) is also using the structure, which will help in sustaining the empowering processes in the long term. Thus, it can be stated the sangha mané has helped in consolidating the MS programme.

Apart from this, the larger community is also seen as acknowledging and using the sangha mané. The range of activities described earlier is imbued with the elements of participation and voluntary work. The sangha mané has become the Samudaya Bhavan in some villages. It is the locus for collecting and disseminating information from the GP. For women hailing from this marginalised socio-economic category, this represents their mainstreaming, as they have become the bridge between the local government and the rest of the village. It is an undisputed fact that these activities have led to the betterment of the sangha women and the community. This reflects an assertion of rights, while acknowledging responsibilities. Therefore, it can be stated that the existence of the sangha mané has enabled effective citizenship. As a result of these citizenship practices, the women feel empowered.

Within the context of empowerment, the notion of power 'with' seems to emerge clearly, as sangha mané construction has entailed a group of women getting organised to achieve a collective goal. This indicates a new ontological validity, which enabled the sangha women to concretely speak of change (or a new way of being) in three domains: acquisition and application of skills associated with construction; enhanced decision-making at the household level; and a changed interaction with the larger community. With regard to the latter two, there are a series of other processes that are underway simultaneously. These may also have contributed to a change in these domains. Yet the women believe that the sangha mané is one of the critical factors for bringing about change.

This 'new way of being' is reflected in the women's voices. With regard to the first domain, they say:

> We have learnt how to manage construction work. We contribute to the building plans in Ashraya Yojana houses. We have learnt how to purchase building material, maintain accounts, documents and even hire vehicles. We know where to place doors and windows in a house. We can follow building plans. We have used this experience while constructing our own homes. We can supervise construction efficiently. We are capable of mobilising funds. We are able to get our work done without paying bribes because we are aware of procedures. We know whom to approach. We do not get cheated any more because we ask for a bill for everything we purchase.

At the household level:

> We participate in all discussions. During rituals and weddings, we decide what should be purchased from where. We choose spouses for our children. If our husbands harass us, we do not get intimidated as we now have a refuge to which we can take recourse. We have begun enrolling our daughters in school. Our families listen to us.

And in the larger community:

> We walk around confidently. We have removed the *pallu* from our heads even when we talk to the Gowda. The Gowdas address us in the plural (that is, using the respectful register in the language). When we visit the GP, the members offer us chairs. We are aware of what language and behaviour are appropriate in different contexts. If we disapprove of something, we are able to express our opinions in the larger community as we have a collective voice. There is no space we cannot access.

The women's influence has even spread beyond the village boundaries, as in some cases they have become a source of inspiration for other sanghas to embark on similar paths. Their own analysis indicates that their 'new way of being' has made the women contributing citizens. It also reflects local notions of empowerment. The women have been able to change the trajectories of their own lives and the lives of people around them through this process. The sangha mané can be concretely seen as a 'stepping stone' leading on to 'potential' citizenship. The 'emancipatory' effect of this structure can be attributed to the fact that the women feel that the sangha mané is a landmark, representing a space in which they are able to play out multiple roles, externalise internal needs and become effective citizens.

ACKNOWLEDGEMENTS

This chapter represents more than a research study. It is the result of the collaboration of many sources. We are grateful to all those who have partaken in this process. We would first like to thank all the sangha women who delved into the recesses of their minds to recreate events that occurred a long time ago. Their narrative has animated the document. We would like to acknowledge all the sahyoginis who requested MSK for training in research and documentation: Renuka (Bijapur), Ratna (Raichur), Zairunbi (Bellary), Shanta (Koppal), Parvati (Bidar), Deviramma (Mysore), Jyothi (Gulbarga) and Sidamma (Raichur). All of them have enriched this study with their ability to internalise research concepts and analyse the data collected in the light of these inputs. Special thanks are due to the District Programme Coordinators of the seven districts for encouraging the sahyoginis to attend the workshops and engage in data collection. We are also grateful to the State Office team, Nagina, Kavita and Nagaratna, for their able translation work. We would like to thank Dr Revathi Narayanan (erstwhile State Programme Director, MSK) for commissioning this study. We are deeply grateful to Dr Suchitra Vedanth (present SPD) for valuable inputs on the report.

REFERENCES

Glover, D. and C. Kaplan. 2000. *Genders*. London and New York: Routledge.
Oxal, Z and S. Baden. 1997. 'Gender and Empowerment: Definitions, Approaches and Implications for Policy', BRIDGE Report No. 40, October.

15

SHGs as Change Agents in Enhancing the Political Participation of Women in Local Self-Governance

Mandakini Pant

INTRODUCTION

Agency is the ability to define needs and priorities and to act upon them. In this chapter, agency refers specifically to women's political participation in decision-making to articulate their rights, entitlements and provision to basic services. Political restructuring and affirmative action have given rural women an opportunity to participate in political decision-making. Not only do they have one-third membership, they are also chairpersons in one-third of panchayats. As gram sabha members, they can actively put forward their concerns in the gram sabha meetings and influence policies in their favour. However, despite the statutory provision for the mandatory participation of women in Panchayati Raj Institutions (PRIs) as elected representatives and as gram sabha members, they are unable to participate effectively in the public decision-making process.

Enhancing the participation of women in PRIs, therefore, calls for alternative organisational forms, such as the grassroots women's collectives. The Self-Help Groups (SHGs), as the grassroots collectives of poor marginalised women organised to act for their own development, assume importance in this context. There are a few cases where women's SHGs have been successfully mobilised to participate in the local governance processes and institutions. The results clearly indicate that these groups have the potential to work cohesively over issues concerning women, as well as go beyond their mandate of promoting savings and micro-finance to local self-governance.

This chapter explores the participation of SHGs in village panchayats and the outcome of this participation to see whether the process contributes to greater agency of women. The chapter also highlights the strategies used by facilitating organisations to organise women purposively around a shared concern, enhancing their participation in PRIs. Such a discussion will facilitate an understanding of the ways in which educational inputs have enabled the SHGs as women's collectives to exercise their agency.

The chapter draws on the findings of a synthesis study undertaken in 2004 by the Society for Participatory Research in Asia (PRIA). The study, 'The Potential of Self-Help Groups in Enhancing Women's Participation in Local Self-Governance', broadly aimed to understand the acts of political participation of SHGs in the process of governance, and analyse the outcomes of their participation. The study specifically analysed the process of external facilitation by the Voluntary Development Organisations (VDOs) to strengthen their collective voice.

The study was conducted in three states, namely, Madhya Pradesh, Uttar Pradesh and Uttarakhand. PRIA purposively selected Samarthan in Madhya Pradesh, Sahbhagi Shikshan Kendra (SSK) in Uttar Pradesh and Himalayan Action Research Centre (HARC) in Uttarakhand to study the SHGs in their respective areas. Each of these VDOs promoted and mobilised the SHGs for political participation. Indeed, promoting SHGs is part of their larger programmatic goal of reforming local-level governance.

HARC in Uttarakhand and Samarthan in Madhya Pradesh chose SHGs purposively from amongst the groups nurtured by them. HARC works with women SHGs of Rawain, a very underdeveloped area in Naugaon Block of Uttarkashi district. It selected five gram panchayats from this region and seven SHGs from these gram panchayats: the Draupadi in Kimi, Yamuna in Upradi, Raj Rajeshwari in Kotyal, Narsingh in Naugaon and Renuka in Naitri. Samarthan purposively selected 10 groups from four villages from amongst the 52 groups it nurtured in Sehore Block. The groups selected for the study were: Nai Roshni and Naya Prakash from Bijora, Lakshmi and Gyan Ganga from Bijori, Chetna and Asha from Heerapur, and Krishna, Durga, Babita and Asha from Khamliya. Sahbhagi Shikshan Sansthan (SSK) randomly selected gram panchayats and SHGs from two sample blocks from the districts of Faizabad and Ghazipur in Uttar Pradesh. PANI in Faizabad district and Purti Sansthan in Ghazipur district of Uttar Pradesh facilitated the formation of SHGs. The groups for the study were randomly selected from eight gram panchayats in Sohawal Block, Faizabad district, and Sadat Block, Ghazipur district, Uttar Pradesh. A total of 67 women's SHGs were studied.

The SHGs were selected on the basis of the following criteria: (*i*) the groups were at least two to four years old; (*ii*) savings were continuous for the last two years; (*iii*) there were no drop-outs for the past two years; (*iv*) the groups received capacity building inputs; and (*v*) they demonstratively undertook some collective action. A combination of data collection methods were used such as purposive sampling, random sampling and focus group discussions with SHGs, interviews with the VDO staff responsible for facilitation, select panchayat members and government officials, and review of secondary sources of information.

The study has also analysed the capacity-building initiatives of facilitating VDOs. These organisations strengthened the collective voice of SHGs. Capacity-building and skills translated into practice increased the economic options of the women's collectives and promoted their sense of worth. It also enabled the women's collectives to participate in the overall affairs of society. Their participation took various forms: (*i*) providing information to the community to raise awareness; (*ii*) discussions in public fora such as gram sabhas; (*iii*) developing as pressure groups to lobby for their interests; (*iv*) leveraging access to resources, setting agendas, rules and norms through active interfacing in discussions.

The case studies, located in three different parts of the country, do not claim to be comprehensive or representative of the participation of SHGs in political processes throughout the country. It is not our intention to make statistically valid generalisations on the basis of these findings, but to provide qualitative insights into women's experiences in particular contexts. Table 15.1 briefly indicates the study areas, key units of study, and methods of data collection and data analysis.

The chapter is organised in six sections. Section one explains the context and conceptual framework. Section two briefly describes the institutions promoting the SHGs, and also gives the profile of the SHGs. Section three describes the nature of participation of SHGs in the processes of governance. Section four focuses on the outcomes in terms of

Table 15.1

The Study Areas, Key Units of Study, Methods of Data Collection and Data Analysis

No. of SHGs Studied	Name of SHG	Name of Gram Panchayat	Facilitating Organisations	Methods of Data Collection and Analysis
State: Madhya Pradesh; District: Sehore; Block: Sehore				
10	Nai Roshni, Naya Prakash, Lakshmi, Gyan Ganga, Chetna, Asha, Krishna, Durga, Babita and Asha	Bijora, Bijori, Heerapur and Khamliya	Samarthan	• Purposive selection of case studies • Interviews and discussion • Qualitative analysis
State: Uttarakhand; District: Uttarkashi; Block: Naugaon				
7	Draupadi, Yamuna, Raj Rajeshwari, Bhagirathi, Surkanda, Narsingh and Renuka	Kimi, Upradi, Kotyal, Naugaon and Naitri	HARC	• Purposive selection of case studies • Interviews and discussions • Qualitative analysis
State: Uttar Pradesh; District: Faizabad; Block: Sohawal				
22	Shiva Dulari, Lakshmi Bai, Jai Kashi, Jai Durga, Mumtaj, Indira Gandhi, Khuba, Meerabai, Ramdulari, Baila, Moona, Kalpa, Lakha Didi, Lakhraji, Lakshmi Bai, Tulsi, Rukmani, Harbansa, Soorsati, Jagrani, Rookmani, Suman	Sarangapur, Deramusi, Rahim Pur Badauli, Deorhi, Mirpurkanta, Pirkhauli, Kareru, Dakshinpara	PANI	• Study by SSK • Purposive selection of case studies • Interviews and discussions • Qualitative and quantitative analysis
State: Uttar Pradesh; District: Ghazipur; Block: Sadat				
22	Ekta, Sakti, Lakshmi, Prayas, Saraswati, Gram Vikas Samiti, Mahila Samaj, Ramabai, Budh, Vaisno, Surya, Lakshmi, Jhakkari, Kishori Panchayat, Prithviraj Chauhan Memorial, Pragatisheel, Sangharshsheel, Dhan Lakshmi, Gram Unnati Samiti, Sadhna, Mahatma Gautam Budh, Chanda	Bahariabad, Akbarpur, Darhwal, Mirzapur, Babura, Gahani, Khazepur, Birbhanpur	Purti Sansthan	• Study by SSK • Purposive selection of case studies • Interviews and discussions • Qualitative and quantitative analysis

the ability of SHGs to exercise their agency. Section five describes the external facilitation processes that enabled SHGs to participate in the affairs of society through the working of the PRIs. Section six highlights presumptions about the SHGs' potential in mobilising women as political participants.

CONTEXT

Decentralisation and micro-finance, the two key interventions that took place in India during the 1990s, have particularly sought to correct the prolonged marginalisation of rural women. The impetus for empowerment came from the state to 'enable women to make strategic life choices, organise and participate in and influence the process of decision-making as per their needs and priorities' (Deshmukh-Ranadive 2005).

Decentralisation means enlarging the space for people's representation in matters of governance and moving decisions closer to people. The 73rd Constitutional Amendment Act (CAA), 1993, and the ensuing state Acts on Panchayat Raj Institutions (PRIs) with their mandatory provisions for one-third reservation of seats for women in local self-governing bodies and the obligatory gram sabha meetings, have provided rural women with the opportunity and space for direct participation in local-level political processes to influence and shape policies as per their needs and aspirations.

Micro-finance seeks to widen the range of options for marginalised people through self-employment and enterprise. Here, it is assumed that power comes inevitably through economic strength. However, bringing the marginalised to a point where they are able to take charge of creating options for themselves requires a combination of confidence, information, analytical skills, ability to tap and identify resources, and an organisation (a collective).

The approaches of both micro-finance and decentralisation strive to build a critical mass that can pull households out of poverty traps and minimise the effects of inequalities. It is assumed that these processes can help less powerful women voice their concerns collectively, or take some sort of collective public action. Such action may eventually challenge the existing power structures.

EVIDENCE OF IMPACT

Women in Panchayati Raj Institutions

A close look at the post-73rd Amendment phase of PRIs vis-à-vis women's participation shows mixed results. On the positive side, we find that women have become more articulate, despite their low levels of literacy. They have begun asserting control over resources. They regularly attended panchayat meetings. In many instances, they have used their elected authority to address issues such as children's education, drinking water facilities, family planning facilities, hygiene and health, quality of health care, and village development such as *pucca* roads and electricity in their panchayat areas. They have also brought alcohol abuse and domestic violence onto the agenda of political campaigns (Nambiar and Bandyopadhyay 2004).

But we also have instances of their passive participation. According to a PRIA study of PRIs in six states, male family members who were previously elected representatives of the panchayats often pushed women to contest elections so that the seat of power could be retained within the family. As a result, women behaved as mere token representatives, that is, dummy candidates (PRIA 1999). When this does not happen, the elected representatives become targets of character assassination. Their male colleagues still treat them indifferently in the meetings. The bureaucracy, too, is less responsive to them. Despite reservations, women from low-caste groups seldom wield any real political power, given the strongly entrenched notions of caste and gender hierarchy (Anandhi 2002; Niranjana 2002).

As gram sabha constituents, the participation of women has been almost invisible. Appeals for an increased political participation of women in gram sabhas generally overlook some ground realities, for instance, the timings of gram sabha meetings, the settlement pattern of the village and the long distances to be trekked, problems of quorum and procedures adopted, the manipulation of discussions by dominant groups, patriarchal snorms restricting the mobility of women outside the home, the crucial loss of daily wages, illiteracy, and lack of awareness about the new system of governance. These severely limiting factors often fuel cynicism amongst women (Sharma 2004).

Despite an enabling environment, created by the legislations, women have, by and large, been unable to be effective participants in local decision-making. Their access to essential services, entitlements and rights has been difficult.

Women in Self-Help Groups

Poor women are mobilised to form SHGs for savings and credit activities. The members take on economic activities in a systematic manner, participate directly in decision-making, and share the risks, costs and benefits on an equitable basis. Enhanced organisational leadership skills increase women's economic options, promote their sense of worth and empower them politically. Studies on SHGs have reported a number of changes in their lives, which could be deemed as empowering. Women have gained control over produce and income. Self-earned income has instilled in them a sense of pride and confidence in their ability to manage on their own. Membership in SHGs, easy accessibility to loans and engagement in micro-enterprise facilitated the women's inclusion in household decision-making. They are now able to negotiate with their husbands on crucial matters. The training programmes have reinforced a collective identity among the members. The learning and exchange between women's groups have enhanced their confidence. Meetings and sharing of experiences have made them sensitive to each other, as well as to the community's needs. They are emerging as strong power groups. They negotiate confidently with government officials, moneylenders and outsiders (Pant 2004). The results clearly indicate that these groups have the potential to work cohesively on issues concerning women, as well as go beyond their mandate of savings and credit activities to local self-governance.

CONCEPTUAL FRAMEWORK

This chapter seeks to document the potential that some SHGs displayed to make PRIs responsive to the concerns of women. The following are its key premises:

- SHGs are an effective interface for poor women to deal constructively with PRIs. They have the potential to: (i) provide a basis for collective action around wider community and gender needs in panchayats and (ii) lobby for the inclusion of women's interests in panchayats.

- For poor women, PRIs as governance institutions are central to the fulfilment of their basic needs as they provide essential services, ensure livelihood and promote sustainable development based on equity and social justice.
- Lack of capability in women is largely due to a lack of resources, agency and organisation. SHGs empower women economically by expanding their individual choice and by fostering self-reliance. Economic empowerment, both depends on, and contributes to social and political empowerment. The formation of groups, and active participation in them, has contributed to women's involvement in political processes. In fact, SHG membership can be seen as a training ground for PRI participation. (Deshmukh-Ranadive 2005).
- Being community-based organisations, SHGs contribute to building social capital by providing the marginalised women in the villages with information, social networks and associations. This in turn helps build their self-confidence and strengthens their ability to exercise agency.
- The participation of SHGs in the planning process and their clear articulation of poor women's concerns can make the governance mechanisms accountable to them. It can enhance the efficacy of PRIs by acting as a pressure lobby to advance the interests of women and their communities.
- The efficacy of SHGs will depend on a number of conditions. These include a strong organisation, access to resources and opportunities, and strong capabilities built through education, information, skills and confidence. External facilitators such as VDOs play a crucial role by educating, organising and mobilising women purposively around a common concern. This can be an effective catalyst in the process of social change, as it strives to bring to the fore women's concerns in local self-governance.

PROFILES OF SHG-PROMOTING ORGANISATIONS AND OF SHGS

In Uttarakhand, HARC promoted the capacity of women's SHGs for collective entrepreneurship. In Madhya Pradesh, Samarthan formed SHGs under the Swa-Shakti project of the Mahila Arthik Vikas Nigam (MAVN).

Swa-Shakti is the project for Rural Women's Development and Empowerment (RWDEP), evolved by the Government of India's Department of Women and Child Development and the Women's Development Corporations of six states: Bihar, Gujarat, Haryana, Karnataka, Madhya Pradesh and Uttar Pradesh. The SHGs under the Swa-Shakti project are linked to banks. Rather than being mere savings and credit collectives, these are intended to play a critical catalytic role for the improvement of women's position in the family and society. PANI in Faizabad district and Purti Sansthan in Ghazipur district of Uttar Pradesh facilitated the formation of SHGs under the Swarna Jayanti Gram Swarozgar Yojana (SGSY). This scheme aims to establish a large number of micro-enterprises in the rural areas, building upon the potential of the rural poor. It covers all aspects of self-employment: organisation of the rural poor into SHGs (with at least half of the groups being exclusively for women), their capacity-building, planning of activity clusters, infrastructure build-up, technology, credit and marketing. District Rural Development Agencies (DRDAs) implement the scheme with the active involvement of PRIs, banks, the line departments and the VDOs.

SHG formation evolves through various phases. What follows is an attempt to define the processes in each phase, based on the study findings.

Group Formation

Members are linked together by various common bonds of age, caste, community, landownership and activity. These 'affinity groups' are critical to the success of SHGs. Members of the SHGs in the study belonged mostly to the Scheduled Castes (SCs) and Other Backward Castes (OBCs). The majority were small landowners with landholdings ranging between one and five acres (0.4–2 ha.). A substantial section of the members were landless agricultural labourers. The average age of SHG members was from 20 to 50 years. The majority of the members were illiterate, followed by a substantial section of those who could only sign their names. Very few of them had studied up to Class VIII.

Group Savings

The groups begin with savings. The group holds regular meetings of members, where they contribute an amount decided as a saving deposit. After about a year, when these savings build up, members are able to access credit through their pooled resources. Members are allocated loans based on group solidarity, instead of formal collateral. By default, the group assumes a political role when it influences decisions relating to the allocation of resources and benefits to its members. Members assess one another's strengths, time the loans, schedule repayments and fix interests rates. The profits, howsoever small, are distributed either among the members or jointly used as per the group's wishes. This strategy promotes self-sufficiency and independence among the poor women. The minimum savings per member in the SHGs under study was Rs 10 per month. The maximum savings were up to Rs 50 per month. The average monthly saving was Rs 20–25 per month.

Micro-credit

The group corpus is supplemented with revolving funds sanctioned as cash credit limit by the banks. The SHGs in the study have received cash credit limit from banks ranging from Rs 15,000 to Rs 25,000.

Micro-Enterprise Development

The SHGs also take up income-generating activities for their members. Samarthan, PANI and Purti Sansthan have facilitated many enterprise activities such as the making of files and folders, durries and soft toys; sewing and embroidery; processed foods such as *badi* and *papad* and pickles; producing incense sticks; animal husbandry; fishery; horticulture; cooperative farming; and setting up general stores, vegetable and furniture shops. HARC has motivated the groups to start collective enterprises based on locally available resources.

Participation in the Public Sphere

The SHGs in this study acted as interest groups to take up their cause either as elected representatives or as active members of gram sabhas. They took part in decision-making processes, raised issues in gram sabha meetings and facilitated the participation of women other than their own group members. Some SHG members in the study are members, sarpanches, or up-sarpanches (vice-heads) of the panchayats. In Sehore

Block, Madhya Pradesh, the women are members of various *samitis* (panchayat committees) such as the *swasthya* (health), *shiksha* (education), *suraksha* (security) and *samajik nyaya* (social justice) samitis.

PARTICIPATION IN POLITICAL SPACES

The SHGs in the study have moved beyond their mandate of economic self-reliance to participate in the overall affairs of society through PRIs. Their participation has taken various forms, such as (*i*) disseminating information in the community to raise their awareness about the issues; (*ii*) deliberation or dialogue in public fora such as the gram sabha where issues for discussion are put forward; (*iii*) activism as pressure groups; (*iv*) leveraging access to resources; (*v*) agenda setting; and (*vi*) altering rules and norms in deliberations through active interfacing.

Attending the Gram Sabha

Prior to the participation of SHGs in the study areas, none of the women had attended gram sabha meetings. Women participated in meetings only to seek approval for their application for social security pensions, or to seek solutions to employment or land-related problems. The gram sabha was seen primarily as a male domain by them.

The SHGs have worked towards making the women realise the importance of the gram sabha. Though many more women are now regular participants in gram sabha meetings, they still remember their first attendance: 'In the first two-three gram sabhas we just sat and came back'. They sat with a *ghoonghat* (long veil) over their faces. Male villagers in particular reacted derisively, remarking, '*Yahan kahan aa gayee ho!*' (How is it that you have come here!') Women members belonging to the Scheduled Castes were subjected to particularly embarrassing remarks.

The sheer persistence of the women members led to a situation where the number of women in a gram sabha was more than the number required for the quorum. Women who were not SHG members also attended the meetings. Sarju Bai, the woman sarpanch of Bijora, Sehore Block, Madhya Pradesh, corroborated the regular attendance of SHG members in the gram sabha: 'The women from the SHGs come regularly to the gram sabha. They have also motivated other women in the village (who are not members of any SHGs) to come and attend the gram sabhas' (Samarthan, interviews, 2004).

The women took conscious steps to ensure that they regularly get information about gram sabha meetings. The members of Gyan Ganga SHG in Sehore Block, Madhya Pradesh, reported that earlier the village chowkidar (security guard) would not come to their locality to announce the gram sabha meetings. They confronted him and made him promise that he would inform them in advance of these meetings. Since then the chowkidar has been coming regularly to inform them personally about the meetings. SHGs in Uttarakhand hired a *paswan* (drummer) to inform all villagers about the agenda of the panchayat meetings.

Speaking out in the Gram Sabha

Initially, women members spoke on SHG proposals, seeking the approval of the gram sabha. The issues were discussed in detail in SHG meetings prior to the gram sabha meeting. The internal meetings helped the women overcome their 'stage fright'. They were prepared with the agenda and the facts. Prem Narayan, up-sarpanch of Bijora, validates this:

> There was apprehension that the sarpanch would siphon off the money received for the construction of the boundary wall of the school building. Since the women from the group (Naya Prakash Group) were regularly attending the gram sabha meetings, they knew the budget and were monitoring the implementation of the scheme, the sarpanch could not do anything. (Samarthan, interviews, 2004)

The construction of the community building and a cement road, approval of the list of Below Poverty Line (BPL) families in the gram sabha, starting the mid-day meal in the school, repair of the hand pump, and disapproval of the quality of toilets constructed in the school are some of the issues the members have addressed in the meetings. For instance, the Gyan Ganga group (Bijori, Sehore Block, Madhya Pradesh) participated in the meeting to consider the construction of a platform within the village where they could hold their group meetings. The gram sabha passed a resolution approving the place for the construction of the platform. While many sabha members dissented when they realised that they would have to contribute monetarily, women members stood strong in their resolve. They contributed money, mobilised additional funds and got the platform constructed.

The SHG in Naugaon Block, Uttarkashi district, Uttarakhand, volunteered to clear paths, lay water pipes for the regular supply of water and collect fodder. They also undertook an anti-liquor drive. They have helped the panchayat to implement a number of government schemes for employment, development, girl children, roads, housing and toilets (Gram Swarozgar Yojana, Gram Samridhi Yojana, Balika Samridhi Yojana, Pradhan Mantri Sadak Yojana, Indira Awas Yojana and Sulabh Sauchalaya), besides the mid-day meal scheme in primary schools.

Claiming Rights and Entitlements

SHGs have articulated demands for services, complained against poor services and claimed entitlements.

Placing Demands for Service: Heerapur village, Sehore Block, Madhya Pradesh, and Kimi, Naugaon Block, Uttarakhand, did not have an *anganwadi* (crèche and infant-care) centre. The women members brought up this issue in the gram sabha and demanded an anganwadi centre in their own village. The SHGs in Kimi, Naugaon Block, Uttarakhand, have also placed demands like the setting up of a dispensary and the laying out of more water pipes.

Making Complaints about Poor Service: The Naya Prakash group, Bijora, Sehore Block in Madhya Pradesh, found that the school was not providing a mid-day-meal to the children. As the mid-day meal was a panchayat programme, they made a complaint to the Jan Shikshak Prabhari (education officer) at the block headquarters. The sarpanch and the panchayat secretary were compelled to start the mid-day meal programme in the school. Members of the Lakshmi group, another SHG in the same block, complained about the defunct hand pump in their village. This complaint was recorded in the gram sabha and a resolution was passed to get the pump repaired. The hand pump was subsequently repaired within three days of the complaint being made.

Demanding Quality Service: The SHGs in Madhya Pradesh found that parents were withdrawing their children from the government school because of a teacher's poor performance, and enrolling them in a newly opened private school. They raised this issue in the gram sabha and demanded that the current teacher be replaced with a better one, and called for an overall improvement in the school's functioning.

Claiming Entitlements: SHGs in Sehore Block have also raised issues related to widows' pensions and employment under government schemes. In one of the meetings of the gram sabha, women SHG members raised the issue of getting employment under the Pradhan Mantri Gramin Sadak Yojana. The sarpanch took this up at the district level. The women from the groups were then employed in road construction.

Raising Issues for Development: The SHGs in Naugaon have helped to get a school sanctioned for the village. They have taken up issues of land and forest rights with the panchayat. Nearly half the SHGs in Ghazipur and Faizabad districts in Uttar Pradesh have raised issues in the panchayats regarding old-age pension, the drainage system, problems of water, health, income-generation, and the villagers' right to information. SHGs in Ghazipur and Faizabad districts have also discussed with government representatives the possibility of arriving at local solutions for local problems. Various health, employment and other socio-economic issues have been discussed (for example, the Pulse Polio programme, the SGSY scheme, and problems related to marriages, housing and development programmes for women and children). They also called for stepping up initiatives for road construction, helping to select the right beneficiaries, monetary help to poor families to marry off their daughters, and public monitoring of the social development projects at the village level.

Interfacing with Representatives of Political Institutions

Putting Pressure on the Sarpanch: In Sehore, Madhya Pradesh, the panchayat was laying a pipeline under a particular scheme. One colony had been completely overlooked, even though the pipeline was passing through this area. The women of the Gyan Ganga group raised the concerns before the sarpanch, who eventually had to succumb to their demands. The women of Nai Roshni group raised their voices against the absence of the sarpanch from gram sabha meetings. Their group facilitator informed them of the particular Act that has provisions related to the recall of the sarpanch. When the women threatened to use the recall provision against the sarpanch, he bowed to this pressure, and now attends the gram sabha meetings regularly.

In many villages, the gram sabha meetings often took place without a quorum. The women members from the groups would return from meetings that were deemed cancelled, after which the sarpanch would conduct the proceedings. He would then send the women the register to record their presence in the meeting. The members refused to sign the register as holding a meeting without the required quorum was illegal. Yielding to their resolve, the sarpanch mobilised the required number of villagers needed to ensure and maintain the quorum.

Developing Linkages with the Sarpanch: Over a period of time, a healthy relationship has developed between the sarpanch and the group members. Three factors seem to have contributed towards the development of this relationship: the role of the intervening agency, the aspiration level of the sarpanch and the motivational level of the women members. The Pradhan of Kotyal panchayat, Naugaon block, Uttarakhand, collaborated with the SHGs and approached the Block Development Council to demand a full-fledged dispensary with a woman doctor for general and reproductive health care, an immunisation drive for women and children, and an adequately staffed anganwadi. The panchayats in Naugaon Block entrusted the SHG with *rakeet bandhaan* through which a person would be hired to guard the crops, and the decision on the terms of payment for the construction of a kitchen for the school.

The sarpanch of Khamliya, Sehore Block, Madhya Pradesh, regularly supported the SHGs in all their endeavours. The SHGs in the village were an important vote bank, representing 40 families. The meeting of the gram sabha was scheduled at about 11 a.m. to suit the women, and would not begin until all women members were present.

Interviews with Pradhans in Uttar Pradesh have revealed that the participation of SHG members in gram panchayats has ushered in some positive changes. Employment opportunities have increased. Migration has been reduced. The village Pradhans wanted the SHGs to raise the issue of allotment of *patta*s (title deeds), ration cards and hand pumps in open meetings of the gram sabha. They looked forward to the cooperation of the SHGs in local resource development and the other developmental works of the gram panchayat. They said that SHGs were important for panchayat development as both charted similar developmental roles.

Developing Linkages with Other Government Officials: SHGs from Naugaon Block, Uttarakhand, interact directly with the block officials at the Nyaya panchayat. The SHG members from Ghazipur and Faizabad districts, Uttar Pradesh, periodically discuss various issues of their village with government officials.

Inter-institutional Membership: Some members of the SHGs in Sehore block, Madhya Pradesh, were also members of the standing committees of the gram sabha such as the *shiksha samiti* for education and *swasthya samiti* for health. According to the panchayat secretary, the women members from the group insisted on knowing why the meetings of the standing committees were not taking place. Parvati Bai of the Lakshmi group is the president of the gram sabha standing committee on education. In one of the meetings of the committee, she complained that the school did not have a proper roof. Other members in the committee did not pay heed to her complaint. She reported this to the group in its routine meeting. The members took up the matter in one of the gram sabha meetings. Gita Bai, a member of the Asha group, Sehore Block, Madhya Pradesh, is also a member of the gram panchayat. She attends the meetings regularly. She signs the documents or the register only after she is apprised of what is written in the document.

OUTCOMES OF POLITICAL PARTICIPATION

The outcomes of SHGs' political participation are visible on two planes: within the group and within the larger community.

Outcomes Within the Group

Increased Self-confidence: Successful implementation of programmes following the gram sabha meetings has increased the self-confidence of the group. Their confidence is apparent in their plans for the future, where they want to undertake a number of community-based activities.

Group Solidarity: All the SHGs in the intervention area of the organisations under study are members of federations who meet regularly. The learning and exchange between women's groups have enhanced the women's sense of solidarity.

Securing Economic Benefits: SHGs have made a significant impact on the wider financial and labour market. The experience of managing collective economic enterprises, such as the weekly market and the trading federation, has brought the groups closer, infusing in them a tremendous sense of confidence to take up future challenges collectively.

A Mutual Support Group: All SHGs in the study are essentially women's collectives whose members are poor. They hold the least political power. As they are, by and large, drawn from marginalised communities such as Scheduled Castes, Scheduled Tribes and Other Backward Castes, they do not have any social standing. The poor and lower-caste women not only interact and organise themselves to manage their own money, but as collectives, they also address social issues, highlight the concerns of the poor women in local planning and development processes, negotiate rights, claim entitlements and interface with authorities concerned to influence governance.

Pressure Groups: The groups in the study have aptly demonstrated their ability to work as a pressure group in the village. They have picked up not only those issues that would have only benefited the group (for example, construction of the platform), but have also taken up issues that benefited the community as a whole (for example, the repair of hand pumps, construction of a cement concrete road). These groups have been able to generate these successes through sheer perseverance and regular follow-up meetings with panchayat representatives.

The SHGs do not rule out the possibility of contesting elections to participate directly in local self-governance as members of gram panchayats. In addition, they are building a consensus among themselves to become members in as many standing committees of gram panchayats as possible, so as to give leverage to development plans in different aspects of village life.

Outcomes within the Larger Community

De Facto Leadership Roles: Many village women share their concerns with SHG members in the hope that group members would speak on their behalf in the sabha meetings. SHGs have also successfully demanded social and political action on issues relating to the rights of women. Thus, they have carved a *de facto* leadership role for the women in the village.

Awareness Generation: SHGs helped to disseminate information on a variety of topics like the gram sabha, health, nutrition, sanitation, education, and various schemes of government departments such as the installation of hand pumps and the mid-day meal programme.

Proactive Citizenship: SHGs took proactive roles in decisions related to the welfare of the village. Their regular and strong presence at the panchayat and gram sabha meetings ensured that village issues were resolved. They voluntarily participated in many community activities such as the plantation of trees, the Pulse Polio campaign, cleaning the panchayat house, repairing damaged and broken roads, and implementation of a number of government schemes.

Building Social Capital: There is a distinct change in the attitudes of villagers towards the activities and meetings of SHGs. The active participation of women's groups and the work undertaken by them has helped in leveraging funds for village development.

Social Inclusion: Past developmental experience has shown that communities are unable to break the cycle of poverty as long as they remain socially excluded from the decision-making processes. Women in rural areas had always formed a large part of this socially excluded group. The SHG has enabled women to bridge this gap and come in contact with institutions of governance, namely, the gram sabha and the gram panchayat. In some cases, they have also been nominated to these institutions. As women make a space for themselves in the institutions where decisions are taken, they have also become recipients of information (for example, process of BPL survey) and have increased access to resources (for example, leveraging panchayat funds for the construction of a road and a boundary wall for the school building).

EXTERNAL FACILITATION PROCESS

The VDOs have played a crucial role by educating, organising and mobilising women purposively and consciously around a common or shared concern for reducing poverty. A strong organisation of their own, access to resources and opportunities, strong capabilities built through education, information, skills and confidence have empowered women with freedom of choice and action.

The VDOs in this study are not micro-finance organisations. They are promoting and supporting the SHG model of micro-finance for the organisation, mobilisation and self-development of marginalised poor women. The organisations started by organising them into small collectives at the grassroots level. The collectives were later formed into federations. The formation of federations has scaled up the 'empowerment process through self-help' from village-level groups to independent community-owned institutions.

Capacity Building Support for SHGs

The VDOs have strengthened the organisational capabilities of women members through education and training; women have gained knowledge and skills related to savings and inter-loaning processes managing records and finances for the group, livelihood enhancement, income-generating activities and entrepreneurship development. They have also built the capacities of field-level workers for effective strengthening of SHGs. The key capacity building areas are summarised in Table 15.2.

Group Formation: HARC, Samarthan and SSK focus on various areas of capacity building by facilitating perspectives on collectivisation, group management including decision-making, problem solving and conflict

Table 15.2
Key Capacity Building Areas for SHGs

Group formation	Formation, management, leadership development, problem solving, conflict resolution, maintenance of records, annual plans, budgets, documenting the minutes of meetings
Federation	Financial management, resource mobilisation, decision-making
Enterprise development	Enterprise promotion, feasibility, other technical and managerial aspects, information and training on techniques to enhance the existing livelihood
Empowerment	Awareness raising on women's issues
Linkages	Linkage building with financial institutions, government schemes
Gram Sabha and Panchayati Raj	Role and function of gram sabha, rights of person attending gram sabha, the proper way of conducting a gram sabha, provisions of gram swaraj under the Panchayat Act, process of removal of sarpanch by a gram sabha, responsibilities of Standing Committees of gram sabha, and micro-planning

resolution, leadership development, self-development, project planning, budgeting and monitoring, report writing and maintaining records, accountancy and bookkeeping, resource mobilisation, legal aspects, project proposal writing and writing minutes of meetings.

Enterprise Development: Enterprise development involves training in enterprise promotion, feasibility and other technical-managerial aspects. VDOs have adopted a livelihood enhancement approach, which involves the upgrading of livelihoods through environmentally sustainable agricultural methods. Training on wastewater structures, vermin composting, bio-fertilisers and non-pesticide management are among the key methods. They have also focused on promoting micro-enterprise development. The Rural Business Development Centre (RBDC) of HARC, for instance, has motivated the groups to start collective enterprises using local resources. It has organised a number of training and orientation programmes, and interfaces with experts on technical skill-building such as grading and packaging; quality control and marketing; government regulatory framework such as registration and preparation of by-laws, sales tax and income tax; strengthening internal processes such as accounts management, maintenance of records and stock registers, inter-loaning system; roles and responsibilities of a cooperative society; and communication and documentation. Samarthan, PANI and Purti Sansthan have facilitated numerous enterprise activities, as mentioned earlier.

Awareness Building: Samarthan provided information to SHGs on personal hygiene, sanitation, nutrition, health, immunisation of women and children, the importance of girls' education, sexual abuse at the workplace, property rights of women, rights of Scheduled Caste communities and dowry. Purti Sansthan and PANI organised training on issues like land rights, Dalit rights, women's rights and gender equity.

Gram Sabha and Panchayati Raj: The organisations also trained SHGs on issues related to the gram sabha and the Panchayati Raj. Samarthan organised trainings on the various facets of local self-governance including the role and function of the gram sabha; rights of persons attending the gram sabha; the proper way of conducting the gram sabha; provisions of *gram swaraj* (self-rule) under the Panchayat Act; the process of removal of a sarpanch by the gram sabha; and the responsibilities of standing committees of the gram sabha. The SHGs, facilitated under the Swa-Shakti project, participated in the preparation of the micro-plan for activities that were part of the other projects of Samarthan in the village. For instance, at Bijora, micro-planning for the construction of the school boundary wall involved the community and the members of the Naya Prakash group. The prepared plan was discussed and presented to the gram sabha for approval. The Samarthan-PACS[1] project provided money for constructing the school boundary wall. HARC has oriented the SHGs on the roles and responsibilities of panchayat representatives and gram sabha members. It mobilised the SHG members through ward-level meetings. Women's groups actively participated in the gram sabha during the Pre-Election Voter Awareness Campaign (PEVAC). HARC also motivated the women's collective in Upradi village to participate in the micro-planning activity of the village. The SHG members prepared the plan to solve the water problem of their village. Purti Sansthan has provided orientation to SHGs on the 73rd Amendment Act. Smooth access to government schemes is difficult because most gram sabha meetings lack quorum. PANI has initiated capacity building among SHG members and has activated SHGs to ensure a quorum. The SHGs are also encouraged to act as a pressure group on panchayats to ensure their just and efficient functioning.

Promoting Linkages: Agriculture is the main source of livelihood in all the study areas. The marginalised communities are either small landholding cultivators or agriculture labourers. The number of working days and the earnings are not sufficient to meet the minimum basic needs of the family. The marginalised are ignorant of development programmes, and, consequently, are not participating in these programmes, affecting their development. To address the immediate needs of poor women, the SHGs were linked to various development schemes and banks. Samarthan facilitated the formation and functioning of 50 groups under the Swa-Shakti project of the MAVN in Sehore Block. Purti Sansthan and PANI leveraged local banks to link with the 'cash credit limit' scheme of the National Bank for Agricultural and Rural Development (NABARD). According to NABARD guidelines, a group of poor people (not more than 20 members) could start their own group savings. After six months, the SHGs could get bank credit if the banker was satisfied with the SHGs' capacity to handle credit. Banks would provide credit to SHGs, which in turn would provide credit to the members who had sought it. SHGs would be responsible to the banks for the repayment of loans. The credit amount would be four times the total savings of the SHGs. The SHG loans would be treated as clean advance and no security would be required for this. Purti Sansthan and PANI motivated and educated the SHGs to make optimal use of the credit amount for economic development. They have also linked the groups to governmental schemes such as the SGSY of the District Rural Development Agencies (DRDAs) to meet their additional financial needs. HARC promoted building linkages with financial institutions, marketing agencies, extension experts, seed and organic fertiliser agencies, and various government machineries.

Developing Networks: The federation of SHGs has led to the development of inter-linkages among SHGs. Networking has enabled women to share their experiences with other groups in different villages that have similar stakes and aspirations. The federations have been trained in financial management, resource mobilisation and decision-making. HARC has enabled the formation of the Rawain Women SHG Federation in Naugaon Block. The federation acts as a trading unit, helping the SHGs to market their products. SHG members have contributed a share value of Rs 500 for a life membership and have started a collective business. HARC is also helping them to deal with banks and other financial institutions. In Sehore Block, the SHGs promoted by Samarthan are federated as 'Cluster Associations', comprising groups from eight to 10 villages. The clusters are so formed that women are able to attend the meetings by commuting less than 3–5 km. Group members who attend the cluster meeting include the office bearers and one other member. The Cluster Association meets in rotation in each of the six villages. Purti Sansthan has promoted cluster-wise networks of SHGs. It has also provided training to cluster associations. PANI has facilitated a confederation of SHGs called 'Lok Sangh' in each gram panchayat. They are also trying to establish various small-scale and cottage industries at the federation level.

Capacity-Building Support to Field-Level Workers and Motivators

Samarthan and HARC have created a cadre of field workers and motivators who act as facilitators. The key capacity building areas are summarised in Table 15.3. The facilitators are trained to motivate other women to organise and form SHGs in the village. They are change agents who strengthen women's groups, help solve their problems, disseminate

Table 15.3

Key Capacity Building Areas for Field Workers and Motivators

Training	Subject
1. Self-development	Knowledge of different development programmes
	Government schemes and related laws
	Organising/re-organising women's group
	Understanding women's issues
	Ways of raising issues at different levels of administration
2. Skills	Communication
	Conflict resolution within the groups
	Micro-planning
	Information dissemination
	Documentation
3. Group management	Understanding group
	Stages of a group formation
	Facilitation capabilities
4. Leadership development	Roles and responsibilities of leadership
	Leadership capabilities and skills of a facilitator
5. Management of local resources	Village ecosystem planning
6. Pre-Election Voter Awareness Campaign	Pre-election awareness issues
	Awareness methods
	Awareness stages
	Documentation
7. International Women's Day	To raise various issues concerning women
	Information about women rights and laws
	Presentations of good efforts by SHGs
8. Panchayati Raj	Roles and responsibilities of panchayat representatives
	How the local Sangathan can be linked with panchayat
	Roles of motivators/field workers in strengthening local self-governance
9. Computer training	Practical knowledge of computers
	Computer literacy
	Typing work on computer

important information, and take up issues at the block and district levels. Their primary role is to enhance the leadership qualities of women, and raise awareness on a number of social and economic issues. They also help group members in the functioning of SHGs such as enhancing awareness of rules and regulations, savings and credit and process of inter-loaning. Their presence has helped the SHGs to get right information on the documents required to seek approval from the higher echelons of the government. The SHGs have also learnt about methods of documentation such as writing the minutes of the gram sabha, and planning and costing of public works.

Under the Swa-Shakti project, Samarthan has trained field workers on the role of women in developmental contexts, government schemes, the process of facilitating SHG formation, the functions and financial management of SHGs, and entrepreneurship development. Similarly, SSK has also provided such training. HARC has provided training to motivators on group management, leadership development, management of local resources and computer training. It regularly monitors the various activities of motivators in their villages. Motivators are linked to HARC's Resource Centre, and get information on various developmental issues, which they convey to the village women. Rawain Mahila Manch organises bimonthly meetings of motivators to share their experiences.

Capacity-building inputs have enabled the field workers/motivators assess their own work in a larger frame of development and empowerment. This has helped them develop a vision for their own work and assign meaning to a number of inputs that they had to provide to SHGs.

Participatory Learning Tools

The capacity-building initiatives were participatory, interactive and inclusive in nature. The training inputs were a combination of classroom training, exposure visits and discussions within the group. The themes and topics for discussion were selected to provide inputs to strengthen the groups (for example, team building, recording of financial transactions, et cetera), to raise their awareness about different developmental issues (for instance health and nutrition of women and children), and on the functioning of PRIs. The organisations created a variety of learning opportunities for women including practical learning through study tours, visits to 'best-practice' projects, hands-on training and demonstration projects, and face-to-face interactions with experts, practitioners, and government officials. HARC organised exposure visits to different small-scale industries, which gave women a practical orientation on grading and packaging. Members of the purchasing committee were taken to an international trade fair in Delhi, where they could get an opportunity to sell their products and build marketing linkages with big traders from across the country. They were also trained at the food-processing unit at HARC. The aim was to upgrade the technical knowledge and skills of the members of the federation and the fruit-processing committee, so that they could utilise the practical knowledge for income-generation activities.

Samarthan conducted training for the members on gram sabha and gram swaraj. The training methodology involved interactive sessions between group members, with the field worker acting as the facilitator and the resource person of the subject. These discussions would normally take place after the routine activity of depositing savings or repayment of loans. Classroom-training sessions also took place. Meetings, awareness camps, trainings, exposure visits and information dissemination were the main instruments of Purti Sansthan's intervention. The capacity-building strategies of PANI aimed to strengthen SHGs towards meaningful participation in panchayats. Hence, their capacity-building strategies included open community meetings, exposure to works done by panchayats and financial statements of panchayats.

POTENTIAL OF SHGs AS CHANGE AGENTS

The experiences of the collective action of SHGs in the study are by no means sufficient to draw a universal conclusion, yet their success offers significant insights into the ways in which they can enhance the political participation of women. Experiences of the post-73rd Amendment phase indicate that women's participation in PRIs has not moved greatly beyond rhetoric. The opportunities for women's participation in deliberations, as well as in the decision-making processes of the gram panchayat, have been minimal. Their participation is not significant enough to make the institutions responsive to their needs and priorities. However, the findings of this study clearly indicate that SHGs are providing a support base to women from marginalised communities by mobilising community-level activism. SHGs can enhance women's participation in PRIs in the following ways:

(a) Ensuring Accountability of the Gram Panchayat

SHGs as active, articulate and organised citizenry have acted on a range of issues, holding the panchayats accountable in terms of the use, production and distribution of public resources for the common public good. Their actions can be classified as those that involve interface with the administrative machinery and those that involve self-help. Among the former, some actions are in the nature of articulation of demands, while others are actions for implementing existing project provisions. Self-help actions include collective problem-solving efforts that are within the reach of citizens. SHGs have taken a proactive role in decisions relating to the welfare of the village. Their regular and strong presence at gram sabha meetings ensures that village issues are resolved. We have seen instances where women have organised themselves to undertake constructive community activities on their own.

(b) Mobilising the Gram Sabha

Acting as pressure groups, SHGs are representing those whose interests have not been articulated earlier. Women from disadvantaged communities in particular are now able to have a say in decision-making processes and take responsibility for changes affecting their lives. Mediation by SHGs has helped sensitise the gram panchayats to local problems, needs and interests. Their concerted action has ensured the development of locality-specific plans, the optimal use of existing resources, the generation of additional resources and their just and equitable distribution.

(c) Support to Elected Representatives

The process of involving women in governance has many critical requirements. They must have the skills and capacities to access information, mobilise and manage resources, and interact with multiple actors. For effective participation, they can rely on the support of SHGs. PRIA's experience of the previous two rounds of panchayat elections clearly shows that women who have been leaders of SHGs, or were supported by SHGs in contesting the local elections, were confident of working better to further their shared interests.

(d) Creating Social Capital

Social reciprocities influence the effective functioning of local governance. This study found that the proactive engagement of SHGs enabled rapid development within the community. The groups have addressed a wide range of women's practical needs by taking on community leadership roles. By effective intervention, they have somewhat reframed the priorities of the village community. The relevance of social correlations in ensuring good governance is evident in this conclusion.

NOTE

1. The PACS (Poorest Areas Civil Society) programme was launched by the Department for International Development of the UK, to fund and support civil society organisations working in the poorest districts of the country, while Samarthan's work focused on strengthening the marginalised groups through capacity building.

REFERENCES

Anandhi, S. 2002. 'Interlocking Patriarchies and Women in Governance: A Case Study of Panchayati Raj Institutions in Tamil Nadu', in Karin Kapadia (ed.), *The Violence of Development*, pp. 425–56. London: Zed Books.

Bandyopadhyay, D., B.N. Yugandhar and Amitava Mukherjee. 2004. 'Convergence of Programmes by Empowering the Self-Help Groups and Panchayati Raj Institutions', in D. Bandyopadhyay and Amitava Mukerjee (eds), *New Issues in Panchayati Raj*, pp. 122–43. New Delhi: Concept Publishing Company.

Deshmukh-Ranadive, Joy. 2005. 'Women in Self-Help Groups and Panchayati Raj Institutions: Suggesting Synergistic Linkages', Occasional Paper No 40. New Delhi: Centre for Women's Development Studies.

Kabeer, Naila. 2003. 'Making Rights Work for the Poor: Nijera Kori and the Construction of Collective Capabilities in Rural Bangladesh', Working Paper 200. Sussex: IDS.

Mayoux, Linda. 2003. *Sustainable Learning for Women's Empowerment: Ways Forward in Micro-Finance*. New Delhi: Samskriti.

Nambiar, Malini and Kaustuv Kanti Bandyopadhyay. 2004. 'Self-Help Groups: Engagement with Governance Institutions', *Participation and Governance*, 10(29): 23–30.

Niranjana, Seemanthini. 2002. 'Exploring Gender Inflections within Panchayati Raj Institutions: Women's Politicization in Andhra Pradesh', in Karin Kapadia (ed.), *The Violence of Development*, pp. 352–92. London: Zed Books.

Pant, Mandakini. 2004. 'Adult Education and Livelihoods: Women as Agents of Change', Occasional Paper Series: Paper No. 1. New Delhi: PRIA.

PRIA. 1999. *Women Leadership in Panchayati Raj Institutions: An Analysis of Six States*. New Delhi: PRIA.

Sharma, Kumud. 2004. 'From Representation to Presence: The Paradox of Power and Powerlessness', in D. Bandyopadhyay and Amitava Mukerjee (eds), *New Issues in Panchayati Raj*, pp. 48–66. New Delhi: Concept Publishing Company.

16

Exploring Linkages between Citizenship, Livelihood Security and Gender Equality

Planned Interventions and Outcomes in Rajasthan

Shobhita Rajagopal

INTRODUCTION

The emerging focus on citizenship within development can be traced to several parallel shifts in the development discourse during the 1990s. The emphasis on participatory development, long rooted in the concern with participation, began to turn towards political participation and increasing poor and marginalised people's influence over the wider decision-making processes that affect their lives. The rise of the 'good governance' agenda, and its concerns with increasing the responsiveness of governments to citizen's voices, also added to the debate (Gaventa 2002).

Citizenship has been defined in myriad ways. Conventionally, the concept of citizenship has been traced to the rise of the nation-state, and taken to refer to membership of a nation-state and the formal rights and duties which this membership carries (Kabeer 2002). Various concepts of citizenship have incorporated ideas of universal citizenship and equal rights for all members. However, the notion of universal citizenship has been challenged on a number of grounds. Feminists, among others, have asserted that such an understanding hides the reality of unequal power on the basis of race, class, ethnicity and gender, which can render women subject to double discrimination (Meer and Sever 2004). It is also criticised for effectively occluding diversity in experiences, identities and welfare needs.

In recent years, popular movements and struggles have highlighted the manner in which citizenship is eroded in various contexts. These movements have stressed that citizenship is not just a set of legal rights and entitlements that individuals possess by virtue of their membership of a state, but is also a set of practices through which individuals formulate or claim new rights or struggle to expand or maintain existing rights. Feminists have been demanding that the notions of citizenship be extended to women, and reconceptualised accordingly in order to achieve greater gender equality and address development goals such as poverty eradication, discrimination and democratisation.

In India, despite constitutional guarantees of full citizenship rights, women continue to face exclusion and marginalisation from the benefits of citizenship. Given their social roles and responsibilities, women are disadvantaged with regard to access to resources and power when compared to men. Looking at citizenship entails understanding women and men, and their activities in a social world. Consequently, development planning and practice have to take into account the unequal gender relations, as social roles and responsibilities are central to the experience of citizenship.

This chapter focuses on exploring the linkage and relationship between citizenship, livelihood security, and promoting gender equality in the context of planned interventions for women's development and poverty alleviation in Rajasthan. It attempts to look at the lessons learnt and the challenges for shaping development initiatives along the lines of gendered citizenship. Section I discusses the emergence of planned interventions in Rajasthan and how they have addressed issues of citizenship, livelihood and gender equality. Section II focuses on the outcomes of these interventions and the lessons learnt.

SECTION I
THE RAJASTHAN CONTEXT

Rajasthan, now the largest state in India, provides tremendous regional variations in terms of ecology, agrarian structures, caste, class and ethnicity. Various pressures on a fragile natural base and limited livelihood opportunities compounded by recurrent droughts make it difficult for the poor and marginalised to cope with shocks. The consequences of drought on the lives of women and children are substantial: it impacts the food intake, health and education, and livelihood options. Caste continues to maintain its hold with reference to marriage, occupational pursuits and relationships. The discrimination, marginalisation, power domination and exclusion that characterise the social and political processes continue to wax strongly.

Gender relations are influenced by both a feudal past and patriarchal rules and norms. Gender inequalities are deeply entrenched, and reproduced through a variety of practices and institutions. Social development indicators reflect that women's access to various resources, that is, education, health, labour and employment, continues to be poor, and that they are marginalised from decision-making positions within the household and the community. The Gender Development Index (GDI) is also indicative of the range of gender inequalities prevalent in the state (HDR 2000).

In the context of policy planning and interventions, the 1980s and 1990s were periods when several innovative programmes were implemented in Rajasthan. The state has served as a laboratory for several experiments in the field of women's development and education. The Women's Development Programme (WDP, 1984), the Shikshakarmi Programme (SKP, 1987) and Lok Jumbish (LJ, 1992) amply proved the success of 'planning from below'. The learnings from these initiatives were taken into account in the design of several national programmes, that is, the Mahila Samakhya and District Primary Education Project. However, the inability of the state to sustain these efforts has come up for a lot of debate.

Rajasthan was also one of the few states to formulate a State Policy for Women in 2000. The policy document reaffirms that it is rooted in a rights perspective. It also informs that 'it is important to create an environment wherein the women do not depend fully on the societal and governmental system, but may become empowered themselves and play a decisive role in the development of their rights and abilities' (GoR 2000).

The state has also witnessed the emergence of several strong community-based movements for the Right to Information and the Right to Food, which have given new meanings to citizenship participation in the development process.

Addressing Citizenship, Livelihoods and Gender Equality through Planned Interventions

The concept of citizenship and its relationship to development (and to gender) is not straightforward and not necessarily positive. Development policy and practice over the past two decades have tried to address the needs of the poor and the marginalised with varying degrees of success. Since the 1980s, when questions related to women's marginalisation in policy and disempowerment in the social, economic and political spheres gained centrality, several interventions were conceived, which laid emphasis on 'empowerment' as a crucial ingredient for positing change. On the other hand, a number of anti-poverty programmes targeted women to provide wage employment, productive assets, skills, and credit and food security. However, experience indicates that these efforts have not succeeded in reducing poverty to the extent necessary. In recent times, the stress has been on applying strong participatory principles for better results.

Mobilising for Social Change: The Women's Development Project (WDP): The WDP was implemented by the Government of Rajasthan in 1984 with the principal aim of 'empowering women through communication of information, education and training and to enable them to recognise and improve their social and economic status' (GoR 1984). Influenced by feminist and liberal discourse, the objective of the programme was to transform the approach to women's issues from one of being powerless and treated with compassion, to operating as equal partners with male members of the family in terms of literacy and in all spheres—cultural, social and economic (Clarke and Jha 2006). The project was initially implemented in six districts of the state with UNICEF support. The beginning of such a development intervention in an extremely feudal Rajasthan was radical, a daring attempt to go to the very roots of the problem of deprivation and subordination of women.

The programme attempted to provide a micro-level alternative and compensate for the institutional failure of the state to meet women's needs and priorities. It was not a service delivery programme with *'targets' or distribution of material resources.* The stress was on intangible resources, such as training-education, communication of information and building supportive networks, with a view to improving women's longer-term access to tangible resources, especially those distributed by the state. Therefore, the programme placed priority on providing support to the needs and demands articulated by rural women, and sought women's participation as never before—seeing them as initiating agents in the move towards greater possibilities (IDS 1991). A predictable support structure at the block, district and state levels helped take forward the issues emerging from the village level.

The village-level *sathin* (change agent), consciously selected from the disadvantaged groups, was expected to facilitate the process of change. The activism of the sathins helped mobilise women on a number of fronts. The sathins raised issues related to the delivery of public services—water, education, health, grazing land, Public Distribution System—and grappled with the day-to-day realities of women from marginalised sections and locations. Many of them took up human rights issues in their villages, raising their voices against atrocities and violence against women. Others were involved in livelihood issues to get pensions for widows and the aged, and ensuring the payment of equal and minimum wages to women, especially from the marginalised sections (see Box 16.1).

Box 16.1
Women Take up Rights Issues

Encroachment of Grazing Land: Twenty women from village Salemabad in Ajmer district met sathin Kamla to discuss the encroachment upon a portion of the village common grazing land by a few upper-caste families from another village. The encroachers would beat up the cattle of the village residents and also put up fencing. This was very upsetting as the women, being poor, were totally dependent on that grazing land for feeding their cattle. The sathin organised a meeting where all the affected women decided to act immediately. They requested the sarpanch to intervene in the matter. Initially the men felt that the women should keep out of this, but the women took a firm, active stand, and said that they were only taking back land which was theirs. The sarpanch feared violence, called the police, and finally the land was returned. The women's persistent efforts prevented the land from being taken away by an exploitative group.

(Box 16.1 continued)

(*Box 16.1 continued*)

Struggle for Fair Wages: In another instance, during the severe drought period in 1986, a *shivir* (intensive camp around an issue) was organised in Ajmer on work and wages at the famine relief work sites. In this camp, the sathins extensively shared information on the irregularities at the sites in their villages and the various ways in which the women were exploited by the 'mates' (male supervisors). The women were not paid the wages due to them. Often a penalty was imposed for not digging the prescribed amount of soil in the stipulated time. A number of cases were collected, which finally led to a new set of guidelines keeping women's concern central, which were proposed to the state government.

(*Source*: 'Exploring Possibilities', IDS 1986)

The sathins also actively voiced their protest against the extreme manifestation of violence against women during the Deorala sati protest movement (1987), and systematically analysed why the incident could not be glorified or be seen as miraculous (see Kavita et al. 1988). Subsequently, in the Bhateri rape case when a sathin was gang-raped after she had prevented a child marriage, the sathins collectively raised the issue of the dignity of women working in government-supported projects and programmes, and demanded justice. There was nationwide protest. The collective pressure of women's groups both within and outside Rajasthan finally led to the Supreme Court order on sexual harassment at the workplace in 1997, popularly known as the Vishakha judgement.

The assertion of and questioning by women from poor and marginalised communities in a highly feudal and patriarchal social environment necessarily meant that entrenched power centres and vested interests operational at the village level were threatened, and the sathins were often identified as 'troublemakers' and 'home breakers'.

The WDP experience clearly established that the poor, non-literate women, given space and support, could reflect, articulate and challenge injustice. The sathins developed skills of communication, mobilisation and reflection. They grew to become 'leaders', assuming a greater degree of control over their lives. There was also a clear recognition that catalysing change would necessitate a change in the self-image, leading to a change in the social image.

In the context of citizenship, the WDP facilitated a process whereby 'development' could be perceived from the vantage point of poor women in Rajasthan, the marginalised citizens. It enabled poor rural women to raise their voices against social injustice, challenge the social and cultural constructions of gender, and articulate their demands through collective action. *It was citizenship in practice.* In subsequent years, some sathins who were elected as panchayat members became active in forums of local governance and continued their struggle for rights.

However, with the failure of constructive engagement with the state, a number of WDP processes could not be sustained and were diluted.

While the WDP aimed at addressing both practical needs and the long-term strategic interest of women by mobilising them, one of the major criticisms levelled against WDP was its inability to address livelihood concerns in a sustained manner. Most WDP functionaries were confronted with the question of how economic status improved after empowerment.

Securing Livelihoods: District Poverty Initiative Project (DPIP): Targeting women in anti-poverty programmes, often through the formation of separate women's groups, has been promoted widely in recent years. These efforts appear to serve a range of policy goals (basic needs, welfare, equity and women's empowerment) by channelling resources through women. The District Poverty Initiative Project (DPIP) was implemented by the Government of Rajasthan in 2000, with support from the World Bank, in seven of the poorest districts in the state. The project has focused on building networks and organisations of the poor at the community level to enable them to plan and implement activities according to their needs. The main objectives of the project were to:

- Mobilise and empower the poor, and help them to develop strong grassroots organisations that facilitate access to and participation in democratic and development processes.
- Expand the involvement of the poor in economic activities by improving their capacities, skills, access to social and economic infrastructure, and services and employment opportunities.
- Improve the abilities of non-government, government and Panchayati Raj Institutions to hear, reach and serve poor clients, that is, to function in a more inclusive and participatory manner.
- Supporting small-scale sub-projects that are priority chosen, planned and implemented by the poor.

The DPIP project document further reiterates that the state government is concerned about the intractability of poverty and is seeking innovative ways to address it. The project aims to meet this need by developing a demand-driven approach, in which the poor themselves identify the actions and investments required, and take responsibility in their implementation. Community ownership and contributions have been seen as the cornerstones of the project. Gender equity has been recognised as an important goal of the DPIP. The project document states that

> DPIP's design to support small community based initiatives is particularly appropriate to meet women's needs. Community Facilitators would be trained to work with women to articulate their needs and priorities, a number of which were identified during the social assessments including, drinking water, income generation, health, literacy, day care and micro enterprise … . At least 30 per cent of the DPIP governing council would be women (World Bank 2000).

The institutional arrangements include the organisations of poor women and men, that is, the Common Interest Groups (CIGs) formed at the village level. The CIGs identify different sub-project activities (SPA), including from infrastructure works, micro-enterprises and land-based activities, according to their needs. At the district level, a District Project Monitoring Unit (DPMU) has been set up for project support, which works along with the NGO partnering in the project. The primary responsibility of the NGOs is to 'mobilise and organise communities'. A State Project Monitoring Unit (SPMU) has been established to oversee the functioning of the project across districts and to monitor implementation. The Institute of Development Studies (IDS), Jaipur, has been involved in Process Monitoring of DPIP since 2002.

By March 2005, more than 18,000 CIGs have been formed in the various DPIP districts, including 7,120 women's CIGs. Many of these CIGs are at different stages of development. The nature of the sub-project activities taken up by women's CIGs ranges from irrigation wells, readymade garments, gem polishing, basket weaving, rope making (*munjban*), to construction of school rooms, livestock rearing/dairying, carpet weaving, horticulture, and so on. While activities such as readymade garments, basket weaving and rope making have been taken up only by women's groups, all other activities have been taken up by men's groups or by mixed groups of women and men.

Women's CIGs in DPIP

The CIG is the key organisation formed with poor women and men to manage and implement small-scale projects of their choice. The cases illustrated in Boxes 16.2 and 16.3 describe the nature of activities that they have undertaken.

As these cases reveal, many of the sub-project activities identified by the women are activities in which they have been traditionally involved. The project built on existing skills with the primary input provided in the form of productive capital for purchasing implements and introducing

---

Box 16.2
Basket Weaving as a Sub-project Activity

Kiron Ki Dhani is a hamlet of Kahwaraoji village in Dausa district. There are 18 households in this *dhani*, all belonging to the Kir caste (traditional basket weavers). The CIG Roshini Samooh was formed in September 2001 with 11 women members. All of them belong to BPL households, are landless and earn their livelihoods through basket weaving. During the period when the raw material for weaving baskets is not available, the women supplement their earnings by performing agriculture labour, or work in the nearby mines as wage labour. The men are largely involved in breaking stones in the local mines. Some have taken land on lease and are growing vegetables, while others work in a nearby dam area and grow *singhadas* (water chestnuts).

After coming together as a CIG, the group started a self-help activity with individual contributions of Rs 50 per month. The group also started inter-loaning small amounts to other community members at an interest rate of 24 per cent per annum. Prior to the CIG formation, the women had received some financial assistance from the partnering NGO for purchasing the raw materials used in basket weaving.

The women selected basket weaving as an SPA since they were traditionally involved in this work. They knew market linkages and they also knew how to procure the raw materials. The SPA was sanctioned in October 2001 with an estimated budget of Rs 300,000.

(Box 16.2 continued)

(*Box 16.2 continued*)

The group purchased various implements/tools such as hammer, water tub, stool, axe and other materials from the stipulated budget. The women fetch the raw material, twigs of the *khajur* (date palm), using a transport (a cart) from villages within a range of 10 km. The women usually pool their resources and purchase the raw material, the twigs, sold at the rate of 50 paise per twig.

The first step is to soak the twigs in water and clean them. They are then cut into equal sizes and woven into baskets. A shed, where women can work together, has been proposed, but at present the work is carried out in individual homes. In a day, the women usually weave two small baskets and one big one, and they work for about 20 days. The cost of one small basket works out to Rs 13, and the bigger basket to Rs 18. These are sold for Rs 20 and Rs 35, respectively. The monthly income is Rs 750 per member. The women said that the tools supplied by the project have improved their work efficiency, so they are able to make more baskets each day. They are now also able to decide the price for the produce and negotiate with the trader. The baskets are sold from home, or the trader visits the village and makes the purchase in bulk. The women go to nearby areas to sell the baskets. However, men take baskets to be sold in Dausa or other far-off places.

Before the project began, the women members did not have the cash to buy the raw materials and often took loans from the local moneylender at high interest rates. Some women had also mortgaged their jewellery. Many group members articulated that earlier they did not interact with men (mostly outsiders), but that now they were less inhibited. While they have to observe purdah in the village, when they go out of the village the observance reduces.

The women members had utilised the income earned from basket weaving for various purposes: for repairing and plastering the house, purchasing goats; and others have used the money for meeting domestic needs. The women are eager to acquire literacy skills, and some have learnt to write their names and put their signatures. An unintended outcome was that all the CIG members wanted their daughters to be educated, so that they could have a better future.

(*Source*: 'Process Monitoring' Reports, IDS 2003–4).

Box 16.3
Rope Making as a Sub-project Activity

The women's CIG in village Alooda, Dausa, has taken up munj-crushing and rope making. The munj (*Saccharum munja*) is a tough grass whose culms are used to make ropes to string charpoys and weave baskets. The tasks primarily include collecting the raw material, crushing the munj and making it into ropes. Traditionally, the crushing is done by hand. The objective of the activity is to increase the manufacturing capacity of the households by introducing simple diesel-operated machines for crushing the munj.

Initially, the group had decided to take up gemstone *bindai* work (beading of gemstones). However, this activity could not be sustained due to the slump in the gemstone market; and because they were not very skilled in the work, their products fetched poor returns. Later on, the group decided that improving on their traditional occupation would benefit them more, and the project proposal of munjban (crushing the culms and rope making) was drawn up with the help of the community facilitator. The estimated cost of the project was Rs 58,000. The machinery and equipment for crushing were purchased from the market. The women members said that the purchasing had been done by the men of their households.

The group shares the crushing machine, but the rest of the work is undertaken individually. The raw munj is usually collected from neighbouring villages and hamlets, or purchased from local businessmen at Rs 5–Rs 7 per kg. The completed rope is sold in the market for Rs 20 per kg. All the members buy or sell according to their capacity and individual requirement. Every member gets a chance to use the machine by rotation after 10 days. The women said that one member uses the machine for a whole day, and then it is her responsibility to fill up the fuel tank for the next person. Girls from the member's households also help in the activity. They felt that the distribution of work and sharing the machine on a rotation basis is beneficial for all. They were satisfied with the increase in production; the machine had helped them work faster and reduced the drudgery.

(Box 16.3 continued)

(*Box 16.3 continued*)

> Earlier, when they used to perform this task by hand, they produced less and it was laborious.
>
> The women said that the project had 'made them financially stronger', and that group members were in a position to save some of their earnings. Due to restrictions on their mobility, it is the men of the household who sell the finished product in the market. Sometimes a truck is hired collectively to take the products to the market. The women leaders of the munjban group had collectively applied for the repair of the well and the installation of a hand pump in their village.
>
> (*Source*: Process Monitoring reports, IDS 2003–04).

technology, that is, the diesel-powered crushing machine. The women already had the necessary information related to the raw material, the market and networks. This made it easier for these poor households to reap some benefits.

In contrast, the experience of groups that have identified other sets of activities has not been so positive. For example, tailoring has been promoted in DPIP as a sub-project activity, which includes manufacturing garments and embroidery work. Many women's CIGs have taken up tailoring of readymade garments as an activity across districts. Most of these women received three months of skills training from a 'Master Trainer' (in most cases a man), from whom they learnt to cut and stitch garments for women, men and children. The training given to the members was designed for learning rudimentary skills in stitching and cutting. Many of the groups have not produced any items for sale. They are only stitching some garments for daily use. The local markets are small, and these groups do not have a niche. The training has not given them the confidence to undertake production for the market, and they have not been able to establish market linkages. Very few women have learnt the art of 'cutting'. The women feel that since they are not equipped with reading and writing skills, they are not able to deal with scales of measurement. No efforts have been made during the training process to create alternative ways of teaching women with minimal levels of literacy. In the local market, to which these groups have access, cutting is a valued activity, and there are professional tailors whose skills these women cannot match. No attempt has been made by the project to link these groups to wholesale producers or firms who can provide cloth that needs to be stitched. Even stitching these high-value goods would require fine skills that the women have been unable to acquire (IDS 2005). In many villages, the sewing machines are lying idle due to lack of work. In Bhagwati Samooh, Piawadi, Rajsamand district, none of the members received any job work after training. They said that everyone in the village has his/her own sewing machine, so it was not possible to get work in the village. One of the members has given her embroidery machine on rent to an embroiderer in the village, where her daughter is reported to be learning embroidery. She also plans to give the interlocking machines to another daughter (ibid.).

The above experience shows that women have hardly gained from the sub-project activity of tailoring. While women who were primarily involved in agriculture and domestic work are now 'owners' of a sewing machine and have learnt to use the machine, no long-term interests are being served. The project functionaries as well as the NGOs have not taken into account the problems faced by these women's CIGs. There are very few instances where the women's CIGs have collectively voiced their concern about the situation they are confronted with and bargained for a better deal. Now, the crucial issue is the economic and social sustainability of these groups. The women's CIGs that have taken up the activity of drilling beads and semi-precious stones have similar experiences. The fact that there has been no economic return is crucial, as many of these women have borrowed money from the moneylenders at high interest rates to pay the 10 per cent contribution for the machines.

Understanding What has Changed

The formation of women's CIGs and the idea that the SPA would help increase women's earning power have various implications for gender relations and women's identity within the household and community, as also for understanding the empowerment potential of the programme. Field-level interactions during process monitoring exercises reveal that involvement in DPIP has led to some changes in women's perception of their own selves and of their role in household decision-making. It needs to be reiterated that these changes are to be understood in relation to the specific social and cultural context in which the women live, and the way they seek to accommodate, adapt to or challenge the gender constraints faced by them.

It is evident that the DPIP had given women an opportunity to work from their own homes. Since they have some income in hand and are contributing to their households, there is a sense of greater self-reliance. The monthly savings have given women some sense of security, and reduced their dependence on the moneylender. Nevertheless, achieving self-reliance is severely undermined by the practice of purdah and the restrictions on mobility in the public domain. This has also been recognised as a central factor contributing to the subordinate status of women in Rajasthan. The women said that before they joined the CIG, most of them observed purdah and could not talk to outsiders, especially men. But now, while they have to observe purdah in front of kin, during the meetings and other interactions they do not strictly adhere to it.

The issue of increased mobility figured commonly across women's CIGs. Some women stated that they have now started going to the market on their own to purchase raw materials. Earlier, a male member used to accompany them. 'People used to make fun of us whenever we used to go to the marketplace as "outside" roles are meant for men and not for "illiterate women".' The chairperson and treasurer of the CIGs have also gone out of the village to attend meetings and training programmes, often accompanied by a male escort. It is evident that women are allowed to go by themselves to neighbouring areas. However, accessing markets at a distance continues to be a male prerogative. A few women have also had to face violence when they stayed away from home to participate in a project activity.

It is also evident that while gender asymmetries in decision-making had not changed drastically, the women now had a greater voice in household decision-making, and that at the household level, men did consult them. However, they also shared with us that while men can take decisions without their consent, women do not have the freedom to do so. Women CIG members in Baran district responded: 'If men spend the money earned from selling the milk on alcohol, we cannot interfere, as it is an age-old practice. We have to accept the situation' (personal communication).

An analysis of how women had used the income generated from the SPA reveals that it has largely been for household consumption, repairing the house, purchase of livestock, and purchasing clothes (this is mostly seasonal, during festivals or marriages). Investing in children's education has emerged as a priority for most women members. Many responded that they have come together so that their children could get a better education: '*Mahare ghar ka to mahane padhaya koni*' ('Our parents never educated us, but we want our children to study'). All the members were aware that education is important. While most women wanted the girls to study and are encouraging them to attend school, the desired education levels for girls continue to be lower than those for boys. Providing better nutrition for children also emerged as an important concern. Milk consumption has increased in households that have taken up the livestock-rearing activity (IDS 2004).

In the public sphere, it is evident that participation of women and men in SPA has led to minimising divisions along caste lines at the workplace. Women and men from various caste groups work together. However, the participation of women at the village-level forums has been limited. Very few women attend panchayat meetings or voice their concerns in the Gram Sabhas regarding issues related to health, nutrition, education, drinking water, et cetera. Many CIG members complained that they are not informed about the meetings and that even if they attend, there is little space for them to raise their concerns. In one district, women CIG members took up the issue of the purchase of bead-drilling machine and approached the district collector with their grievance, demanding that their machines be changed as they were of poor quality. But such instances are few and far between.

It is evident that changing gender relations at the community level require well-designed and sustained efforts. It is necessary to provide an environment where women can demand and question processes around them. More exposure trips, more women's meetings and interactions with other peer groups, and engaging more gender-sensitive staff can help build these CIGs into strong pressure groups in DPIP.

SECTION II
UNDERSTANDING THE OUTCOMES

Differences in the social positioning of women and men are reflected in the unequal distribution of rights, resources and responsibilities. The subordination of women, as represented in cultural norms and behaviour, is reproduced in public policies, legal frameworks and institutional practices. Therefore, granting women and men the same rights in law or the same opportunities in policy do not necessarily translate into equal enjoyments of rights and resources. There is a need to shift from passive citizenship to a situation of not simply asking questions, but demanding answers. In other words, creating a voice that will count is about building a women's constituency that is diverse and broad-based, and reaches out to the excluded.

The WDP aimed at bringing women's voices centre-stage in the policy discourse. The appointment of change agents and facilitators, systematic training and regular interactions helped to nurture associations among women across the state. It was a gender-specific intervention, wherein the processes demonstrated a *transformatory potential,* with women seeking to question the cultural imbalances in gender relations and change their subordinate status through collective reflection and action. The programme helped to establish women as 'active citizens', and sought to transform the perception of women as weak, inferior or limited beings to women who can take decisions and plan for their own development. The sathins' opposition to traditional gender relations and socio-economic hierarchies also resulted in bruising vested interests, and they had to face resistance and backlash from communities.

On the other hand, the DPIP was designed to have multiple impacts on the livelihoods and social conditions of the poor women and men. A direct intended impact was to augment incomes. The project experience suggests that the formation of women's CIGs has helped poor women to put their livelihoods on a more secure basis. A number of changes have also been reported by women at the personal as well as community levels. These changes, however, need to be viewed in the context of the social positioning of women and men, and the space available for taking up the opportunities on offer.

Targeting resources at poor women may help project beneficiaries, but the underlying causes of female poverty remain unaddressed—the deep-rooted inequalities vis-à-vis control over assets, pervasive gender discrimination, and lack of voice in the power structures and public spheres. While women CIG members said they would invest their increased income in the well-being of the family and children's education, the question of how women's personal control over resources will help in altering patriarchal relations and impact on gender asymmetry—the preference for male children, violence against women, as well as ensuring equal opportunities for girls in choosing their future—has not been articulated clearly and remains unclear to programme managers (IDS 2004).

It is clearly evident that the project, while addressing the economic needs of women, has not focused on aspects of women's subordination and the structural causes of inequality that deny women their rights and prevent them from gaining a voice. The CIGs are yet to reach a stage where they can demand and question their social and political contexts, and get into a bargaining position and engage strategically with the state. This in turn would help achieve the objective of sustained and empowered livelihoods.

It is also evident that the need for using the gender lens at all stages of planning, implementation and evaluation has not become an institutional habit, nor is it an assimilated perspective in DPIP. No effort seems to have been made within DPIP to understand the gender-differentiated nature of the experience of poverty and the constraints women face in struggling out of poverty. The experience suggests that issues of gender and poverty cannot be reduced to quotas for women, as in the Integrated Rural Development Programme (IRDP), or women's specific target groups as in the Development of Women and Children in Rural Areas (DWCRA). Such interventions may merely serve to institutionalise the marginal position given to women in official development (Rajagopal 2004).

In contrast, in a recent intervention on poverty alleviation around natural resource management, the effort has been to promote women's collectives for integrated development involving issues of livelihood, environment and the use of local resources. Central to the process is motivating women to take on leadership roles and empowering them instead of creating a dependency on institutions. Convincing men regarding women's role in decision-making is an ongoing activity. In one district (which is common to DPIP) where the project is being implemented, regular trainings and meetings have been organised by the partner NGO, where women have discussed issues related to their participation in village forums, their role in village development, understanding of rights and duties, health issues, right to food, right to work, and issues related to sustainable livelihoods. Capacity-building of women through continuous interactions is an ongoing process. It is expected that these would lead to long-term gains.

CONCLUSION

The two planned interventions discussed in this chapter were implemented at different points in time and at different stages of development. One was in the early 1980s when discourse on women's equality was being refined. The second intervention came at a time when there was a fair clarity on what works and what does not. The WDP experience clearly indicates that the mobilisation of women and collective action enabled women to claim their rights as equals in society. On the other hand, poverty reduction has been the main agenda of DPIP, and the collectives of women and men are yet to reach a stage where they can exercise their voice as empowered citizens.

Gaining recognition as citizens requires an active exercise of citizenship. It implies active and organised participation in processes to strengthen (i) public services to pay attention to women's specific needs and constraints; (ii) a fairer distribution of resources to women and men; (iii) measures to progressively eliminate discrimination against girls; and (iv) redressal of violations (Huq 2000). The Rajasthan experience reveals that promoting citizenship for livelihood security and gender equality would necessarily involve gendered interests being treated as important citizenship rights and valued by policy makers. It involves creating spaces wherein women can define and express their needs and views, and be heard by key institutions. The challenge is to build capacities and abilities wherein marginalised groups can become agents of social change and action, and gain meaningful opportunities as citizens.

REFERENCES

Clarke, P. and J. Jha. 2006. 'Rajasthan's Experience in Improving Service Delivery in Education', in Vikram K. Chand (ed.), *Reinventing Public Service Delivery in India*. New Delhi: Sage Publications.

Gaventa, J. 2002. 'Introduction: Exploring Citizenship, Participation and Account-ability', *IDS Bulletin*, 33(2): 1–11. UK: Institute of Development Studies, University of Sussex.

Government of Rajasthan.1984. *Women's Development Project: Rajasthan.*

―――. 2000. *State Policy for Women.* Jaipur: Department of Women and Child Development.

―――. 2000. *Rajasthan: Human Development Report.* Jaipur: GoR.

Huq, S. 2000. 'Gender and Citizenship: What does a Rights Framework Offer Women', *IDS Bulletin*, 31(4): 74–82. UK: Institute of Development Studies, University of Sussex.

Institute of Development Studies (IDS). 1986. 'Exploring Possibilities: A Review of the Women's Development Programme Rajasthan. Jaipur: IDS

―――. 1991. 'Women's Development Programme: Emerging Challenges', IDSJ Research Report No. 038.

―――. 2003. *District Poverty Initiatives Project: A Report on Process Monitoring.* Jaipur: IDS.

―――. 2004. 'Engaging Women in the Public Sphere: Women CIGs in DPIP', Process Monitoring Report. Jaipur: IDS.

―――. 2005. 'Skill Augmentation of CIGs through RUDA: A Report', Process Monitoring Report 2. Jaipur: IDS.

Kavita, Shobha, Kanchan Shobhita and Sharada. 1988. 'Rural Women Speak', *Seminar*, 342: 40–44.

Kabeer, N. 2002. 'Citizenship, Affiliation and Exclusion: Perspectives from the South', *IDS Bulletin*, 33(2): 12–23. UK: Institute of Development Studies, University of Sussex.

Meer, S. and C. Sever. 2004. 'Gender and Citizenship: Overview Report', *BRIDGE.* UK: Institute of Development Studies, University of Sussex.

Rajagopal, S. 2004. 'Mainstreaming Gender and Development: Policies, Pro-grammes and Outcomes. A perspective from Rajasthan', IDSJ, Working Paper No. 138.

World Bank. 2000. 'Rajasthan District Poverty Initiatives Project', Project Appraisal Document. New Delhi: World Bank.

VI

Dignity in Struggle:
Lessons from the Past

17

Women's Development under Patriarchy
The Experience of the Sathins

Rajesh Ramakrishnan, Viren Lobo and Depinder Kapur

The following article* was written in the mid-1990s when we were working in a Delhi-based NGO that supported grassroots NGOs. This was a time when there was a great deal of introspection among NGOs in Delhi following several incidents of summary dismissal of staff by some leading NGOs. It was a time for reflection on the changing role of NGOs, the position of NGOs vis-à-vis the state, employer-employee relationships in NGOs and the work content of NGO staff. Around the same time, the Women's Development Programme in Rajasthan was also the subject of intense debate among NGOs and activists. The first piece of literature that we came across, which raised fundamental questions about women's development by a state-led programme was Saheli et al. (1993). This encouraged us to look at the Programme deeper. We were working and travelling extensively in Rajasthan during this period, and also personally knew activists of the Sathin Karmachari Sangh. Our sympathies lay with the sathins, whose courageous struggles greatly inspired us, and also illuminated our own life-positions with all their contradictions. This note was both an exercise in self-clarification, and of communication to our colleagues in the NGO sector about the ideological mists in the development sector. The sathins and their organisation taught us that these mists cannot be just analysed away, they have to be challenged through collective action. That lesson retains its validity today.

---

* This chapter, a piece of grey literature from the past, is being published as written a decade ago. A postscript brings it up to date.   —*Editor*

INTRODUCTION

For the past four months, sathins from the Women's Development Programme (WDP) of the Government of Rajasthan have been agitating against the state government's decision to scrap the whole Sathin scheme. Recently, the noted Bengali writer and social activist Mahashweta Devi also extended support to their struggle and spoke to the Rajasthan Chief Minister, but met with stubborn resistance. In this chapter, we will examine the working of this programme since its inception in 1984, and the lessons that the whole experience gives to all democratic-minded people, particularly those working in NGOs.

THE CURRENT TREND OF WOMEN'S DEVELOPMENT

The freedom struggle in India had an anti-imperialist and anti-feudal content, though it was not thoroughgoing. However, it did result in an awakening of women to the possibility of their own emancipation, though again in a limited sense. In 1931, the Fundamental Rights Resolution of the Indian National Congress stated that freedom, justice, dignity and equality for women were essential for nation-building. These ideas were also enshrined in the Constitution of India. But in the decades after independence, women found to their dismay that, as with other oppressed sections, the rights that were guaranteed in the Constitution remained on paper alone. Patriarchal Indian society did not yield easily to the lofty proclamations of the Constitution. The women's movement acquired a new momentum in the early 1970s along with other social and political movements; this period of social ferment culminated in the Emergency. The term 'women's movement' encompassed a wide range of organisations and individuals with varying outlooks, but the movement as a whole raised public consciousness about the many manifestations of patriarchy in Indian society that denied women equal opportunities to develop, even to survive. Violence against women, such as rape, custodial rape and dowry deaths, was the specific point from which many of these movements began.

One outcome of this phase of the women's movement was that the Government of India could no longer remain aloof to the problems of women and had to respond decisively. The Committee on the Status of Women in India (CSWI) set up in 1974 highlighted the decline in the sex ratio, the increasing gender gaps in life expectancy, mortality and economic parameters. The CSWI report also showed the relation between the growing social and economic disparities in society at large, and the declining status of women. The Sixth Five Year Plan (1980–85) included for the first time a chapter on Women and Development; the idea gained ground that many government schemes and projects were adversely affected due to the lack of involvement of women, particularly in the fields of health, education, family welfare, social forestry, animal husbandry and rural sanitation. The reorientation of the government took place in the context of the United Nations' International Decade of Women (1975–85), which was itself an outcome of the international women's movement, particularly in Europe and America.

From the 1980s onwards, there were many government and foreign-funded programmes for women's development in which NGOs and women activists participated. Over the years, there had also been heated debates about the pros and cons of activists joining such government or foreign-funded programmes. But even as these debates continued, the character of the women's movement underwent a change, as did the NGO sector as a whole. While the earlier activists came into the movement voluntarily to protest against injustice, thereby venturing into uncharted territory, the movement later became funded and supported, and relatively more recognised as serving a useful function in society. There emerged a wide-ranging division of labour between organisations (specialising in field implementation, administrative support, training, research, et cetera) and within the same organisation itself. Overall, it can be safely said that today's activist is a 'professional' in the sense that activism is her main source of livelihood and her remuneration comes from her organisation, which in turn is funded by the government or by foreign donors. It is necessary to examine the implications of this change in the character of activism for the goal of women's emancipation. Does the end justify the new means, or are the new means subverting the end? The experience of the Women's Development Programme in Rajasthan gave us an opportunity to examine this question.

THE WOMEN'S DEVELOPMENT PROGRAMME IN RAJASTHAN

Generally speaking, the backwardness of women in Rajasthan is reinforced by a feudal culture. Rajasthan has a limited record of participation in the freedom struggle compared to many other states; nor have there been any other women's emancipation movements except for NGO activity in the past two decades.

In 1983, the Rajasthan Government's Department of Rural Development and Panchayati Raj, which was in charge of implementing the 20-Point Programme, held consultations with NGOs and social workers. It came to the conclusion that for schemes like the emancipation of bonded labour, securing minimum wages, primary education and immunisation to be successful, women would have to be given access to these schemes through innovative means. The project document drafted by the department stated that the main aim of the Women's Development Programme (WDP) was to 'operationalise the policy framework for women's development'. In doing so, it took note of the fact that 'most government schemes were not accessible to women due to a lack of receiving mechanisms, and that it was possible to create such mechanisms through flexible and diversified structures backed by effective participation of women at the grassroots level'. WDP was not meant to take over the responsibility of implementing schemes, but was to improve the participation of women, especially those from disadvantaged communities. The participation of women was to be achieved through their 'empowerment' by means of information, education and training. The meaning of the term empowerment had to be gleaned from the project documents. For example,

> Development is a notion which demands a qualitative shift in the attitudes of the people involved ... to generate experiences which facilitate altered perceptions of the self image as well as social image of women ... to rediscover the lost faith and confidence in ourselves, in our collective strength ... [to create] positive perceptions of a woman's own identity in a larger social process.

The basic concept, therefore, was for the state to support poor women's efforts to organise themselves.

In 1984, WDP was set up in six districts, namely, Bhilwara, Jaipur, Udaipur, Banswara, Jodhpur and Ajmer. Financial assistance for five districts, as well as state-level expenditure, was arranged from UNICEF. By 1995, the programme had spread to 21 districts.

The programme had a four-tier structure through the village, block, district and state levels. At the village level, each selected Gram Panchayat had a trained village-level worker called a sathin, who belonged to one of the villages of the Gram Panchayat. She was responsible for the formation of women's forums at the village level. At the block level, a cluster of 10 Gram Panchayats with 10 sathins was coordinated by a Pracheta, a block-level government functionary, who provided support and guidance to the sathins, and was the communication link with the district. At the district level, there were distinct government and NGO components. The District Women's Development Agency (DWDA) was chaired by the District Collector, and had a Project Director assisted by a Project Officer. Technical resource support was provided by an Information Development and Resource Agency (IDARA). An NGO with experience in the fields of adult education and rural development was designated the IDARA, which was seen as a link between the grassroots and the wider women's movement. Activists from the women's movement served as functionaries and consultants. At the state level, there was a state IDARA, which coordinated all district IDARAs. The WDP Director was overall in-charge. The Institute of Development Studies (IDS), Jaipur, was to carry out the monitoring and evaluation throughout the state.

THE SATHIN AND HER IMPORTANCE IN THE PROGRAMME

The WDP recognised that Rajasthan was a very backward state with highly underdeveloped agriculture. In the arid and semi-arid regions, subsistence agriculture was practised and migration for wage labour was predominant. The social milieu was characterised by feudal values of casteism and feudal patriarchal values. The thinking behind WDP was that these values had led to social fragmentation and acceptance of domination, particularly by the lower castes. In such a situation, work had been deliberately undervalued, statutory minimum wages were not followed, and the rural elite and petty bureaucracy reaped the benefits of development programmes. The condition of women was the worst; as they bore the brunt of both casteist and patriarchal values, their social image and their own self-image was very low.

It was in this scenario that the sathin was seen as a grassroots organiser who would catalyse the shift from acquiescence to self-assertion among women from the most deprived sections of rural society. Women from the Scheduled Castes and Scheduled Tribes in very backward villages were chosen. An honorarium of Rs 200 per month was fixed as incentive to draw women to join as sathins in the programme. The very concept of a sathin as a grassroots organiser was a departure from the accepted practice of using 'professionals' or outside experts. Selected sathins and prachetas received initial training that emphasised experiential learning. Through a process of community living and sharing of life experiences, an atmosphere of mutual trust and understanding was created. The training was the crucial component in building the sathin's self-confidence with a new set of values. When she went back to her village, she had the task of analysing her village situation, particularly to identify the problems of women and their needs, to organise women, and initiate steps to solve their problems and meet their needs.

THE SATHIN'S FUNCTIONING AND SUPPORT FROM THE STATE

The National Commission for Women (NCW) in its report 'The Sathin' had words of high praise for the work of the sathins in the 12 years since the inception of the programme.

> What needs to be re-stated over and over again is that these Sathins have had to deal with tremendous social pressures and economic hardships. Often it has been sheer grit and determination and a test of their courage and endurance that has brought them the successes that they have achieved. Today, they are powerful agents of social change. (NCW 1996)

The NCW report and other case studies also highlighted the support extended to the sathin from the WDP, which is an in-built feature of the programme. For example, the NCW report said that when the sathin took up sensitive issues like the prevention of child marriage, *mrityu-bhoj* (a customary feast thrown after the death of a person by his/her kin) or caste discrimination, the existing traditionally powerful sections of village society reacted, often violently with threats and assault. To protect the sathin and to send out a clear message that the sathin was not alone, the WDP would hold a *jajam* or meeting in the village, where sathins from all over the district and different parts of the state would rally around the local sathin. There were cases of sathins who got hand pumps installed in Harijan bastis in the face of stiff opposition from the upper castes, and of sathins who got encroachments on village grazing lands vacated by mobilising local people and with police back-up.

DIFFERENCES WITHIN THE WDP OVER FORCED STERILISATION

The first signs of a difference in outlook between the higher functionaries of the WDP on the one hand and village people and sathins/prachetas on the other were manifested in 1986–88. There was a widespread need among rural women in Rajasthan for safe contraception, which had been suppressed by feudal and patriarchal values. Helping women meet this need was one of the tasks of the sathin. But, as had been the practice since the days of the Emergency, the government converted this into an exercise to aggressively pursue targets. Each sathin was assigned sterilisation targets, whereas District Collectors were promised rich incentives for exceeding targets. In the severe drought years of the mid-1980s, villagers, particularly women who came for famine relief work, were coerced into undergoing sterilisation in return for the opportunity to work. Moreover, negligence and unhygienic conditions in the sterilisation camps resulted in infection and deaths. Sathins revolted against the targets set for them; villagers entreated them to report the matter to higher authorities in the government.

Higher-level functionaries in the IDARAs (NGOs) encouraged protests and mobilisation outside of the WDP against this coercive policy, but baulked at the prospect of confronting the government directly for fear that the government would cut off the IDARAs from the WDP. Ultimately, the government even withheld two months' salary of the sathins for their refusal to meet sterilisation targets. WDP, thus, became an instrument for what were essentially atrocities against women.

HARASSMENT OF SATHINS BY WDP

The harassment of sathins and prachetas by the WDP reached a flashpoint in 1991 when five sathins and a pracheta were arbitrarily dismissed immediately after they had participated in the National Women's Conference in Calicut (Kerala) in December 1990, under the banner of the Mahila Samooh Kekri (MSK), a separate organisation.

The MSK was a women's organisation of the Kekri Panchayat Samiti (Ajmer district) formed with the laborious efforts of sathins in these villages. This was in keeping with the avowed objectives of the WDP, wherein sathins were expected to organise local-level Mahila Mandals in the villages of their panchayats. Yet, when the sathins led protests against family planning excesses, the decisions of the traditional Jati Panchayats and land grabbing by upper-caste Rajputs, the WDP authorities disapproved of their involvement in 'political' activities and kept aloof. On their return from Calicut, five sathins were arbitrarily dismissed by WDP, after intimidation and harassment and without following any of the procedures laid down in their own documents, such as holding village meetings to test if a sathin had lost the confidence of her village, discussions of other sathins and prachetas with villagers, and discussion in the pracheta meeting. A long legal battle ensued all the way up to the Supreme Court, which upheld the High Court order reinstating the sathins, after four wearisome years. Besides this well-known case, which had a happy ending for the sathins, there had been several other instances of sathins being dismissed in a similar manner.

CHANGE IN THE ORIENTATION OF WDP

About five years into the programme, there was an unannounced shift in its orientation. While the original concept was to turn the notion of development on its head by moving away from centralised policy planning to needs and demands articulated from the village itself, within five years centralised policy planning and a top-down approach reappeared. The sathin, who was earlier viewed by WDP as an agent of social change through *chetna jagran* (awareness raising), began to be viewed as a mere functionary of mainstream development programmes. There was a substantial increase in her workload and the time spent on her work, the nature of which changed from awareness raising to meeting the targets of opening women's bank accounts, participating in awareness campaigns of other government departments and mobilising women to attend them, meeting targets of girls' enrolment in schools, of women's immunisation and sterilisation, et cetera. The sathin's performance assessment now began to be based on how well she fulfilled targets. Village communities also began demanding of the sathin services ranging from information about governmental procedures to the repair of hand pumps and distribution of rations. The sathin was supposed to be doing WDP work in her spare time, but even though the increase in workload necessitated frequent travel and loss of income due to missed work, the sathins' honorarium remained at Rs 250 per month despite persistent demands for an increase. The NCW report said that in the districts where WDP had just begun, the empowerment component was being neglected and there was a reversal to the old view of women as passive beneficiaries of welfare schemes, which was the original point of departure for WDP in 1984.

In the districts covered earlier, the increasing emphasis on the achievement of tangible results and fast expansion had led to the essential component of training and monitoring being weakened. At the district level, the character of the DWDA had changed. While the earlier emphasis was on choosing Project Directors with experience in women's issues (with further gender-sensitisation if necessary), these qualifications had later been given the go-by. New projects had been loaded on to the DWDA, like the Lok Jumbish, anti-AIDS campaigns, literacy missions and campaigns for the girl child. Consequently, responsiveness to field situations and two-way interaction in the form of village visits by Project Directors, letters to sathins by Project Directors, et cetera, had virtually ceased.

If this was the situation within the DWDAs, the situation in the NGOs (IDARAs) was no better. Here, too, new personnel had been selected without regard to their experience in women's issues, and no real orientation was provided after they were appointed. Earlier, IDARAs used to conduct training programmes for sathins spread over a period of one month; these

were carefully designed, value-based and experiential training programmes. However, these had been subsequently replaced by four to five
day training programmes of 'Mahila Samoohs', which had become more
or less mechanical exercises of information dissemination. Once it became
clear that the basic outlook of the WDP was changing, the NGOs' leadership could do little but fall in line, even as the work they were doing became increasingly devoid of content. The government made its message
clear to the IDARAs by clamping down on them. In 1992, the salaries of
all IDARA functionaries were frozen. Those activist IDARAs who challenged this in court were selectively victimised. IDARA budgets were cut
and in 1993 and 1994, no trainings or orientations were conducted. Information about sathin jajams (meetings) was not passed on to IDARAs
to prevent their activists from attending. In the case of Bhilwara district,
citing the absence of a specialist and, therefore, irresponsibility of the
NGOs, all of the remaining staff were terminated and the DWDA took
over the IDARA. The government's idea was now to reduce IDARAs to
reporting organisations, and to use them to publish newsletters and deny
them any proactive role. Some of the activists who quit the IDARAs were
re-employed as project directors to work in DWDAs in newly included
districts. The originally envisaged partnership between government and
NGOs in WDP had been replaced by domination by the government.

The IDS, Jaipur, was entrusted with overall monitoring and evaluation.
IDS, an autonomous research institution, and its women's studies wing,
was actively involved in monitoring the programme. The gap between
field-level problems and the thinking of top-level functionaries of WDP
was also reflected in IDS evaluation, resulting in much soul-searching
among the activist-scholars of the women's studies wing. Seeing the problems and conflicts emerging between IDARAs and DWDAs, between WDP
as a whole and sathins/prachetas, as well as the adamant attitude of the
government, IDS decided to fully dissociate itself from the WDP.

UNIONISATION OF SATHINS/PRACHETAS
AND WDP'S RESPONSE

The change in orientation within the WDP led to an increasing workload
and tightened control over the activities of sathins and prachetas. The
WDP had earlier made them conscious of their status as women who

had to fight for their rights along with other women of their communities. Now the long hours of work at low pay and shabby treatment by their superiors made them conscious of their identities as workers who were being denied their rights. The need to have their own union was keenly felt, and the actual steps were initiated by the Mahila Samooh Kekri and the Mahila Samooh Ajmer. (Some of the activists who had left WDP were members of the Ajmer group.) By July 1993, a state-level sathins' union was formed, which began a programme of staging *dharnas* at the district headquarters and held meetings with MLAs and ministers to press their demands for better pay and terms of work. A prachetas' union was also formed in 1992.

The response of the WDP authorities to the unionisation was similar to that of any management against their workers' unions. Tactics of intimidation and blandishment were used alternately. In Ajmer, letters were sent to the husbands of sathins asking them to allow the women to leave their homes only if they received official letters with WDP seals. So much for women's emancipation! There had been attempts to break the unity of the sathins by selectively choosing some of them for Lok Jumbish programmes on a daily allowance of Rs 50. A rift was sought to be created between sathins and prachetas through the character assassination of prachetas, often by using other prachetas as agents. Large-scale sathin jajams were disallowed, and even large-scale celebrations of International Women's Day were disallowed.

In 1991, seven years after the commencement of the WDP, the authorities woke up to the fact that the post of pracheta was a tenure post and according to the existing rules, the tenure of service of most prachetas had expired. They were asked to re-apply and in the process of re-selection, three militant prachetas (who had served the WDP for two to seven years) were dropped. It may be mentioned here that the strictly illegal practice of contractual appointment was also extended to the lower-level office staff of the DWDAs, many of whom challenged this in court.

CHANGE IN THE STRUCTURE OF THE PROGRAMME

The response to the growing militancy of the sathins and the prachetas was a change in the structure of the programme. It was decided to not fill the vacant posts of sathins, but to substitute them with groups of women (Mahila Samoohs). Officially, it was being stated that the sathin model was a 'lone crusader' model with no support at the village level, leading to incidents such as that at Bhateri (see Box 17.1). It was said that the very training processes of the WDP were elevating the status of the sathin high above that of the other village women. The Rajasthan state Chief Secretary alleged that sathins had been unable to form cohesive groups at the village level. It was further said that despite over 10 years of the

---

Box 17.1
Bhanwari Devi of Bhateri

Bhanwari Devi of Bhateri village (Jaipur district) was chosen as a sathin in the WDP in 1985. She was from a landless family; her husband was a part-time rickshaw puller in Jaipur. Her work as a sathin in investigating the Public Distribution System and payment of wages in famine relief works was outstanding, and she had the support of her villagers, both men and women. In 1992, the Government of Rajasthan went in for a high-profile campaign against child marriages that take place during the traditional festival of Akha Teej. Instructions went down the line from the Chief Minister to the Chief Secretary to the District Collectors. Contrary to the sathins' usual approach of persuasion and moral pressure, the government wanted to go in for a show of force. All sathins were asked to submit lists of people who were planning to perform child marriages. Bhanwari, too, submitted a list, on which one of the names was that of a Gujjar household whom she first approached individually. The whole campaign had evoked considerable resistance in the village, and the local MLA had also threatened Bhanwari. Eventually, on Akha Teej, police presence ensured that the child marriages did not take place; however, the marriages were performed the same night.

Public opinion in Bhateri swung against Bhanwari; a social boycott ensued and there was a threat of violence. Other sathins, prachetas and the Project Director kept calling on Bhanwari to ensure her safety, while Bhanwari herself refrained from complaining to the police

(*Box 17.1 continued*)

(*Box 17.1 continued*)

fearing that this would worsen the situation. Slowly tempers cooled, though the entire Gujjar community remained hostile. When the visits from other WDP functionaries had stopped due to this false sense of security, a very sordid incident occurred. On the evening of 22 September 1992, a group of Gujjar men (including the man against whom the complaint of child marriage had been made) beat up Bhanwari's husband and raped Bhawari in his presence.

What happened afterwards was even more shocking. Though in physical and emotional pain, Bhanwari had the courage to insist on a police complaint and a medical examination to establish the charge of rape. The familiar tale of rape victims enacted itself yet again: Bhawari was shuttled from one police station to another, from one doctor to another, each of whom viewed her complaint with extreme suspicion and dilly-dallied on one procedural pretext or the other. Even as WDP officials and sympathetic bureaucrats could only watch in despair, a section of the administration, the police and politicians went all out to denounce her. The WDP, which was built on the foundation of state support for rural women's struggles, of trust between government, NGOs and people, stood thoroughly exposed.

WDP functionaries also capitalised on the incident. As sathins' tempers were running high, it was possible to instigate sathins against prachetas (who were then agitating for better working conditions) by labelling prachetas as self-seeking, since their work did not expose them to the same level of risk as the sathins.

The final exposition of patriarchy came when the Rajasthan High Court delivered its judgement on the case. All the accused were let off for want of evidence. The investigating agencies, on political instructions, had done a shoddy job. For his part, the learned judge came to the conclusion that the rape seemed *prima facie* impossible as it was inconceivable that higher-caste men would rape a lower-caste woman, that too in the presence of her husband. To the judge's mind, the delay in registering the complaint also gave room for suspicion. Agitating women's groups forced the government to go in appeal to the Supreme Court. No one knew how long Bhanwari Devi's wait for justice would be.

programme, the impact was very meagre, and that the reach of the programme was poor because only 100 sathins had been chosen per district. The Chief Secretary charged the sathins with having stultified the programme by wanting permanent government posts in their villages, and by not moving out to new villages. The Chief Secretary went to the extent of charging sathins with internalising the values of government employees.

It was clear that the government, through the statements of the Chief Secretary, was trying to falsely implicate the sathins for its own unstated policy of scuttling the WDP. Seeing the resistance of the sathins to unbridled exploitation, the WDP itself refrained from meeting the prescribed target of 100 sathins per district. Only about five districts had anywhere close to the required number. The NCW report listed 64 tasks that the sathins performed and noted that these tasks routinely took the sathin to neighbouring villages. The very success of the sathin in combating existing social evils and feudal practices was due to her success in mobilising cohesive groups in the communities.

The idea of Mahila Samoohs replacing single sathins appears correct in principle. Yet, in practice, the operation of these Mahila Samoohs was along the same lines as the routine top-down approach to which the WDP as a whole had reverted.

> Even on an experimental basis, to be effective the Mahila Samooh model requires a completely different approach. The lacunae in implementation have been identified as the arbitrary and mechanical manner in which the Mahila Samoohs have been formed. The formation was done without a detailed planning of the approach, the processes and the training required for facilitation of the empowerment process ... . It is felt that the kind of training that is given is very mechanical and content-based. This is in contrast to the experiential and value-based nature of the earlier training. It has been felt that this kind of training does not bring about an attitudinal shift which is the very crux of the empowerment process ... . This has resulted in various problems at the field level, such as a relative lack of commitment and responsibility, ad-hocism and a high turnover. The fact that the Samooh members do not feel bound to attend meetings and training programmes has been a cause for concern ... . (NCW 1996)

Quite clearly, any stultification of the programme had been done by WDP itself.

NOTICE OF TERMINATION OF THE SATHIN SCHEME

The final blow was then struck by the state government. Having first asked the NCW to study the efficacy of the sathins' working, and having seen that the NCW whole-heartedly endorsed the sathin model, the government chose to reject the NCW report. Instead, the Chief Secretary promised that the government was working on 'an integrated policy for women with focus on their improved targeting through better convergence and inter-sectoral co-ordination'. This semantic smokescreen fooled no one, and women's organisations all over the country roundly condemned the state government. In subsequent years, the state government emerged as the chief agent of oppression of women. Besides the Bhateri episode, there had been instances of atrocities on women in which legislators and their kin and ruling party members had been involved. In all cases, the police were purposefully lethargic. A shocking instance was an acid attack on a schoolgirl by the son of a minister, who was named by the victim; the police dragged their feet over arresting the suspect despite widespread public protests.

In this dark scenario, the sathins who had little formal education but had learnt much more from life than educated activists, carried on a courageous struggle against their two-fold exploitation as women and as workers.

ANALYSING THE WDP EXPERIENCE

So far we have seen how a programme that was supposed to 'empower' women finally ended up oppressing them. Why did it happen? Could it have happened otherwise? These are the crucial questions to be answered.

The WDP began on the premise that rural Rajasthani women face oppression from feudal patriarchal values, that they had internalised these values so much that their sufferings remain unarticulated, that they remain mute even under the most oppressive conditions. Under such conditions, they could not mobilise themselves to receive the welfare programmes that the government ran. In the face of such passivity, the rural elite and the lower-level functionaries of the government connived to corner all the benefits of government welfare and development schemes. WDP conceived that the way to break out of this impasse was to create a trained cadre of village-level organisers among the women. This was to be fortified by creating a support structure at the district and state levels consisting of balanced government and NGO components, the former comprising of gender-sensitised officers and the latter of experienced activists from the women's movement. It should be noted that in concept and in execution, at least in the initial stages, WDP was far bolder than many of the women's development projects today. Many of the programmes, which are basically economic assistance programmes for income-generating activities by women, have gratuitously taken on the label of 'empowerment'.

The cutting edge of WDP was the sathin, who was seen as a village-level volunteer who would organise village women. The process of awakening of the sathins by the WDP training process, and their success in organising women of their village to fight rural elites and corrupt government functionaries surpassed all expectations. But a few years into the programme, the old centralised, top-down and bureaucratic approach re-appeared, and the government began treating WDP as a service-delivery scheme and the sathins as 'volunteers' who could be ordered around at will.

It was when the sathins began contesting their classification as volunteers needing only meagre honoraria that the progressive mask of the government fell and the repressive character of the state came forth. Organising at the grassroots, if done with full seriousness, is full-time work. It was inconceivable that the sathins, hailing from the poorest strata of rural Rajasthan, could do such demanding work at Rs 200 per month and yet be expected to survive. The sathins' demand was that the honorarium should be along the lines of minimum wages and should be raised according to their workload. WDP officials (both government and NGO) began splitting hairs about the difference between a wage and an honorarium, and resorted to the fiction that since there was no master-servant relationship, the sathins were getting an honorarium. This was far from the case as the workload of the sathins was being relentlessly increased, and the payment of those who refused to fulfil sterilisation targets was held up. Officials further argued that sathins were doing 'voluntary' work and an enhanced wage would erode the spirit of *seva* (service) in the work and alienate them from fellow villagers. This line of argument has often been heard by NGO workers when they demand a raise in salaries. Those worthies who put forth this argument pretend not to understand that in a capitalist society like ours, even the spirit of service cannot but become a commodity with a price, for seva too is labour and in order to continue supplying it, the *sevika/sevak* (one who serves) needs means of sustenance. For their own seva, the Project Directors and IDARA co-ordinators were on regular scales, earning twice as much in a month as a sathin would in a year.

The struggle, thus, became a basic class struggle over arriving at a just wage, that is, the price of a special form of labour in capitalist society. WDP officials (both government and NGO) then pulled out the next item from their unending bag of tricks. The very nature of the functions a sathin was supposed to perform made it difficult to gauge the amount of time she would need to spend in fulfilling these. Further, the outcome of her work could not always be measured because these were based on intangibles such as the village women gaining confidence in themselves, and changes in their status in their own eyes and in those of the family, the village. The WDP now began drawing inapt comparisons between the highly skill-intensive work of the sathins and the work of anganwadi workers who had quantifiable, repetitive tasks. The argument now was that since the sathins had no 'defined' work, their meagre honoraria were justified. This was then further justified by changing the nature of the sathin's work by adding on routine tasks of welfare delivery and diluting the training component, thereby striking at the very root of the programme—the skill of the sathins as organisers.

Sathins quickly saw through the argument that their work was not 'defined'. Since the dawn of patriarchal society, the work of women within the household (that is, child rearing, cooking and all housekeeping activities extending to tending of livestock and the homestead farm) has been relegated to the status of a private activity as opposed to the public activity of productions (agricultural or otherwise) engaged in by men. Capitalism, which seeks to buy labour power at the lowest possible wage, has used this patriarchal division of men's and women's labour to cheapen the wage of any home-based production activity undertaken by women. Since the WDP viewed the sathin as a 'volunteer' working in her own village, her organising work, too, was seen as non-work, a hobby for her spare time. In the words of a sathin, 'In the training, we were taught that women's work has no recognition and those very people who taught us this are the ones who are not recognising our work' (NCW 1996).

Similarly, when sathins seriously took up local struggles against politically influential sections or against repressive government policies and formed truly independent and militant women's groups, WDP cracked down on them. The message in essence was that women would be allowed to 'develop' only along the line that the state wanted them to, a line of docility and subservience. What else was this but patriarchal control?

LESSONS FOR ACTIVISTS AND
NGO WORKERS

It is clear from the WDP experience that the state has both a capitalist and a patriarchal character. The Bhateri episode showed up feudal patriarchal values in the legislature, executive and judiciary of Rajasthan. The NGOs attached to the programme also did not stand by the sathins, both when they raised the issue of forced sterilisation to qualify for famine relief and when they raised questions about their own exploitation. On the contrary, the NGOs themselves engaged in patriarchal attacks on the sathins in order to maintain good relations with the government. Only the more conscientious activists forsook their careers and joined the sathins.

It is, therefore, clear that women's emancipation cannot be conferred on them by either the state or NGOs. It has to be fought for and won by women themselves. So closely are capitalism and patriarchy intertwined that the emancipation of women is intertwined with emancipation from capitalism. The unequal and unjust division of labour between men and women in society lies inextricably linked with the unequal and unjust division of labour between toilers and their exploiters. As the sathins have demonstrated, women have a two-fold but integrated struggle—against their exploitation as women and as workers. Their heightened gender and economic consciousness stands on the threshold of a new political consciousness—the consciousness of capitalism as a concrete category and the need to struggle against it. This is, in fact, an old lesson re-learnt in a new context: that only socialism can create conditions for women's emancipation, that the political struggle for socialism is, therefore, linked with the goal of women's emancipation.

The experience of WDP showed that such programmes were meant to prevent the development of this true political consciousness and instead tried to instil a false consciousness. For example, the India Country Paper for the World Summit for Social Development (GoI 1995) said,

> Empowering the poor involves organising them into informal groups, formal associations, trade unions, cooperatives etc. for exerting collective pressure, articulating demand and effectively participating in the decision-making process with the ultimate objective of building foundations of individual and collective self-reliance. NGOs can provide great help in this process, particularly providing the support structures needed for such groups and associations and liaising between them and the Government so that both the groups and the Government are sensitised to an organised approach to development.

To this end, the Country Paper exhorted a trustful partnership between the government and NGOs, with the latter taking on both mobilisation and service delivery activities. Several success stories were cited: WDP itself; the scheme of honorary rural organisers of the Labour Ministry (in the 1980s) extending to 1,500 blocks; CAPART support to voluntary organisations for rural animators, which had resulted in 12,000 animators being trained and 2,000 groups of beneficiaries; thousands of women's groups formed under DWCRA programmes for income-generation activities; the Mahila Samakhya Programme, which sought to establish Women's Activity centres in 2,000 villages of 10 districts of Gujarat, Karnataka and UP; the National Literacy Mission, which had reached 220 districts in 23 states/UTs. Given that the processes in WDP were not accidental but stemmed from the basic character of the state and of NGOs, what were the real stories behind all these programmes?

Those of us who work in NGOs have a good idea of what is actually happening on the ground. We know that many of these success stories are false. Yet, what do we do with our knowledge? Do we challenge the myths spun out by the development sector? The general tendency is to do some elaborate mental calculations and conclude that discretion is the better part of valour. This is where we have much to learn from the sathins of Rajasthan. It would be fallacious to reason that their plight was such that they could not but revolt. In the face of threats and emotional blackmail by their superiors, and out of a dire need for their existing honoraria, they could have silently acquiesced. Yet, they chose the path of struggle without fearing the consequences. In the face of their persistent campaign, the Government of Rajasthan, which once thought of terminating the programme, had to enhance their honorarium to Rs 350 per month. For all our education and so-called enlightenment, we are unable to grasp the higher conception of dignity in the struggle, which the unlettered sathins have. If we follow in their footsteps, we too can possibly emerge as a truly conscious force from the ruins of an increasingly discredited NGO movement.

POSTSCRIPT

The Women's Development Programme continued with the sathins due to pressure from women's organisations, despite neglect and antipathy from the state government. In 2002, the state government again attempted to disband the sathin scheme, and was again forced to backtrack. The Rajasthan Institute of Public Administration (RIPA) commissioned a four-member independent review panel headed by Ms C.P. Sujaya. The findings of the review team once again corroborated what the sathin union had been saying all along. The team traced what it called a 'silent shift' from the sathin to the 'samooh' following a decision to stop recruiting new sathins in 1992. No official document could be found to explain why the shift had taken place; there was only an attempt to explain the rationale for it *post facto* in terms of the sathin model being a 'lone crusader' model, leading to 'occupational hazards' for the sathin. The review team found that the epithet of 'lone crusader' applied to the sathin, and the polarisation between the sathin and the samooh did not stand the test of WDP experience, history and lessons. The sathins had always worked through collective processes with village women and not with individual women as 'targets', planning campaigns and activities on the basis of agreed consensus: *jajams*, where sathins fix the agenda based on extensive and repeated discussions with village women, men and panchayat members, arrive at collective action points where it is emphasised that sathins cannot act alone to meet district officials, call errant line department staff to the village, et cetera (see GoR 2002: 8–9, 20–22).

The team also found that a host of new women's development programmes had been introduced in the state, all of which depended on the mobilisation of women into groups, and insisted on the convergence of all services and programmes for women for greater efficiency and synergy. All these programmes had added to the roles and responsibilities of sathins and prachetas, without any corresponding enrichment of WDP structures, human and financial resources. On the ground, thrift-and-credit societies and Self-Help Groups (SHGs) had overtaken even the samooh concept of village collectives engaged in spreading awareness. The review team found no evidence of these groups acting as a collective for spreading awareness among women of their legal rights or acting as a watchdog body, but found them preoccupied with the details of borrowing, lending and starting enterprises (GoR 2002: 9–11, 18).

Earlier, jajams and village meetings gave a voice to village women, and they prioritised problems based on their local context. Interactions among sathins were also frequent, with information exchange finally translating into campaigns planned by women themselves. The review panel found that the WDP had been critically weakened by the non-recruitment of sathins, the drastically curtailed travel budgets, recruitment of prachetas on short-term contracts, drastic curtailment of jajams, meetings and training programmes, delayed salary and honoraria payments, and replacement of the earlier detailed communication and reporting system from the village upwards by a tabular statement in quantitative reporting format. Earlier, the direction of the programme was bottom-up, with issues raised by sathins after village discussions being central to WDP activity—issues such as local discriminatory practices against women, child marriage, domestic violence, illegal liquor vends and encroachments on village commons. Now, top-down direction had gained ascendancy, with line departments vying to use the competent sathins as frontline workers in their programmes. The World Bank-funded ICDS III in Rajasthan has a 'Women's Empowerment Component and Focus on Adolescent Girl Activities', which basically requires sathins and prachetas to be engaged in a long list of activities that resembles a wish list rather than a carefully thought-out design. At the same time, the WDP structure had been weakened by the state government to such an extent that it could not carry out its core functions (GoR 2002: 12–17, 20–21).

The review team found unclear usage of a number of concepts. 'Economic empowerment' was used synonymously with 'economic activity' and 'economic self-reliance' in the context of women. Policy makers and planners looked at SHGs as mechanisms for women's economic empowerment because they made credit available for economic activities. Members of SHGs received information, resources and inputs only for financial services. Social mobilisation, awareness, or information on legal rights was not part of the information flow at all. Words such as 'convergence', 'integration' and 'merger' were insufficiently differentiated in their scope in the context of programmes for women. The 'merger' of WDP and ICDS in 2000 was found to have created confusion in the work content of project directors, prachetas and sathins in different districts. The review team believed the merger was dictated by a resource crunch in the WDP budget rather than any considered policy decision. According to the sathins, serious issues that require sustained mobilisation have been adversely affected by these changes (GoR 2002: 15–16).

Despite all this, the review team said, 'If work is still being done at the grassroots—and we found plenty of evidence of this—it is because the energy of the sathins, built up through the training, information, communication and other supports in the earlier phase of the programme, has still not completely dissipated' (GoR 2002: 13). It was only in the villages with sathins that the review team found ground rules in place for lending and borrowing in SHGs—no loans for marriages or ostentatious consumption, encouragement of loans for putting girls in schools, for treating illnesses, for childbirth expenses, and domestic emergencies.

The team finally advised the state government to use the lessons from the WDP to develop a critical understanding of the impact of development interventions on poor women and their families, as WDP was the only programme to have a distinctive understanding of and approach to empowerment of women, as well as a dedicated delivery system. The mere recruitment of more sathins by the state government would be inadequate, and the indivisibility of the sathins and other programme support structures had to be understood. Ad hoc efforts to involve WDP functionaries in ICDS III would be ineffective without reviewing the reasons for the low improvement in nutritional and health status despite the rapid expansion of ICDS services. Surveys had found that this was because of the lack of attention paid in the programme to the oppression of women and discriminatory practices, and not the lack of 'receiving mechanisms'.

> The 'receiving mechanism' is not a passive set of women or of community groups. The women or the groups who constitute the mechanism can and do point out the inequities of the system, its irrelevance, its dysfunctional nature, its distanced isolation from the community's actual needs, the prevalence of corruption, and the incidence of violence against women and the marginal communities. The groups expect a response from state agencies. They expect changes to be initiated that bring in greater transparency and accountability at local level .... (GoR 2002: 25)

Importantly, the team also pointed out that the payment of honorarium below the level of a living wage was a violation of the rights of women workers in the programme and contradicted the programme objectives of WDP (ibid.: 31–32)

The state government did not implement the review panel's recommendations entirely. A decision was taken to post a sathin in every Gram Panchayat, but the integration with ICDS continued. To complicate matters further, the administration of the WDP up to the district level was entrusted to PRIs under the scheme of devolution. Selection of new sathins was done by sarpanches and officials of the Panchayati Raj Department, and there were questions about the criteria followed. The training of new sathins was reduced to a mere 10 days, and included only the very tangible tasks, especially those related to ICDS. For all intents and purposes, the sathins have been absorbed into the ICDS and their empowerment role severely diluted.

ACKNOWLEDGEMENTS

This write-up would not have been possible without the valuable inputs of the Sathin Karmachari Sangh and its activists. We are deeply indebted to the late Ashutosh Banerji, a veteran trade union and political leader, who spent innumerable hours with us, patiently providing a broader perspective. Responsibility for errors of facts and perspective is solely ours.

REFERENCES

Saheli, Forum Against Oppression of Women, Sabala Sangh, Action India, Disha, Awaz-e-Niswan. 1993. *Development for Whom: A Critique of Women's Development Programmes*. New Delhi: Saheli.

Government of India (GoI). 1995. *India Country Paper: World Summit for Social Development*. New Delhi: Government of India.

Government of Rajasthan (GoR). 2002. 'The Independent Review of Women's Development Programme, Rajasthan', Commissioned by the Government of Rajasthan under the auspices of the Women's Resource Centre, HCM RIPA. Jaipur: Government of Rajasthan.

National Commission for Women (NCW). 1996. *The Sathin as an Agent of Women's Development*. New Delhi: National Commission for Women, GoI.

About the Editor and Contributors

THE EDITOR

Sumi Krishna, an independent environment-development researcher and gender consultant, currently President of the Indian Association for Women's Studies, has over 35 years of experience at the field, programme and policy levels. Her interests include the gender dimensions of bio-diversity and natural resource-based livelihoods in rural and tribal areas; local knowledge systems and resource rights; participatory governance through community institutions; inter-disciplinary research method-ology; and capacity-building for young professionals. She has served as guest faculty/adviser at various institutions and universities, and earlier worked for several years in development communication. Her major publications include *Environmental Politics: People's Lives and Develop-ment Choices*; *Restoring Childhood: Learning, Labour and Gender in South Asia*; and the edited volume *Livelihood and Gender: Equity in Community Resource Management*. She is a founder-moderator of the e-group 'jivika' on livelihood and gender.

THE CONTRIBUTORS

Chhaya Datar, Professor, Centre for Women's Studies, Tata Institute of Social Sciences (TISS), Mumbai, was also earlier in-charge of the TISS rural campus at Tuljapur, Osmanabad district, Maharashtra. She has fervently promoted women's studies in universities, and is also a grassroots feminist activist. Her interest in rural development grew out of her deep environ-mental awareness and concern for ecological principles. She has focused on women's rights over land and water for livelihood assurance; has edited *Nurturing Nature* and co-authored a monograph, *Women Demand Land and Water.*

Shaila Desouza trained in Social Work from Tata Institute of Social Sciences, Mumbai (1987) and also has a degree in Fine Arts (1985).

Currently a Member of the Goa State Commission for Women, she has been involved with women's issues for over two decades as a social worker, academic and activist and tries to blend these in her research, writing, training, and action projects related to women and children in Goa. She has researched aspects of women's health, and the impact of development and violence against women; her doctoral research is on the way women organise for change. She has edited *Women's Health in Goa: A Holistic Approach.*

Nitya S. Ghotge is a practising veterinarian with a degree in Veterinary Science and Animal Husbandry (1985), and a Masters in Veterinary Surgery (1989). She is Co-Director of ANTHRA, which she started with Sagari R. Ramdas in 1992. ANTHRA works on indigenous knowledge systems, gender-sensitive and sustainable alternatives in livestock development, and also trains para-veterinarians, publishes educational material, and undertakes advocacy on key policy issues on biodiversity and alternative veterinary medicine. She is widely published and has also authored the book *Livestock and Livelihoods: The Indian Context.*

M. Indira, now on the faculty of the Department of Economics and Cooperation, University of Mysore, was earlier also Director of the Women's Studies Centre. She has 20 years of teaching and research experience, and a Ph.D. from the Institute for Social and Economic Change, Bangalore. She has researched and written extensively on aspects of agriculture and natural resources, especially related to Karnataka. Her current research interests are women in development, development approaches, decentralised governance, institutions and participatory methods.

Sandeep Joshi, Senior Fellow at the Madhya Pradesh Institute of Social Science Research, Ujjain, is also Nodal Director, CHILDLINE, Ujjain. He is an Associate Editor of the *Madhya Pradesh Journal of Social Sciences*, and is on the editorial board of the *Madhya Pradesh Samajik Vigyan Anusandhan Journal.* His research areas include rural development, education, decentralised governance and poverty. He has authored *IRDP and Poverty Alleviation* (1999); *Panchayat Raj Institutions and Poverty Alleviation* (2000); has edited *Aspects of Social Justice in India* (2004); and has contributed several articles to academic journals.

Depinder Kapur has worked as a development professional in NGOs since 1988. A postgraduate from the Institute of Rural Management,

Anand, Gujarat, his primary experience has been in rural and urban programmes and projects with NGOs, including the Aga Khan Rural Support Programme, the Society for Promotion of Wastelands Development and CARE. He currently heads WaterAid India and has a keen interest in the political economy of development and secure livelihoods.

Meghana Kelkar is the first woman to be directly inducted (in 1996) as a 'Class 1 Gazetted Officer' in the Maharashtra Agriculture Department. A Masters in Agriculture, she works primarily in agricultural extension and training. In 2002, she was associated with the M.S. Swaminathan Committee to draft an action plan for agricultural development in Maharashtra for the next 25 years. Presently, she is a fulltime Ph.D. scholar at the Tata Institute of Social Sciences, Mumbai, and the University of East Anglia, UK, researching gender, livelihoods and local knowledge of soil management in Maharashtra. She moderates the e-group jivika (http://groups.yahoo.com/group/jivika/).

Seema Kulkarni has a Masters in Social Work from the Tata Institute of Social Sciences, Mumbai. She has worked on gender and livelihood since 1989, and is also an activist with the women's movement, Stree Mukti Sangharsh Chalwal, in southern Maharashtra. She is a core member of the Society for Promoting Participative Eco-system Management, Pune, where she recently coordinated a study on the livelihoods of single and deserted women in Maharashtra. She has published widely on gender and water issues. Presently, she is also the India Coordinator of the 'Women and Water Network', and moderates an electronic discussion group (http://groups.yahoo.com/group/wwn_india2002/).

Kuntala Lahiri-Dutt did her doctoral research on the Lower Damodar Valley in 1985, and has taught geography at the University of Burdwan, West Bengal, since 1982. Currently a Fellow at the Australian National University Research School of Pacific and Asian Studies, she teaches a Master course on Gender and Development, and works on gender and ethnic identities in formal and informal mining practices and water management in India. She is a member of the Steering Committee of the Gender Water Alliance, a global network for mainstreaming gender in water resources management. Her recent publications include *Fluid Bonds: Views on Gender and Water* and *Women Miners in Developing Countries: Pit Women and Others.*

B. Lakshmi teaches Sociology at Aditi Mahavidyalaya, University of Delhi. She was awarded a doctoral degree by the University of Delhi in 2005 on her dissertation titled *Education and Society: A Sociological Study in Chhimtuipui District of Mizoram.*

Viren Lobo is Programme Director, Society for Promotion of Wastelands Development, Udaipur, Rajasthan. He has a Masters from the Institute of Rural Management, Anand, and nearly two decades of experience in natural resources management, especially in dryland areas, and livelihoods. He has formulated and monitored projects in partnership with grassroots-level NGOs on watershed development and joint forest management in Rajasthan, Gujarat and Maharashtra. He is associated with several people's movements on drought mitigation and community-based resource management. He has a special interest in process documentation, and has written extensively on livelihoods in dry-land areas.

Vinalini Mathrani, a freelance social researcher based in Bangalore, is concerned with rural women's empowerment through research and training. She has monitored and evaluated a range of women's empowerment programmes. She has a Masters in Social Work (1988) from the Tata Institute of Social Sciences (TISS), Mumbai, and has worked as lecturer in its Unit for Rural Studies. She is presently pursuing a Ph.D. on women's health issues at TISS. She is also a board member of Sutradhar, an educational resource centre.

Deepak K. Mishra is currently Associate Professor of Economics at the Centre for the Study of Regional Development, School of Social Sciences, Jawaharlal Nehru University, New Delhi. He has worked in the areas of agrarian relations, and gender and livelihood diversification in mountain economies. He is one of the authors of the first *Human Development Report of Arunachal Pradesh.*

Mandakini Pant is Fellow, PRIA Continuing Education at the Society for Participatory Research in Asia (PRIA), New Delhi. She has worked on issues of rights, citizenship and governance, adult education and livelihood, and women's leadership in local self-governance. She has a Ph.D. in sociology, and has been a Reader at the Research Centre for Women Studies, SNDT Women's University, Mumbai.

Vani Periodi, an activist working for women's empowerment with a rights perspective, is based in a village in Karnataka, and is involved with the local government school. She combines interests in research, training and communication. As the Mysore District Coordinator for Mahila Samakhya, Karnataka, she has worked with tribal women. She has edited newsletters and magazines, and works with a street theatre group, Jagruthi; her mono-act *Baki ithihasa* on women's empowerment is popular as a training tool and public performance. Presently, under a fellowship from the Population Council, Delhi, she is developing a training manual for youth on sensitive partnership and responsible parenthood.

P. Ignatius Prabhakar spent his early years in a south Indian village. He has a Masters and a Ph.D. in Anthropology from the University of Madras. His research on grassroots-level democracy and people's participation involved 10 years of fieldwork and academic experience in tribal studies, medical anthropology, development studies and participatory research. He is presently a postdoctoral fellow at the French Institute, Pondicherry, in a Social Water Management Programme, researching the socio-political impact and outcomes of irrigation institutions. Earlier he was with the M.S. Swaminathan Research Foundation, Chennai, working on social capital among self-help groups.

Shobhita Rajagopal, Associate Professor at the Institute of Development Studies, Jaipur, has been a researcher and trainer in women's development and gender issues for 20 years. She has also been active in the women's movement in Rajasthan. Her research has focused on women's sub-ordination, access to crucial resources, modes of collective empower-ment and mainstreaming gender concerns in policy planning and implementation. Her current research includes gender and education, childhood poverty, violence against women, gender poverty and liveli-hoods. She has been involved in the gender training of development plan-ners, practitioners and NGOs at the national, state and international levels, and has published extensively.

Rajesh Ramakrishnan trained as an electronics engineer and turned to rural development and natural resources management after graduating from the Institute of Rural Management, Anand, Gujarat. He worked for the Society for Promotion of Wastelands Development for over eight years, and is now Senior Consultant at Taru Leading Edge, New Delhi, focus-ing on natural resources management, livelihoods and governance. He supports various people's movements; his broader interests include political economy, imperialism, education and Marxism.

Sagari R. Ramdas trained as a veterinarian (1986) and has a Masters in Animal Breeding and Animal Genetics (1991). She has worked with rural and adivasi communities as a field veterinarian, trainer and researcher on livestock and people's livelihoods. Co-Director of ANTHRA, founded with Nitya S. Ghotge in 1992, she has co-coordinated research on the gender, caste and class dynamics of indigenous knowledge systems and livestock production. Currently, her work includes community action-research, training and policy research on livestock production in dryland agriculture. She has significant publications on livestock production in the larger framework of people's rights to food sovereignty.

Gopa Samanta, Senior Lecturer in Geography at the University of Burdwan, West Bengal, has a Ph.D. in rural-urban interaction in Burdwan. She has worked on rural development, poverty, microfinance and gender. In 2004, she was a Visiting Fellow at the Research School of Pacific and Asian Studies, Australian National University, Canberra. Her current research interests are gender, livelihoods and empowerment in Burdwan district. She is exploring, through intensive fieldwork, the dimensions of the life of settlers on the charlands of the Damodar River, jointly with Kuntala Lahiri-Dutt. She has publications in national and international journals, and has also trained as a photographer.

Neera M. Singh is a Ph.D. candidate with the Department of Community, Agriculture, Recreation and Resource Studies, Michigan State University, USA. An alumna of the Indian Institute of Forest Management, Bhopal, she founded Vasundhara, an NGO concerned with natural resources governance and sustainable livelihood issues, in Bhubaneswar. Her many years of work on community forestry issues in Orissa is continued in her dissertation on the emergence of community forestry federations and their role in furthering the democratisation of forest governance. She is interested in the processes of networking, approaches for deepening democracy, participatory action research, and evocative writing.

P. Thamizoli, now a consultant anthropologist, taught for several years at the University of Madras where he had obtained a Ph.D., before moving to the M.S. Swaminathan Research Foundation, Chennai, where he was Programme Director in charge of the tsunami relief and rehabilitation efforts in Tamil Nadu. His specialisation includes participatory rural development, natural resource management, organising village knowledge centres using ICT, and facilitating capacity building for resource-poor women and men to evolve and manage grassroots institutions. His many publications relate to tribals, participatory methodology, gender and livelihoods. He is one of the founders of the e-group jivika.

Vandana Upadhyay is a Senior Lecturer at the Department of Economics, Rajiv Gandhi University, Itanagar, Arunachal Pradesh. In 2006–07, she was a Commonwealth Academic Fellow attached to the Department of International Development, Queen Elizabeth House, University of Oxford. Her research interests include energy security, gender and human development. She is one of the authors of the first *Human Development Report of Arunachal Pradesh*. She has also co-authored a report, *Situational Analysis of Women and Girls in Arunachal Pradesh*, for the National Commission for Women, New Delhi.

Index